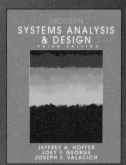
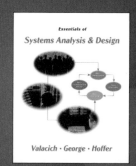

S

FOURTH EDITION

Business Data Networks and Telecommunications

Raymond R. Panko
Ray@Panko.com

University of Hawaii

Prentice Hall

Upper Saddle River,
New Jersey 07458

Library of Congress Cataloging-in-Publication Data

Panko, R. R.
    Business data networks and telecommunications / Raymond Panko.—4th ed.
        p.   cm.
    Includes bibliographical references and index.
    ISBN 0-13-035914-9
    1. Business enterprises—Computer networks—Study guides.   2. Computer
networks—Management—Study guides.   3. Data transmission systems—Study guides.
I.Title.
    HD30.37 .P36   2002
    005.7´1—dc21

                                                                    2001058373

Executive Editor: David Alexander
Executive Editor: Bob Horan
Publisher: Natalie E. Anderson
Editorial Project Manager: Lori Cerreto
Editorial Assistant: Maat Van Uitert
Media Project Manager: Joan Waxman
Marketing Manager: Sharon K. Turkovich
Managing Editor (Production): Gail Steier de Acevedo
Production Editor: Vanessa Nuttry
Permissions Coordinator: Suzanne Grappi
Associate Director, Manufacturing: Vincent Scelta
Manufacturing Buyer: Natacha St. Hill Moore
Design Manager: Patricia Smythe
Designer: Michael Fruhbeis
Cover Design: Michael Fruhbeis
Manager, Print Production: Christy Mahon
Full-Service Project Management: BookMasters, Inc.
Cover Printer: Phoenix Color
Printer/Binder: The Maple Vail Book Manufacturing Group

Pearson Education LTD.
Pearson Education Australia PTY, Limited
Pearson Education Singapore, Pte. Ltd
Pearson Education North Asia Ltd
Pearson Education, Canada, Ltd
Pearson Educación de Mexico, S.A. de C.V.
Pearson Education—Japan
Pearson Education Malaysia, Pte. Ltd

10 9 8 7 6 5 4 3 2 1
ISBN 0-13-035914-9

To Julia, whose insights and diligence made this edition possible.

Brief Contents

Contents

Preface

OUTLINE

- Why a Modular Design?
- Considerations for Potential Adopters
- For Adopters of the Previous Edition
- For New Adopters
- For Students
- Sample Syllabi

WHY A MODULAR DESIGN?

This book has a modular design with 11 core chapters plus additional material, including mini-chapters for hands-on material and case studies, advanced modules, and material at the website (new information, mini-case studies, hands-on exercises).

Tailor the Book to Your Class

This modular design allows you tailor the class to undergraduate MIS majors (using primarily the 11 core chapters), MS/IS graduate students (using selected information from the advanced modules), or MBAs (using case study mini-chapters and mini-case studies at the book's website, www.prenhall.com/panko). Sample syllabi at the end of this preface suggest the type of coverage you might wish in each class.

Select the Emphasis You Want

The modular design was also created to allow you to teach the course your way, covering core material but focusing on a few extra areas you consider to be important without having to create new material yourself.

As the outline before this paragraph indicates, the rest of this Preface is addressed to potential adopters, adopters of the previous (third) edition, new adopters, and students.

CONSIDERATIONS FOR POTENTIAL ADOPTERS

Four things are likely to be of interest to you in evaluating this textbook.

- ➤ The book's core chapters are short enough to be mastered by students, and the book's modular design allows you to enrich the course as appropriate to your students.
- ➤ The content is highly current and reflects what network administrators really do.
- ➤ There is superb teacher support, including full PowerPoint lectures.
- ➤ There is very good student support.

Core Chapters of Reasonable Length

Most teachers hate textbook chapters that are so long that they have to assign only some sections in each chapter. It drives students crazy. So the 11 core chapters in the book are all short enough to assign completely.

What about the other material? With 11 core chapters, most teachers have a week free. The other material in the book allows you to enrich the course in almost any direction you wish without having to prepare a lot of new material yourself. At the end of this Preface there are sample syllabi to indicate typical coverage for different types of courses.

For example, I usually also assign case study mini-chapters (such as Chapters 1a and 5a) as homework and go over them in class, along with the chapter review questions I choose to assign. For hands-on mini-chapters (such as 3a and 4a), I have a wire cutting day in class and give assignments on one or two others. Frankly, most students will read the hands-on mini-chapters on their own because they are so relevant to their lives.

Many teachers cover one of the advanced modules (Module A on TCP/IP and Module D on telephony are the most popular) or parts of a few modules. Or, you can use the freed time to do whatever you like, including spending more time on the most challenging chapters.

How to Use the Modular Design for Emphasis

When I first talked to networking teachers, I was most impressed by how different they were in terms of what they wanted to cover. All wanted to cover some core material, but beyond that, they had very different ideas about what to emphasize.

So I decided to create a modular design that would offer a set of core chapters covering essential information but would also offer other material that teachers could cover selectively in order to do things their way without having to create a lot of new material. Specifically, the book offers the following material beyond the core chapters:

➤ Mini-chapters after many core chapters. These mini-chapters offer either substantial case studies that emphasize the chapter's material or a hands-on lab that students can read or (preferably) do.

➤ Advanced modules keyed to the core chapters. These advanced modules offer material beyond that in the basic chapter. If you think I missed a key concept in a main chapter, there is a good chance I cover it in an advanced module. You can use an advanced module to add emphasis in your class, for instance TCP/IP.

➤ Website material provides new information, photos, mini-case studies that show what real companies are doing, and hands-on exercises (usually dealing with the Internet). If new things become important in the field, mini-chapters dealing with them will be added to the website to keep your course up to date.

Up-to-Date Content

I really hate "core dump" textbooks that tell you about every standard ever created in about equal (lack of) depth. As I did in earlier editions, I spent time with network managers finding out what they really do. This allowed me to cut out never-were products and obsolete products that students will rarely see in the field. Being market focused also allowed me to spend time on topics that really matter even within the constraint of reasonably sized chapters.

➤ For instance, Ethernet is the main LAN focus (Chapters 4 and 5), as it is in life. Students learn Ethernet well.

➤ TCP/IP is the core internetworking focus. It is introduced in the first chapter that deals with standards (Chapter 2) and is discussed in depth in Chapter 8, where students even learn to think like a router. For a really strong TCP/IP focus, there is Module A.

➤ Wireless networking? Sure. And it is integrated throughout the chapters because wireless networking, while new, is no longer a missionary technology. Wireless propagation problems are treated in Chapter 3. Chapter 5 covers 802.11 and Bluetooth. Chapter 6 covers cellular telephony (including 3G). If you prefer to treat wireless in one place, however, there is an online wireless chapter that students can download from the book's website.

➤ Security has become a major IT concern in recent years, and the September 11, 2001, tragedy has intensified concerns about security. The security chapter (Chapter 9) is very rich, and Chapter 7 covers VPNs while Chapter 10 covers server access permissions.

Teacher Support

This is a tough course to teach. To help, I've provided strong support tools.

Full PowerPoint Lectures

There are detailed PowerPoint lectures for each chapter. Not just the "few selected figures" that most books provide but full lectures that I put together (and use) personally. For my students, I print handouts six per page and have students buy them from the copy center to reduce the need for note taking.

By the way, feel free to post these PowerPoint lectures to your local server if you adopt the book. Also, feel free to make changes. However, please don't reuse the clip art (we aren't licensed for that), and please do not remove the copyright notice.

Website Maintained by the Author

The book has a website, www.prenhall.com/panko. I maintain it myself and update it frequently. The website has a number of features for students and teachers.

➤ Photos of equipment. A lot of them. Students really like these things. When I do the PowerPoint presentations, I also bring up the website. I often switch to the browser to show photos of equipment I am discussing.

➤ New information since the book went to press. Assign this material to keep the material completely up to date.

➤ PowerPoint lecture presentation files for downloading.

➤ Word for Windows homework files that have the chapter questions in Word for Windows format. You can assign some or all questions, and students can do their homework on their word processors. (Besides being nice for students, it's a lot easier to grade.)

➤ Small case studies, most of which are articles in the trade press. This material changes too rapidly to print in the book.

➤ Hands-on exercises that typically use the Internet. For instance, students can practice getting a domain name, see how fast their Internet connection really is, and check their home computer for vulnerabilities.

➤ An online glossary organized both by chapter and alphabetically.

Password-Protected Instructor's Part of the Website

There is a password-protected part of the website for adopters. This contains information from the Instructor's Resource CD-ROM (discussed next), but not the sensitive test bank. It has other resources, such as teaching tips and new market data that you can use in class to help students understand the importance of various topics.

Instructor's Resource CD-ROM

The book has an Instructor's Resource CD-ROM that contains material the instructor will wish to have.

➤ A computerized test bank and exam generator, of course.

➤ Answer keys for chapter review questions: test-your-understanding questions in the chapter body and end-of-chapter questions.

➤ PowerPoint presentations. (However, newer ones will be posted to the website to keep the material up to date about every eight months.)

➤ Transparency masters. Some teachers like the freedom of using transparencies compared to PowerPoint presentations. The Instructor's Resource CD-ROM contains transparency masters for *all* figures and tables in the book. They are in Acrobat format.

Chapter Review Questions

Within the chapter's text, there are "test-your-understanding" questions frequently to let students check that they understand the material. These questions cover almost all key points. Quite a few professors assign them selectively for homework and then base their exams on the questions they assigned.

At the ends of chapters, there are enrichment questions, such as troubleshooting questions to help students see how to apply the material to the real world, thought questions that stimulate deeper thinking about the material, and design questions that have them design things (such as a PC network for a small firm in Chapter 4).

Adopters' Mailing List

If you adopt the book, please send me an e-mail (Ray@Panko.com) telling me to put you on the adopters' mailing list. First, this gives me a quick way to communicate with you if there is a major update at the website and (rarely) if there is a really critical piece of networking news you should know about. Second, the list is a great way for me to get feedback from adopters. A number of key design decisions for the current edition were made with input from dozens of adopters of the previous edition.

Student Support

The previous section looked at a number of support tools for students: PowerPoint presentations, downloadable homework questions, and the website with photos, new information, short case studies, hands-on exercises, and an online glossary. In addition, there are a number of mini-chapters (such as Chapter 1a) that are case studies of meaningful length or hands-on activities.

I've also tried to make the book very easy to study. Nearly all important points are covered in the figures. The book has a lot of special "study figures" that outline key points in major sections of chapters (for example, consider Figures 1-1, 1-9, 1-10, 1-14, and 1-17). The test-your-understanding questions cover almost all key points. Chapters begin with objectives. They usually end with a "Market Realities" section that shows students how businesses really use the technologies and standards they learned about in the chapter.

Contact Me

If you have any questions, please send me an e-mail. Again, I'm Ray@Panko.com.

FOR ADOPTERS OF THE PREVIOUS EDITION

Thank you for having used the third edition of the book. I think you will like the fourth even better, although there were quite a few changes.

Chapter Reorganization

Based on comments from adopters of the third edition, I've rearranged some of the material in a way that I think will fit most adopters better.

➤ TCP/IP still begins early, in Chapter 2. However, many teachers asked for a flow of material in the book that would start from bottom layers and then move up the layer hierarchy. So after three introductory chapters, the book focuses first on LANs (Chapters 4 and 5), telephony (Chapter 6), and WANs (Chapter 7), all of which involve the lowest two layers. Then comes internetworking at the internet and transport layers (Chapter 8). Applications come last (in Chapter 11), which is good because applications can be a lot of fun to cover. Security (Chapter 9) and network management (Chapter 10) come just before applications because they involve all layers.

➤ Cheating a little, Chapter 4 covers more than LANs; it discusses the whole task of setting up a small PC network. Perhaps you should think of it as a fourth introductory chapter.

➤ The order of the final two chapters (network management in Chapter 10 and applications in Chapter 11) was selected because many adopters do not cover applications, usually because they are covered in other courses. Putting applications last makes it easiest to drop applications. Network management comes next-to-last because it is the next-most-frequently skipped material.

➤ A good deal of telephony (Chapter 6) is now integrated into the core chapters because Module D was so widely used in the third edition.

➤ There is one fewer core chapter (11 instead of 12), giving you a bit more flexibility. Some teachers will devote extra time to the most difficult chapters. Others will use the reduced number of chapters to add enrichment to their classes.

New and Expanded Material

The book covers several new or expanded topics.

Wireless

Chapter 3 introduces wireless propagation and transmission problems. Chapter 5 presents 802.11 and Bluetooth wireless LANs. Chapter 6 introduces metropolitan wireless networking in the context of cellular telephony (including 3G systems). If you prefer to cover wireless networking all at once, there is an online wireless chapter at the website that students can download.

Security

The security chapter (Chapter 9) is much better than it was in the third edition. In addition, VPNs are covered in Chapter 7, and server access permissions are covered in Chapter 10.

Applications

Chapter 11 covers peer-to-peer (P2P) networking, Web services and .NET, and an integrative section on e-commerce.

PowerPoint Lectures

You'll again get full PowerPoint lectures. They will be a little shorter than the early ones for the third edition. For those who want it, there are notes pages (only available to teachers) containing a script you can use to present each slide.

Adopters-Only Material

The website has an adopters-only section protected by a password. I'll put answer keys there as well as the notes pages for the PowerPoint presentations. I'll also put new market information with facts that you can toss out in class and impress your students. Let me know if there is anything else you would like there.

The Website

Otherwise, the website will look a lot like the current website. It will still have photos, downloadable PowerPoint presentations, downloadable homework, mini-cases, hands-on exercises, and errors pages.

Online Glossary

One major change to the website. The website now has an online glossary organized both by topic and alphabetically. Students can search online or print out the glossary for reading.

Contact Me

If you have any questions, please send me an e-mail. I'm Ray@Panko.com.

FOR NEW ADOPTERS

Thank you for adopting my textbook. If you have any questions or comments, please contact me at Ray@Panko.com. Also, please send me your e-mail address and have me put you on the adopters' mailing list. I'll occasionally send you news of really important new developments in the field (I won't do it often), let you know about major updates to the website, and occasionally send out questions that will help me design the next edition. (Many design choices in this edition are based on adopter feedback.)

If you didn't select the book yourself, you might look at the part of this Preface addressed to potential adopters. It will help you work with this book and its resources. By the way, if you didn't get the Instructor's Resource CD-ROM, you can request a copy from your Prentice Hall sales representative. If you aren't sure who that is, contact Prentice Hall's Faculty and Field Services department by calling 800-526-0485, if you are in the United States.

Selecting Coverage

This book has a modular design to provide teachers with flexibility rather than to present material to be covered in its entirety. At the end of this Preface, there are some sample syllabi indicating typical coverage.

The 11 core chapters provide a complete course in networking, usually with about a week to spare. The rest of the book is for selective enrichment rather than for complete coverage. The modules in particular are designed to let teachers cover extra material selectively without having to produce their own material.

If you have a two-term course, you can cover the entire book, but in a one-term course, most teachers cover the core chapters and a little more. For instance, in the last edition, about half of all adopters covered only the 12 core chapters (one more chapter than this time), and those that went beyond the core chapters usually covered only one or two modules' worth of material. (There were no mini-chapters after the main chapters in the last edition.) Module A (TCP/IP) and Module D (telephony) were the most frequently covered modules, but every module was covered by some adopters. The goal is to let you do things your way.

I personally cover the 11 core chapters plus Module A and the mini-chapters. I merely assign mini-chapters that are case studies as homework, and we go over the students' answers in class. I demo most of the hands-on mini-chapters in class, but I do take one day to have a hands-on class in which my students cut wire and add connectors. Cutting wire is really neat, and students really love it, but it requires about $125 for one set of stripping, cutting, and connectorizing tools to be shared by 10 students, and each student uses about $1.25 in UTP wire and RJ-45 connectors. You'll also need a wiring tester for about $125. (You'll really need a tester because only about two-thirds of all students get it right the first time.)

Using Chapter Review Questions

The chapter review questions are designed to focus student learning. Often, teachers assign a list of chapter review questions for homework or study and then base their exams on those questions. Within the chapters, test-your-understanding questions appear frequently, allowing students to check how well they just learned a section. At the end of each chapter, there are more challenging questions involving trouble-shooting, design, and advanced thinking about the material in the chapter. I also assign mini-chapter case study questions as homework.

Using Figures

To help students organize the material in their own heads, I've covered almost all key points in figures. Many of these figures are study figures (for example, Figures 1-1, 1-9, 1-10, 1-14, and 1-17), which outline key sections. My own students have found these very useful.

Contact Me

Again, if you have any questions, please send me an e-mail. I'm Ray@Panko.com.

FOR STUDENTS

Almost every information systems (IS) program today has a course in networking. Obviously this course is critical to students who will pursue networking as a career. However, programmers increasingly find themselves writing groups of programs on different machines; these programs communicate with each other over a network. Distributed databases are increasing in importance, and help desk personnel today deal as much with networking problems as with application software problems. For better or worse, networking will permeate your working life.

Some Tips on Using this Book

Doing the Review Questions

I've tried to make this book easy to study. First, focus on chapter review questions, which cover almost all key concepts and get you to think about what you have learned. As you go through the chapter, stop and do the test-your-understanding questions after each section before you go on to the next section. Also go back to these test-your-understanding questions when you study each section. In addition, do the end-of-chapter questions to get better insight into the material and how to apply it to real situations.

Study in a Group

I strongly suggest that after you have made up your own answers, you go have a study session with other students in the class and compare your answers. This is a great way to identify holes in your knowledge or at least see where you need to look at the material in more depth.

Study the Figures

In addition, the figures cover almost all important topics in the book, so go over the figures as well as the text itself. Especially important are "study figures" (for example, Figures 1-1, 1-9, 1-10, 1-14, and 1-17) which outline key points in whole sections.

Use the Book's Website

At the book's website (www.prenhall.com/panko), you can download PowerPoint lecture presentation, do hands-on exercises to do fun things (usually over the Internet), download the chapter review questions in Word for Windows format, and read study hints for each chapter. Before you start each chapter, you should check the website for reported errors and correct them in your textbook. Also, use the online glossary to check your understanding of terms. (You can also print out the glossary if you wish.)

Pursuing Networking as a Career

If you are considering networking as a career, you should know that job prospects are excellent, pay is good, and the work is challenging. You should also know that there are some things you should do besides your IS classes to help you land a good job and prepare for that career.

Systems Administration

For better or worse, networking professionals usually also have to manage servers and spend a majority of their time doing this. For historical reasons, this is called systems administration. It would be very good to take practical courses in managing Windows and LINUX servers. At a minimum, you should know how to give basic commands to move around the server's directory structure, how to add and drop users, and how to change user access permissions.

Certification

A major trend in the field is becoming certified to show that you possess a good level of knowledge. The easiest certification to get (note that I did not say easy) is the basic Cisco Systems certification, CCNA (Cisco Certified Network Administrator). With the material students learn in my textbook, you can learn what you need to pass the CCNA in about a normal course's worth of self study. I'd again strongly recommend group study. Todd Lammle has an excellent preparation book (*CCNA Cisco Certified Network Associate: Study Guide with CD-ROM, Deluxe Edition,* Sybex, November 2001). This book can be purchased with a router simulator that is not perfect but it is quite good. A fuller version of the simulator can be purchased from Routersim.com.

Internships

Classes and certification are good, but there is no substitute for experience. It is a very good idea to do at least one meaningful internship in networking while you are in school. Of course, a real job is even better.

SAMPLE SYLLABI

Here is a sampling of what teachers may wish to cover in their courses. Of course, coverage may deepen if students have had more networking background, and some schools cover material in other courses.

Community College or Technical Institute Course

Many community colleges with IT programs and technical institutes cover the 11 core chapters and some of the hands-on exercises (such as Chapters 3a and 4a). They usually cover the hands-on exercises using class demos or, if they have the equipment, using hands-on homework assignments. This gives a solid course in networking and telecommunications. Selective coverage of the hands-on exercises at the website is common.

Introductory Course for MIS Majors

In the general introductory course for MIS majors, it is common to cover the 11 core chapters. Beyond that, it is common to cover a few hands-on mini-chapters (such as Chapters 3a and 4a) using class demos and, if equipment is available, hands-on homework. It is also common to cover the case study mini-chapters (such as Chapters 1a and 5a) by assigning them as homework and going over the results with the students. Selective coverage of the hands-on exercises at the book's website is common.

In addition, there typically is time to cover about one advanced module's worth of material (either an advanced module or parts of a few advanced modules). Some teachers cover Chapter 10 in abbreviated format and cover applications in other classes and so free up another advanced module's worth of material. However, some teachers cover material in the advanced modules only slightly if at all, preferring to focus on the core chapters and the mini-chapters (small chapters that end with an "a"), or preferring to cover other information.

Schools on quarter systems can cover the same material if they have equivalent contact time to semester courses; if they have fewer contact hours, however, their coverage may have to limit their courses to the core chapters.

Two-Term Networking Course

Some schools have two-term networking courses. Those courses can cover the whole book. I find it best to cover the material in the advanced modules after the basic chapter they support. If the core material is covered in one term and the advanced material is covered the next, student forgetting will require going over the first term's material in some detail. Of course, this may be a benefit.

In addition, it would be extremely helpful to give students hands-on systems administration experience with Microsoft Windows and a UNIX network operating system (including LINUX). This knowledge is used widely by systems administrators.

MBA Course

MBAs are difficult to teach because they like technical depth but are more focused on management. The 11 core chapters provide the technical depth they will need. Whether to use the hands-on mini-chapters (such as Chapters 3a and 4a) is a difficult design issue because many MBAs "don't want to be technicians." In many cases, these exercises can be pointed out and left to them to do if they wish, and many will.

Cases studies are very important for MBAs. The mini-chapter case studies (such as Chapters 1a and 5a) are important because they are long enough to generate some class discussion, and the many small case studies at the book's website are attractive because they show the MBAs what real companies are doing. The selective use of hands-on exercises at the website is likely to be valuable.

In addition, in MBA courses, it is common to give term projects in which the MBAs examine an actual networking situation and make recommendations. If they do in-class presentations, this will reduce coverage of material in the book correspondingly.

About the Author

Dr. Ray Panko (Ray@Panko.com) is a professor of IT management in the College of Business Administration of the University of Hawaii. Before coming to the university, he was a project manager at Stanford Research Institute (now SRI International), where he conducted research for nearly every major telecommunications firm. He received his BS summa cum laude in physics and MBA from Seattle University. He received his doctorate in communication from Stanford University, where he graduated with a 4.0 GPA and where his dissertation was conducted under contract to the Office of the President of the United States.

His interest in networking began in the early 1970s, when the interdisciplinary Stanford "communications mafia" was at its peak and when a young doctoral student could work on verifying the effectiveness of the small satellite dishes we use today, could manage the design of a campus-wide LAN using cable television technology, and could pick a dissertation topic relevant enough for the White House to fund. Stanford Research Institute was even more fun because the author got to work on the ARPANET during its first few years, participate in discussions that defined e-mail, and work for Doug Engelbart, who invented the mouse and outline processing and who built the world's first working hypertext system and distributed team support system. In retrospect, it is amazing that many of the things he worked on then took so many years to come to fruition.

At the University of Hawaii, he discovered that teaching networking was even more fun than conducting research in networking and that writing a textbook could introduce thousands of students to this exciting field.

CORE NETWORK CONCEPTS

Learning Objectives:

By the end of this chapter, you should be able to discuss:

- The concept of a "network" and the six major elements in single networks: messages, application programs, stations, trunk links, access links, and switches.
- The client/server architecture that dominates modern networking, including the various types of client and server technologies and the role of directory servers.
- How to increase server scalability (if you study the box feature).
- How packet switching operates, including the general structure of messages and why packet switching saves money.
- Network quality of service (QoS).
- Types of networks by geographical scope.
- The distinction between single networks and internets; the difference between internets in general and the global Internet; and the role of IP addresses.
- The differences between the Internet, intranets, and extranets; the role of firewalls in protecting communities.

INTRODUCTION

The Global Internet: Living in Dog Years

The 21st Century really started in 1995, when use of the World Wide Web exploded on the global Internet. In only a handful of years, "You've Got Mail" became the title of a Hollywood movie, "e-commerce" became a household word, e-mail addresses became de rigueur on business cards, "dot-com" millionaires were created (and in many cases destroyed), and people actually became incensed when they had to go "offline" to find a piece of information. The global[1] Internet lives in dog years,[2] and organizations have been changing almost as rapidly.

Internal Corporate Networks

Although the Internet is glamorous, most of the power in networking today exists within **corporate networks**. Working at their desks, knowledge workers can get the information they need from computer files anywhere in the firm, communicate with one another, and manage their projects with fewer face-to-face meetings. The dull "back office" work in accounting and other clerical activities has become not only more efficient, but also much faster and better able to provide integrated management data. In addition, the Internet has enabled firms to connect their internal corporate networks to the wider world for e-commerce.

The Telephone System

Even the mundane "Plain Old Telephone Service" (POTS) is undergoing a revolution. Technology has slashed long-distance and international calling rates and will continue to do so. Even video transmission may soon be priced attractively. In addition, the worlds of voice and data, which are largely separate today, will **converge** into single networks that support both and that will allow applications to combine voice and data functionality.

Beyond Use Knowledge

The Internet explosion has shown that networking has become easy enough for children and computer novices to use Internet tools on a daily basis. However, this surface simplicity hides a great deal of inner complexity. Home users and marketing professionals may not have to understand how networks work, but you, as an information technology professional, will have to master the details of how networks really operate.

Networking and Programming

Even if you go into programming, networking will be everywhere you look. Today, client/server computing applications require programmers to write pairs of programs that communicate across networks instead of stand-alone programs. In coming

---

[1] The Internet usually is viewed as the transmission system. The World Wide Web, e-mail, and FTP are applications communicating over the Internet. Alternatively, the Internet is sometimes viewed as the transmission system plus all applications.

[2] Dogs are said to live seven years for every calendar year.

Major Network Types

    The Global Internet
    Internal Corporate Networks
    The Telephone System

Telecommunications

    Voice and Video Communication
    Data Communication

Figure 1-1 Major Network Categories

decades, "programs" will be systems of software "objects" scattered over dozens or even thousands of machines that will still work together through intense communication over networks (see Chapter 11).

Telecommunications and Data Networks

Telecommunications is a broad concept that embraces voice and video communication as well as the transmission of **data** (words, numbers, still images, and so forth). Once, there was a stark difference between the **voice and video networking** world and the **data networking** world. As just noted, most corporations still have two separate networks for these two different types of transmission, but in the future, all forms of information are likely to share a single network.

Networks

Figure 1-2 shows the six major hardware, software, and transmission elements found in networks—messages, applications, stations, switches, access links, and trunk links. *A **network** is a system of hardware, software, and transmission components that collectively allow two application programs on two different stations connected to the network to communicate well.*

    In this chapter, we will discuss all of the elements of a network except messages, which are the focus on Chapter 2. Most conversations on a network between applications, stations, and switches are long or brief exchanges of well-structured messages. In this chapter, we will look at two types of messages—frames and packets—and we will discuss the organization of messages in terms of headers, data fields, and trailers. However, the topic of standardized message exchanges is far more complex than we will discuss in this chapter.

TEST YOUR UNDERSTANDING

1. Distinguish between telecommunications and data networking.
2. a) What is a network? b) What are the six main elements of a typical network?

APPLICATIONS, CLIENT STATIONS, AND SERVERS

As Figure 1-2 shows, application programs reside on devices called **stations**.

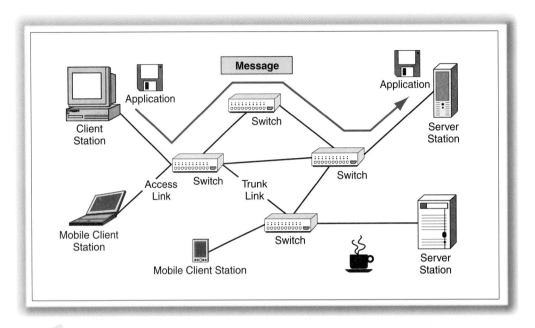

Figure 1-2 Elements of a Network

Applications

Stations are assumed to be **multitasking** computers that may run several application programs simultaneously. Messages must not only get to the correct machine; they also must also get to the correct application program on that machine.

Popular applications include file sharing, printer sharing, e-mail, the World Wide Web, electronic commerce, and access to corporate databases for accounting, payroll, billing, and other important "back-office" matters. Although specific applications are very important, networks usually treat all applications equally. You do not need a separate network for each application. The same network that gives employees access to World Wide Web servers on the Internet can also give them access to local print servers for their word processing documents.

Client/Server Architectures

When you use the World Wide Web, a distant webserver provides services to your PC. You are the client (customer) for this service, and your computer is called a **client station**. The computer that provides service to you is called the **server station**. This is called a **client/server architecture**. This architecture dominates in both large corporate and Internet applications.[3]

---

[3]   In Chapter 11, we will see peer-to-peer (P2P) architectures that eliminate or reduce the need for servers, but these are very uncommon today in corporate environments, so we will focus on the client/server architecture in this book.

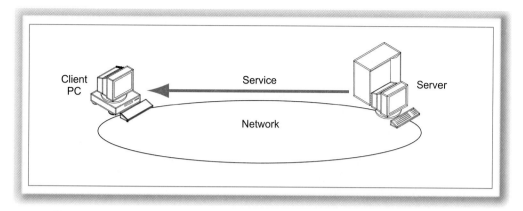

Figure 1-3   Client/Server Architecture

Popular Client Technologies

Desktop PCs: Wintel and Macintosh
The most common clients are desktop computers, which receive that name because they take up your entire desktop. Most desktop clients are **Wintel** computers, which run client versions of the Microsoft Windows operating system[4] and use a standard Intel Pentium microprocessor or a compatible microprocessor from one of Intel's competitors. Some are Macintosh PCs. When we say "PC" in this book, we will be including both Wintel and Macintosh PCs.

Mobile Stations
Desktop PCs are designed to be stationary. Other clients are designed to be mobile. Traditionally, notebook PCs were the only important mobile client computers, and generally they could only use networks through wired connections.

However, **wireless communication** now allows notebook computers to use a network from any location, even while they actually are moving. Wireless networking allows even smaller clients to be networked, including **cellular telephones (cellphones)**, **personal digital assistants (PDAs)**, and other emerging small devices such as **tablet PCs** about the size of a sheet of office paper (although, of course, thicker and heavier).

Network Interface Cards (NICs)
Most clients require a **network interface card (NIC)** to communicate over a network. This is a printed circuit board that usually sits inside the computer and connects to the access line leading to the first switch.

---

[4] Windows 3.X, Windows 9X, Windows ME, Windows NT Workstation, Windows 2000 Professional, and Windows XP.

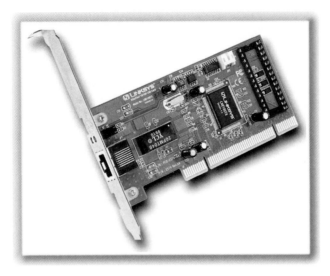

Figure 1-4 Internal Network Interface Card (NIC). Courtesy Linksys

Figure 1-5 PC Card Network Interface Card. Courtesy Linksys

Server Technology

Servers tend to be much more powerful computers than client PCs, although some servers with small and specialized tasks can even be obsolete PCs too slow for corporate client users. Figure 1-6 shows some common types of servers.

PC Servers and Network Operating Systems

PC Servers   PC servers are ordinary Macintoshes and Wintel PCs. Many are designed from the ground up to be servers; they typically have a great deal of RAM, very large and fast hard disk drives, and backup power supplies and fans. However, they still follow the standard Wintel or Macintosh hardware and software architecture.

Network Operating Systems   PC servers must have operating systems that can handle multiple users, rather than the single-user operating systems used on client PCs. For historical reasons, these server operating systems are called **network operating systems (NOSs).** For Intel-compatible PC servers, popular NOSs are Microsoft Windows NT/2000/.NET Server, Novell NetWare, and LINUX.

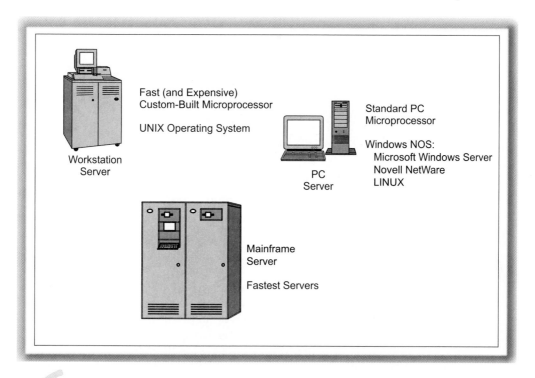

Figure 1-6 Servers

Figure 1-7 IBM eServer x200 PC Server

Workstation Servers and UNIX

As just noted, Wintel PCs use ordinary Intel or compatible mass-market microprocessors. Another type of server, the **workstation server**, uses custom-designed microprocessors. These microprocessors are faster than Pentium and compatible microprocessors but are also more expensive because of their need to push the state of the art in microprocessor

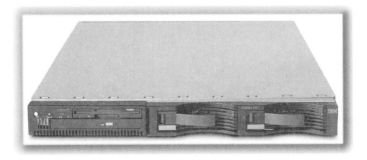

Figure 1-8   IBM eServer x130 Rack-Mountable PC Server

design and because of the limited number of these microprocessors that are sold. Basically, workstation servers are like racing cars in performance and price.

In addition, workstation servers run vendor-specific versions of the **UNIX** operating system. UNIX is extremely reliable and has a rich toolbox of management applications. Although difficult to learn and use, UNIX on a high-speed workstation server is the platform of choice for large enterprise servers.

Figure 1-9   IBM eServer p620 UNIX Workstation Server

Figure 1-10 IBM eServer z900 Mainframe Server

Mainframe Servers

Mainframe computers were designed to work with dumb terminals. However, mainframes can also be used as servers in client/server computing. In fact, IBM, which dominates the mainframe market, now calls its mainframes "enterprise servers." In addition to being faster than UNIX workstation servers, mainframes are even more reliable than UNIX workstation servers. However, mainframe power is more expensive than a comparable amount of workstation server power because mainframe hardware is expensive and because a mainframe requires a large staff of systems programmers.

Server Scalability

In networking, demand sometimes grows explosively within a very short period of time. Consequently, an important consideration for any technology is **scalability**, which is the ability to grow as demand grows. If you only use a single PC server, that is not a very scalable solution. However, if there is a growth path from a PC server to a workstation server, and then to a mainframe, you have a scalable solution. In the box later in this chapter, we will see that increasing scalability by having large numbers of PC or workstation servers work together is another option.

Directory Servers

Small companies may only have a single server at a single site. In contrast, larger companies have networks spanning multiple sites, with many servers at each site.

To manage multiple servers and other resources, firms often create special servers called **directory servers** that store important information about the firm's people and computers in a centralized location. As Figure 1-11 shows, other servers and client computers often ask the directory server for information.

In addition, directory servers store network **policies**, for example, security policies. As Figure 1-11 shows, the directory server sends these policies to other servers. This gives corporations centralized control over the implementation of important policies.

TEST YOUR UNDERSTANDING

3. What is a client/server architecture?
4. a) In this book, what systems are considered to be PCs? b) What is a Wintel PC? c) Give examples of some mobile client stations. d) What is a NIC?
5. a) What are the three types of servers? b) What is a NOS? c) What are the popular NOSs for PC servers? d) Distinguish between PC servers and workstation servers in terms of hardware and software. e) Distinguish between PC servers and workstation servers in terms of ability to handle large processing loads.
6. a) What is scalability? b) Why is scalability important in networking?
7. What are the purposes of directory servers?

Figure 1-11   Directory Server

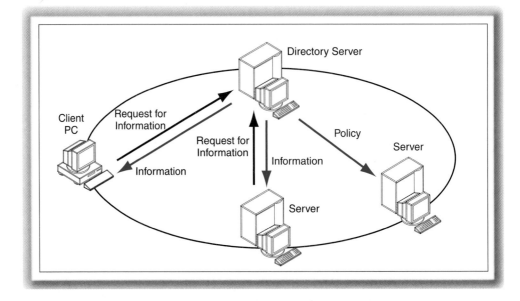

INCREASING SERVER SCALABILITY

As client demand grows, there is pressure to make servers more scalable. Growing from a PC server to a workstation server and then to a mainframe server is one alternative. However, companies can take three approaches to make servers more scalable *within a platform category*. Figure 1-12 shows these three approaches.

MULTIPROCESSING

Traditionally, PCs and workstation servers had a single microprocessor. However, it is now possible to buy **multiprocessing** PCs, workstation servers, and mainframes that have multiple microprocessors to share the workload. Going from one microprocessor to four or from four to sixteen does not quadruple capabilities because of the impossibility of keeping all microprocessors busy all of the time. However, adding more processors does increase the amount of work done substantially, although if one processor fails, the system usually becomes inoperable.

CLUSTERING

PCs, workstation servers, and mainframes can also be **clustered**, which means that a small number of them can be linked together to act as a single large server. In addition to providing scalability, clustering adds reliability. If the hardware in one computer in the cluster fails, others will take over the workload automatically. However, some software faults may cause the entire cluster to crash. Typically, clustering is limited to a small number of servers—generally 2 to 64.

LOAD BALANCING

For large "server farms" (collections of servers), **load balancing** allows dozens, hundreds, or even thousands of servers to be used. Requests come into a device called a load balancer, which typically is a router. (Routers are discussed later in this chapter.) The load balancer, acting like a railroad dispatcher, forwards each incoming request to an available server. As in the case of clustering, load balancing brings reliability. Also, like clustering, load balancing sometimes experiences the crash of all servers due to a common software fault.[5]

TEST YOUR UNDERSTANDING

8. a) What are the three ways to increase server scalability once you have selected a basic platform (PC server, workstation server, or mainframe server)? b) Which of these increases reliability?

---

[5] In both clustering and load balancing, it is possible to store many servers in a standard 19-inch wide equipment rack. The thinnest servers are 1U in height (1.75 inches.) With an 84-inch tall equipment rack, it is possible to install 48 1U servers. Racking servers conserves scarce floor space in equipment rooms. Most switches and routers (discussed later) also are 19 inches wide and multiples of 1U tall to fit into the equipment racks.

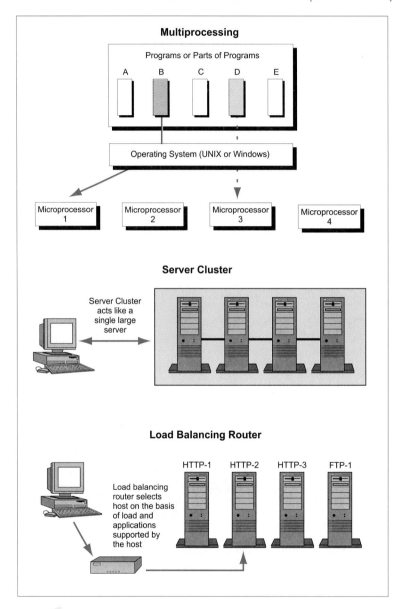

Figure 1-12   Increasing Server Scalability (and Sometimes Reliability)

TRANSMISSION LINKS

Trunk Links

The transmission links *between switches* are called **trunk links**. Trunk links carry the messages of many conversations. Consequently, trunk links usually have high capacity.

Access Links

Access links connect *stations to switches*. Usually, an access link is dedicated to a single user. Consequently, access links usually have less capacity than trunk links, which must carry many conversations.

Transmission Link Technology

Historically, most trunk links and access links used copper wires or optical fiber cabling, which limited transmission to a closed path. However, radio links are beginning to become popular as well, especially for mobile users.

SWITCHES

When trains travel from city to city, they often arrive at switch yards, where they are switched onto tracks that will take them closer to their destination. Switches do the

Figure 1-13   Small Office or Home (SOHO) Desktop Switch with 8 RJ-45 UTP Ports. Courtesy Linksys

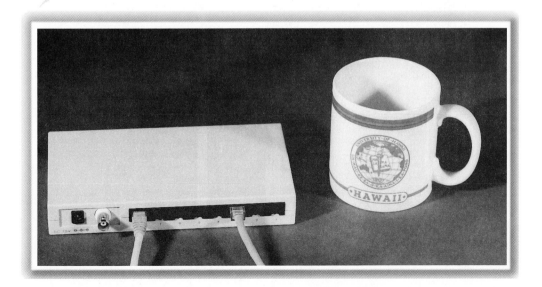

Figure 1-14   Stackable or Rack-Mountable Switches with RJ-45 UTP Ports. 19″ Wide. Courtesy Cisco Systems

Figure 1-15   Chassis Switch with Multiple 19″-Wide Modules. Courtesy Cisco Systems

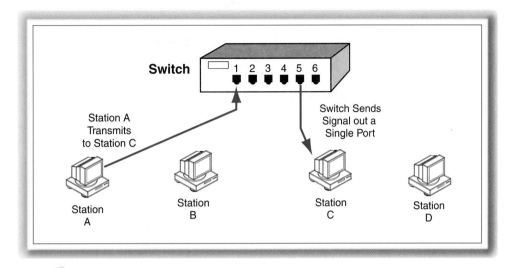

Figure 1-16   Switching Decision

same things for messages within a network. A **switch**[6] accepts a message through one port, makes a **switching decision** to select another port to send the message back out, and transmits the message out that port.

Packet Switching

Packets

For **data networking**, in which at least one of the parties is a computer, most switches are **packet switches**. As Figure 1-17 shows, stations divide transmissions into short messages called **packets**. Actually, "packet" is a generic term for any short message. Within a single network, these messages have a special name: **frames**.

Multiplexing to Reduce Costs

In packet switching, the packets of different conversations share transmission link capacity, much like cars sharing a highway's capacity on their way to work. This is called **multiplexing**. Packet-switched data network customers only pay for the portion of the trunk lines they actually use. This reduces trunk line cost, and this trunk line cost reduction is the main reason for the dominance of packet switching.

---

[6]   In Chapter 4, we will also see simpler devices (hubs) for connecting transmission links. However, modern single networks are "switch rich," meaning that they mostly use switches. The dominance of switches, furthermore, is growing.

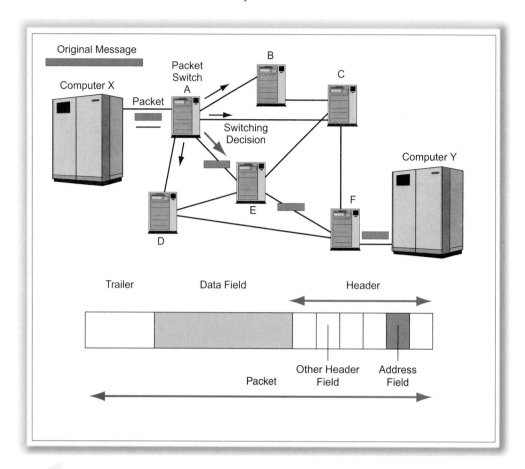

Figure 1-17   Packet Switching

Message Structure

Header, Data Field, and Trailer

Figure 1-8 shows that packets (including frames) can have three parts: a header, a data field, and a trailer.

The **data field** contains the information to be delivered. It usually is far longer than the header and the trailer and usually is the most important part of the message.

The **header** consists of everything coming before the data field, whereas the **trailer** consists of everything after the data field, like the initial and final parts of a postal letter. The header and trailer carry **supervisory information** to govern the communication.

All Three Are Not Always Present

Not all messages contain all three parts. In fact, trailers normally are not used. Furthermore, purely supervisory messages may not have a data field at all, although some purely supervisory messages put their supervisory information in the data field as well.

Fields and Network Addresses

The header and trailer are divided further into parts called **fields**. For instance, the header almost always has destination and source address fields that resemble the address and return address on a postal envelope. Each station in a network has a unique **network address**. For example, in Ethernet networks (Ethernet is the dominant technology for local area networks), every station has a unique 48-bit network address.

Address-Based Operation

To send a frame to another station on a packet-switched network, it is enough to put its network address in the destination address field of the frame. The switches in the network will determine the best way to deliver the frame to that station. The source station does not have to know the internal structure of the network, just as you do not have to know how the postal service functions internally when you send a letter.

TEST YOUR UNDERSTANDING

9. a) What are the two basic types of transmission links? b) Which connects a client to a switch? c) Which connects a switch to another switch?

10. a) What is a switching decision? b) What is packet switching? c) What is a packet? d) How does packet switching save money for data traffic? e) What are the three main parts of a message? f) The header and trailer are further subdivided into sections called what? g) Explain the importance of the address field. h) What is a message in a single network called?

QUALITY OF SERVICE (QoS)

In our definition of a network, we said that the application programs on different stations should be able to communicate *well*. The days when users would put up with slow speeds, long delays, and frequent outages are over. Customers increasingly demand **quality of service (QoS)** improvements and sometimes even QoS guarantees (which require the network provider to pay penalties if QoS guarantees are not met).

Speed

Networks should be fast. Normally, information transmission speed is measured in **bits per second (bps)**, where a **bit** is a single one or zero. Occasionally, speed is measured in bytes per second (Bps).

In increasing orders of 1,000—not 1,024 as in computer memory—we have **kilobits per second (kbps[7])**, **megabits per second (Mbps)**, **gigabits per second (Gbps)**, **terabits per second (Tbps)**, and **petabits per second (Pbps)**.

---

[7]   Americans should note that the standard metric abbreviation for kilo is small k, not capital K. Networking professionals, who deal with international standards, usually use lower-case k. American computer scientists, who tend to be metrically challenged, often retain the capital K they use for kilobytes.

Speed

Bits per second (bps)
Multiples of 1,000 (not 1,024)
Kilobits per second (kbps)
    Note the lower-case "k"
Megabits per second (Mbps)
Gigabits per second (Gbps)
Terabits per second (Tbps)
Petabits per second (Pbps)

Congestion and Latency

Congestion
Latency (measured in milliseconds)

Reliability

Availability (percentage of time the system can accept user data)
    Want 24x7x365 availability
    Telephone network provides "five nines": 99.999% availability
Error Rate
    Percentage of lost or damaged messages or bits

Service Level Agreements (SLAs)

Guarantees for various service parameters
Network provider pays performance penalties if guarantees are not met

Figure 1-18   Quality of Service (QoS)

Congestion and Latency

Even a 16-lane freeway may see traffic grind to a halt during rush hour. Similarly, when there is **congestion** in a network because more traffic is entering the network than the network can handle, speed will not reach its rated capacity. There will be a significant delay (called **latency**) between the time a frame is transmitted to the network and the time it is received.

Latency tends to be a few **milliseconds (ms)** in real-world networks even if there is little congestion. During periods of congestion, latency can reach hundreds of milliseconds. For some applications, such as voice telephony, even a moderate amount of latency can become intolerable.

Reliability

Another key goal of network designers is **reliability**. This means two things: availability and a low error rate.

Availability

First, there is **availability**, which is the percentage of time the network will accept and deliver messages. In the telephone network, the goal is "five nines"—99.999 percent availability. Data networks today fall far below this, and data network availability needs to be improved because corporations are growing ever more dependent on their data networks. In critical applications, $24 \times 7 \times 365$ availability is needed.

Error Rate

Second, there is the network's **error rate**, which is the percentage of bits or messages that are damaged or lost during transmission. On the Internet, for instance, about 6 percent of all messages are damaged or lost. Most networks do much better than this but still tend to have substantial error rates. Errors also increase latency because damaged or lost messages must be retransmitted.

Service Level Agreements (SLAs)

When companies deal with network suppliers, they want guarantees of service quality, not merely vague promises. Many network providers now offer **service level agreements (SLAs)**, which are written guarantees for such matters as speed, latency, availability, and error rates. If guaranteed goals are not met, the network provider will have to pay **performance penalties**. Some firms are even beginning to require their internal networking staffs to provide SLAs for the networks they support.

TEST YOUR UNDERSTANDING

11. a) List and briefly describe the major service quality parameters listed in the text.
     b) What is an SLA? c) What happens if SLA guarantees are not met?

GEOGRAPHICAL SCOPE

Local Area Networks

The smallest networks, in terms of geographical scope, are **local area networks (LANs)**. A LAN may consist of a few computers in a small office, all of the computers in a building, or all of the computers in a university campus or industrial park.

The important distinguishing feature of LANs is that LANs are limited to the **customer premises**, that is, land and buildings owned by the organization that creates and uses the LAN. On your premises, you can select any technology you want and implement it any way you wish. Of course, along with this flexibility comes the need for the organization to maintain the LAN itself.

Wide Area Networks (WANs)

In turn, **wide area networks (WANs)** transmit data *between* customer premises. They carry data between two corporate sites, between the corporation and a business partner, or between a site and a person working at home, in a hotel room, or on an airplane.

Customer Premises Operation Versus Carrier Networks

In addition to being wider in geographical scope than LANs, WANs are different because they are not on the customer premises. To use a WAN, a company must

Local Area Network (LAN)

Customer premises operation
Choice and need to manage
High speed and low cost per bit transmitted

Wide Area Network (WAN)

To link sites
Requires the use of carriers
Limited and complex choices but manage the network
High cost per bit transmitted
Usually low speed (56 kbps to a few megabits per second)

Metropolitan Area Network (MAN)

WAN that serves a single urban area
Usually offers higher speeds than longer-distance WANs

Figure 1-19   Geographic Scope

subscribe to service from a **carrier**, which is an organization with special government-granted **rights-of-way** to carry data where it needs to do so. (Imagine what would happen if you tried to run transmission wires through your neighbor's yard!) Competing carriers in an area tend to offer only a few service options and tend to have complex pricing schemes. On the positive side, they maintain the internal operation of the network, freeing users of that work.

LANs Versus WANs: Speed

Another factor that distinguishes LANs from WANs is speed. Long-distance transmission is far more expensive per bit transmitted than customer premises transmission. Consequently, whereas LANs usually provide 10 Mbps or 100 Mbps to the desktop station, most corporate demand for WANs falls between about 56 kbps and a few megabits per second.

Metropolitan Area Networks (MANs)

A special type of wide area network is the **metropolitan area network (MAN)**, which is a carrier network covering a single urban area. Thanks to the limited distances that must be spanned, MANs tend to be much faster and less expensive per bit transmitted than regional, national, or international WANs. Some analysts feel that we should view the MAN as its own category, so geographical scope should have the hierarchy of LANs, MANs, and WANs.

TEST YOUR UNDERSTANDING

12. a) Distinguish between LANs and WANs in terms of geographical scope. b) In terms of who provides service. c) How do LANs and WANs typically differ in price and speed?

13. Distinguish between WANs and MANs.

INTERNETS

Networks Versus Internets

So far, we have been talking about *single networks,* including individual LANs and WANs. Sometimes, however, it is necessary for stations on different networks to communicate. An **internet** is a group of networks linked together with routers in a way that allows an application program on any station *on any network* in the internet to be able to communicate with an application program on another station *on any other network.* Figure 1-20 shows an internet.

Routers

Whereas switches are used within single networks (LANs or WANs), **routers** are used to connect two or more single networks together into an internet. Routers must work collectively to route packets from the source host to the destination host across multiple single networks connected by routers. This requirement makes routers more complex (and expensive) than switches, which only have to forward frames within a single network.

The path a particular packet takes through an internet is called its **route**. Note that messages in internets really are called *packets,* in contrast to messages in single networks, which are called *frames.*

Packets and Frames

We have just noted that messages in single networks are called frames, whereas messages in internets are called packets. Figure 1-21 shows that frames and packets are related. Specifically, packets are end-to-end messages between hosts, whereas frames carry packets in single networks, much like delivery trucks carry cargo.

The sending host places the packet in a frame whose format is suitable for that network, say an Ethernet frame. When that frame arrives at a router, the router takes the packet out of the Ethernet frame and discards the Ethernet frame, whose work is finished. Suppose the next network is a Frame Relay network. The router will place the packet in a Frame Relay frame and send the frame out over the Frame Relay network to the next router or to the destination host. A packet hopping through 10 routers to get to a destination host will travel in 11 different frames along the way!

Internets Versus the Internet

There are many internets in the world. However, people are most familiar with a particular internet, the worldwide **Internet** that connects hundreds of millions of users around the world to millions of servers. We will use a lower-case "i" to designate a general internet and a capital "I" to designate the worldwide Internet. Figure 1-22 shows the major elements of the Internet.

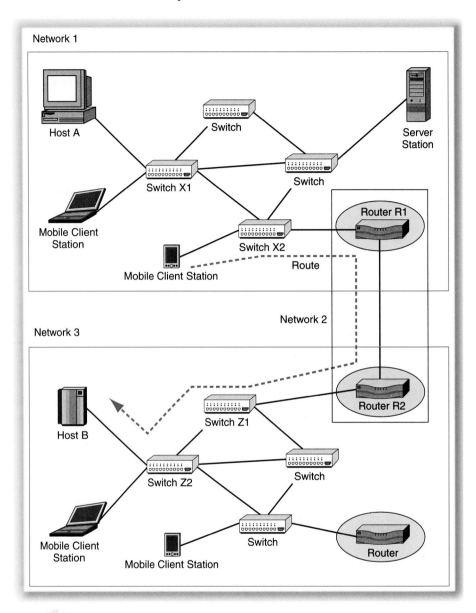

Figure 1-20   An Internet

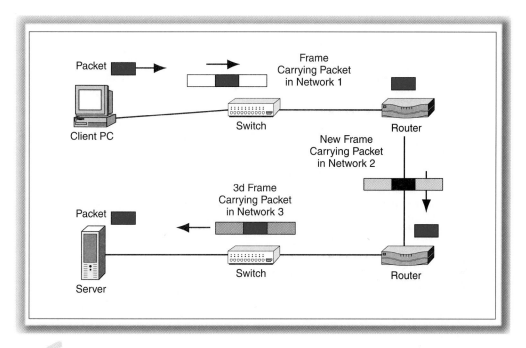

Figure 1-21   Frames and Packets

Figure 1-22   The Internet

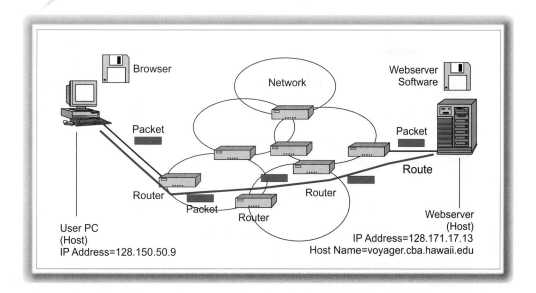

The Internet

Networks on the Internet

The Internet encompasses tens of thousands of individual networks. However, in Internet terminology, a "network" may not be a single network at all. It may itself be an internet owned by an organization, and this internet will have its own internal routers. In other words, in Internet terminology, a network is a collection of resources owned and operated by a single organization. When we are discussing the Internet, we will distinguish between "**Internet networks**" as organizational concepts and **single networks** as individuals LANs or WANs.

Hosts

All stations attached to the Internet are called **hosts**. A server is a host computer. So is a client PC or cellphone that is communicating over the Internet. On the Internet, "host" does not mean "server."

IP Addresses and Host Names

On a network, each station must have its own network address. However, on internets, stations need two addresses. One is their network address on their single network. The other is their internet address, which is unique among all stations on the internet.

IP Address   On the Internet, the official internet address of a host computer is its Internet Protocol address, or **IP address**. It is a 32-bit string of ones and zeros. Every

Figure 1-23   Host Addresses and Host Names

> **HOST IP ADDRESS**
>
> Official address of host on the Internet
> 32 bits long
> Dotted Decimal Notation for human reading (e.g., 128.171.17.13)
>
> **HOST NAME**
>
> Several labels separated by dots (voyager.cba.hawaii.edu)
> Like nickname; easy to remember
> Not the official address of the host
>
> **DOMAIN NAME SYSTEM (DNS)**
>
> You cannot send messages to a host if you only know its name
> Must know its official address (IP Address)
> Provides a way of finding a host's IP address if only its host name is known

host on the Internet, including your home PC or a cellphone, must have an IP address. This IP address must be unique on the Internet.

Dotted Decimal Notation   Routers and hosts work directly with 32-bit IP addresses. To aid human memory, however, IP addresses can be expressed in **dotted decimal notation**. A typical IP address in dotted decimal notation is 128.171.17.13. IP addresses always have four *segments* (numbers) separated by dots.

To change a 32-bit IP address into dotted decimal notation, divide the 32 bits into four 8-bit "segments." Treat each as a binary number and convert it into a decimal number.

It is important to emphasize that hosts and routers never work with dotted decimal notation. They always work in pure binary (ones and zeros). Dotted decimal notation is a way for human beings to represent IP addresses for their use. It is a concession to human memory weaknesses.

Host Names   In addition, a host may have a **host name**, which is easier to remember. Host names have two or more labels separated by dots. Examples are cnn.com, Panko.info, and voyager.cba.hawaii.edu.[8]

However, host names are unofficial. To send a packet on the Internet, the source host must know the destination host's IP address (although not the destination host's network address). Otherwise, routers will have no way to deliver the packet.

Domain Name System (DNS)   As Figure 1-27 shows, there are **domain name system (DNS)** hosts that provide a lookup function for IP addresses if you only know host names. When you type a URL that has the host name of a webserver, your PC's **DNS resolver** software automatically sends a DNS request message to the DNS host. This message contains the host name of the target host and asks for the target host's IP address. The DNS response message contains the IP address of the target host.

Figure 1-24   Small Office or Home (SOHO) Desktop Router with Built-In 4-Port Switch. 8″ Wide. Courtesy Cisco Systems

---

[8]   Voyager.cba.hawaii.edu has four labels. Its IP address, 128.171.17.13, has four segments. However, there is no connection between the four segments and the four labels. In particular, there is no way to compute the segment values from the label values or to do the opposite.

Figure 1-25 Stackable or Rack-Mountable Routers with Various Port Configurations. 19″ Wide. Courtesy Cisco Systems

Figure 1-26 Chassis Routers for the Internet Core with Multiple 19″ Modules. Courtesy Cisco Systems

USING WINDOWS CALCULATOR TO HANDLE DOTTED DECIMAL NOTATION

If you have Microsoft Windows, the Calculator accessory can convert between binary and dotted decimal notations. Go to the Start button, then to Programs, then to Accessories, and then click on Calculator. The Windows Calculator will then pop up.

BINARY TO DECIMAL

To convert eight binary bits to decimal, first choose View and click on Scientific to make the Calculator a more advanced scientific calculator. Click on the Bin (binary) radio button and type in the 8-bit binary sequence you wish to convert. Then click on the Dec (decimal) radio button. The decimal value for that segment will appear.

DECIMAL TO BINARY

To convert decimal to binary, go to View and choose Scientific if you have not already done so. Click on Dec to indicate that you are entering a decimal number. Type the number. Now click on Bin to convert this number to binary.

One additional subtlety is that Calculator drops initial zeros. So if you convert 17, you get 10001. You must add three initial zeros to make this an 8-bit segment: 00010001.

Another subtlety is that you can only convert one 8-bit segment at a time.[9]

---

[9]   Most versions of Excel have BIN2DEC and DEC2BIN functions for converting between binary and decimal. The cell formula "=BIN2DEC(binary number)" yields a decimal number, while the cell formula "=DEC2BIN (decimal number)" produces a binary number. For instance, =BIN2DEC(10) gives 2, while DEC2BIN(2) gives 10.

Figure 1-27   Domain Name System (DNS) Host

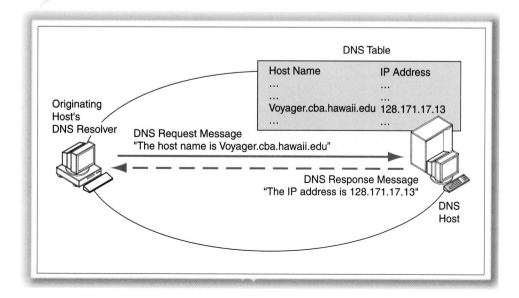

Internet Service Providers (ISPs)

When you connect to the Internet, you actually connect to an **Internet service provider (ISP)**, as Figure 1-28 shows. The ISP's technical function is to connect you to the main part of the Internet, called the Internet backbone.

The ISP charges you a fee. For an individual, this might be about $20 per month.[10] For a large company or a university, it might be a million dollars or more per year. The ISP keeps some of this money to pay for its internal transmission, router, and labor costs. It passes some of this money to Internet backbone companies to pay for their costs of operation. In general, the Internet today is a commercial operation with little government money involved. The ISP's economic function, then, is to fund the Internet.

The Internet Backbone

The Internet backbone, in turn, consists of many carriers that compete with one another to carry data between ISPs. (Some companies are both ISPs and backbone carriers.)

TEST YOUR UNDERSTANDING

14. a) Distinguish between networks and internets. b) What device connects networks in internets? c) Distinguish between internets and the Internet. d) What do we call the path a packet takes through an internet from the source host to the destination host?

15. The source host and the destination host are separated by seven routers. How many packets are sent along the route? How many frames?

Figure 1-28   Internet Service Providers (ISPs) and Internet Backbone Providers

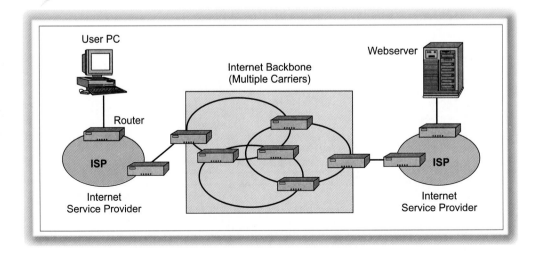

---

[10]   There are also a few "free" ISPs that make their money by requiring users to view advertising as they use the Internet.

16. a) Do you think the router changes the packet as it forwards it? b) The destination address in a packet in Figure 1-12 is the destination address of what device?

17. a) Do you think switches change frames when they switch them? b) In the frame in Network 1 in Figure 1-2, the destination address is the address of what device?

18. a) On the Internet, what is a host computer? b) When you connect to the Internet with a PC in your home or a laboratory, is your PC a host computer? c) What are the two types of host addresses on the Internet? d) Which is a host's official address? e) How long is an IP address? f) What happens if you know a target host's host name but not its IP address?

19. a) What are the two types of carriers on the Internet? b) What is the technical function of an ISP? c) What is its economic function? d) Describe the Internet backbone.

THE INTERNET, INTRANETS, AND EXTRANETS

Just as people were getting comfortable with the idea of the Internet, companies began talking about building "intranets" and "extranets." To understand these distinctions, you need to understand that they describe different types of **communities** whose members can communicate with one another.

Figure 1-29   The Internet, Intranets, and Extranets

Defined by Communities Served

The Internet

  Goal is universal community: include everyone

Intranets

  Community is a single (possibly multi-site) organization
  Use Internet transmission standards (see Chapter 2) and applications
  Limited communication with the outside world via firewalls

Extranets

  Community is a group of sellers and purchasers
  Only some hosts within each company are included
  Single seller with multiple buyers
  Single buyer with multiple sellers
  Marketplace with multiple buyers and sellers

Firewalls

  Protect network from nonallowed messages from the outside

The Global Internet

The goal of the global Internet is universality. By design, the Internet community attempts to include everyone in the world. Although it falls short of this, its goal is to have no limits.

Intranets

"Inter" means "between." The Internet was created to create connections between different networks to achieve universality. In turn, "intra" means "within." In an **intranet**, a firm uses Internet technology, including transmission standards (discussed in Chapter 2) and Internet applications (e-mail, the World Wide Web, etc.) for *internal* communication. The firm is its own limited community. Although employees can communicate internally even if they are at different corporate sites, people from the outside world cannot roam freely through the intranet. Security is extremely important. Outsiders can only come in if authorized.

Extranets

In an **extranet**, in turn, the community is a group of suppliers and purchasers who agree to communicate with one another under a certain set of rules. In one sense, extranets are larger than intranets because they involve multiple companies. In another sense, they usually are narrower than intranets because they only expose some hosts within each company. Some extranets consist of one supplier and its purchasers. Others consist of one purchaser and its suppliers. Still others are marketplaces that connect several purchasers and suppliers. Again, security is very important.

Firewalls

Many intranets use the Internet for transmission between corporate sites. Extranets often use the Internet to connect their firms. As Figure 1-30 shows, companies use devices called **firewalls** to separate allowed and nonallowed traffic. For instance, the firewall in the figure sits at the boundary between the firm and its ISP. Incoming intranet traffic from other sites is passed through the firewall. Outgoing messages to Internet World Wide Web servers and responses to these messages are also passed. However, unauthorized outsiders are denied access to internal intranet servers. Firewalls must examine each incoming and outgoing packet and make a pass-or-deny decision for it. It is like a security guard at the gate of a secure building.

TEST YOUR UNDERSTANDING

20. a) What is the community of the Internet? b) What is an intranet? c) What is an extranet? d) What is the role of a firewall?

GAINING PERSPECTIVE

Market Realities

Many ISPs today offer SLAs guaranteeing good service. Typical SLA values today are 50 ms maximum latency, 0.5 percent maximum packet loss, and 99.7 percent availability. The ISP will pay penalties if these guarantees are not met.

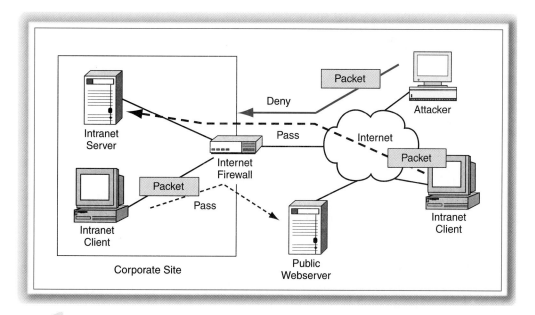

Figure 1-30   Firewall to Pass or Deny Messages

However, these guarantees only apply to the user's connection to the ISP. ISPs cannot guarantee maximum latency, maximum packet loss, and minimum availability for the Internet as a whole because they have no control over the Internet backbone or the other host's ISP. Packet losses on the Internet as a whole, for instance, often average 3 percent to 6 percent, whereas latency typically averages 100 ms to 500 ms.

THOUGHT QUESTIONS

1. Can you think of any mobile client not mentioned in the text?
2. Suggest at least one quality of service measure not listed in the text.
3. a) Express the following IP address in binary: 128.171.17.13. Use the method described in the box. *Hint:* 128 is 10000000. b) Convert the following address in binary to dotted decimal notation: 11110000 10101010 00001111 11100011. (Spaces are added between bytes to make reading easier.) *Hint:* 11110000 is 240 in decimal.
4. Why do you think the Internet is so attractive to businesses?

TROUBLESHOOTING QUESTIONS

1. Troubleshooting is a very important skill. A good idea is to draw a diagram of a system to see what might go wrong. Here is a sample problem for you to solve. You have been using a telephone modem to access the Internet. Its rated

download speed is 56 kbps. You switch to a digital subscriber line (DSL), which allows you to receive at 384 kbps. In general, your download speed for webpages is faster than it was with your modem; however, your actual download rates vary from only 128 kbps to 256 kbps. List likely reasons for your not getting a full 384 kbps. *Hint:* Consider Figure 1-16.

2. In your browser, you enter the URL of a website you use daily. After some delay, you are told that the host does not exist. What do you think happened?

CASE STUDIES

Do the Panko.info case study in Chapter 1a.

For other case studies, go to the book's website, www.prenhall.com/panko, and look at the Case Studies page for this chapter.

PHOTOS

For photos, go to the book's website, www.prenhall.com/panko, and look at the Photos page for this chapter.

PROJECTS

1. **Getting Current.** Go to the book website's New Information and Errors pages for this chapter to get new information since this book went to press and to correct any errors in the text.
2. **Internet Exercises.** Go to the book website's Exercises page for this chapter and do the Internet Exercises.
3. **Hands-On.** Find your computer's IP address. On a Wintel machine in your laboratory or at home, click on Start, and then Run. Run the winipcfg.exe program under Windows. Click on more information. What is your computer's IP address? If you have Windows NT or Windows 2000, go to the command line using CMD and type "ipconfig/all[Enter]".

CASE STUDY: PANKO.INFO

INTRODUCTION

The companion website for this edition is Panko.info. The website includes new information since the book went to press, photographs, short case studies, PowerPoint and Word for Windows downloads, hands-on Internet exercises, error reports, and other information for students. I personally maintain the site, working from my home PC.

WEB HOSTING

It would make no sense for me to have my own server, lease a high-speed connection to an Internet service provider (ISP), and manage this hardware and communication line on an ongoing basis. I do not have the time to do all this, and it would not be cost-effective.

Instead, as Figure 1a-1 shows, I pay a **web hosting company** to maintain my server and its connection to the Internet. In other words, despite being only a one-person company, I outsource my basic web operations.

Servers

The web hosting company has a large **server farm** with thousands of servers on a single local area network. They offer their customers three basic options for using hosting servers.

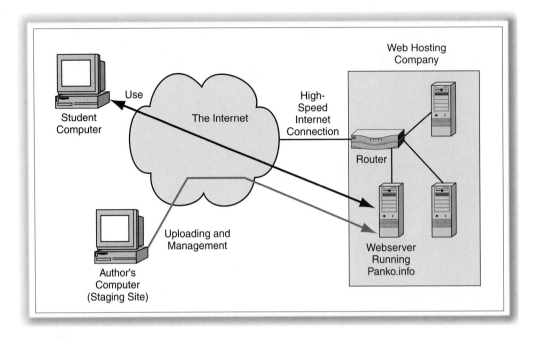

Figure 1a-1   Web Hosting Service for Panko.info

➤ **Co-Location**. In this approach, the client company buys its own server, ships it to the web hosting company, and has the web hosting company install the server. The web hosting company usually manages the server, although the client company sometimes even manages the server remotely. This is the most expensive option, but it gives the most control to the client.

➤ **Dedicated Servers**. This option gives you a server owned by the web hosting company but used by you exclusively. There is no one else on the server whose users will compete with yours, and there are no configuration conflicts.

➤ **Shared Servers**. On a shared server, you are one of a handful of websites being hosted on a single server. Although you have your own domain name, such as Panko.info, you do not have your own machine. This is the least expensive option, but if other websites sharing the server have high-load days, the response time of your users will suffer. Panko.info uses a shared server because of its small size.

Connection to the Internet

Access Line

Web hosting companies have high-speed access lines to their Internet service providers (ISPs). Some even connect to two different ISPs for reliability. Typical access speeds are 45 Mbps and 156 Mbps. These are adequate for excellent response time.

Router

As Figure 1a-1 shows, the web hosting company has a router at its connection to the Internet. When this router receives a World Wide Web HTTP request message addressed to Panko.info, it forwards the message to my server, and my server passes the request to my website.

Security

One advantage of using web hosting is security. Web hosting companies are large enough to have full-time security staffs and strong firewalls to protect their hosts from Internet hackers. In addition, if hackers do break in, they can only break into the web hosting network. They cannot get into your corporate network. On the negative side, a dishonest web hosting employee can read proprietary data on your website.

DOMAIN NAME

Getting a Domain Name

To get the second-level domain name Panko.info, I had to go to an Internet **registrar**—in my case Network Solutions (www.netsol.com). I went to the site, searched on "Panko," and found that both Panko.info and Panko.com were available. I purchased both. I paid $70 per domain name initially for two years, and I pay $20 per year thereafter for Network Solutions to maintain this domain name.

Getting a DNS Host

In Chapter 1, we saw Domain Name System (DNS) servers. These servers know which host is associated with each domain name. My web hosting company, in addition to providing me with a webserver, hosts the IP address of Panko.info's webserver on their DNS server.

MANAGEMENT

The web hosting company allows me to manage my website using my home PC's browser. I can add user accounts, change user access permissions, and do many other things. Of course, what I do only affects my portion of the shared server.

In some cases, however, I have to contact the web hosting companies to do management work. For instance, if the server crashes, I often have to tell them about it.

In addition, because I am a small client, I am not always the first to know what happens at the web hosting company. For instance, the website uses FTP downloading extensively. The web hosting service's FTP capabilities were a major reason for my selecting the site. Without telling me, however, they cut off all anonymous FTP downloading on their servers for security reasons. It took me three days to learn this, and it was several days before I could get another anonymous FTP site established. During that time, students and teachers could not download files.

BUILDING THE WEBSITE

FrontPage

My main website development tool is Microsoft FrontPage. I build the website on my computer at home. Building and testing a website on a separate machine before uploading it to its webserver is called having a **staging site**.

When it is time to upload the website to the host, I simply go to the file menu and choose "Publish." FrontPage then asks me for the name of the website, and I type "Panko.info." It takes me to the website, where I have to give my user name and password for my server.

FrontPage, in cooperation with my shared webserver, then uploads the webpages automatically. It is even smart enough to upload only pages that have changed. To be able to work with me like this, my server must have FrontPage extensions.

E-Commerce

If I wish to add e-commerce capabilities to my website—say if I wanted to sell "I Survived Networking" T-shirts—my web hosting company's servers have this capability. For instance, when a user wishes to make a secure purchase, the transaction must be encrypted so that an interceptor cannot read it.[1] My hosted web server is capable of implementing this. My web hosting company will also allow me to run a database management system program on my server and will facilitate a connection to a credit card company (although I first have to establish a **merchant account** with a bank).

Web Design Service

Web hosting companies will even design and create your website for a fee. As you can see by my website, I did not use this service.

PRICE

What does web hosting cost? The answer is that price depends on what you will be doing.

➤ The sky is the limit for co-location servers, but for shared servers, the price generally ranges from $20 to $200 per month for a website (Panko.info is near the low end of the size range.)

➤ The price is based on download traffic, the number of e-mail accounts you wish to have, and other services.

➤ Most web hosting companies have three to six service bundles in increasing order of capability and cost.

➤ There also is an initial setup fee, which equals a few months' service fees.

➤ There are additional costs for using e-commerce and database capabilities.

➤ If you have the web hosting company design and build your website, you can expect to pay thousands of dollars.

---

[1]   This protocol is called the Secure Sockets Layer (SSL) protocol or the Transport Layer Security (TLS) protocol, depending on its version.

TEST YOUR UNDERSTANDING

1. a) What is web hosting? b) What are the advantages of web hosting?

2. a) What are the three options for web hosting servers? b) In a table, list the advantages and disadvantages of each. c) Which did the author choose? Why? d) Did this choice create any problems?

3. a) How do you get a domain name for your website? b) Who hosts the domain name on their DNS server?

4. a) How do I build my website? b) What is a staging site? c) How do I upload my website to my hosted webserver?

5. Besides hosting your webserver, what service options do web hosting companies provide (for additional fees)?

STANDARDS

Learning Objectives:

By the end of this chapter, you should be able to discuss:

- Layered communication and the purposes of the application, transport, internet, data link, and physical layers.
- What constitutes a physical link, a data link, and an internet link (route).
- Important distinctions between switches and routers, including the highest layer of operation and format conversion.
- Encapsulation and decapsulation processes in vertical layered communication within a single host, switch, or router.
- Differences between the TCP/IP and OSI standards architectures, including layering and standards agencies.
- Minor standards architectures, including IPX/SPX, SNA, AppleTalk, and NetBEUI.

INTRODUCTION

In Chapter 1, we saw the hardware, software, and transmission components of networks. In this chapter, we will look at the standards that govern how these components communicate with one another.

Warning: Difficult Material

You should be warned in advance that the material in this chapter is the most difficult material in networking. It is highly conceptual, and there is a great deal to learn. Most importantly, it is critical to keep looking up from the details to see how each piece you are studying fits into broader patterns.

The Importance of Standards

What Are Standards?

In the last chapter, we covered all of the basic concepts in networking, except for one—the most important concept of all, standards. As Figure 2-1 illustrates, **standards** are rules of operation that govern communication between two (or more) hardware or software processes on different machines.

Benefits of Standards

Standards are critical because they allow hardware and software processes from different vendors to **interoperate** (i.e., work together). Interoperability creates competition, which lowers prices and speeds the pace of technological advancement. It also allows us to buy products secure in the knowledge that if our vendor fails, we can still buy compatible products from other vendors.

Message Exchange: The Internet Protocol (IP) Packet

As Chapter 1 noted, this communication usually involves the exchange of highly structured messages. Figure 2-2 shows perhaps the most important message on the Internet, the **Internet Protocol (IP) packet**. The packet is really a long string of ones

Figure 2-1   Standards Govern Communication

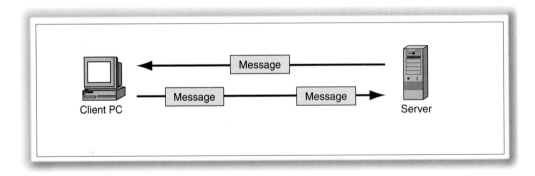

Bit 0			Bit 31
Version (4 bits)	Header Length (4 bits) in 32-bit words	Diff-Serv (8 bits)	Total Length (16 bits) length of entire packet in bytes
Identification (16 bits) Unique value in each original IP packet		Flags (3 bits)	Fragment Offset (13 bits) Octets from start of original IP fragment's data field
Time to Live (8 bits)	Protocol (8 bits) 1=ICMP, 6=TCP, 17=UDP	Header Checksum (16 bits)	
Source IP Address (32 bits)			
Destination IP Address (32 bits)			
Options (if any)		Padding (To 32-bit boundary)	
Data Field (dozens, hundreds, or thousand of bits)			

Notes:

Bits 0–3 hold the version number.

Bits 4–7 hold the header length.

Bits 8–15 hold the Diff-Serv information.

Bits 16–31 hold the total length value.

Bits 32–47 hold the Identification value.

Figure 2-2   Internet Protocol (IP) Packet

and zeros. In this figure, 32 bits are shown on each line. Note that the header is divided into 12 or more fields. The most important of these, the destination IP address field, holds the IP address of the host to which the packet is being sent. Although the header looks large, it is only 20 bytes long without options (which are rare). The data field, in contrast, usually contains dozens, hundreds, or thousands of bytes. Note that there is no trailer in an IP packet.

TEST YOUR UNDERSTANDING

1. a) What are standards? b) What are the benefits of standards?
2. a) How long is an IP header if there are no options? b) What bit number in the header marks the start of the destination address field? (*Note:* The first bit in binary counting is the zeroth bit.)

LAYERED COMMUNICATION

The key concept in this chapter is **layering**. As Figure 2-3 illustrates, the successful delivery of messages from one application layer program to another across an internet requires many different hardware and software processes to talk to one another, using different standards to organize their communication.

Horizontal Communication Through Protocols

Protocols are standards that govern communication between peer processes on different machines but at the same layer (horizontal communication). For instance, communication between the browser on the user PC and the webserver application program on the webserver is governed by the Hypertext Transfer Protocol (HTTP). We

Figure 2-3   Message Communication in the TCP/IP Layered Standards Architecture: An Example

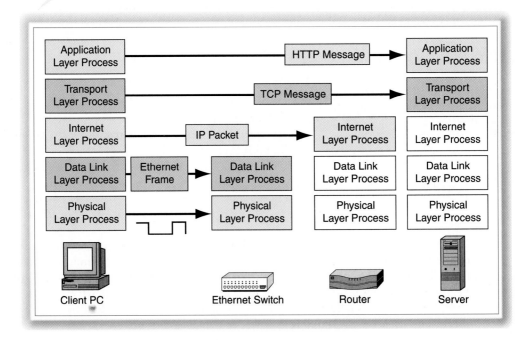

> The purpose of the **application layer** is to allow two application programs on different hosts to work together.
>
> The purpose of the **transport layer** is to allow two host computers to talk to one another even if they have very different internal designs, such as a PC and a workstation server.
>
> The purpose of the **internet layer** is to route packets from the source host to the destination host across one or more routers.
>
> The purpose of the **data link layer** is to govern how the movement of messages from a source station to a destination station or router across a single network containing switches.
>
> The purpose of the **physical layer** is to govern the transmission of bits one at a time over a wire, radio, or other connection between a station and a switch, between pairs of switches, or between a switch and a router.

Figure 2-4   Layer Purposes

will focus on horizontal communication using protocols within single layers in the first half of this chapter.

Layers

The Application Layer

The top layer is the application layer. The purpose of the **application layer** is to allow two application programs on different hosts to work together. When a browser talks to a webserver application program, the standard for communication is the Hypertext Transfer Protocol (HTTP). This is why website URLs begin with HTTP://.

The Transport Layer

The purpose of the **transport layer**, in turn, is to allow two host computers to talk to one another even if they have very different internal designs, such as a PC and a workstation server. If you use HTTP at the application layer, you are required use the Transmission Control Protocol (TCP) at the transport layer.

The Internet Layer

The purpose of the **internet layer** is to route packets from the source host to the destination host across one or more routers. TCP requires the use of the **Internet Protocol (IP)** at the Internet layer.

The Data Link Layer

The purpose of the **data link layer** is to govern the movement of messages from a source station to a destination station or router across a single network containing switches. If the client station is located on an Ethernet LAN, the Ethernet data link layer standard is used (see Chapter 4 for complications to this statement).

The Physical Layer

The purpose of the **physical layer** is to govern the transmission of bits one at a time over a wire, radio, or other connection between a station and a switch, between pairs of switches, or between a switch and a router. For a station on an Ethernet LAN, an Ethernet physical layer standard will be used. (Ethernet offers multiple physical layer standards.)

Only an Example

After seeing the example shown in Figure 2-3, some students get fixated on HTTP, TCP, IP, and Ethernet, believing that they will always be the standards they see. Nothing could be further from the truth. In different situations, you will use different standards at these layers.

For instance, Figure 2-5 shows the protocols you will use if you connect to the Internet via a telephone line and a modem instead of Ethernet and if you are down-loading your e-mail instead of using a webserver. In these examples, only TCP and IP remain. In other situations, you may not even use TCP and IP. Focus on the layers instead of on specific standards.

TEST YOUR UNDERSTANDING

3.   a) What are protocols? b) What are the five standards layers shown in Figure 2-3? c) Define the purpose of each layer.
4.   In layered communication, is HTTP always used at the application layer? Explain.

THE PHYSICAL, DATA LINK, AND INTERNET LAYERS

We will now begin to look at layers in more depth, beginning with the three lowest layers—the physical, data link, and internet layers.

Figure 2-5   Protocols in Two Examples

Layer	Example 1: Internet Web Access from a LAN	Example 2: Downloading Internet E-Mail over a Telephone Line and Modem
Application	HTTP	POP
Transport	TCP	TCP
Internet	IP	IP
Data Link	Ethernet	PPP
Physical	Ethernet	Modem (V.92)

Introduction

The purpose of the three lowest layers is to move messages from the source host to the destination host, across one or more networks. Figure 2-6 illustrates this with a simple situation. Here, messages between the source and destination host must travel across

Figure 2-6   Physical, Data Link, and Internet Layer Transmission

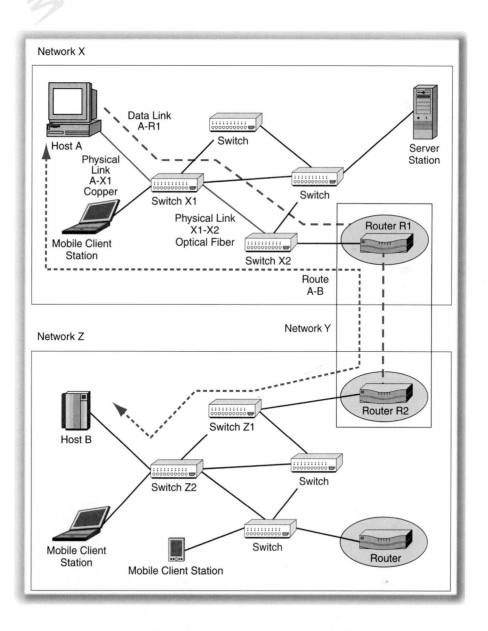

three networks. Networks X and Z are Ethernet LANs with switches. Network Y is a direct high-speed point-to-point connection. In real internets, of course, a dozen or more networks may separate the source and destination hosts.

Figure 2-7 summarizes how the physical, data link, and internet layers differ. In the next section, we will explain this figure row-by-row.

Links and Messages

The three layers differ first in what link (physical or logical connection between devices) each layer governs.

Internet Layer Link: Route

The internet layer is the biggie. It governs the link (connection) between the source and destination hosts across an entire internet. The internet layer link runs from Host

Figure 2-7   Comparing the Physical, Data Link, and Internet Layers

Layer	Physical	Data Link	Internet
Scope	Physical connection between station and switch, switch and switch, switch and router, etc.	Single Network. Station–Station or Station–Router across multiple switches	Internet (Across multiple single networks) Host–Host across multiple networks (route)
Link	Connection between two devices	Path across a single network (Data Link)	Route across an internet
Messages Are Called	None: Bit-by-Bit Transmission	Frame	Packet
Connecting Device	Repeater	Switch	Router
Device Layer	1	2	3
Format Conversion	None	Switches convert between different physical layer connections for different ports.	Routers convert between different networks—different physical and data link layer standards.
Following the Same Standard		All switches within a single network must follow the same data link layer standard.	All routers in an internet must follow the same internet layer standard.

A through Network X to Router R1, then through Network Y to Router R2, and finally through Network Z to Host B.

Routes   The internet layer link that a specific message travels through between the two end hosts is called its **route**. In Figure 2-6, the route runs from Host A to Host B across the connections shown.

Internet Protocol (IP)   All communication along this route is governed by the Internet Protocol (IP) standard, whose packet structure we saw earlier. IP allows host-to-host routing even when routers are connected in very complicated ways. If you are taking a cross-country trip, think of the internet layer as the entire route you will be taking from your home to your final destination.

IP Packets   Internet layer messages in general are called **packets**. Although the Internet Protocol calls its messages IP *datagrams,* nearly everyone calls them IP packets.

Data Link Layer Link

Data Links   Data links are more limited. **Data links** span an individual network, passing through several switches between the two stations, two routers (see Network Y), or a station and a router at the ends of the single network (see Networks X and Z).

A Data Link for Each Network   Along the internet layer route shown in Figure 2-6, there are three data links. The first runs from Host A to Router R1 across two switches. The second runs from Router R1 to Router R2. The third runs from Router R2 to Host B across two switches.

Different Data Link Standards   In different networks, there can be different data link layer standards.

➤ For instance, in Networks X and Z, the switches all follow the Ethernet data link layer standard.[1] This allows them to create an end-to-end path within a single network.

➤ Network Y, in turn, follows the **Point-to-Point Protocol (PPP)** between the two routers. PPP is used in the special case where switches are not used in a network because there is a single physical link between the two end points of the network.

Frames   Data link layer messages in general are called **frames**. Each standard specifies different specific frame organizations. For Ethernet networks, there are Ethernet frames. For direct connections, there are Point-to-Point Protocol (PPP) frames.

Ethernet Frames   Figure 2-8 shows the Ethernet frame containing the IP packet in its data field. Note that the Ethernet frame has a 48-bit MAC destination address.[2] Whereas IP packets have the internet layer address of the destination host, data link layer frames have the destination address of a specific router or host within the single network. In Figure 2-5, when Host A sends an IP packet addressed to Host B, Host A's

---

[1] As we will see in Chapter 4, Ethernet actually divides the data link layer into two layers. However, treating the data link layer as a single layer is a good approximation for our purposes in this chapter.

[2] Why MAC? See Chapter 4.

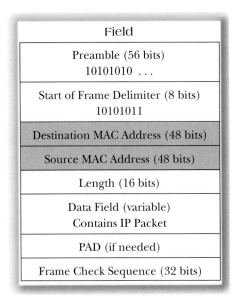

Field
Preamble (56 bits) 10101010 . . .
Start of Frame Delimiter (8 bits) 10101011
Destination MAC Address (48 bits)
Source MAC Address (48 bits)
Length (16 bits)
Data Field (variable) Contains IP Packet
PAD (if needed)
Frame Check Sequence (32 bits)

Figure 2-8 Ethernet MAC Layer Frame

data link layer process carries this packet in a frame addressed to Router R1. Remember that the data link layer is only concerned with transmission across a single network, in this case, Network X.

Physical Links

Finally, each connection between two devices, whether they are hosts, switches, or routers, is a **physical link**.

Different Physical Link Standards Every physical link in the network can follow a different physical layer standard. Although such extreme diversity is rare, it is common to find several different physical links even within a single network.

For instance, consider Switch X1. The physical connection between it and Host A is copper wire. The physical link between Switch X1 and Switch 2, in contrast, is optical fiber.

No Messages At the physical layer and only at the physical layer there are no messages. The transmission is done bit-by-bit.

TEST YOUR UNDERSTANDING

5. a) What two devices do routes connect at the internet layer? b) What two devices do data links connect at the data link layer? c) What two devices do physical links connect at the physical layer?

6. a) What are messages called at the internet layer? b) At the data link layer? c) At the physical layer? (Trick question.)

7. a) A station's MAC address is its address on its _____. b) A station's IP address is the station's address on its _____.

Connecting Devices

Routers

Routing Internet Layer Messages (Packets)   For the internet layer, routers are the connecting devices. Working together, they route internet layer messages (packets) end-to-end between the host computers, across multiple single networks.

Layer 3 Devices   We call routers **Layer 3 devices** because their central function relates to the internet layer. The internet layer is the highest layer that operates in a router during routing (packet forwarding) decision making.

Switches

Switching Data Link Layer Messages (Frames)   At the data link layer, the connecting devices are switches. Switches work together to forward data link layer messages (frames) end-to-end across a single network between a station and a station, between a station and a router, or between a router and a router.

Layer 2 Devices   Switches are **Layer 2 devices** because they handle data link layer functions as their highest layer of operation.

Repeaters

Extending Physical Links   Normally, physical links are single lengths of wire, single lengths of optical fiber, or single transmission paths for radio waves. In some cases, however, devices called **repeaters** can be used to extend the distance of a physical link. Repeaters are rare in corporate networking, except in the case of a device called a hub, which we will see in Chapter 4.

Layer I Devices   Repeaters are **Layer 1 devices** because they operate entirely at the physical layer.

TEST YOUR UNDERSTANDING

8. a) What type of connecting device is a Layer 3 device? b) A Layer 2 device? c) A Layer 1 device?

Format Conversion

Switches Convert Between Different Physical Link Formats

A switch has multiple ports, each connected to a different physical link. What if a switch must pass a frame between an incoming port and an outgoing port that have different physical layer connections? For instance, suppose the incoming port connects to a copper wire physical link and the outgoing port connects to an optical fiber link. As Figure 2-9 shows, there is no problem. Switches perform format conversion between different physical layer standards.

At the same time, all switches within a single network must follow the same standard at the data link layer. All must be Ethernet switches or some other type of switch. Otherwise, they would not even be able to understand the frames passing through them. In Figure 2-10, Network 1 uses Ethernet switches, but Network 2 uses ATM switches.

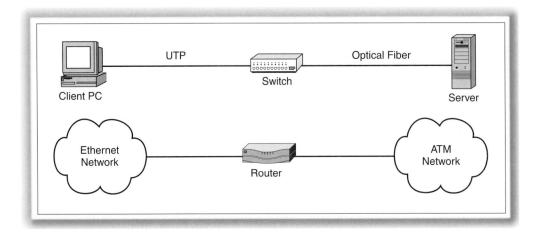

Figure 2-9   Format Conversion

Figure 2-10   All Switches in a Network and All Routers in an Internet Must Follow the Same Standard

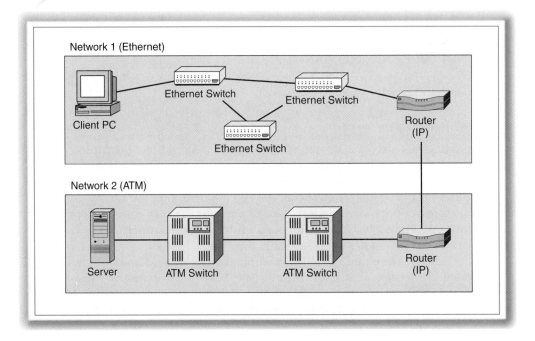

Routers Convert Between Different Network Formats

Routers are even better at format conversion. As Figure 2-9 shows, routers connect different *networks,* not just different physical links. Here, a router connects an Ethernet network to an ATM network.

At the same time, all routers in an internet must follow the same internet layer standard, most commonly IP, as indicated in Figure 2-10.

TEST YOUR UNDERSTANDING

9. a) Switches convert between different ____ formats. b) Routers convert between different ____ formats.

10. a) All switches in a single network must follow the same ____ layer standard. b) All routers in an internet must follow the same ____ layer standard.

LAYER COOPERATION AT THE PHYSICAL, DATA LINK, AND INTERNET LAYERS

In the previous section, we looked at horizontal communication between processes at the same layer but on different machines. That is a valid view of standardized message communication, and it must be understood.

However, message communication also involves communication between adjacent layer processes *on the same machine.* Horizontal and vertical communication processes work together in the total scheme of things, but the human mind finds it easier to move back and forth between horizontal and vertical communication when thinking about standardized message communication.

Vertical Message Communication on the Source Host

Figure 2-11 shows vertical communication on the source host, at the internet, data link, and physical layers.

At the Internet Layer on the Source Host

The internet layer process on the source host (Host A in Figure 2-6) creates the IP packet to be delivered to the destination host. This packet has a header and a data field. The header has a destination address field that contains the IP address of the destination host.

Passing the Packet Down   Now comes the vertical communication part. When the internet layer process creates the IP packet, it immediately passes the packet down to the next-lower-layer process, the data link layer process.

Passing the Message Down Is a General Process   Speaking more generally, whenever any layer process creates a message, it immediately passes it down to the next-lower-layer process. The only exception is the physical layer, because there is no next-lower-layer process.

At the Data Link Layer on the Source Host

The data link layer process now creates a frame, placing the IP packet in the data field of the frame. We now have a frame header, a frame data field (the IP packet), and a frame trailer.

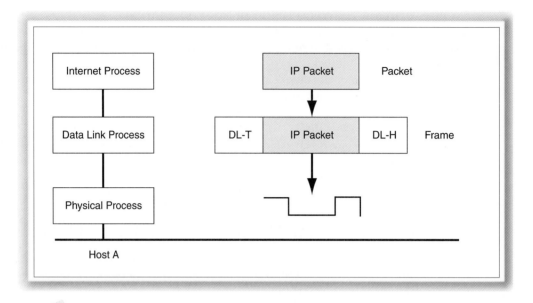

Figure 2-11   Vertical Communication on the Source Host

Encapsulation   This process of placing a message in the data field of another message is called **encapsulation**. It is one of the most common processes in vertical communication.

To use a shipping analogy, the IP packet is like a shipping container, and the frame is like a delivery truck. Encapsulating the IP packet within a frame is like placing the shipping container in the truck's bed.

Passing the Frame Down   As soon as the data link layer process creates the frame (an Ethernet frame, in our example), it does what any good process does. It passes the frame down to the next-lower-layer process, the physical layer process.

At the Physical Layer on the Source Host

The frame is a long string of ones and zeros (usually several hundred bits). The physical layer process converts each bit into a physical layer signal and sends it over the physical link to the next device, in this case, Switch X1.

TEST YOUR UNDERSTANDING

11.   a) What do the application, transport, internet, and data link layer processes on the source host do as soon as they create a message for their peer on another machine? b) What is encapsulation? c) When the Layer *N* process passes the message down to the Layer *N*-1 process, which layer performs encapsulation?

On Switch X1 (and Switch X2)

Figure 2-12 shows what happens when Switch X1 receives the bits of the frame. The port that receives the frame (Port 1) contains a physical layer process. That process converts arriving signals into the bits of the frame and then passes the frame up to the switch's data link layer process.

The Switching Decision

The data link layer process looks at the arriving frame's address field, which contains the 48-bit network address of Router 1. On the basis if this address, the switch decides that it should send the frame back out Port 4.

The Outgoing Port

The data link layer process now passes the frame down to the physical layer process in Port 4. That physical layer process converts the bits of the frame into signals and sends them on to Switch X2, which passes the frame on to Router R1.

Switches Do Not Change Frames

Generally speaking, switches do not change frames. They merely look at them, make a switching decision, and then pass them on. The frame created by the source station gets to the destination station unchanged or with at most minor supervisory information

Figure 2-12   Vertical Communication on Switch X1

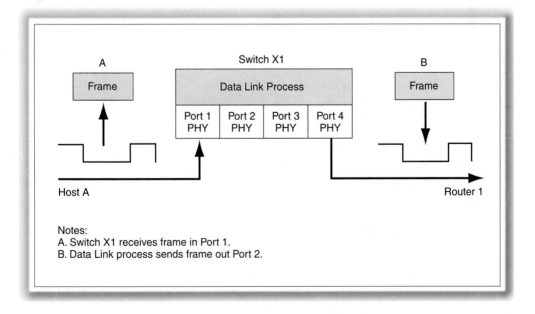

changed. The destination address in the frame is not that of the next switch; the destination address is that of the destination station if it is on the same network or that of a router if the station is sending a frame containing a packet to a router on its single network.

Switches Do Not Worry About Packet Contents

Note that switches do not look at the contents of the IP packet. Switches are Layer 2 devices that concentrate on the data link layer, doing all switching on the basis of the data link layer frame's destination-layer address.

TEST YOUR UNDERSTANDING

12. a) What layers are involved in switching? b) What does the switch look at to make its switching decision? c) What does the switch decide to do in making a switching decision? d) Do switches modify frames when they switch them? e) In a frame, the destination address is the destination of what device? f) Does the switch look at the contents of the internet layer packet?

On Router R1

When the frame travels from Switch X2 to Router R1, the frame has reached its destination on Network X. Figure 2-13 shows what happens on the router. Note that the frame arrives in Port 1.

On the Incoming Port: The Physical Layer

Each port on a router contains both a physical layer process and a data link layer process. (Switch ports only have physical layer process.)

The physical layer process on Router R1's Port 1 receives the signals from Switch X2 and converts the signal into the frame's bits. The physical layer process on the port passes the frame to the data link layer on Port 1—in this case, an Ethernet data link layer process.

On the Incoming Port: Decapsulation at the Data Link Layer

The Ethernet data link layer process on the port checks the frame for errors. If it finds none, it **decapsulates** the IP packet, that is, takes the IP packet out of the data field of the frame. It then passes the IP packet up to Router R1's internet layer process.

The Routing Decision

The router's single internet layer process is concerned with routing across the internet to Host B. It looks at the packet's destination IP address and makes a routing decision—what port to use to send the packet back out again.

When the internet layer process has selected the best route, this means that it has selected a port (Port 4) to use to send the packet back out, so that the packet can travel farther along its route to the destination host.

On the Router's Outgoing Port

Router R1's internet layer process then passes the IP packet down to Port 4. The data link layer process on Port 4 is a PPP process, so it encapsulates the IP packet in the data field of a PPP frame.

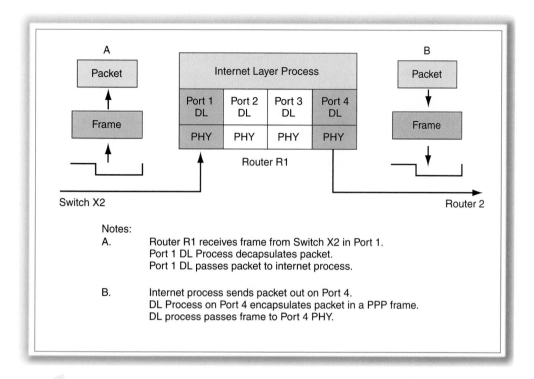

Figure 2-13   Vertical Communication on Router R1

The data link layer process on Port 4 passes the PPP frame to the port's physical layer process. The physical process on Port 4 then encodes the PPP frame's bits into signals and sends the signals on to Router R2 (there are no intermediate switches in Network Y).

Routers Do Not Change Packets

Generally speaking, routers do not change packets. They basically look at them, make a routing decision, and then pass them on. The packet created by the source station gets to the destination station with only minor supervisory information changed to count how many routers the packet has passed through. The destination address in the packet is not that of the next router; the destination address is that of the destination host.

TEST YOUR UNDERSTANDING

13.   a) What layers are involved in routing? b) What does the router look at to make its routing decision? c) What does the router decide to do in making a routing decision? d) What layers do router ports implement? e) Do routers encapsulate first or decapsulate first? f) Does the router change the IP packet as it forwards it? g) The destination address in a packet header is the destination address of what device?

On the Destination Host (Host B)

Router R2 creates a new Ethernet frame addressed to the 48-bit network address of Host B. From Router R2, the frame passes through Switch Z1 and Switch Z2 and then reaches Host B.

Figure 2-14 shows vertical communication between adjacent layer processes on the destination host.

At the Physical Layer on Host B

The signal comes into the network interface card (NIC) of Host B. The physical layer process on the NIC converts the signals into the ones and zeros of the Ethernet frame sent by Router R2.

The physical layer process on the NIC then passes the bits to the data link layer process on the NIC. (NICs implement both physical and data link layer processes in hardware.)

At the Data Link Layer on Host B

The data link layer process on the NIC checks the arriving Ethernet frame for errors. If there are none, it decapsulates the IP packet from the data field of the frame and passes the IP packet up to the internet layer process on Host B.

At the Internet Layer on Host B

The IP packet has arrived at the internet layer process on Host B. Its journey across the internet is complete.

Figure 2-14   Vertical Communication on the Destination Host (Host B)

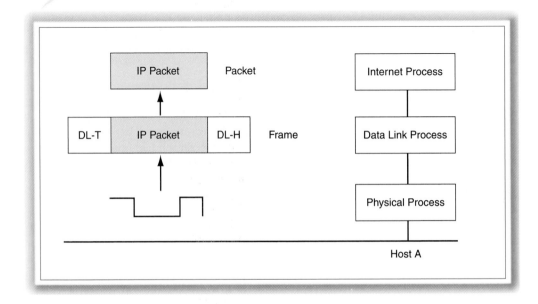

TEST YOUR UNDERSTANDING

14. a) Does the data link process on the destination host encapsulate or decapsulate?
    b) What does it do after that?

THE TRANSPORT AND APPLICATION LAYERS

The physical, data link, and internet layers all deal with transmission over networks and internets. However, end-to-end packet delivery is worthless if the computers and application programs at the two ends cannot understand one another, as Figure 2-15 illustrates. The highest two layers—the transport and application layers—ensure that the computers and application programs can communicate effectively.

Transport Layer Standards

As noted earlier, HTTP requires that the Transmission Control Protocol (TCP) be used at the transport layer.

To Connect Computers of Different Types

The transport layer exists for two reasons. The first is to allow computers of different types to communicate. For instance, when you connect to a webserver, your client machine may be a PC running Microsoft Windows, and the server may be a SUN workstation server running Solaris. Transport standards give these two very different types of machines from companies that largely hate each other the ability to communicate. In fact, when you use a server on the Internet, you do not even know what type of computer it is or what operating system it uses.

Figure 2-15   Transport and Application Layer Standards

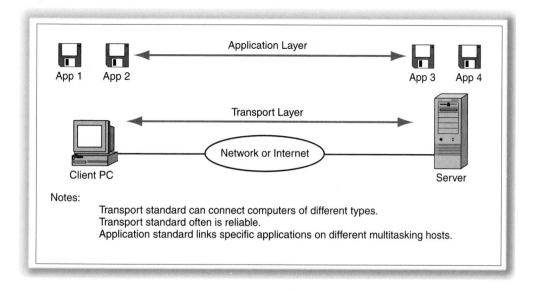

Reliability

Another purpose of most (but not all) transport standards is to give **reliable** communication, that is, to correct transmission errors that occur. The goal is to give the application program clean data. TCP is a reliable protocol that does this.

Typically, the transport layer is reliable whereas lower layers are **unreliable** (i.e., they do not do error correction). Unreliability is not bad per se. Not having to do error checking on each switch and router saves a great deal of money. Making the transport layer protocol reliable will catch all errors at the transport layer and at lower layers as well.

TEST YOUR UNDERSTANDING

15. a) What is a reliable protocol? b) What is an unreliable protocol? c) Why are the data link and physical layers generally unreliable? d) Why is the transport layer generally made reliable?

Application Layer Standards

Multitasking Computers

As Figure 2-15 shows, computers may run multiple application programs simultaneously. (In other words, most computers do multitasking.) Whereas the transport layer standard creates a link between computers, application layer standards create links between specific application programs on the two computers. In Figure 2-15, these programs are App 2 and App 3.

Application–Application Standards

Of course the main job of the application layer is to allow two application programs to talk with each other—a browser with a webserver, for example, or an e-mail client with an e-mail server.

We can say little about application standards in general because there are many different applications, and each has its own standard. Because there are so many applications, there are more application standards than there are all physical, data link, internet, and transport standards combined.

TEST YOUR UNDERSTANDING

16. If the transport layer sets up a connection between two computers, why do we need an application layer standard?

17. a) Is there more than one application layer standard? Explain. b) Are there many application layer standards?

Layering at All Layers

Earlier, we looked at layering in the delivery of IP packets. However, layering also works at the application and transport layers, as Figure 2-16 illustrates.

At the Application Layer on the Source Host

When the browser creates an application message—in our example in Figure 2-16 an HTTP request message—the application layer immediately passes the application message down to the transport layer.

At the Transport Layer on the Source Host

The transport layer process encapsulates the HTTP request message in the data field of a TCP segment. The transport layer process then passes the TCP segment down to the internet layer process.

Figure 2-16   Communication at All Layers on the Source Host

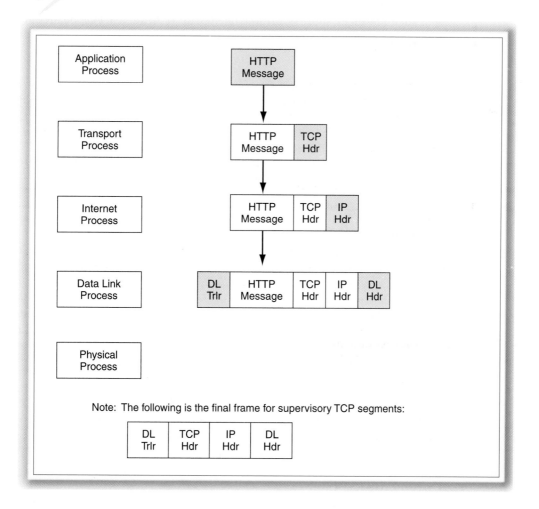

At the Internet Layer on the Source Host

Earlier in this chapter, we saw encapsulation beginning at the internet layer. But what was in the IP packet's own data field? Given the example shown in Figure 2-16, this data field contained a TCP segment, which contains an HTTP message in its data field.

The Final Frame for Application Message Delivery

Therefore, the final frame begins with a frame header, followed by an IP header, followed by a TCP header, followed by an HTTP request message, followed by the frame trailer.

Final Frames for Supervisory TCP Segments

Some TCP segments are not created to carry application data. As Figure 2-16 shows, there can be supervisory TCP messages to govern the communication between the transport processes on Host A and Host B. Supervisory TCP segments have a TCP header but no data field.

For such messages, there is a frame header, an IP header, a TCP header, no TCP data field, and the frame trailer.

TEST YOUR UNDERSTANDING

18. a) When an application layer process creates a message, what does it do immediately afterward? b) When a transport layer process receives a message from the application layer process, what does the transport layer process do?

19. a) In terms of headers and trailers for all involved layers, describe the final frame coming from the source host if the frame is delivering a Simple Mail Transfer Protocol (SMTP) e-mail message. b) Repeat the question if the frame is delivering a TCP supervisory message to control the delivery of the e-mail message.

STANDARDS ARCHITECTURES

It might be nice if there was only one set of standards that governed all network equipment. The reality, however, is that there are several competing **standards architectures**, *which are families of related standards that collectively allow an application program on one machine on an internet to communicate with another application program on another machine on the internet.* To give a non-network example, for physical measurements, there are two competing standards in the United States—the metric system and the English (Imperial) system. Both the metric and English standards architectures contain a number of different and incompatible standards.

TCP/IP and OSI Architectures

Although there are several major architectures, two of them dominate actual corporate use: OSI and TCP/IP. Although they sometimes are viewed as competitors, they actually work together in most networks, as we will see soon.

TEST YOUR UNDERSTANDING

20. a) What is a standards architecture? b) What are the two dominant standards architectures?

TCP/IP	OSI	Hybrid TCP/IP–OSI
Application	Application	Application
	Presentation	
	Session	
Transport	Transport	Transport
Internet	Network	Internet
Use OSI Standards Here	Data Link	Data Link
	Physical	Physical

Notes:

The Hybrid TCP/IP-OSI Architecture is used on the Internet and dominates internal corporate networks.

The standards agencies for the OSI architecture are ISO and ITU-T.

Figure 2-17   TCP/IP, OSI, and TCP/IP–OSI Hybrid Architecture

OSI

OSI is the "Reference Model of Open Systems Interconnection." You can see why it is almost always called OSI instead of being written out.

Standards Agencies: ISO and ITU-T

Standards agencies create and maintain standards architectures. OSI is governed by two cooperating standards agencies. One is the **International Organization for Standardization (ISO)**.[3] The other is the **International Telecommunications Union–Telecommunications Standards Sector (ITU-T)**.[4] No, the names and acronyms do not match, but these are the official names and acronyms for these two organizations. Also, do not confuse OSI and ISO. The former is an architecture; the latter is a standards agency.

OSI's Dominance at Lower Layers (Physical and Data Link)

Although OSI is a seven-layer standards architecture (see Figure 2-17), standards from its five upper layers are rarely used.

However, standards at the two lowest layers, the physical and data link layers, are used almost universally in networks. These two layers govern transmission within a

---

[3]   ISO sets a broad range of industrial standards, including computer standards. And yes, the abbreviation is ISO, not IOS.

[4]   ITU-T sets standards in telephony, television, radio, facsimile, and other public communications services. And yes, the standard abbreviation is ITU-T rather than ITU-TSS.

single network. Almost all single networks—both LANs and WANs—follow OSI standards at the physical and data link layers, regardless of what upper-layer standards they use.

Other standards architectures, realizing the dominance of OSI at the physical and data link layers, also specify the use of OSI standards at these layers.

OSI Network and Transport Layers

The network and transport layers of OSI correspond closely to the internet and transport layers of TCP/IP.

OSI Session Layer

OSI differs most markedly from TCP/IP by having three layers for application programs instead of TCP/IP's single application layer. The **session layer (OSI Layer 5)** initiates and maintains a connection between application programs on different computers.[5] Figure 2-18 illustrates this layer. TCP/IP does not have a session layer, requiring application programs to create, maintain, and terminate application layer transactions if they have the need to do so (few do).

OSI Presentation Layer

The **presentation layer (OSI Layer 6)** is designed to handle data formatting differences between the two computers.[6] As Figure 2-19 shows, the two presentation layer processes communicate using an agreed-upon **transfer syntax**, which may be quite dif-

Figure 2-18   OSI Session Layer

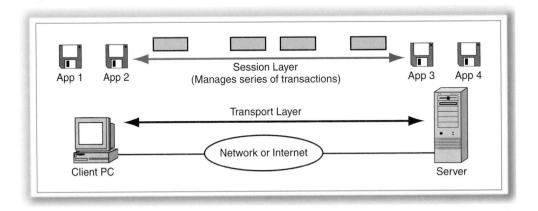

---

[5]   When there is a prolonged period without application traffic, the session layer processes on the two machines send "keep alive" messages to maintain the connection. In addition, there can be "roll-back points," so that if a connection is broken, the application programs only have to start again from the last roll-back point instead of from the beginning of a long series of transactions.

[6]   For instance, most computers store character data (letters, numbers, and punctuation signs) using the ASCII code. In contrast, IBM mainframes store them using the EBCDIC code. Computers also differ in the ways they store numerical data.

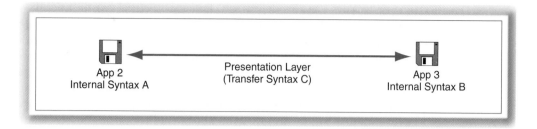

Figure 2-19   OSI Presentation Layer

ferent from either of their internal methods of formatting information. It is as if English and German speakers, who both also speak French and Italian, agree to communicate in French.

The presentation layer also can handle data compression and data encryption for application data. In general, the presentation layer is where many OSI application data formatting standards are placed, such as those for facsimile. TCP/IP has nothing like the OSI presentation layer, and different TCP/IP applications have different data format standards, causing endless confusion for users.

OSI Application Layer
Application-specific communication is governed by the OSI **application layer (OSI Layer 7)**. The OSI application layer is freed from session and presentation matters by the two layers below it.

TEST YOUR UNDERSTANDING

21. a) What standards agencies are responsible for the OSI standards architecture? b) At what layers are OSI standards dominant? c) Describe the functions of the top three OSI layers.

TCP/IP

The TCP/IP architecture is mandatory on the Internet at the internet and transport layers. It also is widely used by companies for their internal corporate networks. It is named after two of its standards, TCP and IP, which we have looked at briefly in this chapter. However, TCP/IP also has many other standards, making its name rather misleading.

The Internet Engineering Task Force (IETF) and Requests for Comments (RFCs)
TCP/IP's standards agency is the **Internet Engineering Task Force (IETF)**. Most documents produced by the IETF are given the rather misleading name **requests for comment (RFCs)**. Each year, the IETF publishes a list of which RFCs are **Official Internet Protocol Standards**. RFCs constantly are being added to this list and dropped from it.

Dominance at Upper Layers (Internet, Transport, and Application)

The physical and data link layers govern the transmission of data within a *single network*. Upper TCP/IP layers govern the transmission of data across an entire internet, ensuring that any two host computers can communicate, and ensuring that the two application programs on the two hosts can communicate as well.

TCP/IP is dominant in corporate networking above the physical and data link layers. It is not universal, but it is by far the most widely used architecture at upper layers, and its dominance is growing. In a few years, the use of other architectures at upper layers in new products will be increasingly rare.

TEST YOUR UNDERSTANDING

22. a) What standards agency manages TCP/IP? b) What are most of its documents called? c) Are all, some, or none of these documents standards? d) At what layers is TCP/IP dominant?

TCP/IP and OSI

Although TCP/IP and OSI sometimes are viewed as competing standards architectures, most organizations use them together. The most common standards pattern in organizations is to use OSI standards at the physical and data link layers and TCP/IP standards at the internet, transport, and application layers. This is very important for you to keep in mind because this **hybrid TCP/IP–OSI standards architecture** shown in Figure 2-17 will form the basis for most of this book.[7]

TEST YOUR UNDERSTANDING

23. a) What layers of the hybrid TCP/IP-OSI standards architecture use OSI standards? b) TCP/IP standards?

A Multiprotocol World

At the same time, quite a few networking products in organizations follow other architectures, as shown in Figure 2-20. Real corporations live and will continue to live for some time in a multiprotocol world in which network administrators have to deal with a complex mix of products following different architectures. In this book, we must focus on OSI and TCP/IP because they are by far the most important. However, a working networking professional also has to be reasonably proficient in standards from other architectures as well.

IPX/SPX

The most common non-TCP/IP standards architecture found at upper layers in LANs is the **IPX/SPX architecture**. This architecture is required on all older Novell NetWare file servers and is a widely used option on new NetWare file servers. Because IPX/SPX is used for file service, it is used mostly in LANs.

---

[7] Another example of cooperation between TCP/IP and OSI is that the ITU-T, recognizing the importance of the IETF, is working with the IETF on standards for sending voice over IP networks (see Chapter 6) and other areas where TCP/IP has potential impacts on traditional telephone and television services.

TCP/IP	IPX/SPX		NetBEUI	OSI	SNA	AppleTalk
Application	NCP*	Various	NetBIOS	Application	No Application Layer**	Uses OSI Layering but proprietary protocols at each layer above the physical and data link layers
				Presentation	Network Addressable Unit (NAU)*** Services	
				Session	Data Flow Control	
Transport		SPX	NetBEUI	Transport	Transmission Control	
Internet	IPX		No Internet Layer	Network	Path Control	
Uses OSI Standards Here	Uses OSI Standards Here		Uses OSI Standards Here	Data link	Uses OSI Standards Here	Uses OSI Standards Here
				Physical		

Notes:

* NCP, which handles file and print service, spans the application and transport layers.

** SNA has no application layer; this is part of IBM's Systems Application Architecture (SAA).

*** A network addressable unit (NAU) is any hardware or software process that can be sent messages by another hardware or software process.

Figure 2-20   Other Standards Architectures

Systems Network Architecture (SNA)

Mainframe computers normally follow the **Systems Network Architecture (SNA)** standards architecture, which actually predates OSI and TCP/IP. Its layering is similar to OSI's because OSI borrowed heavily from SNA. SNA traffic is found mostly in wide area networks because it often serves distant mainframe terminals. In many networks, a significant amount of WAN traffic is SNA traffic.

AppleTalk

Macintosh computers are designed to use Apple's proprietary **AppleTalk** architecture. Macintoshes are rare in corporations today, so AppleTalk is not widely seen. However, some industries, such as publishing, use Macintoshes and AppleTalk extensively, mostly within single LANs.

NetBEUI

For small networks, a stripped-down architecture called **NetBEUI** used to be somewhat common. Having no internet layer, NetBEUI was only good for single LANs. Now that client PCs have ample processing power, there is no good reason to use NetBEUI even in small LANs, despite Microsoft certification indications that it is useful there.

TEST YOUR UNDERSTANDING

24. a) When are you likely to encounter IPX/SPX standards? b) SNA standards? c) AppleTalk standards? d) NetBEUI standards?

GAINING PERSPECTIVE

THOUGHT QUESTIONS

1. How do you think TCP/IP standards will have to change in the future to continue to improve the Internet?
2. OSI offers standards at the transport layer. What problems would you encounter if your firm decided to adopt these standards?

TROUBLESHOOTING QUESTION

1. You have a small LAN with a single Ethernet switch. You discover that your network is highly congested one morning, despite having only a dozen stations. A network protocol analyzer tells you that one of your NICs is malfunctioning, flooding the network with a large number of spurious frames. Your protocol analyzer tells you the 48-bit network address of the NIC, but you do not know what computer has that NIC. How can you find out quickly which PC's NIC is "jabbering?" How can you make it easier to know which PC has which NIC in the future?

CASE STUDIES

For case studies, go to the book's website, www.prenhall.com/panko, and look at the Case Studies page for this chapter.

PHOTOS

For photos, go to the book's website, www.prenhall.com/panko, and look at the Photos page for this chapter.

PROJECTS

1. **Getting Current.** Go to the book website's New Information and Errors pages for this chapter to get new information since this book went to press and to correct any errors in the text.
2. **Internet Exercises.** Go to the book website's Exercises page for this chapter and do the Internet Exercises.
3. **Hands-On.** Learn what standards architectures are used in your college or where you work.

PHYSICAL LAYER PROPAGATION

Learning Objectives:

By the end of this chapter, you should be able to discuss:

- Analog and digital signaling, including reasons for the dominance of digital signaling and the difference between bit rates and baud rates.
- Unshielded twisted pair (UTP) wiring, including relevant propagation effects that must be controlled by limiting distance and by limiting the untwisting of pairs during connectorization.
- The differences between serial and parallel transmission, including the advantage of parallel transmission.
- Optical fiber cabling, including wavelength division multiplexing and relevant propagation effects that can be controlled by using single-mode fiber (where economically feasible) or by using multimode fiber over shorter distances.
- Radio propagation, including reasons for using omnidirectional or dish antennas, the importance of bandwidth, and propagation effects, including fading, multipath interference, and shadow zones.
- Physical layer topologies, including point-to-point connections, stars, extended stars (hierarchies), rings, meshes, and busses (both multidrop and daisy chain busses).

INTRODUCTION

The Physical Layer

Chapter 2 focused on standards, especially layered communication and messaging. Most of the chapter focused on the data link, internet, transport, and application layers. In this chapter, we will focus more closely on the physical layer, which is special in several ways.

> ➤ The physical layer is the only layer that creates a real connection between machines. Other layer processes must rely on encapsulation to talk to their peers on different machines.
>
> ➤ It is the only layer that does not use messages. It merely transmits bits in isolation.
>
> ➤ It alone deals with propagation effects that change signals when they travel over transmission lines.

SIGNALING

Disturbances and Propagation

Jiggling a Rope

Suppose that you and someone else are standing a few feet apart and are holding a rope tautly between you. Now, close your eyes. The other person jiggles the rope for a fraction of a second. That disturbance will **propagate** (travel) down the rope to your hands. When it arrives, you will feel it.

Signal Creation and Propagation

Something similar happens in network transmission. As Figure 3-1 shows, the transmitter creates a disturbance in a transmission medium—wire, optical fiber, or radio. This disturbance is the signal. The signal propagates down the transmission medium to the other side, where it is received.

Figure 3-1   Signal and Propagation

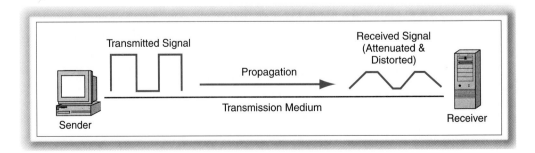

Propagation Effects

Note that the **received signal** is different from the **transmitted signal** because of **propagation effects**, that is, changes in the signal during propagation. In the figure, the signal has **attenuated** (weakened) and is **distorted** (its shape has been changed). If propagation effects are too large, the receiver will not be able to read the signal correctly.

TEST YOUR UNDERSTANDING

1. a) What is a signal? b) What is propagation? c) What are propagation effects? d) Why are propagation effects bad?

Analog and Binary Data

Figure 3-2 shows that networks have to handle two types of user-generated data: binary and analog. **Binary data** consists of a string of ones and zeros. "Binary" is from the Greek word for two, indicating that there are only two possible values. Computers create binary data, and most information submitted to data networks today is binary.

In contrast, **analog data** rises and falls among an infinite number of levels (loudness levels, voltage levels, and so forth). For instance, when we talk, we actually send out pressure waves that rise and fall thousands of times per second, corresponding to the pitch of our voice. The telephone network was designed to carry analog voice signals and analog television signals.

TEST YOUR UNDERSTANDING

2. a) Distinguish between analog and binary data. b) Which type of network usually carries analog data? c) Binary data?

Analog, Binary, and Digital Signals

Binary Data/Binary Signaling

To be transmitted, data has to be converted into physical-level signals that can propagate down transmission media. Figure 3-3 illustrates what is perhaps the simplest example of **conversion**, in which binary data are converted into **binary signals**.

Figure 3-2   Analog and Binary Data

Analog Data

Binary Data

1101011000011100101

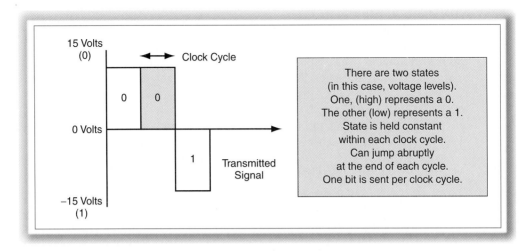

Figure 3-3   Binary Data and Binary Signal

Here, there are two voltage levels. A high voltage is anything between 3 and 15 volts. A low voltage is anything between negative 3 and negative 15 volts. A high voltage represents a zero, whereas a low voltage represents a one. No, this is not a misprint. This is the way **232 serial ports**[1] work on your PC.

Note that binary signal transmission is relatively immune to attenuation errors (loss in signal intensity). If a signal is transmitted at +12 volts and attenuates to +6 volts (a 50 percent loss), it will still be read correctly as a high voltage and therefore a zero.

In binary transmission, time is divided into brief time periods called **clock cycles**. The signal is held constant within each clock cycle. At the end of each clock cycle, the signal either stays the same or changes to the other voltage level (state).

Binary Data/Digital Signaling

Figure 3-4 illustrates a slightly more complex case. Here, the data is binary, but the signal is digital. In binary signaling, shown in Figure 3-3, there are two signal levels. Binary signaling is a special case of **digital signaling**, in which there are a *few* **states** (voltage levels or other line conditions that can be interpreted by the receiver). In Figure 3-4, there are four states. However, digital signaling can have two states, four states, eight states, sixteen states, or more.

As Figure 3-4 shows, having four states allows the sender to transmit two bits in each clock cycle. The four states are mapped into the data groups 00, 01, 10, and 11.

Adding more states allows even more bits to be sent per clock cycle, but there are diminishing returns. Each doubling in the number of states allows only one more bit to be transmitted per clock cycle. For instance, eight states allow three bits to be

---

1   Often called RS-232-C serial ports, they actually follow newer the TIA/EIA-232-F standard.

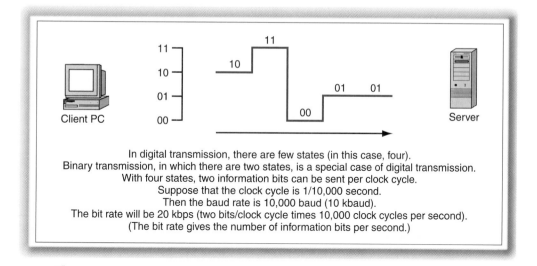

In digital transmission, there are few states (in this case, four).
Binary transmission, in which there are two states, is a special case of digital transmission.
With four states, two information bits can be sent per clock cycle.
Suppose that the clock cycle is 1/10,000 second.
Then the baud rate is 10,000 baud (10 kbaud).
The bit rate will be 20 kbps (two bits/clock cycle times 10,000 clock cycles per second).
(The bit rate gives the number of information bits per second.)

Figure 3-4   Binary Data and Digital Signal

transmitted per clock cycle, and sixteen states allow four bits to be transmitted per clock cycle.

If too many states are transmitted, the states will be very close together. If the signal changes even slightly during transmission, the receiver will record the wrong value. This is why digital signaling only uses a *few* states.

Bit Rates and Baud Rates

Bit Rates   In digital data transmission, the rate at which we transmit data is called the **bit rate**. It is measured in bits per second.

Baud Rate   In digital transmission, in contrast, the **baud rate** is the number of clock cycles the transmission system uses per second. If there are 1,000 clock cycles per second, the baud rate is 1,000 baud (not 1,000 bauds per second).

Binary Data/Analog Signaling

The traditional telephone line going from your home to the telephone network requires **analog signaling**. However, computer signals are almost always binary. As Figure 3-5 shows, a device called a **modem** is needed to transmit binary data over an analog line.

Modems convert signals through **modulation**, in which a pure wave is changed (modulated) to indicate different signal values. Figure 3-5 uses a simple form of modulation called **amplitude modulation**. Here, a loud (high-amplitude) signal is sent to indicate a one during a clock cycle, and a soft (low-amplitude) signal is sent during a clock cycle to indicate a zero.

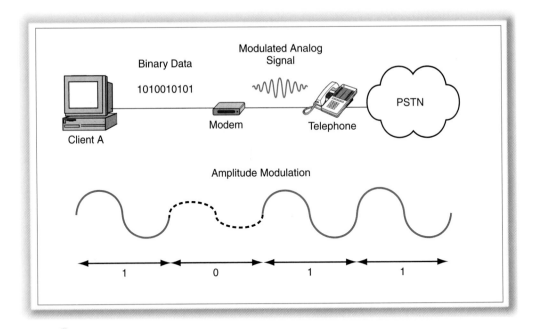

Figure 3-5   Using a Modem to Send Binary Data Over an Analog Transmission Line

Analog Data/Digital Signaling

Suppose you have analog data, such as the human voice, that you wish to transmit over a digital line. Figure 3-6 shows that you need a conversion device called a **codec**.

A codec encodes analog data, converting it into a binary digital signal that can travel over a digital line. Chapter 6 describes how encoding is done in the telephone network.

The codec decodes arriving digital signals, converting them into analog data. The figure shows that decoding does not produce a perfectly smooth analog signal, but if decoding is done well, the human ear will hear the signal as a smooth one.

TEST YOUR UNDERSTANDING

3. a) In 232 serial port binary data conversion for transmission over a binary transmission line, how are ones and zeros represented? b) How does this give resistance to transmission errors?

4. a) Distinguish between binary and digital transmission. b) Is binary transmission digital? c) What is good about having multiple states instead of just two? d) What is bad about having multiple states?

5. a) Distinguish between the bit rate and the baud rate. b) When are the two equal?

6. a) In sending binary data over an analog transmission line, what kind of device does the conversion? b) Describe amplitude modulation.

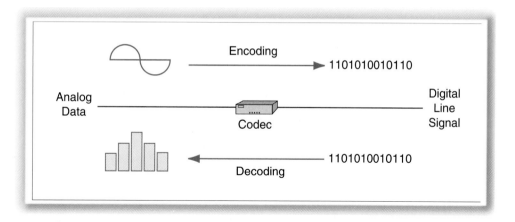

Figure 3-6   Sending Analog Data Over a Digital Line

7.   a) For what kind of signal and data would you use a codec? b) What is encoding?
c) What is decoding?

UTP SIGNAL PROPAGATION

UTP Transmission Standards

LANs need transmission links to connect NICs to switches and switches to one another. Transmission media in the United States are governed by the **TIA/EIA-568**[2] standard. We will look first at UTP wiring, which is the most widely used LAN wiring.

TEST YOUR UNDERSTANDING

8.   What is the standard for transmission media?

4-Pair UTP and RJ-45

The 4-Pair UTP Cable

Ethernet networks typically use **4-pair unshielded twisted pair (UTP)** wiring. This name sounds complicated, but the medium is very simple, as Figure 3-9 illustrates. Each **cord** has four pairs of wires. Each wire is covered with **dielectric** (nonconducting) **insulation.** Each pair's wires are twisted around each other several times per inch. Finally, there is an outer **jacket** that holds the four pairs together and protects them from damage.

---

[2]   TIA is the Telecommunications Industry Association. EIA is the Electronic Industrial Alliance. The standard is a cooperative effort.

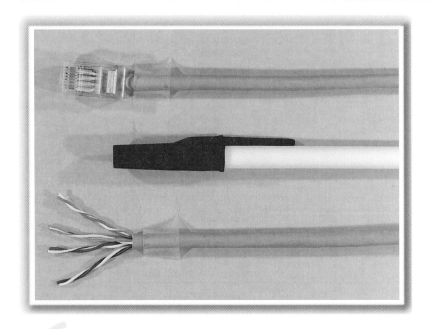

Figure 3-7 Unshielded Twisted Pair (UTP) Cord with RJ-45
Connector, Pen, and UTP Cord with 4 Pairs Displayed

Figure 3-8 Pen and Full-Duplex Optical Fiber Cords with SC Connectors (Left) and
ST Connectors (Right)

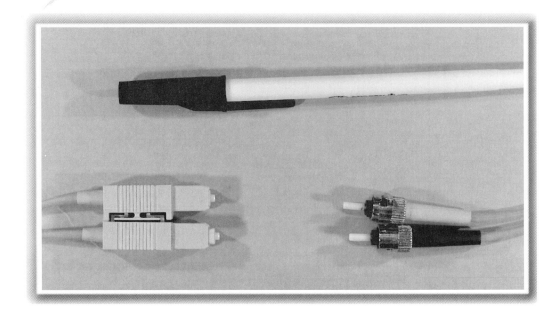

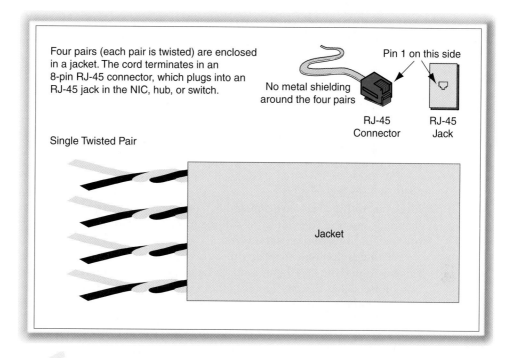

Four pairs (each pair is twisted) are enclosed in a jacket. The cord terminates in an 8-pin RJ-45 connector, which plugs into an RJ-45 jack in the NIC, hub, or switch.

No metal shielding around the four pairs

Pin 1 on this side

RJ-45 Connector

RJ-45 Jack

Single Twisted Pair

Jacket

Figure 3-9   4-Pair Unshielded Twisted Pair Cable with RJ-45 Connector

RJ-45 Connectors

At the ends of a UTP cord, the wires must be separated and placed within an 8-pin **RJ-45 connector**, which is shown in Figure 3-9. The RJ-45 connector at each end of a 4-pair UTP cord snaps into an **RJ-45 port** in the NIC or the switch.[3]

Easy, Inexpensive, and Rugged

UTP is inexpensive to purchase, easy to **connectorize**[4] (add connectors to), and relatively easy to install. It is also rugged, so that if a chair runs over it accidentally, it probably will not be damaged. 4-pair UTP dominates corporate usage in access links from the NIC to the first switch.

TEST YOUR UNDERSTANDING

9.   a) In 4-pair UTP, how many wires are there in a cord? b) What surrounds each wire? c) How are the wires of each pair arranged? d) What is the outer covering called?

10.   Why is 4-pair UTP dominant in LANs for the access line between a NIC and the switch that serves the NIC?

---

[3]   Home telephone connections use a thinner RJ-11 connector and port. It was designed to carry six wires but usually only connects a single pair.

[4]   Don't blame me. I don't make these terms up!

Attenuation and Noise Problems

UTP signals change as they travel down the wires. If they change too much, they will not be readable. As noted earlier in this chapter, there are several of these **propagation effects**. We will look at the most important propagation effects for UTP transmission, beginning with attenuation and noise.

Attenuation

As Figure 3-10 illustrates, when signals travel, they **attenuate** (grow weaker). As noted earlier in this chapter, if a signal attenuates too much, the receiver will not be able to recognize it.

Noise

Electrons within a wire are constantly moving, and moving electrons generate electromagnetic energy. This energy is called **noise**. It adds to the signal, so the receiver sees the total of the signal plus the noise.

Noise is random, spending most of its time near an average that is called a **noise floor**—despite the fact that it is an average and not a minimum. Occasionally, there are brief **noise spikes** that are much higher or lower than the noise floor. If a noise spike is about as large as the signal, the combined signal and noise may be unreadable by the receiver.

Noise, Attenuation, and Propagation Distance

If a signal is far larger than the noise floor (this is called having a high **signal-to-noise ratio**, or **SNR**), few random spikes will be large enough to cause errors. However, as a signal attenuates during propagation, it falls ever closer to the noise floor. Noise spikes will more frequently equal the signal's strength, so errors will become more frequent. In other words, even if the noise *level* is constant, longer propagation distances result in a lower SNR and therefore more noise *errors*.

Figure 3-10   Noise and Attenuation

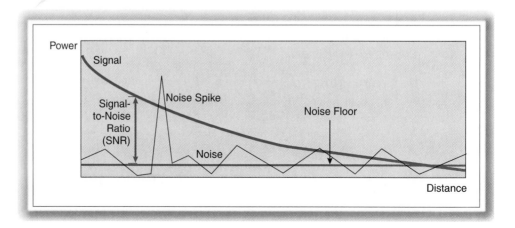

Limiting UTP Cord Distance

Fortunately, attenuation and noise can be controlled fairly simply by limiting the length of UTP cords. The 802.3 standard limits UTP propagation distances to 100 meters. If UTP cords are restricted to 100 meters, the signal will attenuate by no more than two-thirds. It still will be comfortably larger than the noise floor, so there will be few noise errors.

TEST YOUR UNDERSTANDING

11. a) Describe the attenuation problem and why it is important. b) Describe the noise problem and why it is important. c) As a signal propagates down a UTP cord, the noise level is constant. Will greater propagation distance result in fewer noise errors, the same number of noise errors, or more noise errors? Explain.

12. How are UTP attenuation and noise errors kept to an acceptable level? Explain.

Electromagnetic Interference (EMI) in UTP Wiring

General EMI

Noise is unwanted electrical energy *within* the propagation medium. In turn, **electromagnetic interference (EMI)**, or more simply, "interference," is unwanted electrical energy coming from *external* devices, such as electrical motors and fluorescent lights. Like noise, interference can make the received signal unreadable.

Twisting to Reduce Crosstalk Interference

Fortunately, there is a simple way to reduce EMI to an acceptable level. This is to twist each pair's wires around each other several times per inch, as Figure 3-11 illustrates. Consider what happens over a full twist. Over the first half of the twist, the interference

Figure 3-11   Electromagnetic Interference (EMI) and Twisting

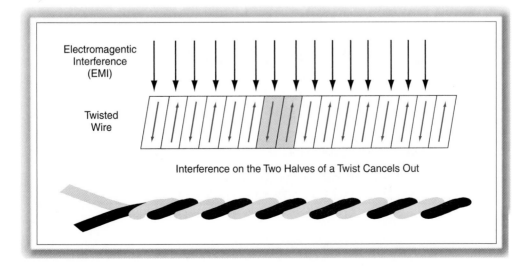

might add to the signal. Over the other half, however, this same interference would sub-tract from the signal. The net impact of the interference would be zero. Does twisting really work this perfectly? No, of course not. However, **twisted pair wiring** dramatically reduces crosstalk interference effects to an acceptable level.[5]

Crosstalk Interference

Standard UTP cords contain four wire pairs, as Figure 3-12 shows. Inevitably, pairs in the bundle will radiate some of their energy, producing electromagnetic interfer-ence in other pairs. This mutual EMI among wire pairs in a UTP cord is called **crosstalk interference**. It is always present in wire bundles and must be controlled. Fortunately, the twisting of each pair normally keeps crosstalk interference to a rea-sonable level.

Terminal Crosstalk Interference

Unfortunately, when a UTP cord is connectorized, its wires must be untwisted to fit into the RJ-45 connector, as shown in Figure 3-12. The eight wires are now parallel within the connector, so there is no protection from crosstalk interference. Crosstalk

Figure 3-12   Crosstalk Electromagnetic Interference (EMI) and Terminal Crosstalk Interference

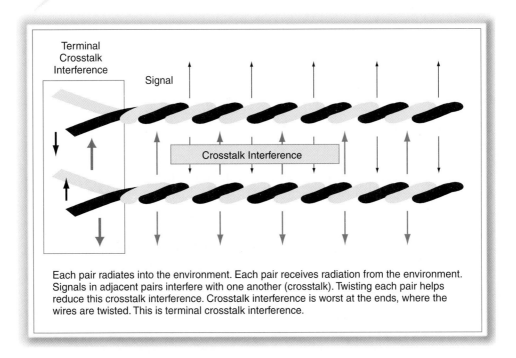

Each pair radiates into the environment. Each pair receives radiation from the environment. Signals in adjacent pairs interfere with one another (crosstalk). Twisting each pair helps reduce this crosstalk interference. Crosstalk interference is worst at the ends, where the wires are twisted. This is terminal crosstalk interference.

---

[5] Alexander Graham Bell himself patented twisted pair wiring as a way to reduce interference.

interference at the ends of the UTP cord, which is called **terminal crosstalk interference**, usually is much larger than crosstalk interference in the entire rest of the cord. Installers must be careful not to untwist wires more than 1.25 cm (half an inch) when adding connectors. This limit will not completely eliminate terminal crosstalk interference, but it should limit it to an acceptable level.

TEST YOUR UNDERSTANDING

13. a) Distinguish between electromagnetic interference (EMI), crosstalk interference, and terminal crosstalk interference. b) How is interference controlled? Explain. c) How is terminal crosstalk interference controlled? Explain.

Serial and Parallel Transmission

Figure 3-13 shows an important distinction in wire communication: serial versus parallel transmission.

Serial Transmission

In the next chapter, we will look at Ethernet standards. In slower versions of Ethernet that run at 10 Mbps and 100 Mbps, a single pair in a UTP cord is used to transmit in each direction, so two-way transmission uses two pairs. The other two pairs are not used, although the standard calls for them to be present.

In each clock cycle, a single state can be transmitted. Ethernet uses binary transmission, so this state indicates a single bit. If one pair of wires is used to send a transmission, this is **serial transmission**, because the signals must follow one another in series.

Figure 3-13   Serial Versus Parallel Transmission

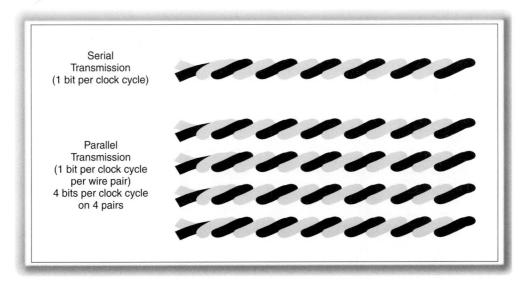

Serial
Transmission
(1 bit per clock cycle)

Parallel
Transmission
(1 bit per clock cycle
per wire pair)
4 bits per clock cycle
on 4 pairs

Parallel Transmission

For gigabit Ethernet, however, when the NIC or switch transmits, it transmits on all four pairs in each direction. This means that it can transmit four bits per clock cycle, even using Ethernet's simple binary transmission. This is **parallel transmission**. It is faster than serial transmission for the same clock cycle duration.[6]

Other forms of parallel transmission use more than four wires. For instance, PC parallel ports use eight wires to carry bits in each direction. (A ground wire avoids the need to send eight pairs of wires in each direction, effectively acting as the second wire for all sixteen of the wires that carry data.) In general, parallel transmission does not mean the use of four transmitting pairs (or grounded wires). It means using more than a single pair or grounded wire.

TEST YOUR UNDERSTANDING

14.   a) Distinguish between serial and parallel transmission. b) At a given clock rate, which is faster? Explain. c) In parallel transmission, how many pairs (or grounded wires) are used in each direction?

OPTICAL FIBER TRANSMISSION LINKS

Optical Fiber

For runs longer than 100 meters, companies turn to **optical fiber** cabling, which is illustrated in Figure 3-14. In LANs, optical fiber is used primarily in trunk links between switches and routers, where its fragility[7] is not as much of a problem as it would be in an access link to the user's desktop. Typical LAN distances for fiber are 200 m to 2 km. In WANs, optical fiber can run hundreds of kilometers.

Core
In optical fiber, a transmitter injects light into a very thin glass tube called the **core**.

Cladding and Perfect Internal Reflection
Surrounding the core is a thicker glass cylinder called the **cladding**. As Figure 3-14 shows, when light begins to spread, it hits the cladding and is reflected back into the core with **perfect internal reflection** so that no light escapes.[8] In contrast, UTP tends to radiate energy out of the wire bundle, causing attenuation.

On/Off Signaling
Optical fiber uses **on/off signaling**. During each bit's clock cycle, a light source is turned on to signal a one or off to signal a zero. Inexpensive fiber uses **light emitting diodes (LEDs)** for its light source. The most expensive fiber uses **lasers**.

---

[6]   Your computer's internal bus, which carries signals among components in your systems unit, has about 100 wires for high-density parallel transmission. SCSI disk drives use 16 parallel wires to communicate with their computers.

[7]   It's made of glass!

[8]   This is based on Snell's Law.

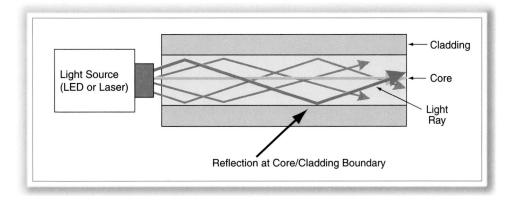

Figure 3-14   Optical Fiber Cabling

Wavelength Division Multiplexing

Installing optical fiber is expensive. One way to leverage your installed base of optical fiber is to replace simple transmitters with transmitters that can transmit several light sources at slightly different frequencies, as Figure 3-15 shows. You can add signal capacity without adding new fiber.

This simple idea is given the complex name **wavelength division multiplexing (WDM)**. Not content with that, marketers created another term, **dense wavelength**

Figure 3-15   Wavelength Division Multiplexing (WDM) in Optical Fiber

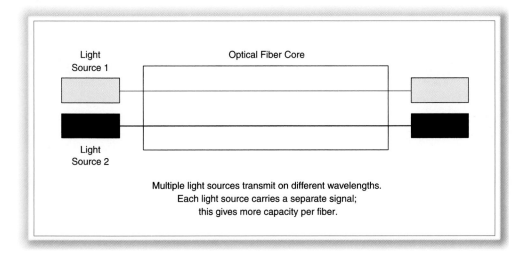

division multiplexing (DWDM) for fiber that carries more than about 40^9 light sources at different frequencies.

Two Strands for Full-Duplex Operation

Note in Figure 3-16 that *two* strands of fiber are needed for **full-duplex** (simultaneous two-way) communication. One fiber carries light signals in each direction. If only a single fiber were used, the two sides would have to take turns talking. This is **half-duplex** transmission.

TEST YOUR UNDERSTANDING

15. a) In optical fiber, what are the roles of the core and the cladding? b) Distinguish between traditional optical fiber transmission, WDM, and DWDM. c) How do WDM and DWDM reduce costs? d) Why do we need two fiber cords for full two-way transmission? e) What is the ability to transmit in both directions simultaneously called?

Distance Limitations with Optical Fiber

Attenuation, Noise, and Interference

Fiber does not have significant problems with attenuation, noise, or interference. The glass is so pure that attenuation is negligible except over distances far longer than those used in LANs. Moving electrons do not create light, so noise is unimportant as well. Also, there is no external interference because a simple opaque covering placed around the cladding prevents external light from entering the core.

Figure 3-16 Full-Duplex Optical Fiber Cord

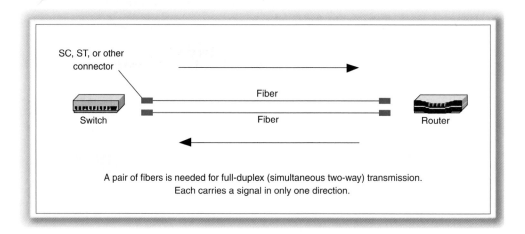

A pair of fibers is needed for full-duplex (simultaneous two-way) transmission.
Each carries a signal in only one direction.

---

9 The minimum number of wavelengths to distinguish between WDM and DWDM probably will increase in the future.

Temporal Dispersion

The main propagation problem for optical fiber is **temporal dispersion**.[10] As Figure 3-17 shows, in multimode fiber, which is the most common type of fiber in LANs, light rays in a pulse can enter at different angles. Light rays going along the axis will travel straight through without reflection. Light rays entering at high angles will be reflected many times as they travel down the fiber, consequently traveling farther. If the difference in arrival times of various rays is too large, the light rays of adjacent pulses will begin to overlap in their arrival time. The signal will be unreadable.

Modes and Multimode Fiber

Actually, the physics of wave propagation limits light rays to a few angles, called **modes**. The thicker the core, the more modes there will be. Most optical fiber used in LANs uses **multimode fiber** with "thick" cores. Multimode cores usually are around 62.5 microns (sometimes 50 microns) in diameter.[11] A thick core is bad in terms of allowing many modes, but it is less expensive to create a thick core than a thin core. Also, it is easier to splice a thick core than a thin core, and it is easier to align the light source exactly with a thick core.

Figure 3-17   Multimode and Single-Mode Optical Fiber

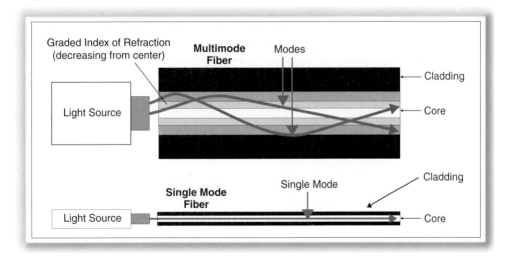

---

10   Temporal dispersion in optical fiber also is called "modal dispersion" because it arises from time differences in the propagation of different modes.

11   In comparison, a human hair is about 75 microns. The cladding extends the diameter to 125 microns, and with the outer jacket, the total diameter of a fiber is about 250 microns. Between a thin opaque coating around the cladding and the outer jacket, by the way, is Kevlar yarn fiber. Yes, Kevlar is the stuff they use to make bulletproof vests. The Kevlar yarn gives some protection to the glass core and cladding. However, the use of Kevlar means that you need a specially hardened tool to cut optical fiber.

Thanks to temporal dispersion, multimode fiber runs usually are limited to between 200 meters and 2 kilometers. However, these distances are more than sufficient for most LANs. Multimode fiber dominates in LANs.

Single-Mode Fiber

For longer distances, say to connect two buildings in a site LAN, **single-mode fiber** is used. Its core is so thin (usually 8.3 microns in diameter) that only a single mode can propagate—the one traveling straight along the axis.[12] Single-mode fiber can run several kilometers, so it is used primarily by transmission carriers for their networks. It can be used in LANs, however, between buildings at a site. WAN carriers use single-mode fiber almost exclusively because their distances are too great for multimode fiber.

TEST YOUR UNDERSTANDING

16. What propagation problems generally are unimportant in optical fiber transmission?
17. a) What are modes? b) What problem do they cause? c) Distinguish between single-mode and multimode fiber in terms of construction. d) Distinguish between single-mode and multimode fiber in terms of transmission distance. e) Distinguish between single-mode and multimode fiber in terms of ease of installation. f) Given your answer in part b, why does multimode fiber dominate in LANs? g) Where is single-mode fiber most commonly used?

RADIO SIGNAL PROPAGATION

Wireless transmission using radio or infrared transmission is exciting because communication is possible even when the user is moving. With UTP and optical fiber, you must be physically connected to the network. With wireless transmission, in contrast, you can use the network anywhere you wish. Cellular telephony has already done this for voice transmission. Wireless LANs, wireless metropolitan area networks (MANs), and satellite-based networks are beginning to do the same for data, and cellular telephone systems are beginning to carry data as well.

Radio Signals and Antennas

Radio Signals

If you cause an electron to oscillate (move up and down rhythmically), it will generate a weak electromagnetic signal. If you can force billions of electrons in an antenna to oscillate together, you will create a signal strong enough to be received several meters away or even many kilometers away.

Omnidirectional Antennas

Figure 3-18 shows that there are two types of antennas: omnidirectional and dish antennas. **Omnidirectional antennas**, as the name suggests, broadcast their signals in all directions. They also receive from all directions.

---

[12] The cladding still has a diameter of 125 microns, and the outer jacket still has a diameter of about 250 microns.

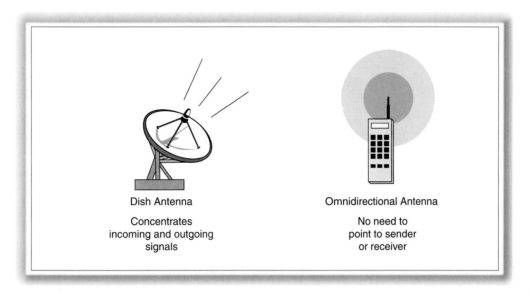

Figure 3-18   Omnidirectional and Dish Antennas

When the signal spreads out from an omnidirectional antenna, it is a sphere. The energy is spread uniformly over the sphere. As the sphere expands, the energy density at a single point grows weaker and weaker. It weakens by an **inverse square law**, so that if you triple your distance from an omnidirectional antenna, you will only get one-eighth $(1/2^3)$ the signal strength. With omnidirectional antennas, you have to be relatively close to your communication partner.

On the positive side, you do not have to aim a dish at your communication partner. Imagine if you had to carry a dish antenna around for your cellular telephone! You would not even know where to point it.

Dish Antennas

As Figure 3-18 shows, dish antennas concentrate incoming and outgoing signals. This generates a much stronger outgoing signal, and it allows your receiver to pick up relatively faint signals. For fixed installations, dish antennas are very desirable.

TEST YOUR UNDERSTANDING

18. a) What is the role of an antenna? b) Distinguish between omnidirectional and dish antennas in terms of operation. c) When would you use an omnidirectional antenna? d) When would you use a dish antenna?

Wave Characteristics

Figure 3-19 shows a simple radio **wave**. It is a classic sine wave, which is created by a constant-intensity signal at a single frequency.

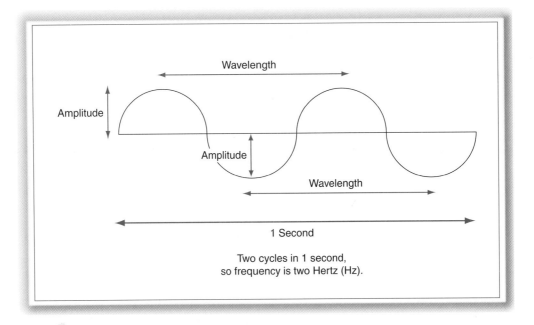

Two cycles in 1 second,
so frequency is two Hertz (Hz).

Figure 3-19   Radio Wave

➤ Its **amplitude** is the maximum (or minimum) intensity of the wave. In sound, this corresponds to loudness.

➤ Its **frequency** is the number of complete cycles it goes through per second. In sound, frequency corresponds to pitch. One cycle per second is one **hertz (Hz)**. Useful radio frequencies for data communications come in the high **megahertz (MHz)** range to the low **gigahertz (GHz)** range.

➤ Its **wavelength** is the physical distance between the corresponding points in adjacent cycles.

Wavelength is not independent of frequency. The wavelength times the frequency equals the speed of propagation through the transmission medium. In other words, the higher the frequency, the shorter the wavelength. This is why bass guitars have longer necks than normal guitars.

By tradition, frequencies are used to describe radio waves, whereas wavelengths are used to describe light waves. This is why wavelength is used in optical fiber transmission, whereas frequency is used in radio LANs, cellular telephone systems, and wireless metropolitan area networks.

TEST YOUR UNDERSTANDING

19. a) What are the three characteristics of radio signals? b) How are two of them related? c) Are the high-pitch strings on a harp the short ones or the long ones? Explain.

d) What is a hertz? e) When would you use frequency to describe propagation? f) When would you use wavelength?

Terminology

The Frequency Spectrum and Service Bands

The **frequency spectrum** consists of all possible frequencies from 0 hertz to infinity, as Figure 3-20 shows.

The frequency spectrum is divided into **service bands** that are dedicated to specific services. For instance, in the United States, the AM radio band lies between 540 kHz and 1600 kHz. The FM radio band, in turn, lies between 88 MHz and 108 MHz.

Channels

Service bands are divided into even smaller ranges of frequencies called **channels**. A different signal can be sent in each channel because signals in different channels do not interfere with one another.

Bandwidth and Transmission Speed

Bandwidth   The **bandwidth** of a channel is its highest frequency minus its lowest frequency. For instance, if the highest frequency of a channel is 88.2 MHz and the lowest frequency is 88 MHz, then the bandwidth of the channel is 0.2 MHz (200 kHz). AM radio channels are 10 kHz wide, whereas FM channels have bandwidths of 200 kHz. Television channels are 6 MHz wide.

Figure 3-20   The Frequency Spectrum, Service Bands, and Channels

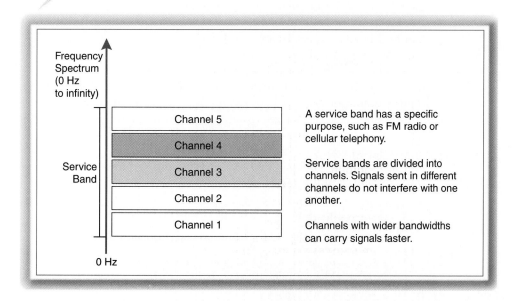

The Shannon Equation   Why are there differences in channel bandwidth? Shannon[13] found that the maximum possible transmission speed for sending data through a channel is directly proportional to its bandwidth, as shown in the equation below. Here, W is the maximum possible speed in a channel with a certain bandwidth (B), signal strength (S), and average noise strength (N).

$$W = B * \text{Log}_2(1 + S/N)$$

If you double the bandwidth, for instance, you can transmit up to twice as fast. Note that this is the *maximum possible* speed in a channel, but modern communication systems come reasonably close to this speed.

Television signals, which carry rich video information as well as audio information, need far more bandwidth per channel than AM and FM radio, which only carry audio signals. FM music quality, in turn, is better than AM quality partly because of the wider bandwidth of FM channels.

Broadband Channels   Channels with large bandwidths are called **broadband** channels. They can carry data very quickly. In contrast, channels with small bandwidths, which are called **narrowband** channels, can only carry data slowly.

Limited Frequency Spectrum Availability

Obviously, we would like each channel to be as wide as possible to provide maximum speed. However, the frequency spectrum at useful frequency ranges is limited, so when the International Telecommunications Union (ITU) designs service bands, there is tension between channel capacity, the number of channels, and the width of the service band.

Frequency and Propagation Characteristics

As just noted, useful radio frequencies for data communications come in the high megahertz (MHz) range to the low gigahertz (GHz) range. This is the **golden zone** of the spectrum because it provides good propagation characteristics, has a large total bandwidth, and has reasonable equipment costs.

Available bandwidth increases as frequency increases. However, propagation characteristics are best at lower frequencies. At lower frequencies, signals travel through walls nicely and bend around obstacles. In contrast, at higher frequencies, the sender and receiver must have an unobstructed **line of sight** because signals will not bend around objects or pass through them. At the high end of the golden zone, even leaves in trees and raindrops begin to cause problems.[14]

Frequencies in the golden zone provide a good compromise between bandwidth and propagation quality. All mobile services and wireless LANs are found in this relatively small part of the spectrum.

---

13   Claude Shannon, "A Mathematical Theory of Communication," *Bell System Technical Journal,* July 1938, pp. 379–423 and October 28, pp. 623–656.
14   If you install an outdoor radio system, measure attenuation in the summer, when trees are full of leaves. Indoor plants also cause problems for wireless LANs. The moisture in leaves absorbs radio signals fairly efficiently.

TEST YOUR UNDERSTANDING

20. Distinguish between the a) frequency spectrum, b) service bands, and c) channels. d) How can multiple signals be sent without interference?

21. a) What is channel bandwidth? b) Why is large channel bandwidth good? c) What do we call a system whose channels have large bandwidth? d) What is Shannon's equation? e) What happens to the maximum possible propagation speed in a channel if the bandwidth is doubled? f) If the signal-to-noise ratio increases? g) If wide bandwidth is good, why do we not use wide bandwidth in all radio channels?

22. a) What is the golden zone in radio transmission? b) Why is it important? c) In general, what bad things happens as frequency increases?

Wireless Propagation Problems

Wireless transmission is good because it allows mobile users to use the network without a cumbersome physical connection. On the negative side, wireless transmission tends to have unpleasant propagation problems, as Figure 3-21 illustrates. With wire or fiber, you know what your signal is going to do. With radio propagation, in contrast, engineering a network capable of reaching everywhere is extremely difficult.

Attenuation

In radio, as noted earlier, signal strength attenuates according to an inverse square law. In wired and optical fiber transmission, however, the signal is confined to a fixed path, so signals attenuate much more slowly.

Shadow Zones

To some extent, radio signals can go through and bend around objects. However, even in the golden zone, if there is a thick wall or a large dense object blocking the direct path between the sender and receiver, the receiver may be in a **shadow zone** where it cannot receive the signal.

Figure 3-21   Wireless Propagation Problems

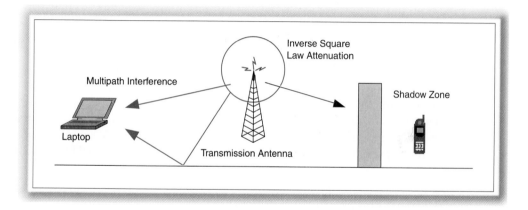

Multipath Interference

In addition, radio waves tend to bounce off walls, floors, ceilings, and other objects. As Figure 3-21 shows, this may mean that a receiver will receive two or more signals—the direct signal and reflected signals. The different signals will travel different distances and so are likely to be somewhat out of phase (one may be at its highest amplitude while the other may be near its lowest, giving an average of zero). This **multipath interference** may cause the signal to become unreadable or to range from strong to nonexistent in the space of a few centimeters.[15]

TEST YOUR UNDERSTANDING

23.   a) Broadly speaking, why are UTP and optical fiber transmission better than radio transmission? b) Describe the three main problems with radio transmission at frequencies used in wireless LANs and MANs.

PHYSICAL LAYER TOPOLOGIES

The term **topology** refers to the way that the wires in a network are connected together. Topology is a physical layer concept.

Major Topologies

Figure 3-22 shows the major topologies found in networking. Some are seen only in older legacy LANs using obsolete technology.

Point-to-Point Topology
The simplest network topology is the point-to-point topology, which connects two points.

Star Topology and Extended Star (Hierarchy) Topology
These are the topologies used by modern versions of Ethernet, which is the dominant LAN standard. In a simple **star**, all wires connect to a single switch or hub (multiport repeater). In an **extended star (hierarchy)**, there are multiple layers of switches or hubs organized in a hierarchy. We will see Ethernet stars in Chapter 4 and Ethernet hierarchies in Chapter 5.

Mesh Topology
In a **mesh topology**, there are many connections among switches, so there are many alternative routes to get from one end of the network to the other. We will see mesh topologies with ATM in Chapter 5, Frame Relay in Chapter 7, and routers in Chapter 8.

Ring Topology
In a **ring topology**, stations are connected in a loop. Messages pass only in one direction around the loop. Eventually, all messages pass through all stations. In LANs, the obsolete 802.5 Token-Ring Networks and FDDI networks use a ring topology, as we will see in Chapter 5. In Chapter 6, we will see that the worldwide telephone network increasingly uses rings to connect its switches, using the SONET/SDH technology.

---

15   Most wireless devices use two or more antennas to average out multipath interference effects.

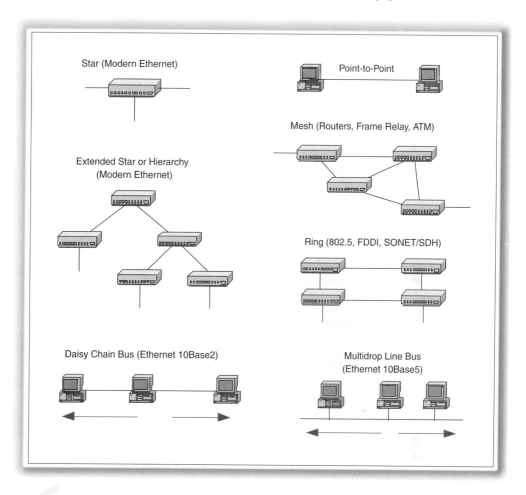

Figure 3-22   Major Topologies

Bus Topologies

In a **bus topology**, one station transmits, and its signals travel in both directions to the end of the transmission segment called a **bus**. Along the way, the signal passes all stations. In a simple **daisy chain**, the wiring passes directly from one station to another. In a **multidrop line**, stations are connected to the main bus via drop lines. Pure bus topologies are found only in obsolete 10-Mbps Ethernet LAN technologies. As discussed in Chapter 5, Ethernet 10Base5 uses a multidrop bus topology, whereas Ethernet 10Base2 uses a daisy chain bus topology.

Physical and Logical Topologies

Ethernet hubs, even when arranged in a star or hierarchy, use a **logical bus topology**. When a station transmits, the hub broadcasts the signal out all ports to all stations.

Although it is wired in a physical star or hierarchical star, the signal travels past all devices as in a physical bus topology.

TEST YOUR UNDERSTANDING

24. a) What is a topology? b) At what layer do we find topologies? c) List the major topologies and give the defining characteristics for each. Please discuss each topology in a separate paragraph. d) What technology is associated with each topology?

25. Distinguish between physical stars and logical busses in Ethernet.

GAINING PERSPECTIVE

Market Perspective

David Passmore,[16] research director for the Burton Group, has noted that SONET/SDH optical fiber technology (discussed in Chapter 6) is quadrupling every two years in terms of the speed it can delivery per wavelength. At the same time, the number of wavelengths that can be supported on a fiber is doubling every two years. This is an eight-fold increase in capacity per fiber every two years. Costs, however, are not rising rapidly. Overall, the cost per bit transmitted though fiber is falling much faster than the cost of computer or router processing capacity.

THOUGHT QUESTIONS

1. Why do you think digital transmission took so long to become dominant?
2. Parallel transmission is faster than serial transmission. Why do you think serial transmission is dominant beyond distances of about 2 meters?
3. Why do you think radio LANs took so long to appear?

TROUBLESHOOTING QUESTIONS

1. A tester shows that a UTP cord has too much crosstalk interference. What is likely to be the problem?
2. What kinds of errors are you likely to encounter if you run a length of UTP cord 200 meters? (The standard calls for a 100-meter maximum distance.)
3. When a teacher lectures in class, is the classroom a full-duplex communication system or a half-duplex communication system?
4. Your wireless notebook computer works on one desk, but when you move it to a nearby desk, you cannot receive a signal. What may be happening? How might you fix the problem?

CASE STUDIES

For case studies, go to the book's website, www.prenhall.com/panko, and look at the Case Studies page for this chapter.

---

[16] Caruso, Jeff, "Today's Focus: Fiber Revolution," *Network World*, Focus on High-Speed LANs, December 16, 2000. E-mail newsletter.

PHOTOS

For photos, go to the book's website, www.prenhall.com/panko, and look at the Photos page for this chapter.

PROJECTS

1. **Getting Current.** Go to the book website's New Information and Errors pages for this chapter to get new information since this book went to press and to correct any errors in the text.
2. **Internet Exercises.** Go to the book website's Exercises page for this chapter and do the Internet Exercises.
3. **Hands-On.** Do the wire-cutting exercise described in Chapter 3a.

CHAPTER 3a

HANDS ON: CUTTING AND CONNECTORIZING UTP[1]

INTRODUCTION

Chapter 3 discussed UTP wiring in general. This chapter discusses how to cut and connectorize (add connectors to) solid UTP wiring.

SOLID AND STRANDED WIRING

Solid-Wire UTP Versus Stranded-Wire UTP

The TIA/EIA-568 standard requires that long runs to wall jacks use **solid-wire UTP**, in which each of the eight wires really is a single solid wire.

However, patch cords running from the wall outlet to a NIC usually are **stranded-wire UTP**, in which each of the eight "wires" really is a bundle of thinner wire strands. So stranded-wire UTP has eight bundles of wires, each bundle in its own insulation and acting like a single wire.

Relative Advantages

Solid wire is needed in long cords because it has lower attenuation than stranded wire. In contrast, stranded-wire UTP cords are more flexible than solid-wire cords, making them ideal for patch cords—especially the one running to the desktop—because they can be bent more and still function. They are more durable than solid-wire UTP cords.

---

[1] This material is based on the author's lab projects and on the lab project of Prof. Harry Reif of James Madison University.

Solid-Wire UTP
　Each of the eight wires is a solid wire
　Low attenuation over long distances
　Easy to connectorize
　Inflexible and stiff—not good for runs to the desktop

Stranded-Wire UTP
　Each of the eight "wires" is itself several thin strands of wire within an insulation tube
　Flexible and durable—good for runs to the desktop
　Impossible to connectorize in the field (bought as patch cords)
　Higher attenuation than solid-wire UTP—Used only in short runs
　From wall jack to desktop
　Within a telecommunications closet (see Chapter 6)

Figure 3a-1   Solid-Wire and Stranded-Wire UTP

Adding Connectors

It is relatively easy to add RJ-45 connectors to solid-wire UTP cords. However, it is very difficult to add RJ-45 connectors to stranded-wire cords. Stranded-wire patch cords should be purchased from the factory precut to desired lengths and preconnectorized.

In addition, when purchasing equipment to connectorize solid-wire UTP, it is important to purchase crimpers designed for solid wire.

CUTTING THE CORD

Solid wire UTP normally comes in a box or spool containing 50 meters or more of wire. The first step is to cut a length of UTP cord that matches your need. It is good to be a little generous with the length. This way, bad connectorization can be fixed by cutting off the connector and adding a new connector to the shortened cord. Also, UTP cords should never be subjected to pulls (strain), and adding a little extra length creates some slack.

STRIPPING THE CORD

Now the cord must be stripped at each end using a **stripping tool** such as the one shown in Figure 3a-2. The installer rotates the stripper once around the cord once, scoring (cutting into) the cord jacket (but not cutting through it). The installer then pulls off the scored end of the cord, exposing about 5 cm (about two inches) of the wire pairs. It is critical not to score the cord too deeply, or the insulation around the individual wires may be cut. This creates short circuits. A really deep cut also will nick the wire, perhaps causing it to snap immediately or later.

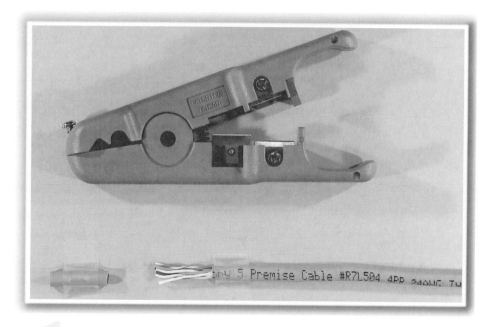

Figure 3a-2   Stripping Tool

WORKING WITH THE EXPOSED PAIRS

Pair Colors

The four pairs each have a color: orange, green, blue, or brown. One wire of the pair usually is a completely solid color. The other usually is white with stripes of the pair's color. For instance, the orange pair has an orange wire and a white wire with orange stripes.

Untwisting the Pairs

The wires of each pair are twisted around each other several times per inch. These must be untwisted after the end of the cord is stripped.

Ordering the Pairs

The wires now must be placed in their correct order, left to right. Figure 3a-3 shows the location of Pin 1 on the RJ-45 connector and on a wall jack.

Which color wire goes into which connector slot? The two standardized patterns are shown in Figure 3a-4. The T568B pattern is much more common in the United States.

The connectors at both ends of the cord use the same pattern. If the white-orange wire goes into Pin 1 of the connector on one end of the cord, it also goes into Pin 1 of the connector at the other end.

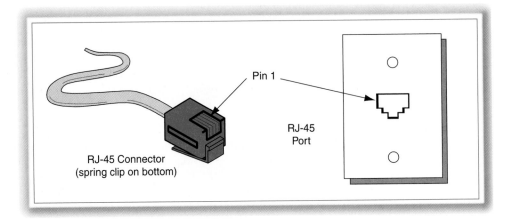

Figure 3a-3   Location of Pin 1 on an RJ-45 Connector and Wall Jack

Cutting the Wires

The length of the exposed wires must be limited to 1.25 cm (half an inch) or slightly less. After the wires have been arranged in the correct order, a cutter should cut across the wires to make them this length. The cut should be made straight across, so that all wires are of equal length. Otherwise, they will not all reach the end of the connector when they are inserted into it. Wires that do not reach the end will not make electrical contact.

Pin*	T568A	T568B
1	White–Green	White–Orange
2	Green	Orange
3	White–Orange	White–Green
4	Blue	Blue
5	White–Blue	White–Blue
6	Orange	Green
7	White–Brown	White–Brown
8	Brown	Brown

Figure 3a-4   T568A and T568B Pin Colors

ADDING THE CONNECTOR

Holding the Connector

The next step is to place the wires in the RJ-45 connector. In one hand, hold the connector, clip side down, with the opening in the back of the connector facing you.

Sliding in the Wires

Now, slide the wires into the connector, making sure that they are in the correct order. There are grooves in the connector that will help. Be sure to push the wires all the way to the end or proper electrical contact will not be made with the pins at the end.

Before you crimp the connector, look down at the top of the connector, holding the tip away from you. The first wire on your left should be mostly white. So should every second wire. If they are not, you have inserted your wires incorrectly.[2]

Some Jacket Inside the Connector

If you have shortened your wires properly, there will be a little bit of jacket inside the RJ-45 connector.

CRIMPING

Pressing Down

Get a really good **crimping tool** (See Figure 3a-5). Place the connector with the wires in it into the crimp and push down firmly. Good crimping tools have ratchets to reduce the chance of your pushing down too tightly.

Making Electrical Contact

The front of the connector has eight pins running from the top almost to the bottom (spring clip side). When you **crimp** the connector, you force these eight pins through the insulation around each wire and into the wire itself. This seems like a crude electrical connection, and it is. However, it normally works very well. Your wires are now connected to the connector's pins. By the way, this is called an **insulation displacement connection (IDC)** because it cuts through the insulation.

Strain Relief

When you crimp, the crimper also forces a ridge in the back of the RJ-45 into the jacket of the cord. This provides **strain relief**, meaning that if someone pulls on the cord (a bad idea), they will be pulling only to the point where the jacket has the ridge forced into it. There will be no strain where the wires connect to the pins.

---

[2]   Thanks to Jason Okumura, who suggested this way of checking the wires.

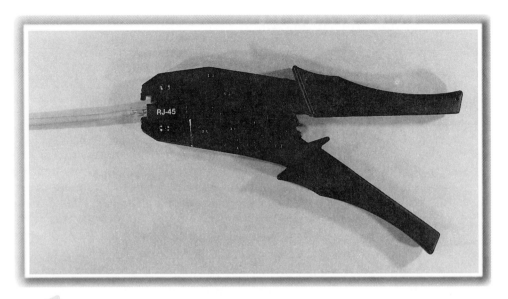

Figure 3a-5   Crimping Tool

TESTING

Purchasing the best UTP cabling means nothing unless you install it properly. Wiring errors are common in the field, so you need to test every cord after you install it. Testing is inexpensive compared to troubleshooting subtle wiring problems later.

Testing with Continuity Testers

The simplest testers are **continuity testers**, which merely test whether the wires are arranged in correct order within in the two RJ-45 connectors and are making good electrical contact with the connector. They cost only about $100.

Testing for Signal Quality

Better testers cost $500 to $2,000 but are worth the extra money. In addition to testing for continuity problems, they send **test signals** through the cord to determine whether the cord meets TIA/EIA-568 signal quality requirements. Many include **time domain reflectometry (TDR)**, which sends a signal and listens for echoes in order to measure the length of the UTP cord or to find if and where breaks exist in the cord.

TEST YOUR UNDERSTANDING

1. a) Explain the technical difference between solid-wire UTP and stranded-wire UTP. b) In what way is solid-wire UTP better? c) In what way is stranded-wire UTP better? d) Where would you use each? e) Which should only be connectorized at the factory?

2. If you have a wire run of 50 meters, should you cut the cord to 50 meters? Explain.

3. Why do you score the jacket of the cord with the stripping tool instead of cutting all the way through the jacket?

4. a) What are the colors of the four pairs? b) If you are following T568B, which wire goes into Pin 3? c) At the other end of the cord, would the same wire go into Pin 3?

5. After you arrange the wires in their correct order and cut them across, how much of the wires should be exposed from the jacket?

6. a) Describe RJ-45's insulation displacement approach. b) Describe its strain relief approach.

7. a) Should you test every cord in the field after installation? b) For what do inexpensive testers test? c) For what do expensive testers test?

A SMALL ETHERNET PC NETWORK

Learning Objectives:

By the end of this chapter, you should be able to discuss:

- The components of a small PC network based on Ethernet 100Base-TX 10/100 Mbps technology.
- Purchasing UTP wiring.
- Differences between hubs and switches and reasons for the growing dominance of switches.
- Network interface card (NIC) operation, including the division of the data link layer into the media access control and logical link control layers, the organization of the Ethernet MAC layer frame, and the use of CSMA/CD to control when a NIC may transmit.
- Operation of the logical link control layer (if you study the box feature).
- Important server services, including autoconfiguration, file service, print service, application service, and Internet access service.
- Popular server network operating systems, including Microsoft Windows, LINUX, and Novell NetWare.

INTRODUCTION

After you take a networking course, a minimum expectation is that you will know how to set up a small PC network. This chapter discusses how to do that. Chapter 4a discusses how to set up a client PC in more detail.

Elements of a Small PC Network

Figure 4-1 shows the elements of a small Ethernet PC network. This network has two client PCs, two servers, and an access router. These are connected by UTP to a device called a hub or a switch. In this chapter, we will look at each of these elements.

Ethernet

This small PC network uses Ethernet for its LAN technology. For a small LAN, this is the only LAN technology that makes sense. ATM and token-ring networks, which we will see in the next chapter, are too complex and obsolete, respectively. The one possible alternative to using Ethernet is to use a wireless LAN technology, which is discussed in Chapter 5.

Standardization

Ethernet was created at the Xerox Palo Alto Research Center in the 1970s. In the early 1980s, its standardization was passed to the **Institute for Electrical and Electronics Engineers' (IEEE's) 802 LAN/MAN Standards Committee.**

The "**802 Committee**," as everybody calls it, is broadly responsible for creating local area network standards and metropolitan area network standards. The 802

Figure 4-1   Elements of a Small Ethernet PC Network

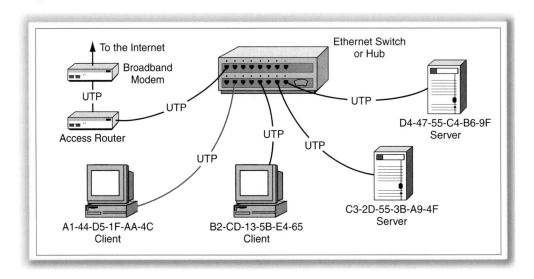

Standardization
    Institute of Electrical and Electronics Engineers (IEEE)
        802 LAN/MAN Standards Committee (802 Committee) creates LAN standards
            802.3 Working Group creates Ethernet standards

Physical Layer Ethernet Standards Using UTP
    10Base-T
    100Base-TX
        10/100 operation thanks to autosensing
    1000Base-T (gigabit Ethernet over UTP)

Figure 4-2   Ethernet Standards

Committee's **802.3 Working Group** creates Ethernet-specific standards. We will use the terms Ethernet standards and 802.3 standards interchangeably.[1,2]

10/100 Ethernet Technology

In this chapter, we will assume that the network uses **100Base-TX** Ethernet technology. This is a 10/100 standard, meaning that most NICs and the hub or switch will operate at 100 Mbps but that the hub or switch will **autosense** the NIC's speed and slow down to 10 Mbps for a NIC following the **10Base-T** standard.[3]

TEST YOUR UNDERSTANDING

  1. What are the elements of a small PC network?
  2. a) Why do we discuss Ethernet in this chapter? b) Who standardizes Ethernet?
  3. Explain 10/100 Ethernet 100Base-TX technology.

UTP TRANSMISSION LINKS

Small LANs use UTP because UTP is inexpensive to purchase and install and is rugged. The "T" in 10 Mbps 10Base-T and 100 Mbps 100Base-TX indicate that these are UTP-based physical layer standards.

In the last chapter, we looked at UTP technology in general. In this chapter, we will discuss how to purchase UTP and present some rules for installation.

---

[1] Properly speaking, the term "Ethernet" should only be used for the Version 1 and Version 2 Ethernet standards created by Xerox, Intel, and Digital Equipment in the early 1980s, before Ethernet standardization was passed to the 802 Committee. However, almost everyone calls 802.3 standards "Ethernet standards."

[2] After a working group creates a standard, it goes to the 802 Committee for approval, then to the American National Standards Institute (ANSI) and finally to the International Organization for Standardization (ISO) for approval. However, these are mere formalities. As soon as an Ethernet standard is created by the 802.3 Working Group, vendors begin to develop products.

[3] Or, if the switch or hub is a 10Base-T device, you can install 10/100 NICs if you anticipate upgrading the switch or hub later. These NICs will slow down to the speed of the switch or hub.

Wiring Quality Categories
   Governed by TIA/EIA-568
   Category 5 and 5e for 1000Base-TX (gigabit Ethernet), but 5 is marginal
   Category 5 and 5e for 100Base-TX
   Categories 3, 4, 5, or 5e for 10Base-T
   Category 6 for high-speed ATM networks; not needed for gigabit Ethernet
   No UTP standard planned for 10 Gbps Ethernet
Plenum Cabling
   Gives off fewer toxic fumes if it burns
   Must be used within air conditioning ducts, false ceilings, false floors, and other airways
   Not for ordinary room wiring
Patch Cords versus Bulk Cable
   Patch Cords
      Precut to certain lengths and connectorized and tested at the factory
   Bulk Cable
      For long runs or to cut a cable to an exact length
      Expensive in terms of labor
      Expensive in terms of cutting, stripping, and connectorizing equipment

Figure 4-3   Purchasing and Installing UTP

Purchasing UTP Wiring

Quality Standards for UTP

When you buy UTP wiring, you need to buy wiring of high quality to carry data at current and future high-speed data rates. The TIA/EIA-568 standard defines several quality standards for UTP wire.

Category 5e UTP   TIA/EIA-568 calls for **Category 5e** (enhanced) UTP wiring quality in new LANs. Almost all UTP sold today is "Cat 5e" UTP.

Category 5 UTP   A large majority of existing LANs already use Cat 5e or **Category 5 (Cat 5)**. Both Cat 5 and Cat 5e can carry data up to 1 Gbps, although for gigabit speed, "Cat 5" has no margin for installation imperfections.

Category 3 and 4 UTP   Some older LANs only have **Category 3** or (rarely) **Category 4** quality wiring. These are only good for an Ethernet LAN running at 10 Mbps.

Category 6 UTP   A new Category 6 quality standard is under development. It may be useful for high-speed ATM networks (see Chapter 5). However, Category 6 UTP will not be required for gigabit Ethernet, and no UTP variant is planned for 10 Gbps Ethernet, so the need for Category 6 wiring is uncertain.

Plenum Cabling

Usually, the outer jackets of UTP (and optical fiber cords) are made of **polyvinyl chloride (PVC)**. PVC is inexpensive, but when it burns, it can give off deadly fumes. Special **plenum** cabling is needed if the cabling is to run through air conditioning ducts, false ceilings, or other areas where smoke can travel quickly. Plenum cabling either uses a non-PVC jacket or a PVC jacket with flame-retardant additives.

Bulk Cable Versus Patch Cords

For short cable runs, it is a good idea to purchase **patch cords**, which are precut to certain lengths up to about 15 meters and are connectorized and tested at the factory. This saves the work of cutting cable, stripping the cable, and adding connectors. It also saves the cost of purchasing tools needed to cut, strip, and connectorize cables.

For long runs, or if cords of exact lengths must be created, it may be necessary to buy **bulk cable**, which comes in large spools. With bulk cable, good tools should be used. A decent tool kit will cost $150, not counting the cost of testing equipment.

TEST YOUR UNDERSTANDING

4. What does the "T" stand for in 10Base-T and 100Base-TX?
5. a) "Category 5e" is a measure of a cord's _____. b) Who creates wiring quality standards? c) What wiring quality standard is now recommended for LANs? d) What wiring quality standards can be used with 10Base-T? e) With 100Base-TX? f) With gigabit Ethernet (1000Base-T)? g) Describe the emerging Category 6 standard and its potential usefulness.
6. a) What is the technical difference between regular wiring and plenum wiring? b) Where must you use plenum wiring? c) Why must you use it there?
7. a) What are the advantages of patch cords? b) Where would you use bulk UTP cabling?

HUBS AND SWITCHES

Figure 4-1 shows that client stations, server stations, and the access router all talk to one another via a central device called a hub or switch. We will look at both of these technologies, which look identical from the outside. (Both are boxes with RJ-45 ports.)

Hubs

Hub Operation

Figure 4-4 shows that hub operation is very simple. First, a NIC (A1-44-D5-1F-AA-4C) transmits a bit to the hub on Pins 1 and 2. The hub then broadcasts the bit out all ports on Pins 3 and 6. All NICs receive the bit on Pins 3 and 6.

Bus Operation   This broadcasting is called **bus operation**. Note that hubs are physical layer (Layer 1) devices that act on bits rather than frames. They are repeaters in the terminology introduced in Chapter 3.

To Read the Frame or Not   Each NIC reassembles the bits of the frame and reads the destination address in the frame (which is discussed a few paragraphs later). If the address is its own, it continues to read the frame. If the address is not its own, it discards the frame.[4]

---

4   Most NICs also can operate in "promiscuous mode," in which they read all frames. This is useful in gathering network statistics. However, it can be a security problem. Transmission using hubs is never secure.

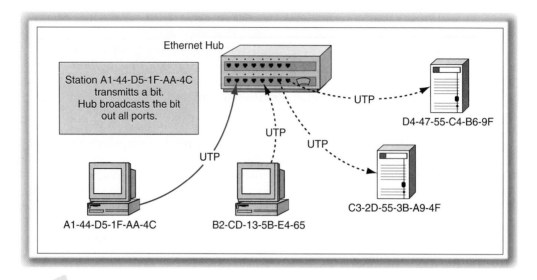

Figure 4-4 Hub Operation

Problems with Hub Operation

Hubs are simple and therefore inexpensive. However, what if two stations wish to transmit at the same time? Their signals would become hopelessly scrambled during broadcasting, and receivers would not be able to read either signal.

Instead, as Figure 4-5 shows, a station must wait if another station is transmitting (Station B2-CD-13-5B-4E-65 is waiting). This creates latency (delay), which grows as the number of stations grows. Another way of saying this is that the speed of the hub is **shared**. A 100 Mbps hub used by several stations will provide considerably less than 100 Mbps to each station on average. Despite what your mother told you, sharing is not always good.

The Prospects for Hubs

Although hubs still make sense for very small networks with only a handful of PCs, the price gap between hubs and more sophisticated switches is falling rapidly. In a few years, you will not even be able to buy a hub.

TEST YOUR UNDERSTANDING

8. a) Describe hub operation, including the pins on which the NIC and hub transmit. b) What is broadcasting called? c) How does a NIC know that an arriving frame is intended for it?

9. a) What happens if two stations connected to a hub wish to transmit at the same time? b) What does it mean that hub speed is "shared?" c) What problem does sharing cause? d) What are the market prospects for hubs?

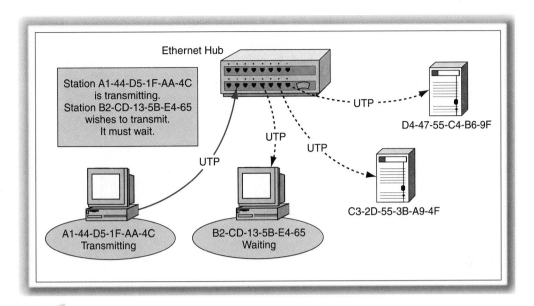

Station A1-44-D5-1F-AA-4C
is transmitting.
Station B2-CD-13-5B-E4-65
wishes to transmit.
It must wait.

Ethernet Hub

UTP

D4-47-55-C4-B6-9F

UTP

UTP

UTP

C3-2D-55-3B-A9-4F

A1-44-D5-1F-AA-4C
Transmitting

B2-CD-13-5B-E4-65
Waiting

Figure 4-5   Waiting to Transmit with a Hub

Switches

Basic Operation

Figure 4-6 shows **Ethernet switch** operation. When a switch receives a frame, it *does not* broadcast the frame. Rather, it sends the frame out a single port—the port to which the destination station is attached. When Station A1-44-D5-1F-AA-4C sends to Station C3-2D-55-3B-A9-4F, the switch only sends the frame out Port 15—the port to which Station C3-2D-55-3B-A9-4F is attached. Note that switches are Layer 2 devices that work with frames.

This approach allows multiple conversations to take place at the same time. In Figure 4-6, Station A1-44-D5-1F-AA-4C is sending to Station C3-2D-55-3B-A9-4F, and Station B2-CD-13-5B-E4-65 is sending to Station D4-47-55-C4-B6-9F simultaneously. There is no need to wait while another station is transmitting.

Consequently, each station can send (and receive) at the full speed of its NIC. Speed is not shared, as it is with hubs. Latency is very small unless the switch has insufficient capacity for its traffic load.

Switching Table

As discussed later in this chapter, each NIC comes from the factory with a unique 48-bit MAC address that becomes its address on its Ethernet network. (We also will see why it is called a MAC address.) A typical address would be A1-44-D5-1F-AA-4C. These addresses appear in both the source and destination address fields in the Ethernet frame discussed later in this chapter.

To do its work, the switch maintains a **switching table**. As Figure 4-7 shows, this switching table has two columns. The right column of the switching table is a particular

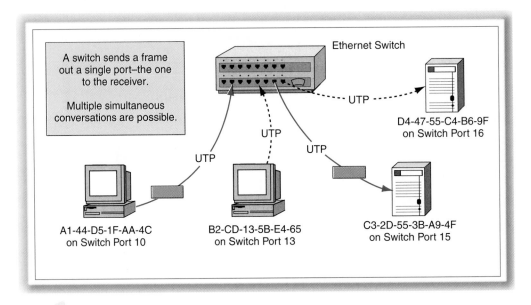

Figure 4-6   Switch Operation with Multiple Simultaneous Conversations

Figure 4-7   Ethernet Switching Table

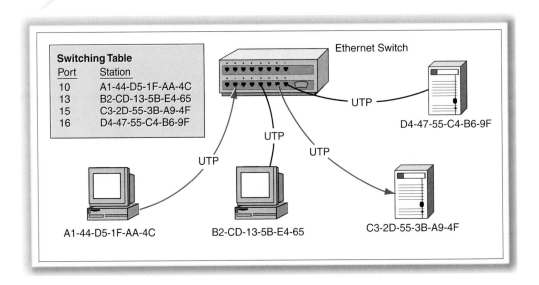

NIC's 48-bit MAC address. The left column holds the port to which that NIC attaches to the switch.

Suppose that Station A1-44-D5-1F-AA-4C transmits a frame to Station C3-2D-55-3B-A9-4F. When the frame arrives at the switch, the switch will look at its switching table. It will note that the station listed in the destination address (C3-2D-55-3B-A9-4F) is out Port 15. The switch will transmit the frame out that port.

TEST YOUR UNDERSTANDING

10. a) Describe basic switch operation. b) Is speed shared on a switch? c) What problem does this reduce?

11. a) What types of information do switching tables hold? b) How are switching tables used in switching decisions?

NETWORK INTERFACE CARDS

Splitting the Data Link Layer: MAC and LLC

As Figure 4-8 shows, the 802 Committee only creates standards for the OSI architecture's bottom two layers because only the physical and data link layers are involved in single LANs.

Figure 4-8   802 Standards Layering

Internet Layer		TCP/IP Internet Layer Standards (IP, ARP, etc.)		Other Internet Layer Standards (IPX, etc.)	
Data Link Layer	**Logical Link Control Layer**	802.2			
	Media Access Control Layer	Ethernet 802.3 MAC Layer Standard			Other MAC Standards (802.5, 802.11, etc.)
Physical Layer		10 Base-T	100Base-TX	1000Base-T	Other Physical Layer Standards (802.5, 802.11, etc.)

MAC and LLC Layers

In addition, the 802 Committee subdivided the data link layer into two layers—the *media access control (MAC)* layer and the *logical link control (LLC)* layer. We will focus primarily on the MAC layer because network administrators have no control over the LLC layer and because the LLC layer has a negligible role.

A Single Media Access Control Layer Standard

Figure 4-8 shows that Ethernet (802.3) has several physical layer standards (10Base-T, 100Base-TX, etc.) but only one MAC layer standard. No matter what physical layer standard you use in an Ethernet LAN, you will use the **802.3 MAC layer standard** at the media access control layer.

TEST YOUR UNDERSTANDING

12. a) What OSI layer did the 802 Committee split? b) What are the two layers into which it split the data link layer? c) Does the LLC layer have practical significance to network administrators? Explain.

13. a) How many MAC layer standards does Ethernet have? b) What is its name?

Media Access Control: The Ethernet Frame

Whereas hubs work with individual bits, switches work with Ethernet frames. Figure 4-9 illustrates the standard **Ethernet frame**, which is, formally speaking, the **802.3 MAC layer frame**.

Octets

In Chapter 2, we saw that field lengths could be measured in bits. Another common measure for field lengths in networking is the octet. An **octet** is a collection of eight bits. Isn't that a byte? Yes. "Octet" is another name for "byte." It is widely used in networking, so you need to become familiar with the term.[5]

Preamble and Start of Frame Delimiter (SFD)

The purpose of the first two fields is to synchronize the sender's clock with the receiver's clock. Each clock cycle is only one 10 millionth to one 10 billionth of a second, and if the senders' and receivers' clocks are even slightly off, bit 1,000 might be read as bit 999 or 1,011, causing an error.

The **preamble** field is a 56-bit (seven-octet) sequence of 10101010 . . . , which gives the receiver a strong repeating pattern it can use to exactly synchronize its clock. The **start of frame delimiter** (SFD), 10101011, continues the pattern but ends in 11 instead of 10 to signal that the main part of the frame is coming next.

MAC Addresses and Hexadecimal Notation

The frame also has source and destination addresses that identify the sending and receiving stations, respectively. Each is 48 bits long. These are called **MAC addresses**

---

[5] "Octet" actually makes more sense than "byte," because "oct" means eight. We have octopuses, octagons, and octogenarians. What is the eighth month? (Careful!)

Field	Description
Preamble (7 Octets) 10101010...	Begins synchronization
Start of Frame Delimiter (1 Octet) 10101011	Ends synchronization Signals start of content of frame
Destination Address (6 Octets)	48 Bits Expressed for humans in Hexadecimal Example: A1-34-CD-7B-DF h Unique value set at factory
Source Address (6 Octets)	48 Bits Expressed for humans in Hexadecimal Example: A1-34-CD-7B-DF h Unique value set at factory
Length (2 Octets)	Length of Data Field in octets 1,500 (decimal) maximum
Data Field (variable)	LLC Frame
PAD	(Needed if Data Field is less than 46 octet Minimum; Data Field plus PAD Will be 46 Octets)
Frame Check Sequence (4 Octets)	Error Detection Field

Figure 4-9   Ethernet Frame

because they are addresses at the media access control layer. Each NIC has a unique MAC address when it leaves the factory.

For humans, we normally represent MAC addresses in **hexadecimal** (Base 16) notation. Figure 4-10 shows how "**hex**" represents all possible groups of four bits with the numbers 0 through 9 and letters A though F.

To represent a MAC address in hex, you first divide it into 12 groups of four bits apiece. You then represent each group by a hexadecimal symbol. This gives you 12 hex symbols.

Next, place a dash after every second symbol, and place "h" after the symbol string to indicate that it is hexadecimal notation. A typical 48-bit MAC address would be "A7-BF-23-D4-33-99 h." It is common to drop the h.

Remember that computers and switches work directly with 48-bit sequences of ones and zeros. Only humans use hex representation.

4 Bits (Base 2)*	Decimal (Base 10)	Hexadecimal (Base 16)
0000	0	0 hex
0001	1	1 hex
0010	2	2 hex
0011	3	3 hex
0100	4	4 hex
0101	5	5 hex
0110	6	6 hex
0111	7	7 hex
1000	8	8 hex
1001	9	9 hex
1010	10	A hex
1011	11	B hex
1100	12	C hex
1101	13	D hex
1110	14	E hex
1111	15	F hex

*2^4=16 combinations

For example, A1-34-CD-7B-DF hex begins with 10100001

Figure 4-10   Hexadecimal Notation

The Length Field

Coming just before the data field, the two-octet **length field** gives the length of the data field in octets. (Note that it gives the length of the *data field,* not the length of the *entire frame.*)

Data Field

The **data field** has variable length. It can range in length from a few octets to as many as 1,500 octets.

PAD Field

If the data field is too short, this will cause problems, so if the data field is less than 46 octets, the sender must add a **PAD field** to bring the total length of the data field plus the PAD field to 46 octets.

Frame Check Sequence Field

Following the data field is a single trailer field, the **frame check sequence field**. This four-octet field holds a number that the sender calculates from all of the other fields (except for the preamble and start of frame delimiter fields). The receiver recomputes the number and compares its calculation to the value in the frame check sequence field. If the two numbers match, then no error has occurred during transmission. However, if the numbers do not match, an error occurred during transmission. The receiving NIC simply *discards* the frame. There is no request for retransmission.

TEST YOUR UNDERSTANDING

14. a) What is an octet?

15. a) What is the purpose of the Ethernet preamble and start of frame delimiter fields? b) What is the total length of the combined preamble and start of frame delimiter fields?

16. a) How long are MAC addresses? b) Where are MAC layer addresses set on NICs? c) Do computers work with them in hex representation? d) Do people tend to work with them in hex representation? e) Convert the following to hex (spaces are added between octets to ease your burden): 10101010 00001111 11011110 00010010 11111111 00000000. *Hint:* The first octet is AA.

17. a) How long is the Ethernet length field? b) It tells the length of what?

18. a) Is the Ethernet data field of fixed or variable length? b) What is its maximum length? c) What is the minimum length of the data field and the PAD? d) Is the PAD always present? e) If not, under what circumstances is it added? f) Does the sender or the receiver add it?

19. a) How long is the Ethernet frame check sequence field? b) What is its purpose? c) How is it used? d) What happens if a receiving NIC detects an error?

Media Access Control: CSMA/CD

With hubs, only one station can transmit at a time in an Ethernet LAN. Others must wait, or their signals will collide and be unreadable. The purpose of the **media access control (MAC) layer** is to ensure that only one station transmits at any moment.

1. Carrier Sense Multiple Access (CSMA)

The mechanism that Ethernet uses to control media access is called **CSMA/CD**, which stands for **Carrier Sense Multiple Access with Collision Detection**. We will begin by looking at the CSMA part of this protocol.

Multiple access means that multiple stations may wish to transmit at any moment. (Note that this is "multiple" access, not "media" access.) **Carrier sense** means that the NICs "sense the carrier," which is a fancy way of saying that they listen to (sense) the signal (the carrier) on the LAN.

Quite simply, the NIC listens for traffic on the LAN. If the NIC wishes to transmit and there is no traffic, the NIC may transmit. If the NIC wishes to transmit and there is

Carrier Sense Multiple Access (CSMA)
1. If a NIC wishes to transmit, it must listen for traffic
    If there is no traffic, the NIC may transmit
    If there is traffic, the NIC must wait until there is no traffic to transmit
Collision Detection (CD)
2. If there is a collision,
    All NICs stop transmitting
    All wait for a random amount of time
    The first NIC that finishes its wait may transmit
        but only if there is no traffic
    If there is traffic, the NIC must wait until there is no traffic
3. If there are multiple collisions
    The random wait is increased each time
    After 16 attempts to transmit, the sending NIC discards the frame
NICs Implement CSMA/CD
    Hubs do not
    Switches do not

Figure 4-11   Carrier Sense Multiple Access with Collision Detection (CSMA/CD)

traffic, the NIC must wait until there is no traffic; then it may transmit. In other words, NICs follow the rule of polite conversation.

2. Collision Detection (CD)

While a station is transmitting, two or more other stations may be waiting to transmit. As soon as the transmission ends, both NICs may begin transmitting. Their signals will collide, becoming unreadable.

Stations are always listening to traffic on the network, so the stations involved in the collision will engage in a **collision detection** procedure.

First, the NICs involved in the collision will stop sending their messages. Second, all NICs set a random timer. Third, the NIC wishing to transmit whose timer finishes first may transmit—but only if it hears no incoming traffic.

3. Multiple Collisions

It is possible that another collision will occur because the waiting period is too brief. In that case, stations will again engage in collision detection, this time using a longer random period of time. This can happen multiple times, but after 16 collisions, the transmitting NIC stops trying and discards the frame.

CSMA/CD, NICs, and Hubs

Note that CSMA/CD controls how *NICs* behave. It does not specify how hubs or switches behave.

Furthermore, NICs implement the physical, MAC, and LLC layers. Properly speaking, it is not the NIC that implements CSMA/CD, but rather the MAC layer process on the NIC.

TEST YOUR UNDERSTANDING

20. Describe the three main phases in CSMA/CD.
21. a) If CSMA/CD is implemented, is it implemented on NICs, hubs, switches, or all three?

THE LOGICAL LINK CONTROL LAYER: 802.2

Although the MAC layer is the most important layer in the data link layer, there also is the logical link control layer, as shown in Figure 4-12.

802.2: PROVIDING A SINGLE CONNECTION BETWEEN MAC AND INTERNET LAYER PROCESSES

The figure shows that there is a single LLC standard, **802.2**. Having a single LLC standard means that internet layer processes only have to interface with a single next-lower-layer standard, 802.2, regardless of what MAC layer standard is in use. In addition, MAC layer processes only have to interface with a single next-higher-layer standard regardless of what internet layer standard is in use.

OPTIONAL ERROR CORRECTION

The LLC layer also offers optional error correction, including the retransmission of damaged or lost LLC frames. However, this function is almost never used. In fact, there usually is no way for a network administrator to turn on error correction in a NIC, so it is irrelevant.

TEST YOUR UNDERSTANDING

22. a) What is the only LLC standard? b) What are the two purposes of the logical link control layer?

> **802.2 LLC Standard is Used in All 802 LANs**
> All MAC layer standards interact only with 802.2 at the layer above them
> All internet layer standards interact only with 802.2 at the layer below them
> **Optional Error Correction**
> Almost never used
> NICs do not allow user to control LLC functionality

Figure 4-12   Logical Link Control (LLC) Layer

SERVER SERVICES

In PC networks, servers provide services to client PCs. Among these services are autoconfiguration, file service, print service, application service, and Internet access service. In a small PC network, using a single server provides all of these services except Internet access.

TCP/IP Autoconfiguration

You will almost certainly install TCP/IP. To make it work properly, you also need to configure your PC's TCP/IP protocol—that is, set a number of parameters, including your own IP address, a default router's IP address, your DNS server's IP address, and several other parameters that we will discuss in Chapter 8.

Manual Configuration

One option is to type in all of these configuration parameters manually. **Manual configuration** has two drawbacks. First, it is time-consuming if you have many PCs. Second, if one of the parameters changes—say the IP address of the DNS server—then all manually configured PCs will have to be manually reconfigured.

Autoconfiguration

Client PC Setup   For client PCs, **autoconfiguration**, which Figure 4-13 illustrates, supplies TCP/IP parameters automatically. The client PC asks an autoconfiguration host to send it an IP address and usually other configuration parameters as well.

The IP address that the client receives may be different each time it autoconfigures, so this method cannot be used with servers, which need a permanent IP address.

Conserving IP Addresses   In addition, autoconfiguration conserves IP addresses. Suppose that a department has 300 client PCs but only 254 IP addresses. Computers that are not booted up (or in some cases are not using TCP/IP currently) will not be assigned temporary IP addresses. This advantage is fading now that most office computers are left on and connected to the Internet all day or are set up at boot time to talk with file servers, most of which today use TCP/IP.

DHCP   The **Dynamic Host Configuration Protocol (DHCP)** is almost universally used for TCP/IP autoconfiguration because Microsoft Windows requires it.

Figure 4-13   Autoconfiguration with DHCP

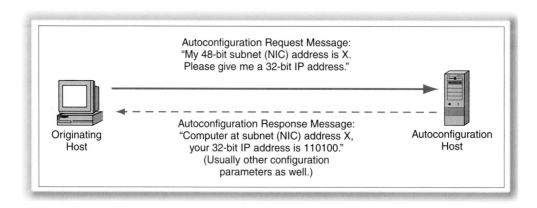

TEST YOUR UNDERSTANDING

23. To turn a typical PC you buy from the store into a client PC, what else may you have to purchase?

24. a) Distinguish between manual configuration and autoconfiguration. b) Why is auto-configuration good? c) Explain how the DHCP autoconfiguration protocol works. d) Why is DHCP so popular?

File Service

File service stores files on a file server. File service is the most basic service in PC networking. It also is heavily used—even more heavily than Internet access. File service is built into the NOS, so there is no extra charge for it.

Access from Anywhere for Individuals and Backup

One advantage of a file server is that an individual user can access his or her data files from anywhere—at work, at home, or while traveling. These data files, furthermore, are backed up frequently and therefore are relatively safe.

Shared Access

Another advantage, shown in Figure 4-14, is that team members can work with shared directories that only authorized people can access. Even within a project team, there can be different access permissions, the most limited being **read-only** access in which a user can read files but not change them or create new ones.

Figure 4-14   File Service for Data Files

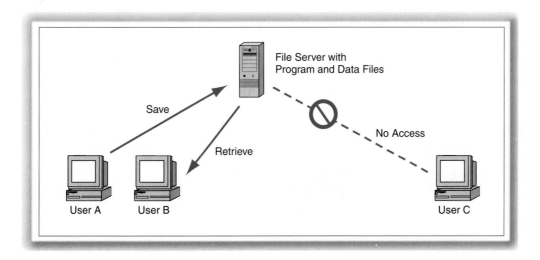

TEST YOUR UNDERSTANDING

25.   a) What is file service? b) Do you have to buy a file service application program for a server? Explain. c) Why is file service good for groups? d) Will all members of a group typically have the same access permissions for all the group's files? Explain.

Print Service

Print service also is built into NOSs. When a user prints, his or her output is printed on a network printer. By sharing printers, users can have higher-quality printers than they could afford if everyone had to have his or her own printer.

As Figure 4-15 shows, some high-end printers are **network-capable**, meaning that client PCs can send their print jobs directly to these printers.

In other cases, the print job is sent to a **print server**, which feeds the print output to the printer. Print servers may be file servers, client PCs, or dedicated print server boxes.

Note that print servers connect to a printer via a parallel cable. Print servers also connect to a hub or switch via a UTP cord. Parallel cables must be very short, so print servers usually are located within 2 meters of the printer. They can be up to 100 meters away from the hub or switch.

TEST YOUR UNDERSTANDING

26.   a) What is print service? b) Describe print service with a network-capable printer. c) Describe print service if a printer is not network capable. d) Where are print servers located?

Figure 4-15   Print Service

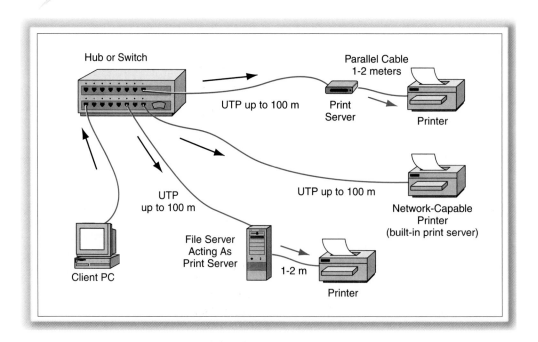

Application Services

There can be a number of application services, such as e-mail, database, and word processing. Servers that run such services are called application servers. Application servers that run database programs are called database servers. In Chapter 11, we will see another use for the term "application server."

File Server Program Access

Figure 4-16 shows that PC network application servers usually do not execute applications themselves. Most application servers really are file servers. They merely store program files.

Instead, in a process known as **file server program access**, when the user runs the program, the file server sends the program across the network to the client PC. The client PC then executes the program on its own hardware. For instance, if you are running an e-mail program, that program will execute on your client PC. The file server will supply you with the program and associated data files.

Limits of File Server Program Access

Only relatively small programs such as word processing and e-mail can use file server program access because client PCs are not large enough to execute large programs.

Advantage of Single Installation

Although file server program access is limiting, it allows systems administrators to install a program or update only once—on the file server. As Figure 4-17 shows, this means that there is no need to install each new program or update on each client PC.

➤ Single installation greatly reduces client administration costs.

➤ New programs and updates are available to users as soon as they are installed on the file server.

➤ Everyone in the organization uses the same version of the program.

Figure 4-16   File Server Program Access

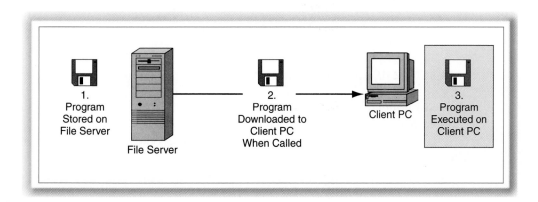

1.
Program
Stored on
File Server

File Server

2.
Program
Downloaded to
Client PC
When Called

Client PC

3.
Program
Executed on
Client PC

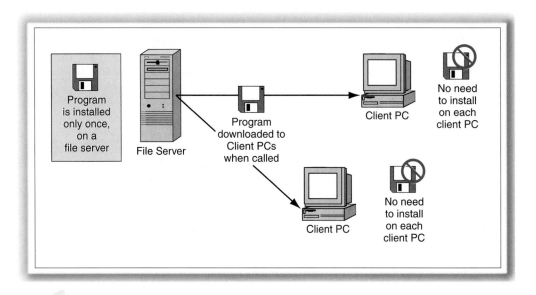

Figure 4-17   Single Installation of a Program or Update

TEST YOUR UNDERSTANDING

27.   a) Is a server offering e-mail an application server? Explain. b) Describe file server program access. c) What limit does it create? d) Why is it good?

Internet Access

As Figure 4-1 shows, internet access normally runs on a separate device called an **access router**. Costing between about $100 and $2,000, this access router connects the LAN to the firm's Internet service provider via one of the transmission lines or WANs we will see in Chapters 6 and 7. An access router connects to a hub or switch through one port and to the transmission line or WAN to the ISP through its other port.

TEST YOUR UNDERSTANDING

28.   a) What will you need for Internet access if you have an Ethernet LAN? b) An access router has two ports. To what do these ports connect?

POPULAR NETWORK OPERATING SYSTEMS FOR PC SERVERS

The most popular network operating systems (NOSs) for PC servers are Microsoft Windows Server, LINUX, and Novell NetWare.

Microsoft Windows Server

For small businesses, the best choice usually is **Microsoft Windows Server**, which comes in three versions: NT, 2000, and .NET.

	Microsoft Windows	**LINUX**	**Novell NetWare**
Ease of Learning	Very Good	Poor	Good
Ease of Use	Very Good	Poor	Good
Reliability	Very Good in the Most Recent Versions	Excellent	Very Good
Standardization	Excellent	Poor (Many Distributions)	Excellent
Availability of Device Drivers	Excellent	Poor	Very Good
Price	Moderate	Low or Free	Higher than Windows

Figure 4-18   Popular Network Operating Systems (NOSs)

Ease of Learning and Operation

Windows Server is the most popular NOS because it is the simplest NOS to learn and operate. This is crucial in small businesses. Its interface looks like client versions of Windows (95, 98, ME, NT, 2000, and XP), and almost all management functions are executed from a single program group.

Reliability

Early versions of Windows Server, through NT, had poor reliability. Newer versions have made Windows Server sufficiently reliable for departmental and small business needs, although for central corporate servers, UNIX is the gold standard for reliability.

LINUX

LINUX was created as a freeware version of UNIX.[6] Unlike most versions of UNIX, which run on workstation servers, LINUX is one of a handful of UNIX variants that runs on standard PCs.

Cost and Reliability

A principle attraction of LINUX is its cost. It can be downloaded for free, although boxed versions with instructions and phone-in support tend to cost $100 or more. Another benefit is that LINUX has the legendary reliability of UNIX.

---

[6] Linus Torvalds, who created LINUX, pronounces it "Lee-nucks." In English, it usually is pronounced with a short "i," "Li-nucks" (with a stress on the first syllable).

Diversity and Configuration Problems

When you buy Microsoft Windows Server, you know what you are getting. However, LINUX really is only an operating system kernel. What you actually buy or download for free is a **LINUX distribution** consisting of the kernel plus a collection of many other programs, which usually are taken from the GNU project.[7] Different distributions contain different programs, causing endless confusion. For example, LINUX offers two competing graphical user interfaces and a command-line language.

In addition, configuring LINUX to run on a server can be very difficult. Often, there is no device driver for a particular NIC, or you must compile a device driver from source code.

LINUX Overall

For small businesses, the low cost of LINUX is a false savings because of the learning, configuration, and maintenance headaches the business will have to face. This may change as LINUX matures.

Novell NetWare

Novell NetWare once dominated the NOS market. It still has the best file and print service. However, high pricing led to a catastrophic loss of market share. Although NetWare still is an excellent product, Windows Server generally is a better choice for small businesses because of its greater ease of installation and use and because there now are many more consultants who can provide help if a Windows Server has problems.

TEST YOUR UNDERSTANDING

29. a) On what type of machine does the NOS run? b) Describe the strengths and weaknesses of Microsoft Windows Server. c) Describe the strengths and weaknesses of LINUX. d) Describe the strengths and weaknesses of Novell NetWare.

GAINING PERSPECTIVE

Market Realities

In February 2001, 250 network executives were asked to describe their networks.[8] For file and print service, Windows Server had 53 percent market share, Novell NetWare had 36 percent market share, and all other operating systems combined—including LINUX—had 11 percent market share.

The survey also confirmed the dominance of 100 Mbps switched Ethernet to the desktop. First, it noted that 96 percent of all traffic between client stations and the nearest switch was Ethernet traffic.

---

[7] Often, there are different distributions for clients and servers.

[8] "How Does Your Network Stack Up?" Network World, February 19, 2001. http://nwfusion.com/research/2001/0219feat.html.

Second, for LAN traffic to the desktop, switched 100 Mbps accounted for 45 percent of the traffic, while switched 10 Mbps accounted for 24 percent, shared 10 Mbps accounted for another 28 percent, and gigabit Ethernet accounted for 3 percent. Among new LANs, 100 Mbps switched Ethernet dominated even more.

For connections to servers, 100 Mbps was even more dominant, accounting for 82 percent of all installations, followed by rapidly growing gigabit Ethernet at 21 percent.

THOUGHT QUESTIONS

1. a) Convert the following binary strings to hexadecimal: 0001, 1001, 11100111, and 1. *Hint:* The first answer is 1 h. b) Convert the following hexadecimal values to binary: 00-00-00 hex, 03 hex, and AA hex. c) (A tough one. You will not be penalized if you cannot answer it.) What types of games use Base 13? How do they handle the values 11, 12, and 13?

2. a) Describe, field-by-field, what a receiving NIC will do when it receives a frame not addressed to it. *Hint:* Begin with what the NIC does when it reads the preamble. b) Describe, field-by-field, what a receiving NIC will do when it receives a frame that is addressed to it.

3. a) One octet per line, give the contents of an Ethernet frame whose data field is 20 octets, whose contents are all ones. Use zeros for the PAD field. Use ones for the frame check sequence field. The destination MAC address is A1-34-CD-7B-DF-7A h. The source MAC address is BB-CC-47-40-AA-A7 h. *Hint:* the binary value for 21 is 10101. b) How long is the entire frame? For a), the first two lines are:

   10101010
   10101010

DESIGN QUESTIONS

1. Your organization has 10 employees, each with his or her own stand-alone PC running Windows 98. a) List *all* the additional hardware and software you would have to buy to install a simple PC network. Be very sure that you list all the things the organization will have to buy. The organization wishes to use e-mail, word processing, file sharing, Internet access, and print sharing with three laser printers in different parts of the office. b) How many ports on the hub or switch will your organization use? Explain.

2. Using the links at the Internet Exercise for this chapter, cost out the LAN you just specified. For installation labor, assume $125 per client PC or server. Assume $500 per UTP cord for installation. For application software, assume $2,000. a) Cost out your system except for the hub or switch. Be very specific. b) How much will a 10Base-T hub add? c) A 10Base-T switch? d) A 100Base-TX hub? e) A 100Base-TX switch? Do not use managed hubs or switches, which are much more expensive and unnecessary for a system this size. Note that 10/100 equipment is 100Base-TX equipment. Do not use such equipment for your 10Base-T hub or switch estimates.

3. Your small business has a 10Base-T switched network. a) If you upgrade to 100Base-TX switches, must you change your wiring? b) Must you change all of your NICs? Explain.

TROUBLESHOOTING QUESTION

1. You use an ISP to connect your home to the Internet. You have a high-speed connection to your ISP. You set up a server and tell your friends its IP address. They use it effectively. The next day, however, they cannot reach your server. What probably happened?

CASE STUDIES

For case studies, go to the book's website, www.prenhall.com/panko, and look at the Case Studies page for this chapter.

PHOTOS

For photos, go to the book's website, www.prenhall.com/panko, and look at the Photos page for this chapter.

PROJECTS

1. **Getting Current.** Go to the book website's New Information and Errors pages for this chapter to get new information since this book went to press and to correct any errors in the text.
2. **Internet Exercises.** Go to the book website's Exercises page for this chapter and do the Internet Exercises.
3. **Hands-On.** Set up a client PC as described in Chapter 4a.
4. **Hands-On.** In a Wintel client machine in your laboratory or at home, click on Start, and then Run. Run the winipcfg.exe program under Windows. Click on More Information. Describe what you learned. For a Windows 2000 PC, run CMD to go to the command line. Type "IPconfig/All[Enter].

4a

HANDS ON: CONFIGURING A MICROSOFT WINDOWS 98 PC AS A CLIENT

INTRODUCTION

This chapter discusses how to set up an ordinary Wintel PC running Windows 98 to be a client PC on a LAN. The process is similar in other versions of Windows.

Microsoft Windows Layering

Microsoft Windows clients can work with many different types of servers via several different types of standards architectures. As Figure 4a-1 shows, Microsoft has its own form of layering, into which it maps all architectures.

Protocol Stacks

This layering scheme fits the realities of protocol stacks—if you use an architecture at the physical layer, you will use it at the data link layer; and if you use an architecture at the internet layer, you will also use it at the transport layer. A **protocol stack** is two or more layer processes from the same standards architecture.

Adapters

The Microsoft **adapter** layer embraces the physical and data link layers. For telephone modems, you create a **dial-up adapter**, which includes physical layer modem standards and the Point-to-Point Protocol at the data link layer. If you have a NIC, which implements LAN communication at the physical and data link layers, you choose an adapter that corresponds to your particular NIC. The name "adapter" reflects the fact that NICs are classified as adapters in PC design.

Microsoft Layer	TCP/IP	IPX/SPX	SNA	OSI
Application (Client or Service)	Application	Application	Not Applicable	Application
			Network Addressable Unit (NAU) Services	Presentation
			Data Flow Control	Session
Protocol	Transport (TCP)	Transport (SPX)	Transmission Control	Transport
	Internet (IP)	Internet (IPX)	Path Control	Network
Adapter	Data Link	Data Link	Data Link	Data Link
	Physical	Physical	Physical	Physical

Note: The Microsoft Application Layer is only for file server clients (clients) and peer–peer PC networking (services).

Figure 4a-1   Microsoft Layering

Protocols

Standards at the internet and transport layer also come as a protocol stack. Oddly, Microsoft calls an internet–transport layer stack a **protocol**. This is a terrible name, because, as noted in Chapter 2, "protocol" means something very different. (Protocols are standards that govern communication between peer processes on different machines but at the same layer.) The adapter layer also implements protocols, as does the application layer.

Clients and Services

In Microsoft terminology, clients and services form a sort-of application layer, although the focus is on file and print sharing, not on applications in general. **Clients** allow the user PC to connect to various types of file servers. We will focus on client setup in this chapter. **Services**, in turn, make the user's PC a peer–peer network member that offers services to other PCs in the workgroup. Chapter 11a discusses this aspect of Microsoft networking.

Bindings

Clients, services, protocols, and adapters must be bound together to work. **Bindings** create communication paths between a particular adapter and a particular protocol and between a particular protocol and a particular client or service, as Figure 4a-2 shows.

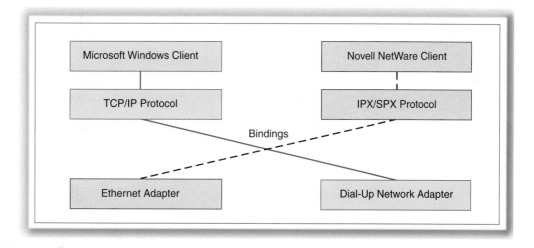

Figure 4a-2   Bindings in Microsoft Windows

Installing the NIC

Physical Installation
The first step is to physically install the NIC with the computer's power turned off. To install an internal NIC, you must remove the cover from the computer's systems unit. As Figure 4a-3 shows, the computer has a **mother board** with a number of **expansion slots**. Install the NIC in a slot that fits it.[1]

Grounding
When installing any expansion board or when going inside your PC's systems unit for any reason, be sure you touch a grounded device to release any static electricity in your body. Otherwise, static electricity may create a spark that can destroy the NIC's sensitive electronics.

PC Card Modems
Figure 4a-4 shows that internal NICs, which sit inside a desktop systems unit, are not the only type of NIC. PC Card NICs are simply snapped into a PC Card slot on a notebook PC, personal digital assistant, or other small device.

Plug and Play Device Driver Installation
The NIC requires a piece of software called its device driver. To install the device driver, first turn on the PC. Windows Plug and Play functionality should discover the NIC, alert you to this fact, and lead you through a series of dialog boxes that will install the NIC's device driver and set up the NIC and its device driver as an adapter. One dialog box (see Figure 4a-5) will show a "Have Disk" button that you click on if you have a disk containing the device driver.

---

[1]   There are two basic types of slots. Traditional ISA slots are longer than newer PCI slots, which are for faster NICs. Most mother boards have both types of slots, but many new mother boards only have PCI slots.

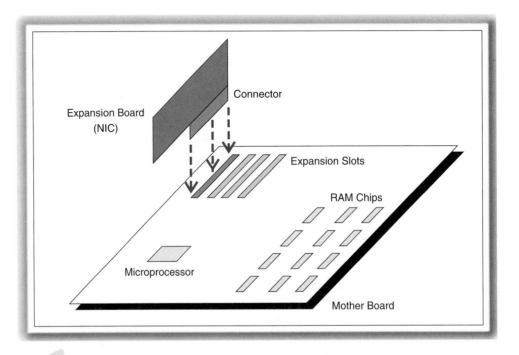

Figure 4a-3 Mother Board and Internal NIC

Vendor-Specific Device Driver Installation
Some NICs have their own installation software. If it exists, it should be used instead of the standard Plug and Play installation.

Perspective
If everything works as it should, the process will be very simple. Otherwise, your life will be ruined, although you will learn a great deal about your computer's hardware organization and its operating system.

Adding Clients and Protocols
Next, you need to install a client and protocols (the first two steps installed the adapter for your NIC). Click on the *Start* button, point to *Settings,* then *Control Panel.* When the Control Panel appears, double click on the *Network* icon.

You will be taken to the **Network dialog box**, shown in Figure 4a-6. This will show you a list of installed adapters, protocols, clients, and services. Hopefully, the components you need will already be installed and bound together.

Selecting a Client or a Protocol to Add
If the client or protocol you need is not shown in the Network dialog box, click on the *Add* button. You will be taken to a new dialog box, the **Select Network Component Type** dialog box, shown in Figure 4a-7. Select *Client* or *Protocol.*

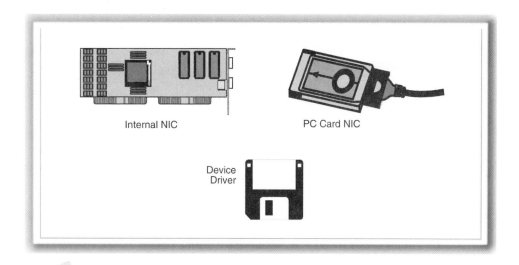

Figure 4a-4   Internal NIC and PC Card NIC

Figure 4a-5   Dialog Box for Installing a Device Driver

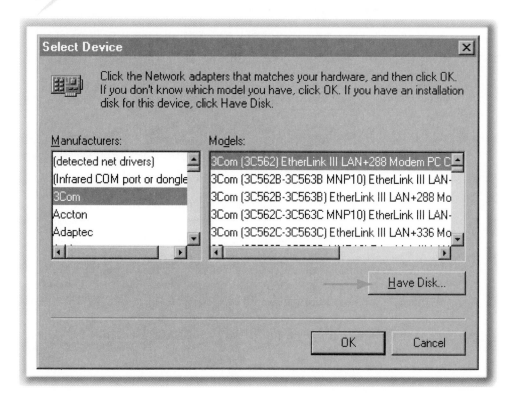

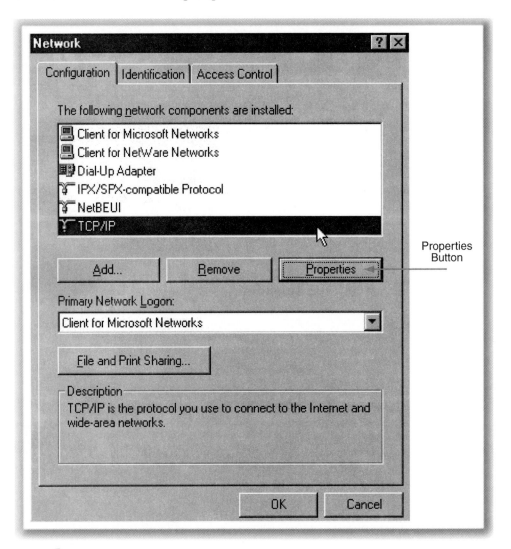

Figure 4a-6   Network Dialog Box in Windows 98

As Figure 4a-8 shows, you will then see a list of manufacturers (creators of components). Click on one, such as Microsoft. Then click on the component you wish to have from that manufacturer, for instance the Microsoft TCP/IP protocol stack.

Autoconfiguration

As Chapter 4 noted, PCs can have their IP addresses assigned via autoconfiguration. The autoconfiguration host also supplies all other parameters, including the local network mask, the IP address of a default router (Microsoft calls routers "gateways"), and

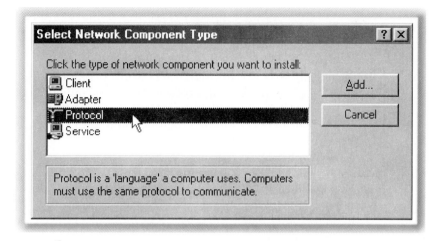

Figure 4a-7   Select Network Component Type Dialog Box in Windows 98

Figure 4a-8   Select Network Component in Windows 98

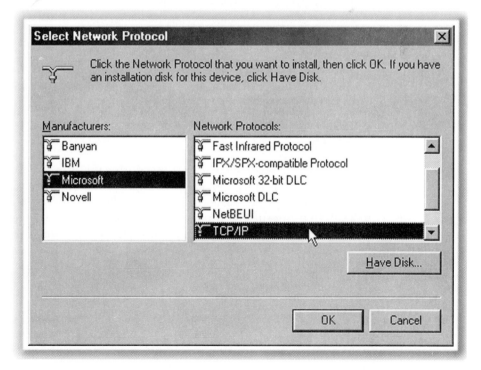

the IP address of a DNS host and perhaps a backup DNS host. Microsoft Windows requires DHCP autoconfiguration. The alternative to autoconfiguration is to type in all information manually, then retype it whenever configuration information changes.

Configuring the Computer for DHCP Autoconfiguration

If you use TCP/IP as a Microsoft protocol, you must configure it, usually using DHCP autoconfiguration. In the Network dialog box shown in Figure 4a-6, click on the TCP/IP protocol and click on the Properties button. You will be taken to the **TCP/IP Properties** dialog box shown as Figure 4a-9.

Normally, the IP *Address tab* will be selected. If not, select it. As Figure 4a-9 shows, you can check a radio button marked "Obtain an IP address automatically." This has DHCP autoconfigure not only your IP address, but also other TCP/IP parameters.

If, on the other hand, you select "Specify an IP address," you will have to manually enter not only the IP address, but all other TCP parameters as well. Generally, you only do this for servers, which must have permanent IP addresses.

Checking Bindings

In Figure 4a-6 (The Network dialog box), you can click on any component's Properties button to see if it is bound to the component it needs to be bound to for your application. For instance, if you are connecting to a file server, your client must be bound to the protocol the file server requires, which in turn must be bound to your NIC adapter.

TEST YOUR UNDERSTANDING

1. a) What is a protocol stack? b) What three protocol stacks are used in Microsoft networking? c) What is a protocol in Microsoft networking? d) What do bindings do?

2. a) Describe the steps to add a NIC. b) Compare internal NICs and PC Card NICs in terms of ease of installation. c) In what types of devices are PC Card NICs used?

3. a) Describe the steps to add a client or service. b) Describe the steps to add a protocol.

4. a) Describe the steps to set up the TCP/IP protocol to use autoconfiguration. b) How would manual configuration change the setup process?

PROJECTS

1. Caution: Be sure not to change anything during this exercise. a) On a computer at home or in your lab, go to Start, Settings, Control Panel, Networking. List the clients, services, protocols, and adapters installed on the computer. b) Next, go to TCP/IP properties. Is the computer set up for DHCP autoconfiguration? Explain. c) Next, go to properties for an adapter. What are its bindings?

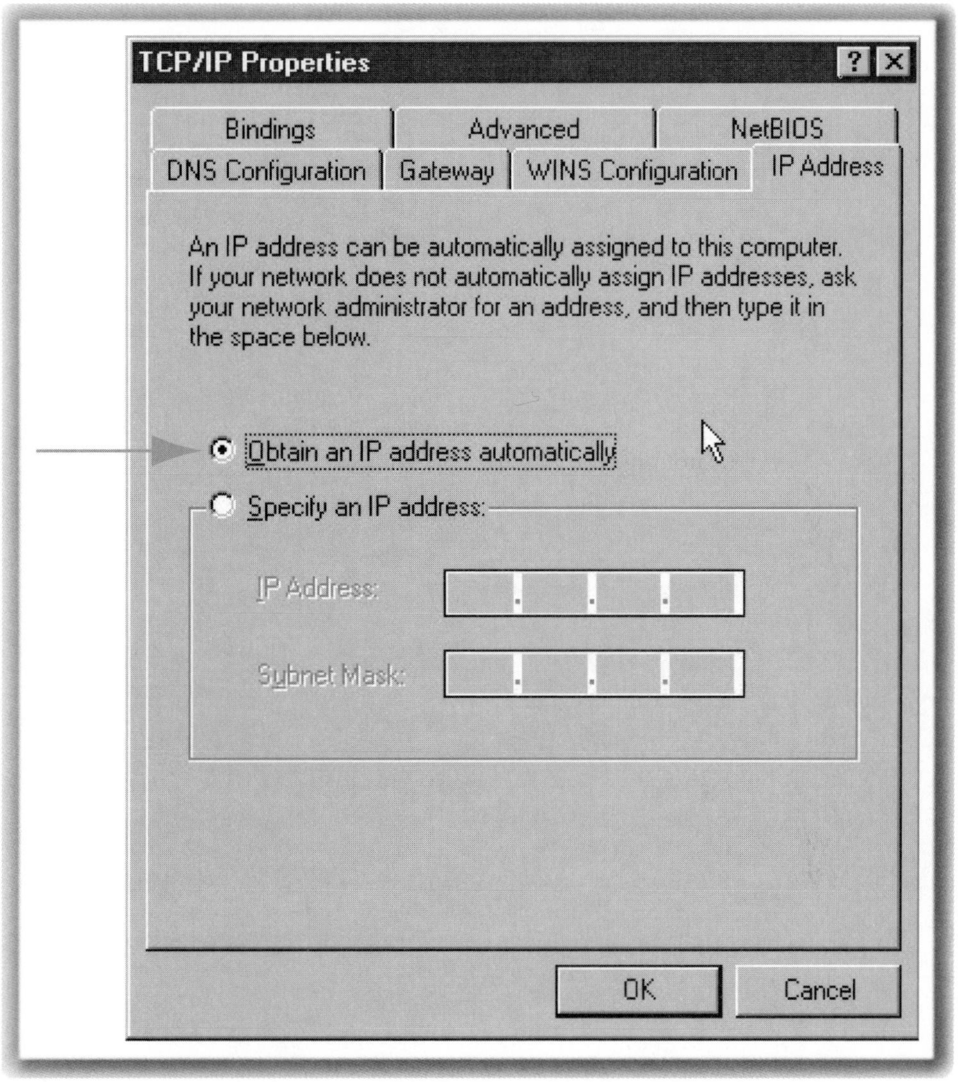

Figure 4a-9 TCP/IP Properties Dialog Box in Windows 98

CHAPTER 5

OTHER LAN TECHNOLOGIES

Learning Objectives:

By the end of this chapter, you should be able to discuss:

- Large Ethernet networks, including hierarchical switch organization to reduce cost, single points of failure, workgroup versus core switches, virtual local area networks, and Ethernet physical layer standards.

- Wireless LANs, including 802.11 speeds, 802.11 access points and handoffs, CSMA/CA+ACK, Bluetooth master/slave operation, and spread spectrum transmission (box feature).

- ATM LANs, including quality of science (QoS) guarantees for voice and video (but not necessarily for data), ATM operation using meshes and virtual circuits to reduce switching costs, and comparisons between ATM and Ethernet in handling brief traffic peaks.

- Legacy LANs, including token-ring networks and early Ethernet standards.

INTRODUCTION

In Chapter 4, we looked at a small PC network based on a single-hub or single-switch Ethernet LAN. In this chapter we will look at larger Ethernet LANs, wireless LANs, ATM LANs, and several older "legacy" LAN standards, including 802.5 Token-Ring Networks, FDDI, and Ethernet 10Base5 and 10Base2 (box feature). In the discussion of ATM, we will compare ATM and Ethernet approaches to the important problem of how to deal with momentary traffic peaks that exceed the capacity of the network.

LARGER ETHERNET NETWORKS

Multiple Ethernet Switches

Figure 5-1 shows an Ethernet LAN with three switches. Larger Ethernet LANs have dozens of switches, but the operation of individual switches is the same as when there are only a few switches.

Suppose that Station A1-44-D5-1F-AA-4C on Switch 1 transmits a frame destined for Station E5-BB-47-21-D3-56, which is attached to Switch 3. The frame will have to pass through Switch 2 along the way.

Switch 1 will look at its switching table and note that Station E5-BB-47-21-D3-56 is out Port 5. The switch will send the frame out that port. The link out that port will carry the frame to Switch 2 instead of directly to the destination station.

Switch 2 will receive the frame in Port 3. It will note that the destination address of the frame is E5-BB-47-21-D3-56. It will look up this address in its own switching table and see that it should send the frame out Port 7. This will take the frame to Switch 3.

Switch 3 will receive the frame in Port 4. It will note the destination address and look this address up in its own switching table. It will see that Station E5-BB-47-21-D3-56 is out Port 6. It will send the frame out that port, to Station E5-BB-47-21-D3-56. This completes the frame delivery process.

TEST YOUR UNDERSTANDING

1. In a single switch LAN, the switch reads the address of an incoming frame, looks up an output port in the switching table, and sends the frame out that port. Do individual switches work differently in multiswitch LANs? Explain.

Reliability in a Hierarchical Switched Network

Hierarchical Switch Organization

Note that the switches in Figure 5-1 are organized in a **hierarchy**. In fact, Ethernet *requires* a hierarchical arrangement for its switches. Otherwise, loops would exist, causing frames to circulate endlessly from one switch to another around the loop. Figure 5-2 shows a larger switched Ethernet LAN.

Single Possible Path Between Any Two Stations

In a hierarchy, there is only one possible path between any two stations. Trace any path between any two stations in Figure 5-2, and you will see that this is true.

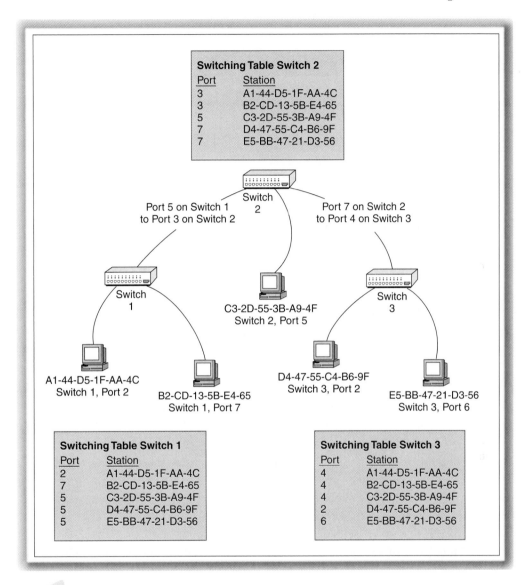

Figure 5-1   Multiple-Switch Ethernet LAN

Low-Cost Switching

The advantage of having only a single possible path between any two stations is that Ethernet switches only have to do simple table lookups when a frame arrives, as we saw last chapter and in the discussion of Figure 5-1. Simple table lookups are very fast, allowing Ethernet switches to be very inexpensive for the traffic load they handle. In Chapter 8, we will see that routers have to do much more work when a packet arrives,

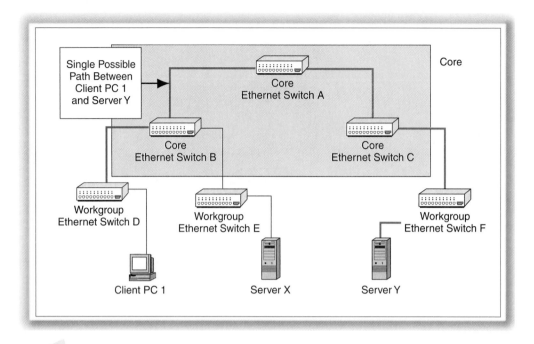

Figure 5-2   Hierarchical Ethernet LAN

because there are multiple alternative routes between any two stations. Therefore, a router must first identify all possible routes and then select the best route. This makes routers very expensive for the switching load they handle. Network professionals say, "Switch where you can; route where you must."

Single Points of Failure

The danger of having a single possible path is that it is vulnerable to **single points of failure**. Suppose that Switch 2 in Figure 5-3 fails. Then the stations connected to Switch 1 will not be able to communicate with stations connected to Switch 2 or Switch 3.[1]

TEST YOUR UNDERSTANDING

2.   a) How are switches in an Ethernet LAN organized? b) Therefore, how many possible paths can there be between two stations? c) In Figure 5-2, what is the single possible path between Client PC 1 and Server Y? d) Between Client PC 1 and Server X? e) What is the benefit of having a single possible path? f) Why is having a single possible path good between any two stations dangerous?

---

[1]   As discussed in Module C, the 802.1D Spanning Tree protocol can add some back-up links between switches that turn on automatically if a link or switch fails.

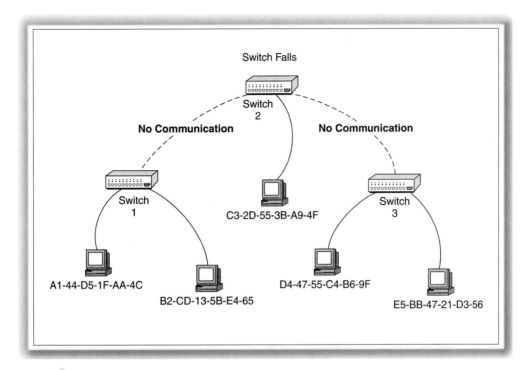

Switch Falls

Switch
2

No Communication   **No Communication**

Switch
1

C3-2D-55-3B-A9-4F

Switch
3

A1-44-D5-1F-AA-4C

B2-CD-13-5B-E4-65

D4-47-55-C4-B6-9F

E5-BB-47-21-D3-56

Figure 5-3   Single Point of Failure in a Switch Hierarchy

Workgroup Versus Core Switches

Switches tend to be divided into two basic categories—workgroup switches and core switches. Figure 5-4 shows how they differ.

➤ **Workgroup switches** are the ones that stations connect to directly (Switches D, E, and F in Figure 5-2). These switches carry traffic to and from their stations. The switches we saw in the previous chapter were workgroup switches.

➤ **Core switches**, in turn, are switches farther up the hierarchy (Switches A, B, and C in Figure 5-2). They carry traffic between one switch and another.

Core switches must work faster than workgroup switches because core switches have to handle the traffic of many workgroup switches. To give an analogy, large hub airports like O'Hare in Chicago have to handle many more aircraft per hour than small feeder airports. The dominant port speed for workgroup switches today is 100 Mbps. In contrast, the emerging dominant port speed for core switches today is 1 Gbps, and some core switches already use port speeds of 10 Gbps.

TEST YOUR UNDERSTANDING

3. a) Distinguish between workgroup switches and core switches in terms of what devices they connect. b) How do they compare in terms of port speed?

	Workgroup Switches	Core Switches
Connects	Client of Server to the Ethernet Network	Ethernet Switches to One Another
Typical Port Speeds	10/100 Mbps	100 Mbps, Gigabit Ethernet, 10 Gbps Ethernet
Switching Matrix	Lower Percentage of Nonblocking* Capacity	80% or More of Nonblocking* Capacity

Figure 5-4   Workgroup Switches Versus Core Switches

Virtual LANs and Ethernet Switches

We will close the discussion of Ethernet switching with the option of creating virtual LANs (VLANS).

Broadcasting

Ethernet NICs normally wish to **unicast**, that is, send a frame from one station to one other station. Ethernet switches support unicasting, sending the frame out of a single port.

However, sometimes stations wish to **broadcast** messages, that is, send them to all stations, as Figure 5-5 illustrates. Most notably, Novell NetWare servers may advertise their presence every 60 seconds or so by broadcasting a server advertisement message that is designed to go to all other stations. The station that wishes to broadcast sets the frame's destination MAC address to 48 ones (FF-FF-FF-FF-FF-FF h). When an Ethernet switch sees this address, it broadcasts the frame out all ports like a hub. All NICs, in turn, process frames addressed to FF-FF-FF-FF-FF-FF h as if it was their own address.

Congestion

Broadcasting is fine in small networks. However, in a large switched Ethernet LAN, broadcasting will produce a tremendous amount of traffic and therefore congestion.

Virtual LANs

As Figure 5-5 illustrates, most Ethernet switches allow stations to be grouped into sub-collections of servers and the clients they serve called **virtual LANs (VLANs)**. When Server E (on VLAN 1) transmits, its frames only go to the clients on its VLAN (Client A and Client C). Sending to multiple stations but not to all stations is called **multicasting**. Multicasting greatly reduces congestion compared to broadcasting.

Connecting VLANs

What happens if a client on one VLAN wishes to connect to a server on another VLAN? Some Ethernet switch vendors allow stations to be members of multiple VLANs. Another option is to use routers to connect VLANs, just as routers connect different LANs.

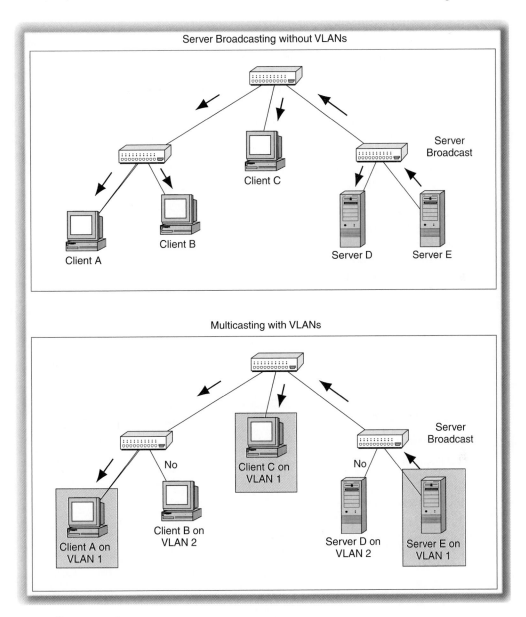

Figure 5-5   Virtual LAN with Ethernet Switches

Standardizing VLANs

Until recently, there was no standard for VLANs, so if you used VLANs, you had to buy all of your Ethernet switches from the same vendor. However, as Figure 5-6 shows, the **802.1Q standard** is extending the Ethernet MAC layer frame to include two optional **tag fields**. The first tag field (**Tag Protocol ID**) has the value 81-00 h, which indicates that the frame is tagged. The second tag field (**Tag Control Information**) contains a 12-bit VLAN ID that it sets to zero if VLANs are not being implemented. If VLANs are being used, each VLAN will be assigned a different VLAN ID. With 12 bits, there can be 4,095 ($2^{12}-1$) different VLANs on an Ethernet network. Switches from different vendors can all build switching (see Figure 5-5) using standardized VLAN ID numbers. This will allow them to interoperate.

VLAN Security

If an employee attempts to log into a server in another VLAN, he or she will find it difficult to do so. However, this is only a slight augmentation to security because a technically savvy attacker can easily defeat it.

Figure 5-6 Tagged Ethernet Frame

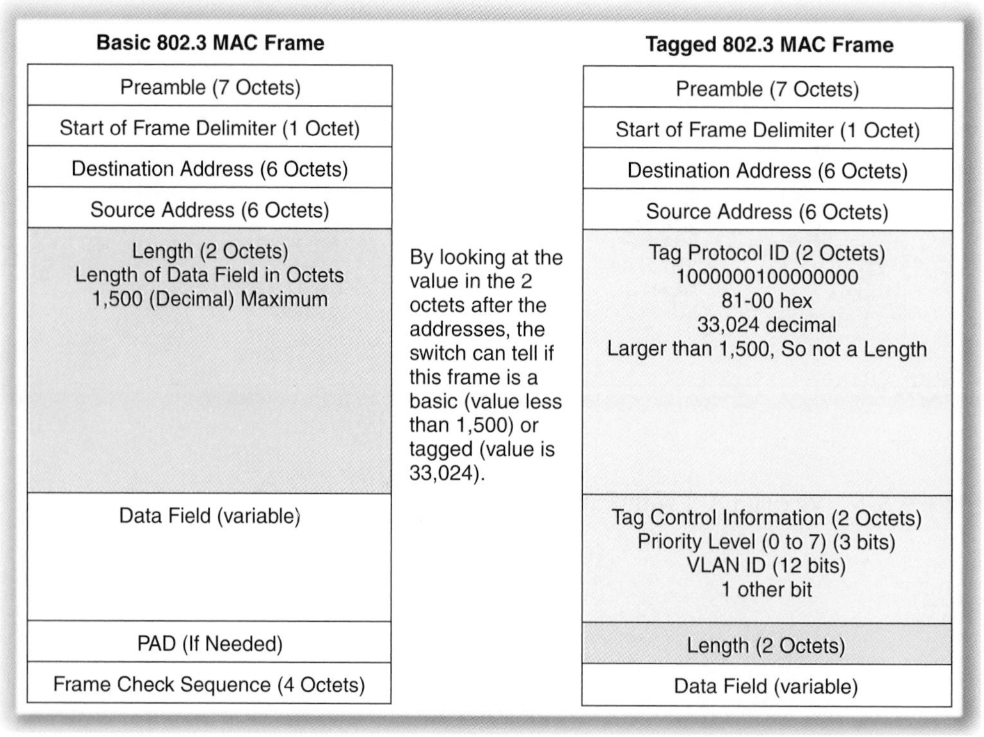

TEST YOUR UNDERSTANDING

4. a) What problem do VLANs address? b) How do they address it? c) Describe VLAN interoperability. d) Describe the VLAN tagging standard. e) When a server on a VLAN broadcasts, what stations receive its message? f) Do VLANs increase security?

Ethernet Physical Layer Standards

Many Standards

As Figure 5-7 shows, there are many Ethernet physical layer standards for connecting users, switches, and hubs. This gives network designers flexibility in tailoring physical links to distance requirements and other needs.

Optical Fiber Wavelengths

Optical fiber has three "windows" in which propagation is exceptionally good. These are spectrum regions around 850 nm, 1300 nm, and 1550 nm. From Figure 5-7, you can see that light with longer wavelengths can travel farther than shorter-wavelength light. On the other hand, longer-wavelength light sources are more expensive than shorter-wavelength light sources. Light sources at 850 nm are especially inexpensive. For wavelength, then, there is a strong trade-off between propagation distance and cost.

TEST YOUR UNDERSTANDING

5. a) What is the relationship between wavelength and distance of propagation in optical fiber? b) What is the drawback to using longer wavelengths? c) What are the three main spectrum windows in optical fiber?

WIRELESS LANS

Wireless LANs replace wires with radio waves or (rarely) with infrared light.

Advantages

Freedom of Movement

The obvious benefit of wireless LANs is that they can support mobile stations. There is no need to find an RJ-45 LAN outlet, stop to plug the station into the outlet, and then work in one position while you are connected to the outlet.

Avoiding Wiring Costs

Another potential benefit of wireless LANs is that they can reduce the cost of wiring, which is about $1,000 per wall jack in a typical corporate building.

Disadvantage

Propagation Difficulties

However, as we saw in Chapter 3, radio and infrared transmission have propagation problems, including shadow zones and multipath interference. Designing a wireless LAN to give good coverage throughout a building is difficult and expensive.

Physical Layer Standard	Speed	Maximum Run Length	Medium
UTP			
10Base-T	10 Mbps	100 meters	4-pair Category 3, 4, or 5
100Base-TX	100 Mbps	100 meters	4-pair Category 5
1000Base-T	1,000 Mbps	100 meters	4-pair Category 5. 4-pair enhanced Category 5 is preferred
Optical Fiber			
10Base-F	10 Mbps	Up to 2 km	62.5/125 micron multimode, 850 nm.
100Base-FX	100 Mbps	412 m	62.5/125 multimode, 1,300 nm, hub
100Base-FX	100 Mbps	2 km	62.5/125 multimode, 1,300 nm, switch
1000Base-SX	1 Gbps	220-275 m	62.5/125 micron multimode, 850 nm. Distance depends on fiber quality.
1000Base-LX	1 Gbps	550 m	62.5/125 micron multimode. 1,300 nm.
1000Base-LX	1 Gbps	5 km	9/125 micron single mode, 1,300 nm.
10GBase-SR/SW	10 Gbps	65 m	62.5/125 micron multimode (850)
10GBase-LX4	10 Gbps	300 m	62.5/125 micron multimode 1310 nm, wave division multiplexing
10GBase-LR/LW	10 Gbps	10km	9/125 micron single mode, 1310 nm.
10GBase-ER/EW	10 Gbps	40 km	9/125 micron single mode, 1550 nm.
40 Gbps Ethernet	40 Gbps	?	9/125 micron single mode.****
Other Media			
10Base5	10 Mbps	500 meters	Thick co-axial cable
10Base2	10 Mbps	185 meter	Thin co-axial cable

Notes:

Longer wavelengths (1550 nm) allow longer distances than shorter wavelengths (1300 nm and 850 nm). Several 10 Mbps fiber standards were defined in 10Base-F. 10GBase-X descriptions are preliminary. LAN versions transmit at 10 Gbps. WAN versions transmit at 9.6 Gbps for carriage over SONET links (see Chapter 6). The 40 Gbps Ethernet standards are still under preliminary development.

Figure 5-7   Ethernet Physical Layer Standards

Figure 5-8   802.11 Wireless Access Point and Wireless PC Card NIC. Courtesy SMC Communications

TEST YOUR UNDERSTANDING

6. a) What are the advantages of wireless LANs? b) What is the average cost to wire an RJ-45 LAN outlet? c) What are the disadvantages of wireless LANs?

802.11 Wireless LANs

Recall from the previous chapter that the IEEE 802 LAN/MAN Standards Committee sets LAN standards and that individual working groups create specific standards. For example, the 802.3 Working Group produces Ethernet standards.

A newer working group, the **802.11 Working Group**, creates **wireless LAN standards** for networks that use radio or infrared instead of wires to connect stations. Their 802.11 radio standards dominate commercial wireless LAN usage.

Speeds

The first 802.11 standard specified a maximum speed of only 2 Mbps for both infrared and radio LANs, but few organizations purchased such slow products. Most current installations run at 11 Mbps (802.11b).

802.11b: 11 Mbps   In the **802.11b** standard, although the technology is rated as 11 Mbps, practical maximum speeds are much less. Wireless transmission is very inefficient, for reasons we will soon see. Overall, average throughput often is only 300 kbps to 500 kbps, so 802.11b can support only a few stations in each area.

802.11a: 54 Mbps   New 802.11a^2 systems operating at 54 Mbps are beginning to appear on the market. These will offer far greater capacity than 11 Mbps wireless LANs.[3]

Channels

The 802.11b standard can use three 11 Mbps channels, multiplying its throughput. The 802.11a standard can use eleven 54 Mbps channels, multiplying its throughput even more.

Unlicensed Radio Bands

Standards for 11 Mbps specify the use of the 2.4 GHz unlicensed radio band. In turn, the 54 MHz 802.11a standard specifies the use of the 5 GHz unlicensed radio band. (Specific frequencies vary by country.)

In **licensed radio bands**, stations must have government licenses and must have their licenses modified every time they are moved. This would make no sense for mobile devices. However, although operating in an **unlicensed radio band** allows mobility because there is no need to license stations, nothing prevents your neighbor from transmitting on the same unlicensed band you are using and, in doing so, interfering with you.

Typical Operation

As Figure 5-9 shows, an 802.11 wireless LAN typically is used to connect a small number of mobile devices to a large wired LAN—typically, an Ethernet LAN—because the servers that mobile client stations need to use usually are on the wired LAN.

Stations   Each mobile station must have a **wireless NIC**. Mobile stations tend to use PC Card NICs, which simply snap into the station. Fixed stations normally use internal NICs.

Access Points   When a wireless station wishes to send a frame to a server, it transmits to an access point. The **access point** is a bridge to the wired LAN. **Bridges** connect different types of LANs—in this case, an 802.11 LAN and an 802.3 LAN. The access point converts an 802.11 frame into an 802.3 frame and passes the Ethernet frame over the wired LAN to the server. When the server replies, the access point converts the frame and forwards it out to the wireless station.

The access point also controls stations. It assigns transmission power levels to stations within its range and does a number of other supervisory chores.

Handoff   When a mobile station travels too far from an access point, the signal will be too weak to reach the access point. However, if there is a closer access point, the station will be **handed off** to that access point for service. This aspect of 802.11 LANs is not yet standardized.

---

[2]   Why has "a" come after "b"? Actually, the *a* standard was created first, but it was not technically feasible or fully defined until after the *b* version was complete.

[3]   In Europe, there may be competition from a competing high-speed wireless LAN standard, HiperLAN/2, which also operates at 54 Mbps. As the book went to press, the 802.11 Working Group released the 802.11g standard that provides a speed of 54 Mbps in the 2.4 GHz unlicensed band used by 802.11b. However, the total bandwidth of this band is limited.

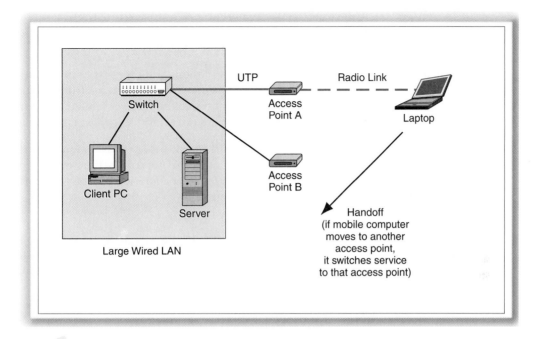

Figure 5-9   Typical 802.11 Wireless LAN Operation with Access Points

Access Point Placement   Placing access points relative to one another can be difficult. For instance, 802.11b access points can only use three channels, and adjacent access points must use different channels. In three-dimensional buildings, this creates real design problems for where to place access points.

In turn, 802.11a provides eleven channels for access points, making access point placement and channel selection less problematic. However, as speeds rise in a wireless LAN, the maximum distance from the station to the access point shrinks. In 11 Mbps networks, distances of 100 meters are said to be possible, although 30 meters is more realistic. With 54 Mbps networks, maximum distances will be even smaller, so many more access points will be needed.

CSMA/CA +ACK Media Access Control

In 802.11 wireless LANs, only one station can transmit at a time in each channel, so there must be media access control discipline.

Problems in Hearing Collisions   The access point assigns each station a power setting so that the access point can hear all stations equally loudly. Unfortunately, this means that stations cannot necessarily hear one another, so collision detection is impossible.

CSMA/CA   Instead, 802.11 LANs use CSMA/CA, where CA stands for **collision avoidance**. With CSMA/CA, if the wireless NIC does not hear transmissions, it may transmit. However, it does not transmit immediately. Instead, it waits a random amount of time *before* transmitting. Only if there still are no transmissions after this wait does it transmit. This minimizes the likelihood of collisions.

ACK Actually, 802.11 uses **CSMA/CA+ACK**. Collisions and other types of signal loss still are possible with CSMA/CA. When the access point receives a frame from a station, or when a station receives a frame from an access point, the receiver immediately sends an acknowledgement frame, an **ACK**. A frame that is not acknowledged is retransmitted.

Inefficient Operation CSMA/CA+ACK works well, but it is inefficient. Waiting before transmission wastes valuable time. Sending ACKs also is time-consuming. Overall, an 11 Mbps 802.11 LAN becomes congested far more rapidly than a 10 Mbps wired Ethernet LAN as the number of stations grows.

TEST YOUR UNDERSTANDING

7. a) Which 802 Working Group creates wireless LAN standards? b) What is the speed of most 802.11 installations today? c) Compare 802.11a and 802.11b in terms of transmission speeds, number of channels per access point, and propagation distance.

8. a) Describe the elements in a typical 802.11 LAN today. b) Why is a wired LAN still needed? c) What do access points do? d) What is handoff?

9. a) Why can't wireless networking use CSMA/CD? b) Describe CSMA/CA+ACK. c) Why is CSMA/CD+ACK inefficient? d) Does CSMA/CA+ACK govern transmission by NICs, access points, or both?

Bluetooth

Personal Area Networks

Although 802.11 is good for fairly large wireless LANs, another wireless networking standard, **Bluetooth**,[4] was created for wireless **personal area networks (PANs)** to be

Figure 5-10 CSiMA/CA+ACK in 802.11 Wireless LANs

CSMA/CA+ACK in 802.11 Wireless LANs

CSMA/CA (Carrier Sense Multiple Access with Collision Avoidance)
Sender listens for traffic
If there is traffic, waits before sending
If there is no traffic, first waits a random amount of time to avoid collisions
If there still is no traffic, transmitts

ACK (Acknowledgement)
Receiver immediately sends back an acknowledgement
If sender does not receive the acknowledgement, retransmits using CSMA/CA

---

[4] Bluetooth is named after King Harald Bluetooth, a Danish king in the tenth century. As you might guess, Bluetooth was developed in Norway, but it is now under the control of an international consortium.

	802.11	Bluetooth
Focus	Local Area Network	Personal Area Network
Speed	11 Mbps to 54 Mbps in both directions	722 kbps with back channel of 56 kbps. May increase.
Distance	100 meters for 802.11b (but shorter in reality)	10 meters
Number of Devices	Limited in practice only by bandwidth and traffic	10 piconets, each with up to 8 devices
Scalability	Good through having multiple access points	Poor
Cost	Probably higher	Probably lower
Battery Drain	Higher	Lower
Discovery	No	Yes

Figure 5-11   802.11 Versus Bluetooth LANs

used by a single person. Figure 5-12 illustrates several uses of Bluetooth. For instance, in Piconet 1 (Bluetooth calls PANs "**piconets**"), a notebook computer wirelessly prints to a printer and synchronizes its files with those on a desktop computer. In Piconet 2, a cell phone prints to the same wireless printer and places a call through the firm's telephone system instead of paying to make a call.

Costs
Bluetooth basically offers **cable replacement**—a way to get rid of cables between devices. Unfortunately, Bluetooth is much more expensive than cabling, and this may limit its acceptance. In addition, Bluetooth is developing more slowly than 802.11. If 802.11 costs fall rapidly because of economies of scale, limited Bluetooth networking may offer no cost savings compared to full 802.11 networking.

Battery Life
Bluetooth is designed to operate at lower power than 802.11, thanks to Bluetooth's shorter range. This will extend battery life—a crucial consideration in portable devices such as notebook computers and PDAs.

Discovery
Bluetooth offers one very important thing that 802.11 does not—ways for devices to **discover** one another automatically and exchange communication parameters automatically. For instance, you could take your notebook computer to a new printer and print as soon as the two devices become acquainted, without installing

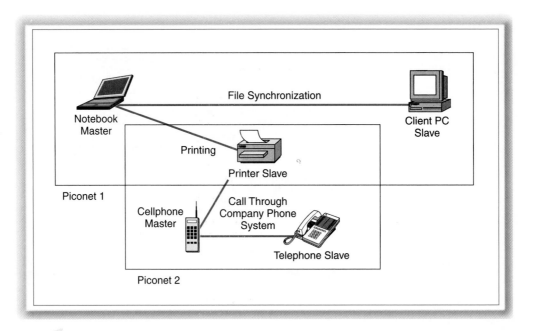

Figure 5-12   Bluetooth Operation

printer drivers on the notebook computer. The 802.11 standard has nothing like this currently.

Low Speed

Bluetooth currently offers a speed of 722 kbps (with a back channel of 56 kbps) and a maximum distance of 10 meters.[5] In addition, there can only be 10 piconets in an office area. Each piconet can have only eight devices. Faster versions with longer distance spans may appear in the future.

Master-Slave Architecture

In Bluetooth, one device is a **master**—generally the mobile PC, PDA, or cell phone. The other device, such as a printer, becomes the **slave**. As Figure 5-11 shows, a slave may have multiple masters, masters may have multiple slaves, and two masters may have the same slave simultaneously. A piconet includes one master and all of its slaves.[6]

---

[5] This is with standard 1 milliwatt power. This can be raised to 50 meters using 100 milliwatt power, although this drives down battery life.

[6] Bluetooth can use access points, which are not shown in the figure.

Interference with 802.11 Networks

Another problem is that Bluetooth and 802.11b both operate in the 2.4 GHz un-licensed radio band, so they may interfere with one another. The 802.15 Working Group is now working on ways to allow coexistence.[7]

TEST YOUR UNDERSTANDING

10. a) What are the advantages of 802.11 over Bluetooth? b) What are the advantages of Bluetooth over 802.11? c) What problem may occur if both are used in the same office?

ATM LANS

A competitor of Ethernet for switched corporate LANs is **Asynchronous Transfer Mode (ATM)**, which is administered by the ITU-T rather than the IEEE 802 Committee.

Complexity

Whereas Ethernet was created for LANs, ATM was created as a road to a new worldwide telephone network that would replace today's telephone system and provide higher-quality voice and video transmission. Unfortunately, the requirement to be able to serve the entire world required a great deal of complexity in the design of ATM networks. This has made ATM technology extremely expensive compared to Ethernet technology, and it has also made the cost of managing ATM networks much higher than the cost of Ethernet networks. Consequently, ATM has done poorly in the LAN market.

A Lost Speed Advantage

Typical ATM speeds are 1 Mbps, 25 Mbps, 156 Mbps, 622 Mbps, 2.5 Gbps, 10 Gbps, and (soon) 40 Mbps. Once, ATM speeds were far higher than Ethernet speeds. Today, however, both ATM and Ethernet are about equally scalable.

Quality of Service (QoS) Guarantees

The one concrete advantage that ATM has over Ethernet is **quality of service (QoS)** guarantees. Ethernet offers no guarantee that your frame will get through with low latency, which is very important for voice and video traffic. In contrast, we will see that ATM offers strong QoS guarantees, at least for some traffic.

TEST YOUR UNDERSTANDING

13. a) What is the advantage of Ethernet over ATM? b) What is the advantage of ATM over Ethernet?

---

[7] Another potential competitor for 802.11 in small offices is *HomeRF*, which, as its name suggests, is designed for the home market. "RF" means "radio frequency." HomeRF is likely to offer 802.11b speeds at a lower price because HomeRF equipment does not have to do things needed in larger wireless LANs. However, HomeRF is not scalable to the corporate environment.

SPREAD SPECTRUM TRANSMISSION

Both 802.11 and Bluetooth operate in radio bands that do not require a license for each station. To operate in these bands, computers and access points must use a form of transmission called spread spectrum transmission.

NORMAL TRANSMISSION

As noted in Chapter 3, if you want to transmit at a given bit rate, you will need a channel whose bandwidth is sufficiently wide. To allow as many channels as possible, channel bandwidths normally are limited to the data requirements of the user's signal in normal radio transmission, as Figure 5-12 illustrates.

SPREAD SPECTRUM TRANSMISSION

In spread spectrum transmission, however, the original signal, called a **baseband signal**, is passed through a **spreader circuit** before transmission. As Figure 5-13 shows, this spreads the signal energy over a much larger bandwidth. As a result, the average energy per hertz is lower.

Frequency Hopping Spread Spectrum (FHSS)

In the simplest form of spread spectrum transmission, the signal keeps the bandwidth required by the signal but hops frequently among different radio channels within the spreading range, as

Figure 5-13   Normal Radio Transmission and Spread Spectrum Transmission

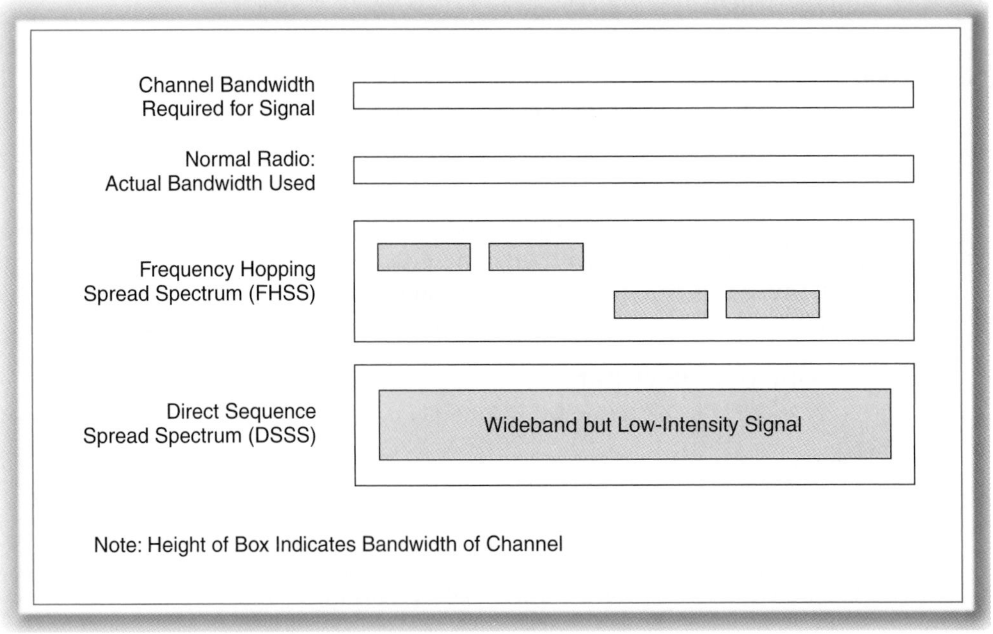

SPREAD SPECTRUM TRANSMISSION (*continued*)

Figure 5-13 illustrates. This is **frequency hopping spread spectrum (FHSS)** transmission. If the signal runs into strong EMI or multipath interference in one of these channels, that part of the message will be lost, but parts of the message in other channels will get through.

The 802.11 standard specifies **slow frequency hopping**, in which one or more frames will be sent in each hop. Slow hopping allows for simple circuitry in the sender and receiver, but because whole frames are lost, there needs to be extensive error correction to give an acceptable error rate.

One reason why frequency hopping is undesirable is that the transmitter must be retuned with each frequency hop. This takes a small but distinct amount of time, slowing the transmission rate. Consequently, the 802.11 Working Group only specified frequency hopping spread spectrum transmission for speeds of 1Mbps and 2 Mbps. Few products operating at these low speeds were adopted.

Direct sequence spread spectrum. In **direct sequence spread spectrum (DSSS)**, a transformation is applied to the original signal to create a wide-bandwidth signal with low signal density per hertz. The receiver, which uses the same transformation in reverse, gets the original signal back. Although there may be slight damage, the natural error resistance of spread spectrum signaling to narrowband EMI and multipath interference effects (discussed later) normally makes the received signal readable. Although DSSS is more complex than FHSS, 802.11 standards require DSSS at 11 Mbps and higher speeds.

Figure 5-14   Code Division Multiple Access (CDMA) Spread Spectrum Transmission

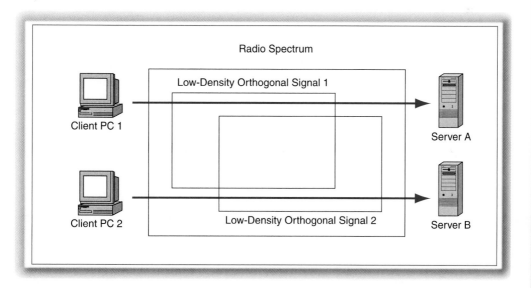

SPREAD SPECTRUM TRANSMISSION (*continued*)

Code Division Multiple Access (CDMA)

In the simple form of DSSS used in 802.11, if two or more parties transmit at the same time, their signals will interfere with one another's. This is why 802.11 uses CSMA/CA to reduce the likelihood of a collision.

Cellular telephone systems, however, use a more sophisticated DSSS system, called **Code Division Multiple Access (CDMA)**. In CDMA, each pair of stations uses a different transformation code. If the transformation codes are taken from a set in which the codes are sufficiently orthogonal, two stations will be able to transmit to their partners simultaneously and each partner will be able to decode the other's signal successfully, as Figure 5.13 indicates. CDMA is *not* used in 802.11 LANs, but it is used in some cellular telephone systems.

WHY SPREAD SPECTRUM TRANSMISSION?

Why use spread spectrum transmission? The simplest answer is that it is required in unlicensed radio bands. However, there are strong technical reasons for using it.

Reduced Multipath Interference

Chapter 3 described multipath interference, in which reflected waves interfere with direct waves. At any location, this interference is frequency-specific. Spreading the frequency range of the signal reduces the likelihood that most of the signal will be subject to destructive multipath interference.

Reduced Electromagnetic Interference (EMI)

Electromagnetic interference (EMI), which we saw in Chapter 3, comes from many sources, such as electrical motors. Usually, the frequency ranges of interference produced by EMI sources are rather limited and will affect only part of the spectrum, allowing most of the spread signal to get through. In fact, spread spectrum transmission was invented in World War II by actress Hedy Lamar as a way for Allied radio signals to "burn through" narrowband enemy jamming.

Security?

The military uses spread spectrum transmission to avoid detection by enemy listeners. In FHSS, if the enemy listens to a channel, they will only hear an occasional burst of traffic and may pass this off as noise. In DSSS, the amount of energy in each channel will be so small that the receiver probably will not be able to pick it out. However, 802.11 spread spectrum technology is *not* designed for security but rather to make it easy to detect and receive signals. Security in wireless LANs requires messages to be encrypted if secrecy is important.

TEST YOUR UNDERSTANDING

11. a) In normal radio operation, how does channel bandwidth usually relate to the bandwidth required to transmit a data stream of a given speed? b) How does this change in spread spectrum transmission? c) Describe FHSS. d) Describe DSSS. e) Which is used at higher speeds? f) Distinguish between DSSS and CDMA.

12. What are the advantages of spread spectrum transmission?

	Ethernet LANs	ATM LANs
Designed for	LANs	Worldwide Telephone Network
Complexity	Low	High
Equipment Cost	Low	High
Management Cost	Low	High
Scalability	High	High
QoS Guarantees	None, but Overprovisioning and Priority make Ethernet competitive even for latency-intolerant applications	Excellent for voice Usually not for data

Figure 5-15   ATM Versus Ethernet LANs

Handling Traffic Peaks

Traffic Peaks

If traffic volume is comfortably below a network's capacity, *all* traffic will get through quickly. However, sometimes there are brief **traffic peaks** that exceed the network's capacity, as Figure 5-16 illustrates. Although these peaks normally last only a fraction of a second to a few seconds, they can be highly disruptive for some applications, especially voice and video. For other applications, such as e-mail, however, users will not even notice brief delays.

Quality of Service in ATM

When a brief traffic peak exceeds network capacity, as shown in Figure 5-16, ATM will ensure that traffic with QoS guarantees will get through without increased latency.

Class A (Constant Bit Rate) for Voice and Video   ATM offers excellent QoS guarantees for voice and video transmission. For voice and video, ATM offers **Class A Constant Bit Rate (CBR)** service. CBR guarantees a specified level of speed and maximum latency.

CBR also guarantees that ATM frames (called cells) will arrive with the same inter-frame time spacing that they had when they left. This low **cell delay variation tolerance** is important for voice and video. If inter-frame time spacing varies too much between the sender and the receiver, voice will sound jittery and video will look jerky.

Class D for Data   Unfortunately, *data* traffic in ATM usually gets **Class D** service, which receives little or no guarantee of throughput. Capacity on ATM switches and trunk lines is reserved first for CBR voice and video traffic, and Class D data usually gets whatever is left over. Data transmission on ATM actually can be worse than over Ethernet during traffic peaks.

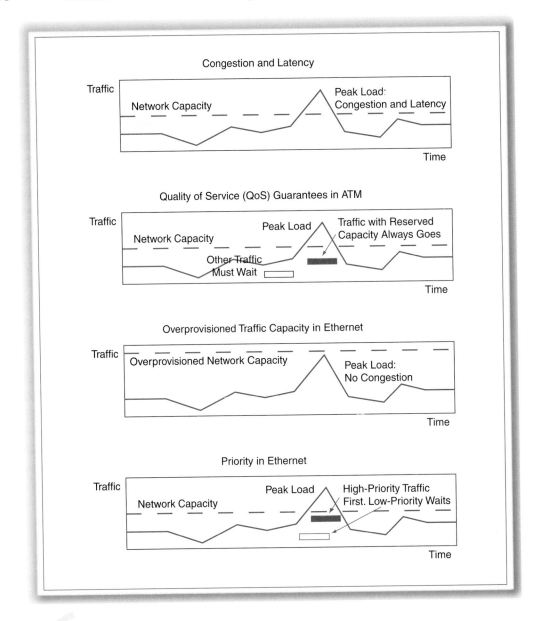

Figure 5-16   Handling Brief Traffic Peaks

Improving Ethernet

Overprovisioning   Most organizations have discovered that the way to get around Ethernet's lack of QoS guarantees without spending the money required for ATM is to **overprovision** the Ethernet network, that is, to install much more capacity than will be needed most of the time. If 10Base-T would be sufficient most of the time, for example, they install 100Base-TX. When there are brief traffic bursts, these bursts will rarely exceed capacity. Although this method is not elegant and wastes capacity most of the time, it has proven to be the least expensive way to handle traffic bursts.

Priority   In addition, Figure 5-6 shows **802.1Q** Ethernet frame tagging. The Tag Control Information field contains not only a 12-bit VLAN ID, but also a 3-bit priority field that can be used to give a frame one of eight **priority** levels from 000 to 111. The definition of these policy levels is given in the **802.1p** standard.

When brief traffic peaks occur, higher-priority traffic will go first. If high priority is given to latency-intolerant applications, such as voice communication, and if low priority is given to latency-tolerant traffic, such as e-mail transmission, applications for which latency is a problem will experience no latency, and users of latency-tolerant applications probably will not even notice brief delays during the momentary traffic peak. Priority also guarantees that network control messages get through, which may be crucial during periods of high congestion.

Figure 5-17   ATM Network with Virtual Circuits

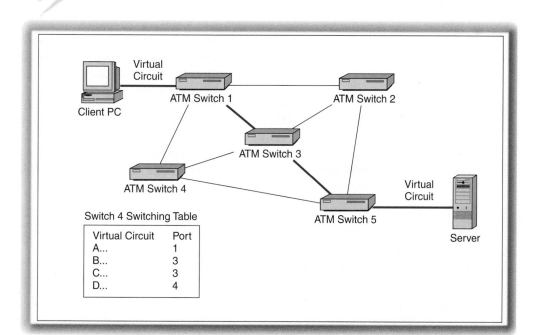

However, priority has proven difficult to manage. Its management costs have made priority substantially more expensive than overprovisioning Ethernet. In addition, prioritizing traffic can lead to pitched political battles within a firm over whose traffic should have the highest priority.

TEST YOUR UNDERSTANDING

14. a) What are brief traffic peaks? b) What problem do they create? c) How does ATM address brief traffic peaks? d) Describe the two classes of service named in the text. e) Is ATM's approach better for voice or data? f) In what two ways does Ethernet address traffic brief peaks? g) What is the advantage of each? h) Overall, what is the most economical way today for most firms to address the problem of traffic peaks in LANs?

ATM Network Operation

Meshes and Alternative Paths

As Figure 5-17 shows, ATM networks can have switches arranged in a **mesh**, in which there are many connections between switches. A mesh creates the potential for multiple **alternative paths** between the sender and the receiver.

As we saw earlier in the chapter, Ethernet switches are arranged in a hierarchy. In a hierarchy, there is only one possible path between any two stations, and this makes Ethernet vulnerable to single points of failure—a fault that mesh networks do not share.

However, pure meshes make switching decisions complicated and slow because the switch must evaluate all possible alternative paths for each arriving frame. It must then select the best path for each frame. This process is processing-intensive and therefore expensive. Consequently, ATM networks resort to using virtual circuits, which are illustrated in Figure 5-17.

Virtual Circuits

Each station in an ATM network has a unique 20-octet (160-bit) **ATM address**.[8] However, switches only use this address to establish a path between the sender and the receiver. This path is called a **virtual circuit**. Once the virtual circuit is established, all traffic between the two stations flows over that virtual circuit.

Virtual circuits reduce the workload of ATM switches. Instead of having to deal with multiple alternative paths, ATM switches merely look at the virtual circuit number in the frame's header. They then do a simple and quick lookup in a table that has one row per virtual circuit–port combination. (In comparison, Ethernet switching tables have one LAN address–port pair per row.) This is much less work than identifying all possible paths and then selecting the best one.

Failure Recovery

If a switch or trunk line along the virtual circuit fails, communication can no longer take place using that virtual circuit. However, the switches can use available alternative paths to create a new virtual circuit and send subsequent cells along that virtual circuit.

---

[8] This allows multiple levels of hierarchy in addresses, as in the telephone system (In the United States, country code, area code, exchange, and specific telephone). Again, ATM was designed for the needs of worldwide service, not for LAN needs.

TEST YOUR UNDERSTANDING

15. ATM switches can be arranged in a mesh. a) What is the advantage of this? b) What is the disadvantage? c) How does ATM address the disadvantage? d) How does this approach save money? e) What element of the network costs less as a result—switches, trunk lines, access links, etc.?

ATM Cells

Figure 5-18 shows an ATM frame, which is called an ATM cell. **Cells** are fixed-length frames, and all ATM cells are 53 octets long. There are five octets of header plus a **payload** (data field) of 48 octets.

Fixed Length

Fixed length allows switches to operate very quickly, for instance by processing different fields of the cell in parallel. The switch knows exactly where each field will appear in the cell.

Short Length

Also, the small size of the ATM cell minimizes latency at each switch. Until an entire frame arrives, a switch may not be able to send it back out again. This produces latency. Having small cells minimizes this latency at each switch. This latency reduction is very important for telephone calls—the primary application for which ATM was created.

Figure 5-18   ATM Cell

Bit 1	Bit 2	Bit 3	Bit 4	Bit 5	Bit 6	Bit 7	Bit 8
Virtual Path Identifier							
Virtual Path Identifier				Virtual Channel Identifier			
Virtual Channel Identifier							
Virtual Channel Identifier			Payload Type		Reserved	Cell Loss Priority	
Header Error Check							
Payload (48 Octets)							

This is the call structure for the network–network interface (NNI) between the switches of different carriers. There is a different cell structure for the user–network interface (UNI) between the customer premises and the ATM carrier.

Virtual Circuits Number

Instead of a destination address, each ATM cell header contains a two-part virtual circuit number consisting of a **virtual path identifier (VPI)** and a **virtual channel identifier (VCI)**. Together, these numbers identify a particular virtual circuit. The ATM address of the destination station is not used in ATM frames.

Unreliable Service

Like Ethernet, ATM is an unreliable service. It does not do error correction on a hop-by-hop basis between switches. This reduces switching costs by not requiring switches to do the complex work of error correction.

TEST YOUR UNDERSTANDING

16. a) Briefly describe the sizes of ATM headers, payloads, and cells. b) Why are they so short? c) Do they contain the destination station's network address? d) In what two ways does ATM reduce switching cost?

LEGACY LAN TECHNOLOGIES

Today, Ethernet dominates local area networking, although wireless LANs are growing in importance and ATM is used in some LANs where QoS guarantees are critical. At the same time, there are several legacy LAN technologies that have enough market presence to be important to know at least in overview.

Token-Ring Networks

Rings

Some networks connect their stations or hubs in a **ring**, as Figure 5-20 shows. Signals travel in one direction around the ring. Only one station at a time may transmit, or a collision will result. This is called a **ring topology**.

Ring Wrapping

Actually, these networks use two rings—usually an active main ring and an inactive backup ring. If a connection breaks, the ring can be **wrapped**, as Figure 5-20 illustrates. This will create a full loop, allowing continued communication until the break is fixed.

Token Passing Media Access Control

How does a station know when it may transmit? For media access control, a special frame called a **token** circulates around the ring when there is no traffic. When a station wishes to transmit, it waits for the token. It then transmits, sending the token back out when it is finished transmitting.

802.5 Token-Ring Networks

When the 802 Committee was formed, it created two LAN standards. One was Ethernet. The other was the **802.5 Token-Ring Network** standard, which initially operated at 4 Mbps but which quickly grew to 16 Mbps. 802.5 was faster and a

Token-Ring Networks
      Physical topology is a ring
      Ring wrapping for reliability
      Token passing for media access control
      802.5 Token-Ring Networks
            4 Mbps initially, soon 16 Mbps
            More expensive than Ethernet; has died in the Market
      FDDI (Fiber Distributed Data Interface)
            100 Mbps
            200 km circumference is possible
            Had core niche
            Losing out to gigabit and faster Ethernet
Early Ethernet Standards
      General
            Before switches and hubs
            Only 10 Mbps
            Used coaxial cable
    10Base5
            Multidrop topology
            Thick trunk cable uses coaxial cable technology; 500-meter limit
            Drop cable has 15 wires
            15-hole Attatchment Unit Interface (AUI) connector
    10Base2
            Daisy chain topology
            Thin coaxial cable between stations
            Circular BNC connector

Figure 5-19   Major Legacy LAN Technologies

more reliable technology than 802.3, but it also was substantially more expensive. Although it still has a niche in companies with strong IBM mainframe groups, it has largely died in the marketplace.

Fiber Distributed Data Interface (FDDI)

Another legacy of token-ring network technology, **Fiber Distributed Data Interface (FDDI)**, operates at 100 Mbps and can have an amazing circumference of 200 km. FDDI was quite popular as a core LAN technology when most desktop switches only operated at about 10 Mbps. However, it is being pushed out of the core by gigabit Ethernet because 100 Mbps is too slow for core usage.

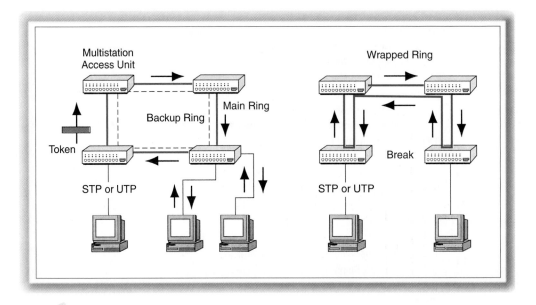

Figure 5-20   802.5 Token-Ring Network

TEST YOUR UNDERSTANDING

17. a) What is the attraction of dual rings? b) Explain wrapping. c) Explain token passing.

18. a) Which working group created the token-ring network standard for LANs introduced at about the same time as 802.3? b) How was it superior to Ethernet? c) Why did it not fare well in the marketplace?

19. a) Describe the speed and distance capabilities of FDDI. b) What was its main niche? c) Why is it not being installed in new LANs?

Early Ethernet 802.3 Physical Layer Standards

Today, Ethernet uses switches or hubs and operates at high megabit to low gigabit speeds. However, the first versions of the Ethernet 802.3 standard—802.5 and 802.2—did not use switches or hubs. In addition, they only operated at 10 Mbps. However, some of these legacy technologies are still in place, so you need to be broadly familiar with them.

Coaxial Cable

Both of these standards use coaxial cable instead of UTP or optical fiber. You use coaxial cable to connect your VCR to your television. If you receive cable television service in your home, this also comes in through coaxial cable. Coaxial cable has a thin central wire and a metallic ring as its two conductors.

Figure 5-21   Ethernet 802.3 10Base2 NIC and Connections

Ethernet 802.3 10Base5

As Figure 5-22 shows, Ethernet **10Base5** uses a multidrop line bus topology (see Chapter 3). The main trunk link is thick coaxial cable. This cable can be up to 500 meters long (hence the "5" in 10Base5). The drop cable running from the NIC to the trunk link has 15 wires. The NIC must have a 15-hole **attachment unit interface (AUI)** plug to connect to the drop cable. When one station transmits, its signal travels along the trunk line in both directions, to all stations. This is a multidrop line bus topology, as discussed in Chapter 3.

Ethernet 802.3 10Base2

As Figure 5-22 shows, **10Base2** dispenses with the complication of having separate trunk lines and drop cables. Rather, it uses thinner coaxial cable to connect stations directly in a daisy chain bus. This is a multidrop line bus technology, as discussed in Chapter 3.

The thinner cable and the simpler connectivity make 10Base2 less expensive than 10Base5. However, a segment (daisy chain) in 10Base2 can only span 185 meters (giving the "2" in 10Base2). Ethernet 802.3 10Base2 uses tubular **BNC** connectors. A **t-connector** connects a NIC with the two cable links to the two adjacent stations.

TEST YOUR UNDERSTANDING

20. a) What is the transmission speed of 10Base5 and 10Base2? b) What transmission medium do they use? c) Which standard uses a multidrop line bus topology? d) Which standard uses a daisy chain bus topology? e) What plug do 10Base5 NICs

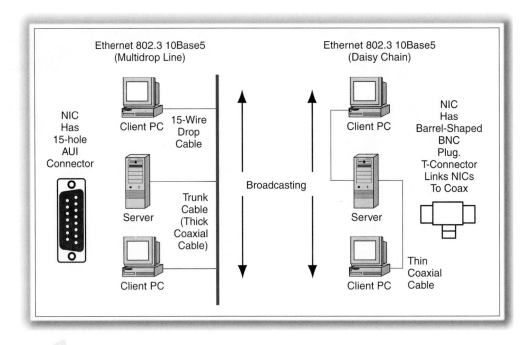

Figure 5-22   Ethernet 802.3 10Base5 and 10Base2

use? f) What plug do 10Base2 NICs use? g) What connects the NIC to the two segments linking the NIC to adjacent NICs?

GAINING PERSPECTIVE

Market Realities

In this chapter, we focused primarily on Ethernet, touching more lightly on other LAN technologies. This reflects the realities of corporate use. *Network World* asked 240 network executives to describe their LAN traffic in 2001.[9] For workgroup hubs and switches, 96 percent of the traffic was Ethernet, while 4 percent was 802.5 Token-Ring Network traffic.

Similarly, in the core of the network, Gigabit Ethernet was twice as popular as ATM and FDDI combined. Ethernet is growing, while FDDI is fading, and ATM is used mostly in situations where voice or video is crucial.

According to the International Data Corporation, wireless LAN revenue should double from $768 million in 2000 to over $1.5 billion in 2004.[10]

---

[9] "How Does Your Network Stack Up?" *Network World*, February 19, 2001. http://nwfusion.com/research/2001/0219feat.html.

[10] International Data Corporation, Document #23431, December 2000.

THOUGHT QUESTIONS

1. a) Can you think of a way in which Ethernet switches could build their switching tables automatically, just by examining arriving frames? b) What might they do with a frame addressed to a station whose destination address that is not in their switching table?
2. Why do you think Ethernet is flourishing in the LAN environment while ATM is not?
3. Create a flow chart of CSMA/CA.

TROUBLESHOOTING QUESTION

1. A firm buys an inexpensive Ethernet switch to place in its core. After installation, performance actually degrades. What might the problem be, and why does it cause degradation in performance?

DESIGN QUESTION

1. Design an 802.11a wireless LAN for a building at your school with a wired backbone connecting access points but wireless connections to all stations. Assume a maximum transmission distance of 10 meters. Don't forget that in a multistory building, nearby access points on the same and different floors must use different channels.

CASE STUDIES

Do the XTR Consulting case study in Chapter 5a.

For case studies, go to the book's website, www.prenhall.com/panko, and look at the Supplementary Readings page for this chapter.

PHOTOS

For photos, go to the book's website, www.prenhall.com/panko, and look at the Photos page for this chapter.

PROJECTS

1. **Getting Current.** Go to the book's website's New Information and Errors pages for this chapter to get new information since this book went to press and to correct any errors in the text.
2. **Internet Exercises.** Go to the book's website's Exercises page for this chapter and do the Internet Exercises.
3. **Hands-On.** Go to a computer store and note the availability and prices of wireless LAN equipment.

CASE STUDY: XTR CONSULTING'S PC NETWORK

INTRODUCTION

XTR Consulting (name changed for confidentiality) is a small environmental consulting company with four professionals and a secretary. They have an office suite in a large downtown office building. This is called a **SOHO (small office or home)** environment. It is quite different from the large networks we will see in later chapters.

INITIAL SITUATION

PCs and Printers
Initially, each staff member had a good personal computer and a printer. Victor Chao, XTR's president, had a laser printer. So did Ann Jacobs, the secretary. The other consultants had color dot matrix printers.

Sneakernet
When a consultant with a dot matrix printer needed laser printout, he or she saved the file onto a floppy disk and gave it to Ann. Similarly, when consultants wanted to share a file, one had to save it to disk and walk it to the other consultant. Walking files around was jokingly called "**sneaker-net.**" It wasted time and created confusion over who had the most current version of each file.

Remote Access
The consultants, who frequently are on the road, had to copy files they would need to the firm's one "loaner" notebook computer. If they needed an unexpected file on the road, there was no good way to retrieve it.

Internet Access

Although all PCs had modems, only one could dial into the Internet at a time, and telephone access was very slow for the large maps they often had to download.

Maintenance

One of the consultants, Kumiko Touchi, is very good with computers. However, there were many problems that Kumiko could not fix. Also, pulling Kumiko away from highly paid consulting work to fix a computer problem was absurd financially.

NETWORK DESIGN

To improve their computer service, Victor Chao hired a network consultant, Robert Blanco, who created the design shown in Figure 5a-1.

Switch

An Ethernet switch connects all of the elements. It has ports for 12 devices, leaving room for growth. It operates at 100 Mbps.

Wires

A UTP wire cord runs between the switch and each computer. The company bought precut UTP cords of the correct length for each run. These cords came with connectors already installed. The cords ran over carpets, creating a mild safety hazard. Neater but more expensive installation was put off because the firm might be moving soon.

Network Interface Card (NIC)

Mr. Blanco had to install a NIC in three of the firm's current desktop PCs, now renamed client PCs. The other two desktops came with NICs when they were purchased. The firm also installed a NIC in its notebook PC and in its new server. NICs, like the switch, operated at 100 Mbps.

SERVER

The firm purchased a new computer to be a server. It was only about as powerful as the clients. It ran the Windows 2000 Server network operating system instead of the desktop versions of Windows that the client computers used.

File Service

The main job of this server is to provide **file service**, meaning that the consultants can store their files on the server. Consequently, the main server is called a **file server**. File service is good because the server is backed up nightly.

Print Service

As Figure 5a-1 shows, the firm connects both one laser printer and one color dot matrix printer to small boxes called **print servers**. When client users print, their printout comes out on one of these printers.

Each print server connects to the switch with UTP wiring and to the printer through an ordinary parallel cord. Parallel cables are very short—only one or two meters. Consequently, print servers sit right next to the printer, and there is a long UTP wiring run to the switch.

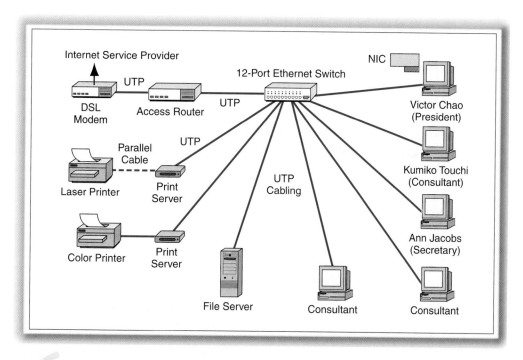

Figure 5a-1   XTR Consulting's SOHO Network

Internet Access

For Internet access, the firm replaced slow telephone access with high-speed DSL service from their local telephone company. Several client PCs can use this access line simultaneously. As Figure 5a-1 shows, this required purchasing an access router. One end of the access router plugs into the DSL modem via a UTP cord. The other end plugs into the switch via another UTP cord.

E-Mail

The server also is used as a mail server, storing incoming mail for all users. It communicates over the Internet with mail hosts in other companies.

Remote Access Service (RAS)

Victor decided not to install **remote access service (RAS)** because he was concerned about security. He did not want a hacker breaking in and stealing critical files.

THE CURRENT SITUATION

XTR Consulting generally is very happy with the new network. The switch works quite well and rarely needs maintenance. Unfortunately, managing the server has been a problem. Ann Jacobs went to a Windows 2000 Server training course. The company reluctantly also sent Kumiko Touchi to the course to provide backup expertise. The company also has Robert Blanco on retainer and frequently has to use him.

THE FUTURE

Wireless LAN

In a few months, the company may be moving to a new office. Laying wiring neatly will be expensive, costing as much as $1,000 per wired client PC and server. The company may wish to install a wireless LAN that would replace most or all UTP cords with radio waves.

Remote Access Service

Victor Chan still wants to add remote access service for his traveling consultants. However, he has heard horror stories about hackers breaking into remote access systems that are not set up correctly and doubts that he can build the needed expertise internally.

TEST YOUR KNOWLEDGE

1. Describe the problems that led to the installation of the PC network.
2. Describe the services offered by the PC network.
3. Describe the hardware and software components of the PC network.
4. Do you agree with there being a file server that also runs e-mail, or should there be a separate e-mail server?
5. Is the company having any problems with the network? If so, how are they being managed?
6. What next steps may the company take? Do you agree or disagree with them? Explain.

CHAPTER

TELEPHONY: INTERNAL AND EXTERNAL

Learning Objectives:

By the end of this chapter, you should be able to discuss:

- The importance of telephone service and the growing integration between voice and video services on the one hand and data networks on the other hand.

- Internal customer premises telephone systems, including PBXs and building wiring. (LAN wiring is based on traditional building telephone wiring.)

- The technology of the public switched telephone network (PSTN), including the local loop, switches, trunk lines (including SONET and SDH), circuits, and circuit switching.

- The digital nature of the PSTN, except for the local loop to the residential customer premises; PCM conversion of customer signals at the end office.

- Cellular telephony, including handoffs, roaming, channel reuse, and generations of cellular telephone service, including the emerging third-generation (3G) service that will provide data transmission speeds up to 2 Mbps.

- Regulation and carriers, including the need for regulation, deregulation, and types of carriers.
- Converged voice and data services (voice over IP, IP telephony), including how it can be implemented, reasons why convergence may save money, and how latency and jitter can be controlled.

INTRODUCTION

This is a bridge chapter. The last two chapters have dealt with LANs. In this chapter, we will look first at internal telephone wiring, which is the basis for UTP LAN wiring. We will then introduce carriers and long-distance technology as a prelude to Chapter 7, which deals with WANs.

Public Switched Telephone Network (PSTN)

In this chapter, we will look at the worldwide telephone network, which is officially called the **Public Switched Telephone Network (PSTN)**. Although the PSTN's technology may seem ho-hum (we will see that it is not), companies spend a great deal of money on telephony. Companies would very much like to control and reduce these costs.

WANs and Telephone Technology and Regulation

Another reason to study telephony is that most wide area networking is built on top of the PSTN's switches, trunk lines, and access lines. In terms of both technology and carrier regulation, you cannot understand WANs unless you first understand telephony. This makes a chapter on telephony a good precursor to the next chapter, which deals with WANs.

LANs and Building Telephone Wiring

Even for LANs, telephony is influential. The 4-pair UTP LAN wiring we have seen in the last two chapters is based on standard building telephone wiring, which we will look at in this chapter.

Converged Services

In addition, companies realize that it is expensive to build and maintain two separate networks, one for voice and one for data. Companies are now moving slowly toward **convergence**, in which they will create a single network to handle both voice and data.

Figure 6-1   Telephony

High cost for corporations
LANs and telephone building wiring
Wide area networking and telephone technology and regulation
Converged services (integrating voice and data)

Integrated Management of Voice and Data Networks

Finally, many organizations put telephony under the networking function (or do the opposite). Just from a pragmatic point of view, then, networking people need to understand telephony and telephony people need to understand networking.

TEST YOUR UNDERSTANDING

1. a) Explain why it is important for data networking professionals to understand telephony. b) Explain why it is important for telephone specialists to understand data networking.

INTERNAL TELEPHONY

Our focus in the last two chapters has been local area networking, so we will begin with the **customer premises equipment (CPE)** needed for internal telephony. In a sense, corporations set up and maintain their own internal telephone companies, with switches, wires, telephone handsets, and even operator services.

Private Branch Exchanges (PBXs)

A Private Switch

As Figure 6-2 shows, the heart of customer premises telephony is the **private branch exchange (PBX)**.[1] It is a company's own internal telephone switch. ("Exchange" is another word for "switch.") The PBX will connect all of the site's telephones and link the site to the outside PSTN.

4-Pair UTP

From the PBX, wires fan out to individual offices. There, they terminate in individual telephones jacks. The wiring, by the way, is 4-pair UTP. Business telephony has long used 4-pair UTP. LAN standards makers adopted this wiring to take advantage of installers' familiarity with it.

TEST YOUR UNDERSTANDING

2. a) What is the function of a PBX? b) What type of wiring is used in building telephone wiring?

Building Wiring Distribution

Entrance Facility

The **entrance facility** is the place where carrier access lines come into the buildings, as Figure 6-2 shows. Special **termination equipment** protects the external telephone network from nonallowed signals the company might transmit to the carrier.

Equipment Room

The PBX is located in a central **equipment room**. From this room, wires fan out throughout the building.

---

[1] Small businesses and branch offices use smaller devices called key telephone systems, which give each telephone access to two or more telephone lines.

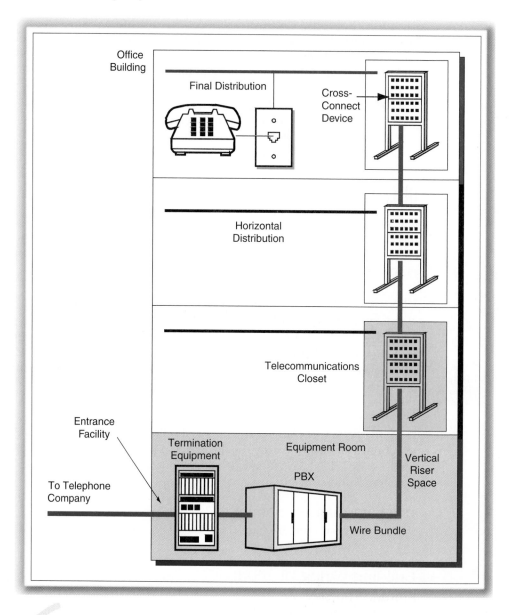

Figure 6-2   Internal PBX-Based Telephone Wiring

Risers and Backbone Cabling

From the PBX, several thick cables that are bundles of 25 to 250 UTP pairs run through a vertical **riser** space between floors. The bundles that run through the risers are known, collectively, as the **backbone** cables.

Telecommunications Closet

On each floor, there is a **telecommunications closet**, also called a *wiring closet*.[2] In this closet, some wires in the bundle are terminated (cut). A **cross-connect device** connects these terminated wires to the 4-pair cords that will serve this floor.

Horizontal Cabling

From the telecommunications closet, wires spread out to each telephone wall outlet. This is called **horizontal cabling**. Usually, the cabling runs through false ceilings or through the walls to the **wall jack**. Sometimes, near the end, it is run on visible walls through enclosed raceways that are simply rectangular coverings like the ones used to cover electrical wiring.

TEST YOUR UNDERSTANDING

3. Explain the following concepts in building wiring. a) Entrance facility. b) Termination equipment. c) Equipment room. d) Riser. e) Backbone wiring. f) Telecommunications closet. g) Cross-connect block. h) Horizontal cabling. i) Wall jack. j) In Figure 6-2, how many UTP pairs will run from the PBX through the vertical riser space if there are 25 telephones on each floor (and no telephones in the equipment room)?

Data Cabling

Data cabling follows this same general pattern with some important changes.

Vertical Distribution is Different

Typically, the equipment room holds a central router and switch. Figure 6-3 shows a single core switch connecting to workgroup switches on each floor. The core switch is a chassis switch that can take many plug-in cards, each with multiple UTP or optical fiber ports. In the figure, a router connects the switched network to the outside world.

Note that only one cord (4-pair UTP or optical fiber) runs from the core switch through the riser to the workgroup switch in the telecommunications closet on each floor. There is no large bundle of wires containing four pairs for each telephone in the building. The single cord between switches multiplexes all traffic between the workgroup switch and the core switch.

Horizontal Distribution Is the Same

UTP cables go from the floor's workgroup switch out to the wall jacks on the floor. For horizontal distribution, then, LAN building wiring is exactly like telephone building wiring. In fact, if you have unused installed telephone wires and wall jacks in place, you can use them for data without change if they are sufficient quality.

---

[2] The equipment room is sometimes called the main distribution facility (MDF). The telecommunications closets are then called intermediate distribution facilities (IDFs).

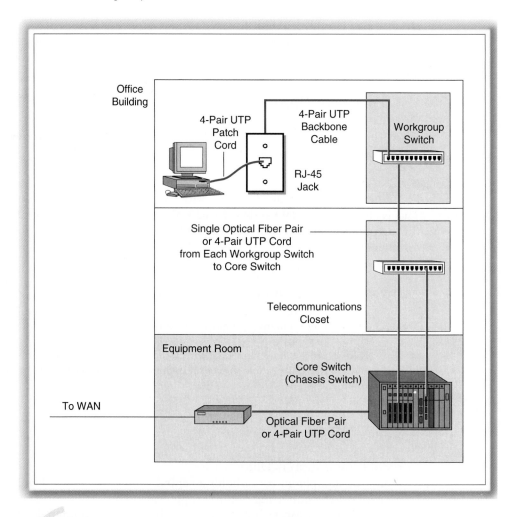

Figure 6-3   LAN Building Wiring

TEST YOUR UNDERSTANDING

4. a) Compare how data cabling and telephone cabling are different for vertical runs.
    b) Compare how data cabling and telephone cabling are similar for horizontal runs.
    c) In Figure 6-3, how many 4-pair UTP cords will run from the core switch through the vertical riser space if there are 25 computers on each floor (and no computers in the equipment room), and if UTP is used for vertical communication? d) If optical fiber is used in place of UTP. How many optical fiber cords will run through the vertical riser?

Building Cabling Management

Structured Cabling Plans

The TIA/EIA-568 standard is only one of several TIA/EIA standards that govern building wiring. Within each of these standards, furthermore, there usually are several options, and it is important to select among these options and apply them consistently throughout a site (and in sites of a multi-location firm). It is important to have a **structured cabling plan** that documents all of the options an organization selects.[3]

Testing

It is important to test each wire run. As noted in Chapter 4, simple testers only test whether the wires are making proper contact in the RJ-45 connector and whether the wires are inserted in the correct pins. To test the quality of transmission, companies need much more expensive testers.[4]

Documentation and Neatness

Given the enormous amount of wiring in even small buildings, of course, it is crucial to have good documentation for wire runs. It is also important to lay wires neatly. Without neatness and documentation, it will be very difficult to identify which cord serves a particular wall jack, switch, or other termination point.

TEST YOUR UNDERSTANDING

5. a) What is a structured cabling plan, and why is it important? b) Why is documentation critical?

THE TECHNOLOGY OF THE PSTN

Having looked at the customer premises equipment (CPE) needed for internal telephony, we are now ready to look at the broader world of telephone carrier technology. Figure 6-4 shows the main technical elements of the worldwide public switched telephone network.

Customer Premises

The first element in the system is the **customer premises**, which for some reason is always spelled in the plural. It is also known as the subscriber premises. This is a residential home, a business building, a college campus, or an industrial park. We have just finished looking at CPE technology, including PBXs and wiring.

---

[3] Some vendors offer structured cabling systems, which are complete plans for all aspects of cabling. Different vendors have different structured cabling systems.

[4] These will test compliance with TIA/EIA-568 propagation criteria. It will also test the length of the connection to ensure that it is not over the maximum length.

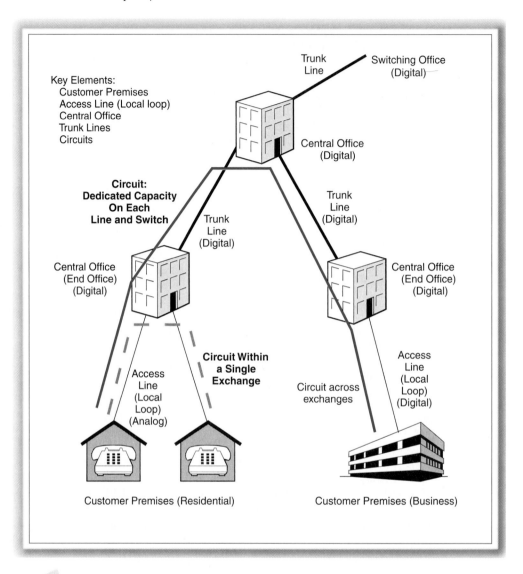

Figure 6-4   Public Switched Telephone Network (PSTN)

Local Loop

The transmission link to the customer premises is called the **local loop**. This access line usually is a single pair of UTP wires. For large customers, however, it may be a pair of optical fibers to multiplex many telephone calls. As we will see in the next chapter, wireless local loops may be increasingly popular in the future.

Switch Hierarchy

Switches are located in buildings called **central offices (COs)**. As Figure 6-4 shows, telephone company switches are arranged in a *hierarchy*. At the bottom are **Class 5 switches.** These are **end office switches**, in which the local loop terminates. Many Class 5 switches connect to a few **Class 4 switches,** which connect to fewer **Class 3 switches.** In Hawaii, for instance, there are about 80 Class 4 and Class 5 switches but only a single Class 3 switch. **Class 2 switches** span large regions. The **Class 1 switch** is at the top of the switching hierarchy.[5] There are only a few Class 1 switches in the world.

TEST YOUR UNDERSTANDING

6.   a) What is a central office? b) How are switches organized in the telephone network? c) What are the classes of switches? d) Which class of switches is highest in the hierarchy?

Trunk Line Technologies

High-speed **trunk lines** are transmission links that connect pairs of central offices. Trunk lines today operate at speeds from 56 kbps to 40 Gbps, as Figure 6-5 illustrates.

North American Digital Hierarchy

In North America, most trunk lines traditionally have been 56 kbps, T1 and T3 links. All are point-to-point links. A **56 kbps** trunk line can carry a single telephone conversation. **T1** links operate at 1.544 Mbps, allowing them to multiplex 24 voice conversations. **T3** lines operate at 44.7 Mbps, allowing them to multiplex 672 voice conversations.

Both 56 kbps and T1 trunk lines bring two data-grade twisted copper pairs to the subscriber premises (one pair for traffic in each direction). Data-grade copper is carries signals farther than the voice-grade copper pairs normally run to residential dwellings but is much more expensive. T3 lines normally use optical fiber.

Conference of European Postal and Telecommunications (CEPT) Multiplexing Hierarchy

In Europe and many other parts of the world, there is a different but similar traditional hierarchy defined by the **Conference of European Postal and Telecommunications (authorities), CEPT**. The slowest link is the **64 kbps** trunk line, which again carries a single voice call. **E1** links operate at 2.048 Mbps, allowing them to multiplex 30 voice channels plus a control channel. **E3** links, in turn, operate at 34.4 Mbps. These CEPT standards define point-to-point connections between switches.

SONET/SDH

Higher Speeds   As telephone companies saw the need for ever faster trunk line speeds, they developed a new set of high-speed optical fiber trunk line standards that operate at multiples of 51.84 Mbps, which is designed to multiplex 672 telephone calls—the same as a T3 circuit. Typical speeds are 155 Mbps, 622 Mbps, 2.5 Gbps, 10 Gbps, and 40 Gbps.[6]

---

[5]   Although this system is primarily hierarchical, telephone companies sometimes put in cross-links. For instance, if two Class 3 switches send a great deal of traffic to each another, there may be a direct connection between them, instead of going through a Class 2 switch.

[6]   So SONET and SDH speeds really are 155.52 Mbps, 622.08 Mbps, 2.49 Gbps, 9.95 Gbps, and 39.82 Gbps.

Trunk Line	Speed
North American Digital Hierarchy	
56 kbps (DS0)	56 kbps (sometimes 64 kbps)
T1 (DS1)	1.544 Mbps
T3 (DS3)	44.7 Mbps
CEPT Multiplexing Hierarchy	
64 kbps	64 kbps
E1	2.048 Mbps
E3	34.4 Mbps
*SONET/SDH**	
OC3/STM1	156 Mbps
OC12/STM4	622 Mbps
OC48/STM16	2.5 Gbps
OC192/STM64	10 Gbps
OC768/STM256	40 Gbps

Notes
    SONET and SDH speeds are multiples of 51.84 Mbps. OCx is the SONET designation. STMx is the SDH designation.

Figure 6-5   Trunk Line Technologies

SONET and SDH   In the United States and Canada, this system became the **Synchronous Optical Network (SONET)**. In Europe, it became the **Synchronous Digital Hierarchy (SDH)**. Despite small technical differences and many naming differences, SONET and SDH are almost the same technology. Consequently, we will refer to them collectively as SONET/SDH.

Dual Ring Technology   As Figure 6-6 shows, SONET/SDH is designed to operate as a dual ring, although it can be used in point-to-point connections. As we saw in the last chapter, dual rings can be wrapped if there is a break in a transmission link between switches. This is important in telephony because the most common cause of telephone disruptions is line breaks by construction backhoes whose operators have not checked local maps of underground telephone lines. This dual ring architecture underlies the telephone system's traditional aggressive concern for reliability.

TEST YOUR UNDERSTANDING

7. a) What are the designations and speeds of the two fastest trunk lines in the North American Digital Hierarchy? b) Are they designed for point-to-point service? c) What

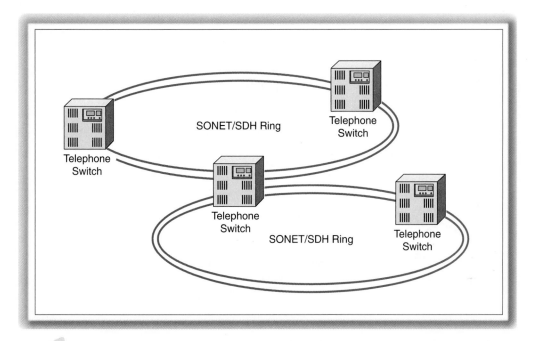

Figure 6-6   SONET/SDH Dual Rings

transmission medium do 56 kbps and T1 trunk lines use? d) What are the designations and speeds of the two fastest trunk lines in the CEPT Multiplexing Hierarchy? e) What trunk line technology do carriers use for SONET and SDH? f) Are SONET and SDH designed for point-to-point service? g) Explain why your answer to the previous part of this question (f) is important.

Circuits and Circuit Switching

Circuits
When one subscriber calls another, the switches of the PSTN set up a connection between the two subscribers. As Figure 6-4 showed, this connection, which is called a **circuit**, may pass through several switches and trunk lines as well as the two subscribers' local loops. However, to the two callers, the circuit appears to be a simple direct connection between them.

Circuit Switching and Its Benefit
This process is called **circuit switching**. Capacity is reserved (dedicated) at each switch and trunk line along the circuit's path. Once a circuit is established, this **reserved capacity** is always available to the subscribers. There is no possibility of a slowdown due to congestion as there is in the packet-switched networks used for most modern data transmission.

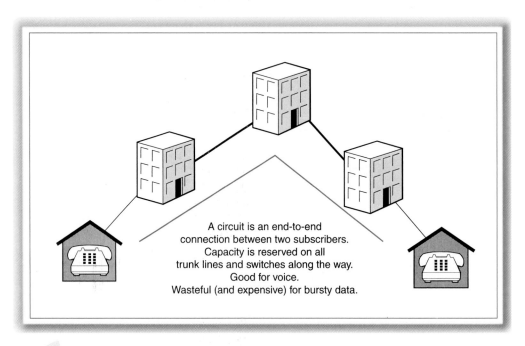

A circuit is an end-to-end
connection between two subscribers.
Capacity is reserved on all
trunk lines and switches along the way.
Good for voice.
Wasteful (and expensive) for bursty data.

Figure 6-7   Circuit Switching

Circuit Switching: The Problem of Reserved Capacity

The problem with reserved capacity is that you still pay for it even if you are not using it. For voice, this is not a serious problem, because one side or the other nearly always is talking. However, data transmission tends to be bursty, with short bursts of traffic separated by long silences. For instance, if you are using a webserver, each download will be a fast burst lasting a few seconds. You will then read the webpage for about half a minute before doing another download. During that reading time, you generate no traffic.

Packet switching does not reserve capacity. Rather, it multiplexes packets from many conversations on trunk lines. Each call only uses the capacity that it needs, with the consequence of lower trunk line costs.

TEST YOUR UNDERSTANDING

8. a) What is a circuit? b) Why are circuits good? c) Why is circuit switching bad for data transmission?

ANALOG AND DIGITAL TRANSMISSION IN THE PSTN

Mostly Digital

As Figure 6-8 shows, the PSTN, which was originally completely analog, is almost entirely digital today. Almost all of its switches are digital, as are almost all of its trunk links. Larger businesses even get digital access links for their local loop communication.

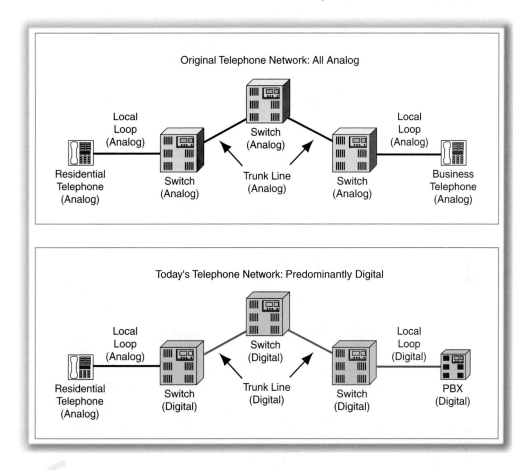

Figure 6-8   The PSTN: Mostly Digital with Analog Local Loops

The local loop that connects residential customers to the nearest end office is a single twisted pair of wires. The customer's telephone sends and receives analog signals, so the end office switch has analog termination equipment and equipment to convert between analog local loop signals and the digital signals of the end office switch.

Codec

Analog-to-Digital and Digital-to-Analog Functions

This termination equipment is called a **codec**. The codec converts incoming analog subscriber signals into digital PSTN signals. This is the **analog-to-digital (ADC)** conversion process, which is called *coding*. In turn, the codec converts digital signals from the switch into analog subscriber signals. This is the **digital-to-analog (DAC)** conversion process, which is called *decoding*. Hence the name "codec."

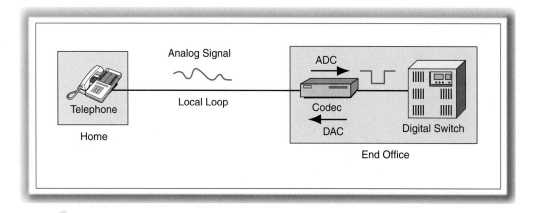

Figure 6-9   Codec at the End Office Switch

Bandpass Filtering

Before a codec codes an incoming subscriber signal, it passes the signal through a **bandpass filter** that only allows frequencies from 300 Hz to about 3.4 kHz to pass into the codec. In Chapter 3, we saw that increasing bandwidth allows higher transmission speeds. It is also true that limiting bandwidth limits the transmission rate so that that fewer bits have to be transmitted, thus reducing transmission cost within the network's digital core. If the top range of frequencies were increased to 20 kHz, four times the traffic would have to be carried per conversation by the digital core, substantially increasing the cost of a telephone call.

Four kHz Channels

The codec treats this bandpass-filtered signal as a channel whose width is 4 kHz. This provides "guard bands" around the 300 Hz–3.4 kHz voice signal.

Sampling

To digitize voice, the ADC samples the voice signal 8,000 times per second, as Figure 6-10 illustrates. Nyquist showed that if you sample at twice the highest frequency in the signal (in this case 4 kHz), you will collect all necessary information. This is why we need 8,000 samples per second.[7]

Encoding Signal Intensity

During each sampling period, the intensity of the signal is measured. The ADC represents the intensity of each sample by a number between 0 and 255, with 255 being the

---

[7] For audio CDs, which can record up to 20 kHz, the sampling rate is 44,100 samples per second. This often is called 44.1 kHz.

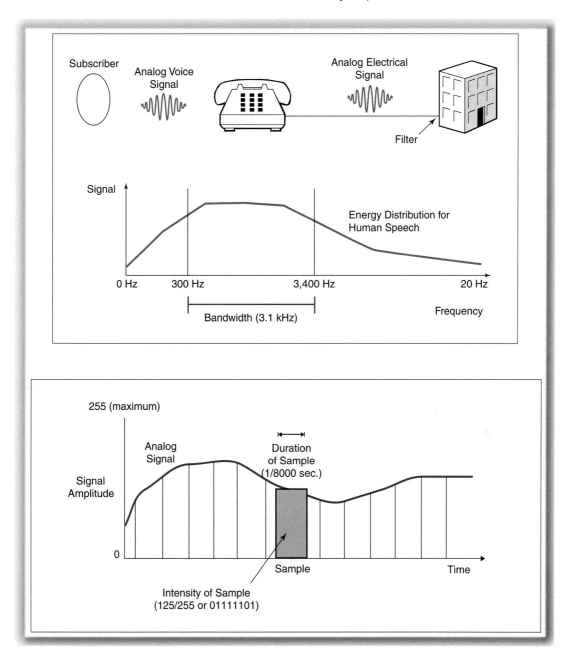

Figure 6-10   Sampling for Analog-to-Digital Conversion (ADC) using Pulse Code Modulation (PCM)

highest possible intensity. With 255 possible values, a single octet of binary data is needed to store each sample's value.[8]

64 kbps for Pulse Code Modulation (PCM)

If you multiply 8 bits per sample times 8,000 samples per second, you get 64,000 bits per second. In other words, using this ADC technique, called **pulse code modulation (PCM)**, ADCs produce a data stream of 64 kbps for voice.

In many cases, 8 kbps will be "stolen" for supervisory signaling, leaving 56 kbps for transmission. This is why the telephone system is built around units of 56 kbps or 64 kbps. This also is why trunk line speeds typically are multiples of 56 kbps or 64 kbps, plus some supervisory bits.

Perspective on Bandpass Filtering

A perfect human ear can hear frequencies up to 20 kHz. However, for most humans, the maximum is only about half that, and most energy in the human voice falls below about 4 kHz. So bandpass filtering reduces signal quality only very slightly.

However, suppose that the full 20 kHz were allowed on each subscriber channel. Then instead of needing 8,000 samples per second, we would need five times as many—40,000 samples per second. At 8 bits per sample, voice would require 320 kbps instead of 64 kbps.

Digital-to-Analog Conversion (DAC)

ADCs are used for transmissions from the customer premises to the end office switch. In contrast, digital-to-analog converters (DACs) are for converting transmissions from the digital telephone network's core to signals on the analog local loop (see Figure 6-9). Figure 6-11 shows that as the DAC reads each sample, it puts a signal on the local loop that has the intensity indicated for that sample. It keeps the intensity the same for 1/8000 of a second. If the time period per intensity level is very brief, the amplitude changes will sound smooth to the human ear.

TEST YOUR UNDERSTANDING

9. a) What parts of the telephone system are largely digital today? b) What parts of the telephone system are largely analog today? c) What are the roles of the codec in the end office switch? d) Explain why the ADC generates 64 kbps of data for voice calls. e) Why do we need DACs? f) How do they work?

CELLULAR TELEPHONY

Cells

Wireless LANs

In Chapter 5, we saw that wireless LANs have a number of access points, which usually are connected together and to servers through a wired LAN. The nearest access point will serve your mobile client. As you move through a building, your mobile

---

[8] For audio CDs, there are two octets per sample, giving 65,536 possible intensity levels for finer resolution. This is called oversampling.

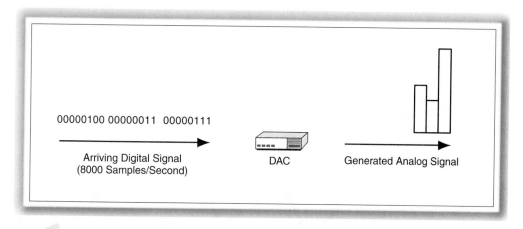

Figure 6-11 Digital-to-Analog Conversion (DAC)

client will be handed off to successive access points so that you always have a strong signal.

Cells and Cellsites

Figure 6-12 shows that cellular telephony works in a similar way. A metropolitan service territory is divided into areas called **cells**.[9]

Near the middle of each cell is a **cellsite**, which contains a **transceiver** (transmitter/receiver) to receive cellular telephone (**cellphone**) signals, send signals out to the cellphone, and supervise the cellphone's operation (setting its power level, initiating calls, terminating calls, and so forth.)

Mobile Telephone Switching Office (MTSO)

All of the cellsites connect to a **mobile telephone switching office (MTSO)**, which connects cellular customers to one another and to wired telephone users. The MTSO also controls what happens at each of the cellsites.

Handoffs Versus Roaming

If a subscriber moves from one cell to another within a system, the MTSO will implement a **handoff** from one cellsite to another. For instance, Figure 6-12 shows a handoff from Cell O to Cell P. In contrast, if a subscriber leaves a metropolitan area and goes to another area or country, this is called **roaming**.[10]

---

[9] The figures shows these cells with regular shapes and sharp boundaries, but they really are overlapping irregular shapes because radio does not propagate evenly in all directions and because radio waves attenuate continuously with no sharp ending distance.

[10] Handoffs always work, but roaming often is problematic. Roaming requires the destination cellular system to be technologically compatible with the subscriber's cellphone and requires administration permission from the destination cellular system.

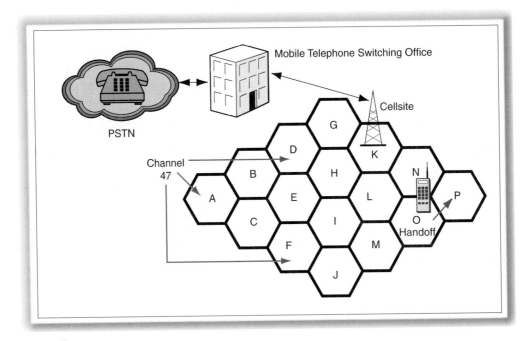

Figure 6-12   Cellular Telephony

Why Cells?

Why not have a single transmitter/receiver in the middle of the metropolitan area instead of dividing the area into cells and dealing with the complexity of cellsites?

Channel Reuse

The answer is **channel reuse**. The number of channels permitted by regulators is limited, and the number of potential subscribers far outstrips the number of channels that regulators will allow. Cellular telephony uses each channel multiple times in different cells in the network. This multiplies the effective channel capacity.

No Channel Reuse in Adjacent Cells

You cannot reuse the same channel in adjacent cells, because there will be interference. For instance, in Figure 6-12, suppose you use Channel 47 in Cell A. You cannot use it in Cells B or C.

Channel Reuse in Nonadjacent Cells

However, you can reuse the same channel in nonadjacent cells because they are too far away for interference. For instance, you can reuse Channel 47 in Cells D and F, which are separated from Cell A by Cells B and C, respectively. Cells D and F, in turn, are separated from each other by Cell E. Overall, Channel 47 can be used several times in the system shown in Figure 6-12.

TEST YOUR UNDERSTANDING

11. a) Why does cellular telephony use cells? b) If I use Channel 3 in a cell, can I reuse the channel in an adjacent cell? Explain.

Generations of Cellular Telephony

Figure 6-13 shows that there have already been two generations of cellular telephony technology and that we are about to enter a third.

Figure 6-13   Generations of Cellular Telephone Service

Generation	First	2nd	2.5G	3G
Technology	Analog	Digital	Digital	Digital
Data Transfer Rate	Data transfer is difficult	10 kbps*	20 kbps to 384 kbps	384 kbps to 2 Mbps
Channels	~800	~800+2,500	~800+2,500	?
Cells / Channel Reuse	Large / Medium	Large / Medium and Small / High	Based on 2G	?
Voice Compression	None	3.1	NA	NA
World Standardization (and therefore roaming)	Poor	Good (GSM)	Based on 2G	? (W-CDMA, CDMA-2000, and other systems may compete)
U.S. Standardization	Good (AMPS)	Poor (GSM, CDMA, TDMA, and CDPD)	Based on 2G	?

*Sufficient for Short Message Service (SMS) and wireless Web access using the Wireless Access Protocol (WAP) or i-mode

First-Generation Cellular Telephony

Analog Service   When cellular telephony first appeared, its **first-generation (1G)** systems were analog. Consequently, their voice quality was only fair. In addition, data transmission was difficult, requiring an additional device—a modem—to be used.

Large Cells Limiting Channel Reuse   In addition, cells were quite large, limiting channel reuse. For instance, Honolulu, which is a mid-size city, only had about 20 cells in its first-generation system. Large cities only had 50 cellsites or slightly more.

Limited Bandwidth   Also, only about[11] 50 MHz of bandwidth was provided for first-generation service, which was only enough for about 800 channels. These channels use an 800 MHz or 900 MHz frequency band.

Incompatible Global Standards   Different countries around the world used different first-generation cellphone standards, making international roaming difficult. In the United States, there was a single standard, AMPS.

Second-Generation Cellular Telephony

Digital Service   **Second-generation (2G)** cellular systems, in contrast, are digital. This dramatically increases signal quality.

Digital service also allows voice to be compressed and multiple conversations to share channels. This allows at least three times as many subscribers to be served for a given amount of bandwidth.

Digital technology also allows new services, such as **Short Message Service (SMS)**, which allows subscribers to type brief messages to one another.

Another new service is **wireless Web** service, in which webpages can be shown on the cellular telephone screen. Given the tiny size of cellular displays, webpages need to be specially formatted. The main standard for wireless webpages is the **Wireless Access Protocol (WAP)**,[12] which also standardizes other aspects of wireless Web access. In addition, the competing **i-mode** wireless Web technology developed in Japan is being extended to systems in other countries.

Additional Bandwidth   Second-generation digital systems can and do operate in the service band created for first-generation systems. In addition, second-generation systems have been allocated an additional service band around 1,800 or 1,900 MHz, depending on the country in which the system is deployed.

The second service band has a bandwidth of 150 MHz, giving about 2,500 channels. This alone tripled the number of potential subscribers.

Smaller Cells for Greater Channel Reuse   In addition, in this new frequency band, cellsites can be much smaller, giving more cellsites in a city and therefore increasing channel reuse and the number of possible subscribers. For instance, whereas Honolulu carriers had about 20 cellsites for their 800 MHz systems, they have about 100 in their 1,900 MHz systems.

---

[11] Different systems in different parts of the world received somewhat different bandwidth allocations.

[12] WAP represents websites as stacks of cards. Each card contains a few short lines of information. Navigation buttons allow the reader to move between cards. There are no hyperlinks.

Compression   Second-generation cellular systems use more efficient codecs to reduce the amount of bits per second generated by a call. Effectively, second-generation cellular telephony sends only about a third of the bits per calls that a second-generation system does.

Good Global Standards (GSM), Except in the United States   Almost the entire world standardized on the **GSM**[13] technology for the second generation. This permits roaming across most of the world with a single telephone.

In the United States, however, the Federal Communications Commission (FCC) permitted open competition in technology, resulting in four main incompatible systems: GSM, CDMA, TDMA, and CDPD (which is only used for data). This chaotic situation limits roaming, keeps U.S. cellphone prices high, and it has lost the United States its early leadership in cellular technology.

Third-Generation Cellular Telephony: High-Speed Data
Although the first two generations were good for voice calling, even 2G systems could only transmit data at about 10 kbps. This is far too slow for general data networking.

Third Generation (3G) for 384 kbps to 2 Mbps   The world telecommunications community is now developing **third-generation** (**3G**) cellular technologies that will increase speeds to up to 384 kbps for mobile stations and 2 Mbps for fixed stations. Third-generation service will require a new service band in the frequency spectrum.

Competing 3G Technologies   Currently, two technologies are competing for 3G dominance. The winner in most countries is likely to be **Wideband CDMA (W-CDMA)** (see Chapter 5 for information about CDMA). W-CDMA is seen as a growth path for GSM carriers. Qualcomm, which created the CDMA technology used in many U.S. 2G carriers, has a competing technology, **CDMA 2000**. A few countries, including China, are developing other technologies. Consequently, standardization across the world is uncertain.

2.5G for 20 kbps to 384 kbps   In addition, some second-generation systems are being upgraded to **second-and-a-half generation** (**2.5G**) technologies that will send and receive data at between about 20 kbps and 384 kbps. The main 2.5G technology is likely to be the **General Packet Radio Service (GPRS)**.[14] GSM service providers can switch some of their channels to GPRS while continuing to use GSM in other channels, so evolution from GSM to GPRS should be smooth.

The Need for New Spectrum   An attraction of 2.5G technology is that it will use the existing 2G spectrum. Providers will convert some of their channels to 2.5G service, and users will need new 2.5G cellphones. Existing 2G users will be unaffected. They will use remaining 2G channels, and they will not have to change their cellphones. The MTSO will allocate the proper channels to 2.5G and 2G users.

---

[13]   Global System for Mobile (communication).
[14]   Another contender is the High-Speed Circuit-Switched Data (HSCSD) standard, which will not use packet switching but will offer a circuit-switched connection at up 57.6 kbps by adding several 14.4 kbps GSM circuits. However, circuit switching is wasteful for bursty data.

For 3G technology, however, new spectrum allocations will be needed in the crowded golden band of the radio spectrum, as noted previously. Finding room in this part of the spectrum is proving difficult in many countries.

Perspective   Third-generation technologies and even 2.5G technologies should bring a revolution in the type of services available to mobile data clients.

TEST YOUR UNDERSTANDING

12. a) Which generation of cellular technology is analog? b) What are the two service bands for 2G systems? c) How do they differ in bandwidth? d) How do they differ in cell size? e) How do 2G systems serve more customers than first-generation systems? (There are several parts to this answer.) f) What is SMS? g) What is wireless Web access? h) What is the international standard for wireless Web access? i) Why do we need 3G service? j) What speeds will 3G service bring? k) What is 2.5G service? l) Why is it attractive?

REGULATION AND CARRIERS

Figure 6-4 showed that switches and trunk lines connect calling parties, creating a complete circuit. At a technical level, the call will be able to go through no matter who owns the switches and trunk lines.

However, at a practical level, subscribers must deal contractually with the many different carriers that own telephone facilities. In addition, government regulation determines the carriers that will be allowed to provide service, what services they will be allowed to provide, and how they can price their services. Service and pricing differences around the world can be very substantial because of differences in regulatory decisions. In many countries, data and business telephone service prices are kept high in order to subsidize residential telephone service. Gone is the simple rationality of LAN decision making based on real costs and performance.

Regulation and Deregulation

Rights of Way

We need carriers for transmission beyond our premises because we do not have **rights of way** (government permission) to lay our wires along roads and in other public and private areas. The government only grants these rights of way to carriers.

Regulated Status

In return for receiving rights of way, the carrier agrees to become subject to **regulation** to prevent the abuse of its power.

Tariffs

Usually, the government oversees pricing. Carriers usually must submit **tariffs** for each service. The tariff specifies the exact details of the *service* to be provided so that customers will have a basis for complaining if service conditions are not met. The tariff also specifies the *fees* to be charged, preventing preferential pricing for some customers. Only if the government accepts the tariff may the carrier offer the service.

> **Regulation**
>   Carriers
>   Rights of way
>   Monopoly
>   Regulation
>   Tariffs
> **Deregulation**
>   To increase competition
>   Varies by country
>   Varies by service
>   Data, long-distance, and customer premises deregulation is high.
>   Local voice service deregulation is low.

Figure 6-14   Regulation and Deregulation

Monopolies

Traditionally, almost all carriers were given protected **monopoly status**. For agreeing to accept **rate regulation**, they were given protection from competition. Most countries (but not the United States) originally had a single monopoly telephone carrier called the **Public Telephone and Telegraph authority (PTT)** that handled all domestic telephone service.

Deregulation

In recent years, governments around the world have begun to repeal price control and monopoly protections, including the need to file tariffs for all services. This **deregulation** allows new carriers to offer services, hopefully brining price competition and speeding the pace of innovation.

Deregulation Differences by Country   Deregulation varies greatly among countries. For instance, it is very high in the United States and high in Europe but low in many countries. Doing business in the United States and then expanding globally can bring some unpleasant service and price surprises.

Deregulation Differences by Service   In addition, deregulation varies widely by service. Deregulation usually is complete for customer premises telephony, and it usually is high for data transmission and long-distance voice telephony.

However, regulators have been slower to introduce competition in local voice service. They are afraid that unfettered local voice competition might leave poor subscribers, whose service is subsidized today by charging other residential users higher fees, without service.

TEST YOUR UNDERSTANDING

13. a) Why do we need to use carriers? b) What are rights of way? c) Why are carriers regulated? d) Why are data and business service prices set high in many countries? e) What two things do tariffs specify? f) Why are tariffs required?

14. a) Why is a good deal of telecommunications being deregulated? b) What are the implications of the fact that deregulation varies widely around the world? c) In what services is deregulation generally high? d) In what services is deregulation generally low?

Carriers in the United States

Local Exchange Carriers (LECs)

In the United States, there are two tiers of service, as Figure 6-15 shows. **Local exchange carriers (LECs)** serve a region that generally spans a few hundred miles. This region is called the **local access and transport area (LATA)**. Small states such as Hawaii have only a single region. Large states have one to two dozen regions. The traditional monopoly telephone company in the region is called the **incumbent local exchange carrier (ILEC)**. Other regional carriers are called **competitive local exchange carriers (CLECs)**.

Inter-exchange Carriers (IXCs)

In turn, service between local regions is provided by carriers called **inter-exchange carriers (IXCs)**. Major IXCs for telephony are AT&T, Sprint, and WorldCom.

Figure 6-15   Carriers in the United States

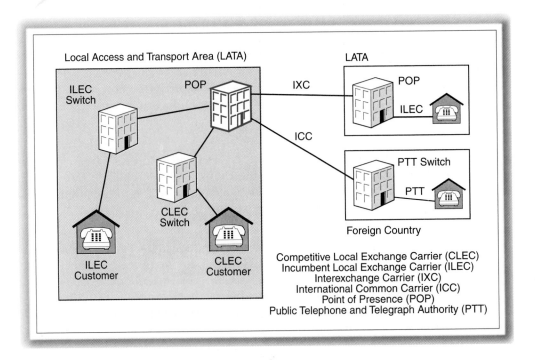

Competitive Local Exchange Carrier (CLEC)
Incumbent Local Exchange Carrier (ILEC)
Interexchange Carrier (IXC)
International Common Carrier (ICC)
Point of Presence (POP)
Public Telephone and Telegraph Authority (PTT)

Points of Presence (POPs)

In each region, there is at least one **point of presence (POP)** where the carriers inter-connect, so that any subscriber can reach any other. For instance, a circuit may begin at an ILEC in one region, pass through an IXC to another region, and terminate in a CLEC in that other region.

International Common Carriers (ICCs)

POPs can even connect **domestic carriers** (carriers that provide service within the country) with **international common carriers (ICCs)**, which provide service between countries.

TEST YOUR UNDERSTANDING

15. a) What are the two tiers of carriers in the United States? b) What are U.S. intra-regional carriers called? c) Distinguish between an ILEC and a CLEC. d) What are U.S. inter-regional carriers called? e) What is the name of the location where different U.S. carriers interconnect?

Data Networking

Data networking generally is less regulated than voice service. However, building a corporate data network also tends to involve multiple WAN carriers operating under different regulatory categories. Generally, carriers for data networks are divided into the same regulatory categories as telephone carriers.

In addition, many data carriers use telephone carrier circuits for transmission, adding their own switching. Consequently, what they can offer and how much it will cost depends on services and prices set through regulation. Even more directly, as we will see in the next chapter, customers almost always connect to WANs through leased lines, which normally are provided by telephone carriers on a regulated basis.

TEST YOUR UNDERSTANDING

16. a) Compare regulation for telephone service and data service in general. b) Why are distinctions between types of voice carriers important for companies purchasing data service?

CONVERGENCE

One of the hottest (and most frustrating) networking topics today is **convergence**—the combining of a firm's data and voice networks. Typically, voice is carried over an IP network, giving rise to the names **voice over IP (VoIP)** and **IP telephony**.

Saving Money

The main reason for convergence is to save money. VoIP saves money in three ways: reducing staff and other economies of scale, implementing efficient encoding, and multiplexing through packet switching.

Reducing Staff and Other Economies of Scale

Operating separate voice and data networks requires a great deal of redundant labor. In addition, there are economies of scale in purchasing or leasing switching and transmission equipment and services for a single converged network.

Integrate voice and data networks
  Often referred to as voice over IP (VoIP) and IP telephony
Save money compared to traditional telephony
  Reducing staff and economies of scale in purchasing with one network
  Encoding voice to less than 64 kbps so fewer bits need to be sent
  Packet switching to reduce transmission costs for bits sent
Other advantages
  Computer-telephony integration (CTI)
    Provide integrated voice and data applications
Implementation
  PBX-to-PBX connectivity is easy and saves money on long-distance calls
  LAN implementations are more difficult, less well-developed, and may not save money
Will cost savings be realized?
  Falling traditional telephone prices
  Packet transmission inefficiency
Service quality
  Availability (less than the PSTN's 99.999%)
  Sound quality (latency and jitter)
  Sound quality is addressed by using a single ISP to connect all sites
    Service Level Agreements (SLAs)

Figure 6-16 Converged Services

Efficient Encoding

As noted earlier in this chapter, telephone voice channels generate 64 kbps of traffic because of PCM encoding. Using newer technology, VoIP systems can encode voice at 6 kbps to 12 kbps.

Packet Switching

In addition, VoIP uses packet switching, which shares the cost of transmission lines so that there is no cost during silences.

Improving Applications

Another reason for using combined voice–data networks, besides saving money, is to support new applications. For instance, a customer support specialist can talk to someone while automatically seeing information about that customer based on his or her telephone number. This is called **computer–telephony integration (CTI)**. Supporting new CTI applications is likely to be more important than cost savings in the long term.

TEST YOUR UNDERSTANDING

17. a) What is VoIP or IP telephony? b) What are the three ways in which IP telephony saves money? c) Besides saving money, what do companies find attractive about VoIP? d) What is CTI?

PBX–PBX IP Telephony

The simplest way to implement IP telephony is to install it only in PBXs, as Figure 6-17 illustrates. Most PBX vendors now offer optional IP telephony modules. Confining IP telephony to PBX–PBX links makes sense because only long-distance transmission is expensive, so this approach saves money where the potential cost savings are greatest. In addition, the technology is fairly mature.

In contrast, computer–telephony integration requires bringing converged services to every desktop, presumably using LAN technology. Unfortunately, this technology is still in its infancy, different vendors take very different approaches, and building telephone transmission is already inexpensive. Unless a firm has strong reasons for implementing desktop convergence immediately, it generally is best to wait until the technology matures.

TEST YOUR UNDERSTANDING

18. a) Why is VoIP for PBX–PBX transmission attractive? b) Why is VoIP less attractive for LAN transmission?

Will Cost Savings Be Realized?

Initially, it appeared that long-distance telephone savings would be extremely large with converged networks. However, two factors have emerged to reduce cost savings.

Falling Traditional Telephone Prices

The biggest attraction of VoIP is its low cost relative to long-distance and international telephone calling rates. However, carrier telephone transmission prices have fallen dramatically in the last few years. As a result, expected costs savings from converting to VoIP have shrunk accordingly.

Figure 6-17   PBX-PBX IP Telephony

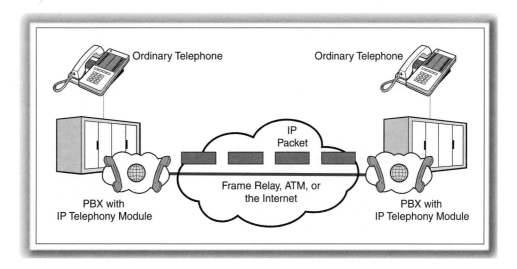

Packet Transmission Inefficiency

Also, reducing the encoding rate from 64 kbps to 8 kbps does not really reduce traffic by a factor of eight. At lower data rates, systems often have a difficult time loading the data fields of IP packets efficiently. In addition, TCP/IP has other sources of overhead, in the form of supervisory messages. Often transmission capacity reductions are only a small fraction of encoding reductions.

Service Quality

The telephone system works so well that we sometimes take its service quality for granted. However, any telephone engineer will tell you that such high service quality is very difficult to achieve.

Availability

The telephone system is available 99.999 percent of the time. (This is called the "five nines.") Data networks do not approach this level of reliability. Corporations are understandably reluctant to accept reduced availability for telephone service, which is critical to business functioning—especially in light of possibly marginal cost savings.

Sound Quality

Another quality of service issue is that sending voice IP packets across a long series of routers creates two problems for sound quality. First, this process causes delay (latency).[15] Such delays cause serious problems with turn taking in conversations. When you think the other person has stopped talking, they may have started again. Not hearing this because of the lag, you begin talking. As soon as you do, you hear their voice and realize that you have interrupted. At the other extreme, you hesitate to talk when the other party stops for fear of interrupting them.

Another problem, mentioned in Chapter 5, is that adjacent packets do not arrive with exactly the same time difference they had when they started. This inexactness in timing causes voices to sound jittery, and it is called **jitter**.

Using a Single ISP

One way to reduce latency and jitter is to attach all sites to a single Internet Service Provider (ISP), as Figure 6-18 illustrates. The biggest delays in Internet transmission come at the connections between ISPs and backbone providers and in backbone provider networks. As transmission problems are reduced by avoiding connection points and backbone carriers, both latency and jitter usually decline to an acceptable level. For an additional fee, most ISPs even offer service level agreements (SLAs) that guarantee maximum latency and jitter.

TEST YOUR UNDERSTANDING

19. a) Why may expected cost savings from VoIP compared to traditional long-distance telephony not be realized? b) What service quality problems does VoIP face? c) How can these service quality problems be reduced?

---

[15]   On the Internet, latency often can be 500 milliseconds or even higher. That is a half-second delay.

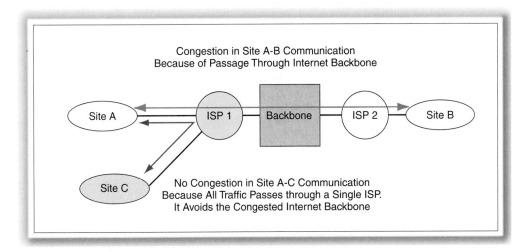

Figure 6-18 Using a Single ISP for VoIP

Perspective

Overall, convergence is an area that every firm has to explore today. However, the technology is still immature. Although some applications, notably PBX–PBX communication, can produce benefits today, much more work has to be done before businesses can evaluate converged voice–data networks with confidence.

GAINING PERSPECTIVE

THOUGHT QUESTIONS

1. a) Your city has 100 cells in one of its second-generation cellular telephone systems. As a rough rule of thumb, you can divide the number of cells by seven and get the average number of times you can reuse each channel throughout the system. In other words, if you have 21 cells, you can reuse each frequency about three times on average. There also is a 3:1 compression ratio for voice conversations relative to what a channel would be able to carry without compression. There are 2,500 channels in the frequency spectrum allotted for this service. On average, subscribers will only be using their cellphones 3% of the time, but call this 5% to be on the safe side. Consequently, each channel can support 20 subscribers and still give good service. How many subscribers can the system support? Show your work. Hint: The answer is about two million. b) Redo your calculation for a first-generation system with 20 cells. Your calculation should reflect other differences between first-generation and second-generation systems. Hint: this system can serve only about a tenth as many subscribers.

2. In Figure 6-12, you use Channel 47 in Cell A. List the other cells where you can use it. Pick the selection of cells to maximize channel reuse. How many times does this allow you to reuse the channel?

3. Trace, in order, the carriers a circuit will go through for a telephone call placed from a CLEC in a U.S. city to a telephone number in another country.

DESIGN QUESTION

1. For a building, design where the equipment room, vertical runs, telecommunications closets, and horizontal runs should go. Determine how many wall outlets you would need. Estimate lengths of UTP wire and optical fiber you would need for data transmission. Determine the number of switches you would need. Where would you place a router to connect your building to the outside world?

CASE STUDIES

Do the College of Business Administration wiring case study in Chapter 6a.

For case studies, go to the book's website, www.prenhall.com/panko, and look at the Case Studies page for this chapter.

PHOTOS

For photos, go to the book's website, www.prenhall.com/panko, and look at the Photos page for this chapter.

PROJECTS

1. **Getting Current.** Go to the book website's New Information and Errors pages for this chapter to get new information since this book went to press and to correct any errors in the text.

2. **Internet Exercises.** Go to the book website's Exercises page for this chapter and do the Internet Exercises.

CHAPTER 6a

CASE STUDY: REWIRING A COLLEGE BUILDING

INTRODUCTION

The College of Business Administration (CBA) building at the University of Hawaii has the shape of a "C." The farthest parts of the building are 230 meters apart. The building actually consists of several adjacent towers, which are labeled A, B, C, D, E, and G. The F tower had to be demolished a few years after the building was constructed[1] in the mid-1970s, changing the building from a circle to its current C shape. The towers range from three to six stories in height.

UTP Wiring
In the 1980s, the building was rewired for telecommunications using UTP. In every room there are two RJ-45 wall jacks. One is for telephone use, the other for data use. Unfortunately, the quality of the wiring is well below Cat5e. In fact, it has been characterized as "Cat3 on a good day." In addition, until recently, the university's central telephone services group managed all of this wiring and gave the college no control over data usage. This central control issue has disappeared in recent years, but the wiring quality problem remains.

Ethernet 10Base5 and 10Base2
To circumvent central control, the college created its own data network. Built before 10Base-T was created, the network has a central 10Base5 backbone whose thick and bright yellow coaxial trunk cable snakes through the

---
[1] Don't ask.

corridors of the building. At various points in the building, a repeater connects the 10Base5 trunk cable to 10Base2 daisy chains that run to college offices, broom closets (which are used as faculty offices), and classrooms. A router connects the CBA network to the campus network via optical fiber.

Congestion

The network's performance (shared 10 Mbps) was adequate when it was constructed in the mid-1980s and for several years after that. By the mid-1990s, however, the number of computers attached to the network had passed 200, and performance slowed to a crawl. LED collision lights on the repeaters glowed red all day long. Sometimes, the network would freeze up for several seconds at a time. It was time for a new network.

OPTION 1: STATE-OF-THE-ART REWIRING

One option is to do things right and rewire the entire building with modern technology. From the building's equipment room, optical fiber would run out to telecommunications closets in each tower. From there, Cat5e UTP would run to individual wall jacks. Users would receive dedicated (nonshared) 100 Mbps service to the desktop. The wiring would be sufficient if switches were upgraded later to provide gigabit speed to the desktop or at least to servers.

Optical Fiber Runs

This approach would be best, but it faces a number of obstacles. The most important is cost. Installing the optical fiber backbone alone would cost $200,000. This cost is somewhat unrepresentative because the building was built without false ceilings, duct spaces for wiring, or wiring closets. However, this cost would not be far lower if the building's designers had been smarter. The cost of the fiber itself would be a large part of the total in any case.

UTP Runs

From switches in each tower, Cat5e would run to individual offices and classrooms. The cost to install the UTP wiring was estimated at $1,000 per wall jack. This is typical for UTP building wiring. About 300 wall jacks will have to be installed.

Switches

The switches themselves would cost about $50,000.

Telecommunications Closets

To house the switches and fiber/UTP connections, telecommunications closets would have to be built. They would have to be built as cabinets attached to corridor walls because room was not created in the building design for them. The expensive part would be providing them with the electrical power they would need for the switches and other equipment they would contain. Creating the telecommunications closets would cost about $50,000.

Considerations

One consideration is that the CBA is seeking funds for a new building. Therefore, the CBA is reluctant to invest heavily in a built-from-scratch LAN.

OPTION 2: USING THE EXISTING UTP DATA WIRING

10 Mbps
Testing has shown that most of the building's UTP data wiring is capable of carrying data at 10 Mbps without excessive error rates. One option is to install Ethernet switches to give unshared 10 Mbps service to each wall jack via the existing data UTP lines.

Assessment
This would end the current congestion problem, which exists because 10Base5 and 10Base2 are shared 10 Mbps technologies. Runs to some offices, however, might not work. In addition, it would only bring 10 Mbps to each desktop.

Cost
The total cost would be around $150,000. A switch with many ports would have to be purchased, and considerable rewiring would be needed to connect existing UTP wire runs to the switch.

OPTION 3: RESEGMENTATION

A Single Collision Domain
The network's main problem is that it is a single large network with over 200 stations. In Ethernet terminology, it is a single **collision domain**. If any of the 200 stations is transmitting, all other stations will wait. In addition, because of the long distances involved, when one station starts to transmit, signals will not get to other stations for a while. These stations may begin transmitting in the meantime, causing a collision.

Resegmenting the Network
One option is to divide the entire network into four parts, called segments, each of which would have only 50 to 75 stations. This would only give rise to modest congestion.

To connect stations in different parts of the network, each of the four segments would be connected to a central switch via optical fiber. This switch would allow cross-traffic between the four segments. Even with cross-traffic, traffic should be low enough in each segment to allow reasonable service.

Again, users would only get 10 Mbps to the desktop. In addition, all stations in a segment would share this speed, so the throughput for individual stations would be much lower.

Resegmentation can be done for about $75,000 using optical fiber connections from a switch at a central point to a repeater in each of the four areas. The repeater would connect the segment to the switch. This cost would be small, in part because three of the optical runs from the central switch to a repeater would be short runs. The network staff would buy fiber pre-cut to the desired length and run the optical fiber through the building without bothering to hide it inside ducts or other enclosures.

TEST YOUR UNDERSTANDING
1. Why is the college's data network not adequate for its needs?
2. a) What would be the cost of a completely new network with Category 5 UTP and an optical fiber backbone? b) What would be the components of that cost? c) What

would be the capital investment per user? d) In what ways is complete rewiring the best option?

3. a) What would be the cost of using existing data UTP lines? b) What would be the components of that cost? c) What problems would this option create?

4. a) What would be the cost of a resegmentation? b) Would it reduce congestion to an acceptable level? c) What problems would this option create?

5. What about installing a wireless LAN? a) What costs would this reduce compared to the state-of-the-art wiring option? b) What additional costs would it create? c) What problems would this option create? d) What problems would you foresee in implementing it?

6. Put on your consultant's hat. Which option would you recommend and why? You can also offer another option.

CHAPTER 7

WIDE AREA NETWORKS (WANs)

Learning Objectives:

By the end of this chapter, you should be able to discuss:

- Differences between LANs and WANs, including the high cost of WANs per bit transmitted and consequently the dominance of low-speed transmission (56 kbps to a few megabits per second) in WAN service.
- The three purposes of WANs and the four basic WAN technologies.
- Telephone modem communication.
- Trunk line-based leased line networks using data-grade UTP and fiber; broadband digital subscriber lines (ADSL, HDSL, HDSL2, and SHDSL) using voice-grade copper; cable modem service; and satellite service using GEO, LEO, and MEO satellites.
- Public switched data networks (PSDNs), including how they minimize cost; X.25; Frame Relay; ATM; ISDN; Ethernet (for MANs); access devices; Frame Relay pricing.
- Virtual private networks (VPNs), including reasons for using VPNs, types of VPNs, PPTP and IPsec security, and latency control.

INTRODUCTION

Chapter 6 began to take us beyond the customer premises, to telephone services provided by carriers. This chapter looks at carrier services designed for data instead of voice.

WANs and the Telephone Network

Many of these wide area network (WAN) services are built on top of the telephone network's technology that we saw in the last chapter. Sometimes companies lease circuits from the telephone company to carry their internal data. In other cases, WAN carriers lease telephone circuits, add their own switching, and offer data networking services to user corporations.

Reasons to Build a WAN

There are three main reasons to build a WAN.

> ➤ The first is to link two or more sites within the same corporation.
> ➤ The second is to provide remote access to *individual* employees or customers.
> ➤ The third is to provide access to the Internet.

WAN Technologies

There are four basic ways to create WANs. This chapter looks at each of these technologies in turn.

> ➤ The first, which is only useful for low-speed remote access and Internet access, is to use an ordinary telephone line and a *telephone modem*.

Figure 7-1   Wide Area Networks (WANs)

The Telephone Network
    WAN technology often is based on telephone technology
WAN Purposes
    Link sites within the same corporation
    Provide remote access to individuals who are off-site
    Internet access
WAN Technologies
    Ordinary telephone line and modem (low-speed access only)
    Network of leased lines
    Public switched data network (PSDN)
    Send your data over the Internet securely, using Virtual Private Network (VPN) technology
Low Speeds
    High cost per bit transmitted compared to WANs
    Lower speeds (most commonly 56 kbps to a few megabits per second)

➤ The second, which is used mostly to link sites within a company, is to create a *network of leased lines.*

➤ The third, which is good for both internal site-to-site networking and customer access, is to use a *public switched data network (PSDN).*

➤ The fourth is to send your data over the Internet securely, using *virtual private network (VPN)* technology.

Low Speeds

LAN users are accustomed to 100 Mbps service to the desktop, or at least 10 Mbps service. In contrast, long-distance communication is much more expensive per bit transmitted, so companies content themselves with slower transmission speeds in WANs. Most WAN communication takes place between 56 kbps and a few megabits per second.

TEST YOUR UNDERSTANDING

1. a) How are telephony and wide area networking related? b) What are the three main reasons to use a WAN? c) What are the four technologies for WANs? d) What is the main speed range for WAN communication? Why?

TELEPHONE MODEM COMMUNICATION

The simplest way to transmit data over long distances is to use a computer with a telephone modem. Telephone modem communication is very slow and is limited to remote access for individuals and individual Internet access.

As Figure 7-2 illustrates, either both parties in the communication must have compatible telephone modems (Client A and Server A) or one of the parties must have a digital connection to the telephone network (Server B). The latter is the case for the two newest telephone modem standards, V.90 and V.92, which can deliver data at up to 56 kbps. If there is a digital connection, it is on the side of the ISP or a corporate server site.

TEST YOUR UNDERSTANDING

2. a) In telephone modem communication, does the home user use a modem? b) Does the ISP or a corporate site use a modem?

Modulation

The most important telephone modem standards are modulation standards. These standards set the maximum speed of communication because different modulation methods can produce different exchange speeds. In Chapter 3, we saw amplitude modulation. Modern modems use more complex forms of modulation.[1] However, such details are hidden from users and purchasers.

---

[1] They use two carrier waves, a sine wave and a cosine wave. The receiving modem can tell the two apart easily. Each carrier wave can have four or more possible amplitude levels. The two amplitude-modulated waves are independent, so having four possible amplitude levels for each gives 16 possible states, and having more possible amplitude levels for each gives more possible states. Having 16 states allows four bits to be sent per clock cycle, and having more states allows even more bits to be sent per clock cycle. This approach, called Quadrature Amplitude Modulation (QAM), also is used in many digital subscriber lines and cable modem systems. QAM is discussed in Module B.

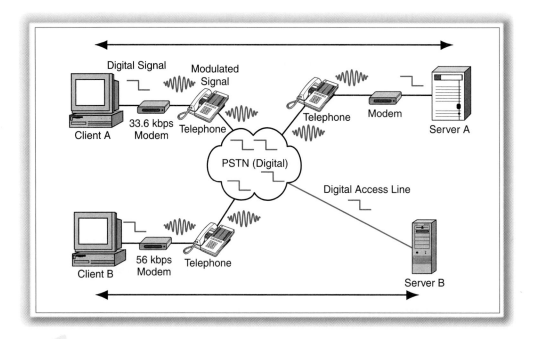

Figure 7-2   Telephone Modem Communication

Modulation Standards

V.34

The slowest telephone modems in wide use today are **V.34** telephone modems, which can send and receive at up to 33.6 kbps. If line conditions are not optimal, V.34 telephone modems will fall back to 28.8 kbps or even lower speeds. This falling back is present in all modems.

V.90

Like V.34 telephone modems, **V.90** telephone modems can send at 33.6 kbps. However, they can *receive* at a faster speed, up to 56 kbps. This type of **asymmetric** speed support, with higher **download** speeds than **upload** speeds, is useful for World Wide Web access. **Upstream** requests tend to be relatively small, so there is no need for high upstream speeds. In contrast, downstream transmissions may include large webpages and associated files, so fast downstream speeds are essential.

The party at the other end of the circuit, usually an ISP, must have special equipment and a digital connection to the Internet (see Figure 7-2) to support 56 kbps download speeds. Fortunately, almost all ISPs have this today. A bigger problem is that not all telephone lines can support high downstream speeds. In such cases, V.90 telephone modems slow down to V.34 (33.6 kbps) downstream speeds.

V.34
Send and receive at up to 33.6 kbps
Fall back in speed if line conditions are not optimal
V.90
Receive at up to 56 kbps
Send at up to 33.6 kbps
Other party must have a digital connection to the PSTN
V.92
Receive at up to 56 kbps
Send at up to 33.6 kbps or higher if the line permits
Other party must have a digital connection to the PSTN
Modem on hold
Cuts call setup time in half
Usually uses V.44 compression, which downloads webpages twice as fast as the old standard for compression, V.42 *bits.*

Figure 7-3   Telephone Modem Modulation Standards and Speeds

V.92
The newest telephone modem standard is **V.92**. On a very good telephone line, it can support upstream transmissions at up to 48 kbps. However, few telephone lines will support such speeds, but modest speed gains above 33.6 kbps may be possible. In addition, if you use V.92 capabilities to increase upstream speeds beyond 33.6 kbps, your downstream speeds will be less than 56 kbps. V.92 would be best for something like videoconferencing, in which you need more equal speeds in both directions.

As in the case of V.90 telephone modems, the other party, usually an ISP, must have special equipment and a digital connection to the Internet. V.92 is still new, so many ISPs do not support it yet.

One nice feature of V.92 is that it is very smart about call setup; V.92 cuts call setup time in half.

In addition, if you have an incoming voice call, V.92 telephone modems will allow you to answer your telephone and talk briefly without ending your telephone modem connection. However, ISPs set the time limit for such **modem on hold** calls, and they are likely to make it very brief.

Most V.92 modems come with new **V.44** compression, which allows webpages to be downloaded about twice as fast as with V.42 *bis* compression, which was the main standard before 2001.

TEST YOUR UNDERSTANDING

3. a) What is the fastest modulation standard that is symmetrical in sending and receiving speeds? b) What is fall back? c) What is the fastest modulation standard that does not require the other side to have a digital connection to the telephone system?

d) What are the speeds of V.90 modems? e) What are the speeds of V.92 modems? f) What is modem on hold? Which standard supports it? g) Which standard reduces call setup time? h) What is the advantage of the new V.44 data compression standard?

LEASED LINE NETWORKS

Telephone modem communication is good for light use, but it is far too slow for most corporate data communications.

Leased Lines

We saw in Chapter 6 that the public switched telephone network (PSTN) creates a circuit between two subscribers. Capacity on this circuit is dedicated (reserved) for the duration of a call. To the subscribers, it is as if they have a simple point-to-point pipe.

Dedicated Circuits

Leased lines also are circuits between two sites. However, unlike traditional telephone dial-up circuits, leased line circuits are permanent. The telephone company **provisions** them (sets them up), and they remain in operation for weeks, months, or even years. They are always on.

Reduced Cost for Intensive Point-to-Point Communication

Leased lines, which are also called private lines or dedicated lines, are good if you have a great deal of traffic between two points, say between two corporate sites or between your site and your ISP. They offer high transmission speeds, and telephone companies charge far less per bit transmitted for leased lines than for ordinary dial-up service—essentially giving a bulk discount to high-value customers.

TEST YOUR UNDERSTANDING

4. a) How are leased lines like dial-up telephone circuits? b) How are they different in terms of operation? c) How are they different in terms of speed and cost?

Trunk Line-Based Leased Lines

Operation

In the last chapter, we saw the technologies that telephone carriers use to build trunk lines between pairs of switches. As Figure 7-5 shows, carriers create end-to-end circuits with trunk line capacity running through the telephone network's trunk lines and switches to another site. For instance, a T1 leased line provides 1.544 Mbps of capacity between two customer premises. We use T1 lines in this example because it is the most common trunk line-based leased line.

Data-Grade Copper and Optical Fiber

To provide trunk line-based leased lines to the customer premises, the telephone company has to connect the customer premises to the telephone network's end office with optical fiber or at least (for T1 service) special **data-grade copper**, which normally uses two high-quality twisted pairs and so is called **4-wire service**. In contrast, the standard telephone local loop to residences and businesses is a single pair of inferior **voice-grade copper** wires.

Leased Lines (Private Lines or Dedicated Lines)

Point-to-point connection

Always on

Lower cost per minute than dial-up service

Must be provisioned

Trunk Line-Based Leased Lines

Based on trunk lines discussed in the previous chapter

Extend trunk line speeds to circuits between two customer premises

Require expensive data-grade copper or optical fiber

For data, clear circuits do not use multiplexing but present a single data pipe

Fractional T1 lines offer low-speed choices: 128, 256, 384, 512, and 768 kbps

Digital Subscriber Lines (DSLs)

Broadband speeds over voice-grade copper

Does not always work: distance limitations, etc.

Where it does work, much cheaper than trunk line-based leased lines

Asymmetric DSL (ADSL)

Asymmetric speed

Downstream (to customer): 256 kbps to over 1.5 Mbps

Upstream (from customer): 64 to 256 kbps

Simultaneous telephone and data service

DSL access multiplexer (DSLAM) at end telephone office

Speed not guaranteed

HDSL

Symmetric speed (768 kbps) over one voice-grade twisted pair

HDSL2: 1.544 symmetric speed over one voice-grade twisted pair

Needed in business (ADSL primarily for home and small business access)

Speed guaranteed

SHDSL

Super high rate DSL

Singe voice-grade twisted pair; longer distances than ADSL, HDSL

Symmetric speed

Variable speed ranging from 384 kbps to 2.3 Mbps

Speed guaranteed

Cable Modem

Delivered by cable television operator

High symmetric speed: up to 10 Mbps downstream, 64 kbps to 256 kbps upstream

Speed is shared by people currently downloading in a neighborhood

In practice, medium ADSL speed or higher

Figure 7-4   Leased Line Networks

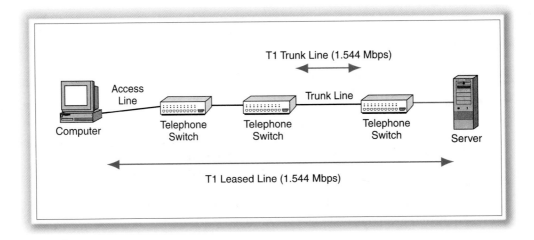

Figure 7-5 Trunk Line-Based Leased Line

Fractional T1 Leased Lines

As noted earlier, most demand for WAN service lies between 56 kbps and a few megabits per second. The gap between 56 kbps and 1.544 Mbps leased line speeds is fairly large, so many carriers offer **fractional T1** leased lines operating at 128 kbps, 256 kbps, 384 kbps, 512 kbps, or 768 kbps. These provide intermediate speeds at intermediate prices.

TEST YOUR UNDERSTANDING

5. a) What is the difference between trunk lines and trunk line-based leased lines? b) What is provisioning? c) If a trunk line-based leased line uses UTP, what type of UTP will it use? d) What are fractional T1 lines, and why are they desirable?

Digital Subscriber Lines (DSLs)

Broadband Transmission Over Voice-Grade Copper

In recent years, signal processing has matured to the point where we now can send high-speed (broadband) data over inferior-quality media. This has prompted carriers to offer broadband data services over the ordinary voice-grade wiring running to individual homes and businesses. To differentiate this use of ordinary voice-grade wire from normal analog telephone use, such lines are called **digital subscriber lines (DSLs)**.

ADSL

The term "digital subscriber line" embraces several different services. One is the **asymmetric digital subscriber line (ADSL)**, which offers high download speeds (256 kbps to over 1.5 Mbps) but limited upload speeds (typically 64 kbps to 256 kbps). This asymmetry is good for World Wide Web access and FTP downloading. For most other services, such as e-mail, upstream speeds are fast enough for interactivity.

As Figure 7-6 shows, ADSL puts a splitter at the end of the line. This allows an ADSL to carry voice as well as data. This eliminates the need for a separate telephone line.[2]

At the end office of the telephone company, there is a **DSL access multiplexer (DSLAM)**, which sends voice signals over the ordinary PSTN and sends data over a data network such as an ATM network.

HDSL

ADSL is fine for home Internet access, but heavy business use requires symmetric speeds and higher speeds. The most popular business DSL is the **high-rate digital subscriber line (HDSL)**. This standard allows symmetric transmission at 768 kbps (half of a T1's speed) in *both directions*. A newer version, **HDSL2**, transmits 1.544 Mbps in both directions using a single voice-grade twisted pair. Many of the "T1" lines now being installed are actually HDSL lines using two pairs of voice-grade UTP or HDSL2 lines using a single pair.

SHDSL

The next step in business DSL is likely to be **SHDSL (super high rate DSL)**, which can operate symmetrically over a single twisted pair and over a speed range of 384 kbps to 2.3 Mbps. In addition to offering a wide range of speeds and a higher top speed than HDSL2, SHDSL can operate over somewhat longer distances.

Figure 7-6   ADSL with Splitter

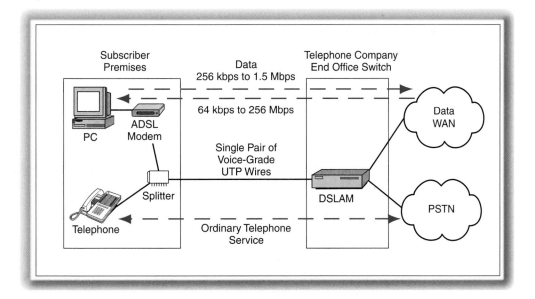

---

[2] You need a splitter in all of your telephone outlets.

Guarantees

Generally, there are no hard guarantees for ADSL speeds, which are aimed at the tolerant home market. However, speeds for HDSL, HDSL2, and SHDSL generally are guaranteed because they are sold to businesses, which require predictable service.

Limits

Although modern signal processing now allows us to send high-speed data over the ordinary voice-grade lines of the local loop, there are limits on what voice-grade lines can do. Many local loop lines will not support DSL service. The most common reason is that they are too far from the end office of the telephone company, but there are other limitations as well. Overall, DSLs are good where they can be used, but they cannot be used everywhere.

TEST YOUR UNDERSTANDING

6. a) How do trunk line-based leased lines and DSL lines vary in terms of transmission media? b) Describe ADSL speeds and technology. c) Does ADSL disable your telephone line when you are using the Internet? d) Describe HDSL and HDSL2 in terms of speed. e) Describe SHDSL in terms of speed. f) Can you always get a DSL to your premises? g) What is the biggest determining factor for whether you can? h) Which DSL services usually offer performance guarantees for speed?

Cable Modem Service

Cable Modems

Cable television operators, besides bringing television into homes, also offer high-speed Internet access, as Figure 7-7 indicates. From the cable television's headquarters building, called the head end, optical fiber runs out to a neighborhood with about 500 households. Within the neighborhood, a standard coaxial television cable comes into the subscriber's house. It plugs into a device called a **cable modem**. The cable modem usually has an RJ-45 port that you connect to your PC's NIC with Cat5e UTP. Some cable modems, however, have USB ports for connection to your PC's USB port.

High Shared Speed

Cable modem service normally provides downstream speeds of 10 Mbps. (Upstream speeds typically are 64 kbps to 256 kbps.) However, this capacity is shared among all devices in a user's neighborhood that happen to be sending or receiving at any given moment. This can reduce effective throughput, but cable modems still usually provide medium to high DSL speeds.[3]

TEST YOUR UNDERSTANDING

7. a) Which of the following is shared: cable modem service or DSL service? b) What are the implications of this sharing?

---

[3] The author usually gets at least 300 kbps and often gets much higher downstream speeds.

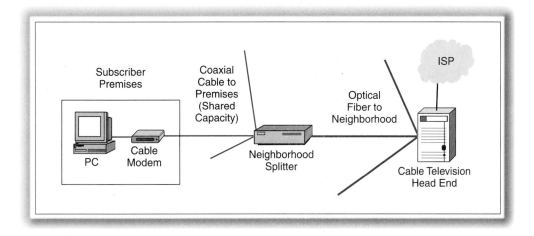

Figure 7-7   Cable Modem Service

Satellite Access

One way to use wireless transmission is to avoid **terrestrial** (earth-bound) communication entirely and communicate via satellite, as Figure 7-8 illustrates. Satellite users typically get 500 kbps in downstream speed and about 64 kbps in upstream speed. In other words, they get ADSL-like service.

Geosynchronous Earth Orbit (GEO) Satellites

Figure 7-8 specifically shows a **geosynchronous earth orbit (GEO)** satellite system. The satellite orbits at 36,000 km (22,300 miles) above the earth. At this height, its orbital time equals the earth's rotation, so the satellite appears fixed in the sky. This allows dish antennas to be aimed precisely.

However, 36,000 km is a long way for radio waves to travel. Even with a dish antenna, considerable power is required. In addition, mobile devices cannot use dish antennas.

Low Earth Orbit (LEO) and Medium Earth Orbit (MEO) Satellites

As Figure 7-9 shows, most communication satellites operate at much lower orbits. This means that they only are over a receiver a few minutes before passing below the horizon. Because of this, satellites must hand off service to one another. As one satellite passes over the horizon, another satellite will take over a customer's service. The user will not experience any service interruption. This is reminiscent of cellular telephony, except that here the customer remains relatively motionless while the satellite (the equivalent of a cellsite transceiver) moves. (A transceiver is a transmitter/receiver.)

Satellites for mobile users operate in two principle orbits. **Low earth orbit (LEO)** satellites operate at a few hundred kilometers (a few hundred miles) above the earth. **Medium earth orbit (MEO)** satellites, in turn, operate at a few thousand kilometers (a

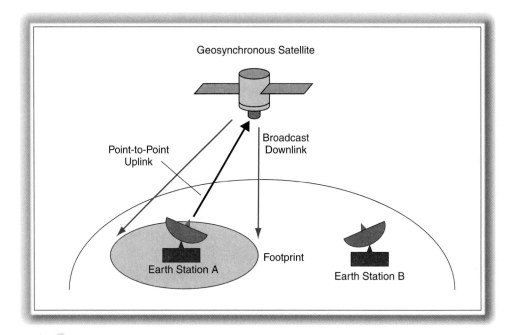

Figure 7-8   GEO Satellite System

Figure 7-9   LEO and MEO Satellite Systems

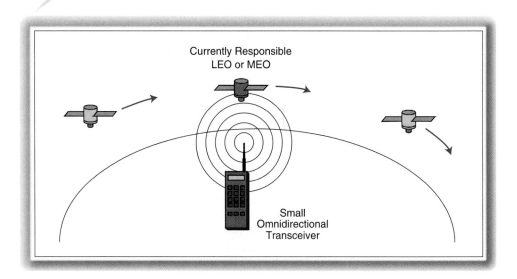

few thousand miles) above the earth. LEOs are closer, so signals do not attenuate as much, allowing receivers to be smaller and lighter. In contrast, MEOs have longer orbital periods, so they stay in sight longer, reducing the frequency of handoffs.

TEST YOUR UNDERSTANDING

8. a) What is a transceiver? b) Which of the following uses dish antennas: GEOs, LEOs, or MEOs? c) Which of the following is good for mobile stations: GEOs, LEOs, or MEOs? d) What are the heights of GEO, LEO, and MEO orbits?

PUBLIC SWITCHED DATA NETWORKS (PSDNS)

Leased Lines Versus PSDNs

Meshes of Leased Lines

Figure 7-10 compares using a mesh of leased lines to connect multiple corporate sites with using a **public switched data network (PSDN)** for this purpose. A traditional leased line creates a single point-to-point circuit between two subscriber sites. If the two sites are far away, this will be an expensive circuit because leased line prices depend heavily on distance. Each site, furthermore, will need several leased lines running to other sites. Some or most of these lines may have to span long distances between sites.

Leased Lines in PSDNs

In contrast, with a PSDN, each site only needs one leased line circuit to connect it to the PSDN. For a large number of sites, this brings a dramatic reduction in the number of leased lines needed, compared to meshes of leased lines.

In addition, these circuits usually only have to span a short distance and so are (relatively) inexpensive. Most PSDNs have many access points, called **points of presence (POPs)**. Leased lines only have to run from a site to the nearest POP.[4]

Any-to-Any Connectivity with PSDNs

Also, whereas leased line connections only connect two sites, after you connect to a PSDN using a leased line from your site, you can use the PSDN to connect that site to many other sites.

Reduced Management Costs with PSDNs

Figure 7-10 shows that a PSDN normally is drawn as a cloud. This signifies that the subscriber does not care about what goes on within the PSDN network. The PSDN handles all of the internal details. The subscriber merely has to format data at the data link layer to the PSDN vendor's specifications. As noted later in this chapter, an access device does physical and data link layer data formatting. This reduction in labor compared to a network of leased lines dramatically reduces management costs.

---

[4] In Chapter 5, we saw that the term point of presence (POP) also is used in telephony as a place where various LECs, IXCs, and ICCs interconnect.

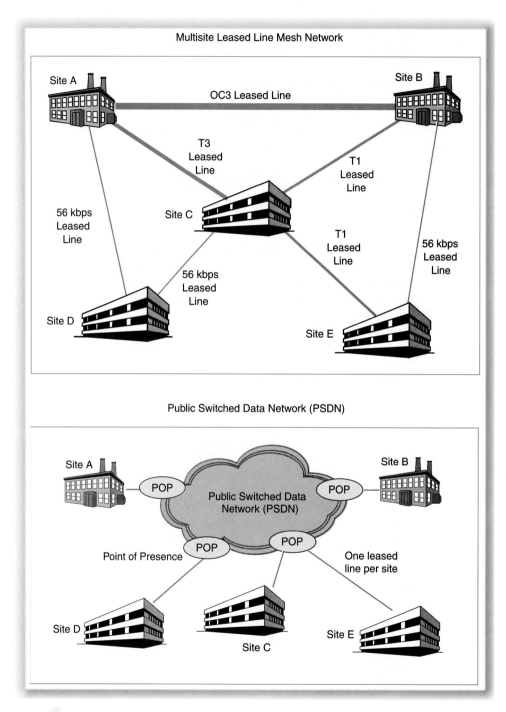

Figure 7-10   Leased Line Networks Versus Public Switched Data Networks

The PSDN Cost Advantage

For most corporations in most countries, PSDNs are less expensive for connecting multiple sites than leased line meshes. They greatly reduce labor costs because carriers do most of the work. In addition, competition among the multiple PSDN carriers that operate in most markets has created highly aggressive PSDN pricing.

The Market Situation

Although leased lines and PSDNs will both remain popular in the foreseeable future, PSDN use is growing rapidly, whereas the number of leased line installations is growing more slowly, and in many markets actually is falling. In new corporate networks, leased lines are used primarily to connect very large sites because leased line prices may still be competitive with PSDN prices for high-volume connections.

TEST YOUR UNDERSTANDING

9. a) Describe how corporate WANs use meshes of leased lines to create their WANs. b) Describe PSDN technology. c) Describe how PSDNs use leased lines. d) Do these two types of WANs use the same number of leased lines for a given number of sites? Explain. e) Do their leased lines have about the same average distance? Explain. f) How do PSDNs reduce labor costs?

Popular PSDN Services

If you decide that you will use a PSDN service, the next step is to decide which type of service you will use—X.25, Frame Relay, ATM, or ISDN. Figure 7-11 compares these services.

X.25

The first public switched data network was **X.25**. Created in the 1960s, X.25 is quite slow, usually operating at speeds of about 9,600 bps to about 64 kbps. This was sufficient for terminal–host communication, but it is inadequate for modern corporate networking. It is found today mostly in countries with primitive networking infrastructures because this old technology is very easy to implement today. It is also found in some places in Europe today; speeds there tend to be somewhat faster.

Like ATM, X.25 uses virtual circuits. (In fact, X.25 introduced virtual circuits.) Unlike ATM, X.25 is reliable, checking for errors during each hop between its internal switches. This was necessary in the 1960s when transmission errors were more common. However, reliable service requires extensive switch processing power, so X.25 is slow and expensive per bit sent.

Frame Relay

Today, the most widely used PSDN service is **Frame Relay**, which operates between 56 kbps and about 40 Mbps, with most communication taking place below 2 Mbps. As noted earlier, most corporate networking today takes place at 56 kbps to a few megabits per second. This close fit with corporate speed requirements and the low price of Frame Relay has made it the dominant PSDN service.

Cost Minimization: Unreliability, Virtual Circuits, and Multiplexing

The high cost of long-distance transmission requires Frame Relay to focus heavily on cost minimization.

Service	Typical Speeds	Circuit-or Packet-Switched (a)	Reliable or Unreliable (b)	Virtual Circuits? (b)	Relative Price
ISDN	Two 64 kbps B channels One 16 kbps D channel	Circuit	Unreliable	No	Moderate
X.25	9,600 bps to 64 kbps	Packet	Reliable	Yes	Moderate
Frame Relay	56 kbps to about 40 Mbps	Packet	Unreliable	Yes	Low
ATM	1 Mbps to about 156 Mbps	Packet	Unreliable	Yes	High
Ethernet	10 Gbps and 40 Gbps	Packet	Unreliable	No	Probably Low

(a) Packet switching allows multiplexing, which reduces transmission line costs for bursty data.

(b) Unreliability eliminates error-checking work on switches. Virtual circuits restrict transmission to a single possible path, reducing switching work. Both reduce the work that switches must do and therefore the cost of switches, which are the most expensive components in PSDNs.

Figure 7-11   Popular PSDN Services

➤ Frame Relay uses virtual circuits. As discussed in Chapter 5, virtual circuits reduce costs by limiting communication to a single path. This simplifies switching decisions and therefore *switching costs.*

➤ Frame Relay is an unreliable service, meaning that it does not check for errors at each hop between internal PSDN switches. This reduces *switching costs* by eliminating the high processing load of error checking at each switch.

➤ Finally, Frame Relay uses packet switching, which reduces *trunk line costs* by sharing trunk line capacity.

ATM

For higher speeds, there is **ATM**, which stands for asynchronous transfer mode.[5] We saw ATM before in the context of LANs, but it has been more successful as a WAN service.

Speeds   Like Frame Relay, ATM uses virtual circuits, unreliable service, and multiplexing to reduce costs. Unlike Frame Relay, however, ATM is designed to operate at

---

[5]   Don't ask. It's really complicated, and learning why they call it asynchronous transfer mode won't enlighten you much.

very high speeds: 156 kbps, 622 Mbps, 2.5 Gbps, 10 Gbps, and 40 Gbps. Commercial ATM WAN services also offer lower speeds, beginning at about 1 Mbps.

A Growth Path from Frame Relay   For companies that need more speed than Frame Relay can provide, ATM is the obvious option. As demand for higher speeds increases, ATM revenues should exceed those of Frame Relay.

Unfortunately, ATM is a complex and expensive technology to purchase and manage. However, some of this complexity exists because ATM was created by the ITU-T specifically as an eventual replacement for today's worldwide telephone network. This will make it very useful in the future as WANs continue to grow in size.

Not a Competitor for Frame Relay   Frame Relay and ATM are not really competitors. Most carriers offer both. To their customers with modest needs for speed, they offer Frame Relay. To customers with greater transmission needs, they offer ATM. Some carriers even offer ATM–Frame Relay translation services so a customer's site with low speed requirements can use Frame Relay and a customer's site connections that require high speeds can use ATM.

ISDN

2B + D   As Figure 7-12 shows, **Integrated Services Digital Network (ISDN)** service was designed to bring two 64 kbps **B channels** into the home—one for voice, the other

Figure 7-12   Integrated Services Digital Network (ISDN)

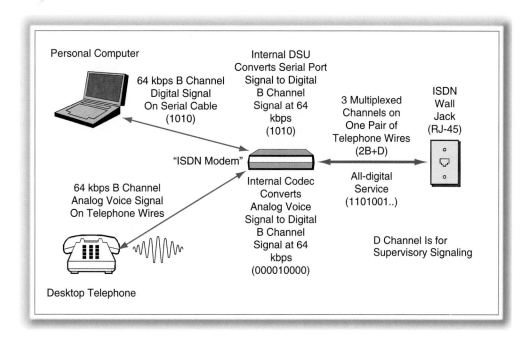

for data. The single pair of wires coming into the home also multiplexes a 16 kbps D channel for supervisory control signals. In practice, however, it is common to **bond** the two B channels into a single symmetric 128 kbps channel.

However, even 128 kbps is slow by modern broadband standards, and ISDN is also more expensive than ADSL and cable modem service for heavy Internet access. ISDN has a reasonable installed base of users, but it is not flourishing.

Good Backup Service   However, one characteristic of ISDN continues to make it popular in a niche market. X.25, Frame Relay, and ATM are **always-on** services that are available all the time. In contrast, ISDN is a **dial-up** service, like the ordinary telephone network. You pay a modest monthly fee, but the real cost is the transmission cost when you use it. Consequently, ISDN tends to be used most heavily as a backup service. For instance, a bank's branches may communicate with headquarters using Frame Relay, but if the Frame Relay connection fails, they can activate the ISDN connection.

Ethernet

We saw in Chapter 4 that Ethernet was created for local area networking. However, 10 Gbps Ethernet is being created primarily for longer-distance communication. Some versions of 10 Gbps Ethernet can have links as long as 40 km.

In Chapter 1, we saw that a metropolitan area network (MAN) is a special case of wide area networking. Operating at shorter distances than national or international WANs, MANs offer correspondingly higher transmission speeds and lower transmission costs.

Before 10 Gbps Ethernet, it was widely assumed that ATM operating over SONET would be the basis for metropolitan area networking. However, 10 Gbps Ethernet is likely to be a serious MAN competitor because of its relative simplicity and therefore its lower price. In addition, a 40 Gbps version of Ethernet for MANs is also under development.

TEST YOUR UNDERSTANDING

10. a) What is the speed range of X.25? b) Is it reliable or unreliable? c) Where is it likely to be available?

11. a) What is the most widely used PSDN technology? b) What is its speed range? c) Why is it the most widely used PSDN technology?

12. a) What is the speed range of ATM? b) Why is ATM usage likely to grow in the future? c) Are Frame Relay and ATM competitors? Explain.

13. How does Frame Relay, like most other PSDNs, reduce costs? Be sure to specify which element of the network costs less as a result of each action.

14. a) What is the highest speed you can have to and from an ISP using ISDN? b) Is ISDN an always-on service? c) How is it likely to be used in corporations? Why?

15. a) Explain why Ethernet is attractive for WANs. b) For what type of WAN is Ethernet likely to be attractive?

Access Devices

As Figure 7-13 illustrates, usually there is only one connection from each corporate site to the outside world. There, **access devices** connect the internal network to a leased line.

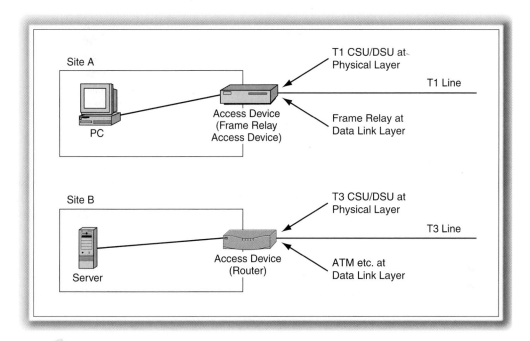

Figure 7-13 Access Devices

Data Link Layer

At the data link layer, access devices implement the data link layer protocol required by the PSDN standard if a PSDN is used. This usually is Frame Relay or ATM, although Ethernet is beginning to be used at the data link layer.

Physical Layer

At the physical layer, the connection uses a leased line whether a PSDN is being used or the company is using a mesh of leased lines. At the physical layer, access devices need a **CSU/DSU**. As its name suggests, this device has two functions: channel service and data service.

Its **channel service unit (CSU)** component is there to protect the telephone network from improper voltages and signals that a subscriber might accidentally transmit.

The **data service unit (DSU)**, in turn, formats physical layer signal to travel over the leased line. Each leased line requires a particular signal format, and some offer several options. In carrier networks, the carrier determines what formatting options will be used, so the DSU must be compatible with the telephone company's standards.

Dedicated Access Devices and Routers

Some access devices are dedicated access devices operating at the physical and data link layers. For example, you might use a dedicated Frame Relay access device (FRAD) to connect your site to a Frame Relay service. Often, however, routers are used as access devices. They have one port connected to an internal network switch—probably an Ethernet switch—and one port connected to the external network. The output port to the PSDN will function as an access device.

TEST YOUR UNDERSTANDING

16. a) What is the purpose of an access device? b) At the physical layer, what is a DSU? c) A CSU? d) What type of broad-purpose networking device often is used as an access device?

Frame Relay Pricing

Purchasing a PSDN is complex because there are several pricing elements and because different vendors emphasize different elements in their pricing. In this section, we will look at Frame Relay pricing because it is the most popular PSDN. Figure 7-14 shows the main elements in Frame Relay pricing for most vendors.

Access Device

If you use a Frame Relay network, you will have several costs. The first is the cost of your access device. You may purchase your access device from a vendor other than the

Figure 7-14 Pricing Elements in Frame Relay Service

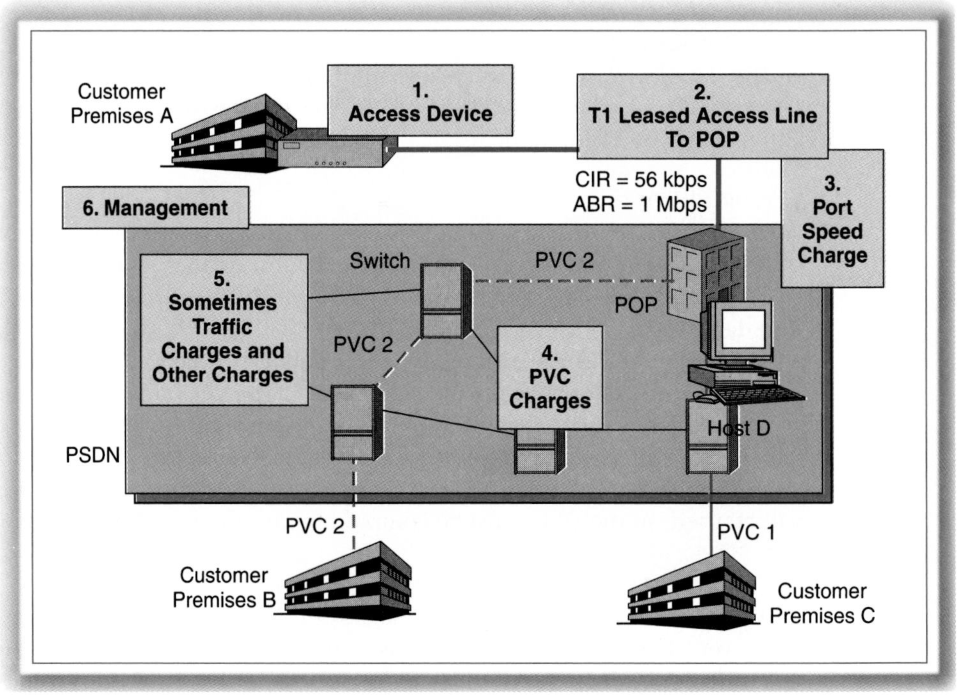

PSDN carrier, or you may lease it from the PSDN. Your **edge router** (the router that connects your site to the outside world) may be your access device, as noted earlier.

Leased Access Line Charge

Second, you need a leased access line to the POP. This line's monthly charge will depend on both speed and distance. Generally, you get your leased line from a local telephone carrier instead of from the Frame Relay carrier, although some Frame Relay carriers will handle the lease for you in bundled pricing. In general, it is important to know what the Frame Relay network's prices cover and do not cover.

Port Charge

At the POP, the subscriber connects to a port in the Frame Relay network's edge switch. Ports come in different speeds, such as 56 kbps, 1 Mbps, or faster. You must get a port whose speed matches your needs. Determining the port speed you need is very important because the **port charge**, which depends heavily on the speed of the port, usually is the largest element in the price you will pay for your Frame Relay network.

Permanent Virtual Circuit (PVC) Charges

We saw in Chapter 5 that ATM creates paths called virtual circuits between two stations. In fact, most PSDNs create virtual circuits between sites. Usually, these are **permanent virtual circuits (PVCs)**, which are set up for weeks or months at a time instead

Figure 7-15   Frame Relay Pricing Details

Frame Relay Access Device (FRAD) or Router
Leased Access Line Charge to the POP
Port Charge
   The largest part of the price
Permanent Virtual Circuit (PVC) Charges
Determining Site Requirements
   Determine traffic demand to each other site
   You need a PVC of the required speed to each other site
   Sum the speed of the PVCs from a site
   You need a port speed for that site equal to at least 70% of that total
   You need a leased line for that site at least as fast as that port speed
Other Charges
   Flat rate versus traffic volume charges
   Installation charges
   Managed service charges
   Service level agreement (SLA) charges
Geographical Scope

of on a call-by-call basis. Most PSDNs charge you a certain amount of money for each PVC you use, and this charge usually depends on the speed of the PVC. Aggregate PVC charges usually rank second to port charges in Frame Relay prices. In Frame Relay, virtual circuit numbers are called **data link connection identifier (DLCIs)**, usually pronounced "dullsees."

Determining Your Speed Requirements

Determining a Site's PVC Needs   Given the importance of pricing, how do you determine your needs? You begin by looking at each site individually. You first ask what connection speeds that site needs to other sites. You usually find that you need PVCs to each of several other sites. These PVCs must be fast enough to serve those needs. For instance, suppose that you determine, based on traffic patterns, that you need five 56 kbps PVCs from a site, one to each of five other sites.

Determining a Site's Port Speed Requirement   Next, you determine the port speed requirement for the site. The port speed must be fast enough to handle your PVCs. If you have five 56 kbps PVCs running from one site to other sites, this would suggest that you would need a port speed of at least 280 kbps to serve all the PVCs.

However, not all of these PVCs will be carrying data simultaneously. A common rule of thumb—that must of course be modified by actual traffic patterns in real firms—is that 70 percent of aggregate PVC capacity is sufficient for a site's port speed. So instead of needing 280 kbps of capacity in our port, we would only need 70 percent of this amount, or 199.5 kbps. A 256 kbps port speed would be sufficient if it is available. If that port speed is not available, you would have to move up to the next-higher port speed.

Determining a Site's Leased Line Speed Requirement   Your last design task is to determine your leased line speed requirement for the site. Port charges are higher than leased line charges, so you need a leased line at least as fast or faster than your port speed. For example, if your port speed is 1 Mbps, you would need a T1 line operating at 1.544 Mbps.

Other Charges

Flat Rate Versus Traffic Volume Pricing   Most Frame Relay networks use **flat rate pricing**, meaning that you pay a predetermined amount per month. The amount will depend heavily on port and PVC speeds.

In some cases, there will be two speeds. For instance, many Frame Relay vendors offer a **committed information rate (CIR)**, which is pretty much guaranteed. The other is a faster **available bit rate (ABR)**, which allows you to send bursts of limited duration at a higher rate. For instance, you might have a CIR of 56 kbps and an ABR of 1 Mbps. It is important for port and leased line speeds to support ABRs because if they are set on the basis of CIRs, there will be no additional capacity to send bursts at the higher ABR speed.

Some Frame Relay networks also have a traffic volume charge based on how much traffic you transmit. However, this is less common than flat rate pricing and usually occurs as a way to modify flat rate pricing instead of replacing it.

Installation Charges   You will also face installation charges from your telephone company for the leased access line and from your PSDN for the initial setup and for each PVC you create. PVC deletions are also charged.

Managed Service Charges   Some PSDN vendors offer **managed services**, in which they will actually manage your entire network, including your access lines and access devices. They charge extra for the service.

Service Level Agreements (SLAs) Charges   Most Frame Relay vendors offer service level agreements (SLAs) that guarantee maximum latency, minimum reliability, minimum throughput, and other service parameters. Companies must pay more for such guarantees.

Geographical Scope
When comparing the prices of Frame Relay services, you must only compare services of comparable geographical scope. Naturally, Frame Relay services that only serve a single MAN are much less expensive than nationwide or worldwide services.

Overall Pricing
Although Frame Relay pricing has many elements, overall, connecting several sites with a Frame Relay network usually is substantially cheaper than connecting them with a mesh of leased lines. Frame Relay networks and other PSDNs multiplex traffic efficiently on the trunk lines between their internal switches, dramatically reducing long-distance costs compared to leased-line transmission, which uses reserved capacity.

TEST YOUR UNDERSTANDING

17. a) What are the main elements in Frame Relay pricing? b) What usually is the largest component of Frame Relay pricing? c) What usually is the second largest component of PSDN carrier pricing? d) To what company do you usually pay leased line charges? e) What is managed Frame Relay? f) Distinguish between CIRs and ABRs. g) Is there generally a charge for an SLA? h) What is a DLCI? i) From a site, you need one PVC of 256 kbps, one of 128 kbps, and four of 56 kbps. What port speed would you select if your choices were 56 kbps, 128 kbps, 384 kbps, and 1 Mbps? Explain. j) In another situation, you have a port speed of 200 kbps; what leased line would you select if your choices were 56 kbps, 128 kbps, 500 kbps, and 1 Mbps? Explain.

VIRTUAL PRIVATE NETWORKS (VPNS)

PSDN Lack of Connectivity
The main problems with PSDNs are that there are many of them and that they generally are not interconnected. This is not too much of a problem for connecting sites within a single company, but it is a serious problem for connecting different firms, which are likely to use different PSDNs.

Advantages of Using the Internet for Internal and Customer Communication

Reaching Everywhere

However, almost all sites of most corporations today are linked to the Internet. Virtual private networks (VPNs) use the Internet to link sites together—both sites of the same firm and sites of different firms. Unfortunately, the Internet has little security, so VPNs must add security to Internet transmissions. As Figure 7-17 illustrates, a **virtual private network (VPN)**, then, is transmission over the Internet with added security.[6]

Low Transmission Cost

One advantage of the Internet, besides universal connectivity, is low cost. Transmission over the Internet tends to be much less expensive than transmission over PSDNs.

Latency Control

One problem with the Internet is latency. As we saw in the previous chapter, firms can control latency by having all users attach to a single ISP that offers a service level agreement (SLA) that guarantees low latency (plus reliability, throughput, and other service parameters.) Of course, this approach is only useful for site-to-site service and remote access service within single firms. Customers and suppliers are likely to be using different ISPs than the company is using.

Security

There are several ways to add security to Internet transmission, allowing VPNs to be a viable solution.

TEST YOUR UNDERSTANDING

18. a) What is a VPN? b) Why are VPNs attractive? c) What problems do they face? d) How can latency be controlled for intranets?

Remote Access VPNs

Figure 7-17 shows that there are three basic forms of VPN: site-to-site networks, remote access service, and extranets. We will look at each in turn.

Remote Access

Given the high cost of remote access for employees dialing into a remote access server from distant cities, the most popular use of VPNs to date has been remote access by users.

Also, long-distance telephone calling is limited to telephone modem speeds. Many telecommuters have high-speed DSL and cable modem connections at home. VPNs allow remote access at broadband speeds.

TEST YOUR UNDERSTANDING

19. a) What is a remote access VPN? b) Why is it attractive?

---

[6] Some say that the use of a PSTN with added security is also an example of a virtual private network.

Virtual Private Network (VPN)
　Transmission over the Internet with added security
Why VPNs
　PSDNs are not interconnected
　Internet reaches almost all sites
　Low transmission cost
VPN Problems
　Latency
　Security
Remote Access VPNs
　User dials into a remote access server (RAS)
　　RAS often checks with RADIUS server for user identification information
Point-to-Point Tunneling Protocol (PPTP)
　Built into all versions of Windows since Windows 95
　　No need for added software
　Provided by many ISPs
　PPTP access concentrator at ISP access point
　Secure tunnel between access concentrator and RAS at corporate site
　Some security limitations
　　No security between user site and ISP access point
　　No message-by-message identification of user
Site-to-Site VPNs and Extranets
　Site-to-site networks link sites within a single company
　　Often part of an intranet—use of TCP/IP transmission and applications internally
　　TCP/IP transmission is low in cost
　　TCP/IP applications are good, standardized, and inexpensive
　Extranet: communication with customers and suppliers with security over the Internet
IP Security (IPsec)
　At internet layer, so protects information at higher layer
　Tunnel mode: sets up a secure tunnel between IPsec servers at two sites
　　No security within sites
　Security associations
　　Agreement on how security options will be implemented
　　Governed by corporate policies

Figure 7-16　Virtual Private Network (VPN)

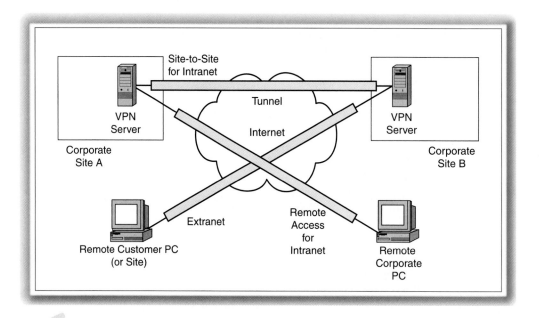

Figure 7-17 Virtual Private Network

Point-to-Point Tunneling Protocol (PPTP)

Built into Windows

The dominant VPN standard for remote access is the **Point-to-Point Tunneling Protocol (PPTP)**. This protocol is popular because it works quite well and has been included in every client and server version of Windows since Windows 95. Therefore, there is no need to add software to the many remote client PCs a firm may have to serve.

ISP Implementation

Another reason why PPTP is popular is that many ISPs implement it, freeing corporations from a great deal of work. Figure 7-18 shows that the remote user dials into the ISP's nearest access point as if there were no VPN in place. The ISP connects them automatically to a **PPTP access concentrator** at the client's ISP access point.

    The ISP creates a secure PPTP connection between the PPTP access concentrator and the **PPTP remote access server** at the corporate site. This connection is called a **tunnel** because it is a secure connection in the middle of the nonsecure Internet—as if the data were traveling through a secure pipe in a turbulent ocean.

RADIUS

Figure 7-18 shows that many companies have a RADIUS server that stores information to identify users, such as passwords. PPTP remote access servers often check with the central RADIUS server when deciding whether to accept a user's connection. RADIUS is not part of PPTP, but it is widely used whenever there are remote access servers.

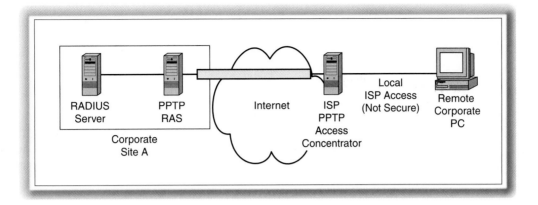

Figure 7-18   ISP-Based PPTP Remote Access VPN

This means that wherever a user comes into the network, the RAS will check with the RADIUS server and will base the accept/reject decision on the account's profile stored on the RADIUS server. A hacker cannot simply try different RASs until he or she finds one with incorrect information, as a hacker could before RADIUS, when each RAS kept its own profiles. The difficulty of keeping many RASs synchronized before RADIUS often meant that some RASs would almost inevitably be misconfigured and therefore easy to get through.

Security Limitations

PPTP is something of an interim standard because it lacks message-by-message authentication, potentially allowing an adversary to insert a message into the message stream. However, this is difficult to exploit.

Another threat is that the connection between the user and the ISP's access point usually is not secure. Again, this security weakness is difficult to exploit.

TEST YOUR UNDERSTANDING

20.   a) What is PPTP? b) Where is it likely to be used? c) Can ISPs provide the PPTP access concentrator? d) Describe the components of a PPTP system that uses a RADIUS server. e) What is a tunnel? f) Why is PPTP attractive? (Give two reasons.) g) Describe PPTP's two security limitations. h) Why do remote access servers usually check with RADIUS servers before accepting a user connection?

Site-to-Site Networking and Intranets

A growing use of VPNs is site-to-site networking. Given the large volume of data that companies typically send between sites, site-to-site (also called LAN-to-LAN) transmission will soon be the most important corporate use of VPNs.

However, site-to-site transmission is already efficient thanks to the use of leased lines and PSDNs. The cost savings per bit transmitted for site-to-site VPN transmission are not as dramatic as those from remote access transmission. However, the high volume of site-to-site traffic can still produce substantial cost savings.

TEST YOUR UNDERSTANDING

21. Why are site-to-site VPNs likely to become the most important corporate use for VPNs?

IPsec

Internet Layer Security

For site-to-site networking, the dominant security standard is **IP Security (IPsec).** As its name suggests, IPsec is an internet layer security standard. It protects everything contained in secured packets, including TCP segments, UDP segments, and application messages.

Tunnel Mode

Normally, IPsec operates in **tunnel mode**, in which packets are only secured between the IPsec servers at the two sites. Figure 7-19 illustrates IPsec's tunnel mode. This mode is suitable if internal security at the sites is not a serious issue or is handled outside of ISP tunnel mode operation.[7]

The computers within each site are unaware that the security tunnel even exists. The IPsec servers handle everything. They intercept messages, tunnel them, and then pass them on to the intended receiver. Clients do not require special software.

Figure 7-19   IPsec in Tunnel Mode

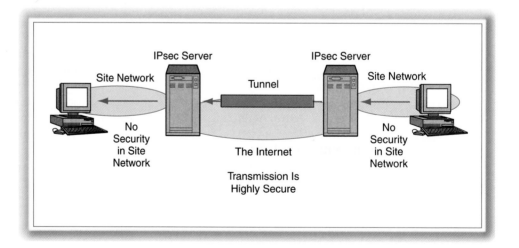

---

[7]   IPsec also offers a transport mode that offers full host-to-host security. However, transport mode requires that the client and server know how to implement IPsec transport mode. Windows 2000 introduced IPsec to the Windows line of operating system. Earlier clients need to have IPsec software installed.

Some companies implement transport mode IPsec from host to host but also add IPsec tunnel mode operation to carry the traffic across the Internet because tunnel mode offers some security that transport mode does not.

Security Associations

One major advantage of IPsec is that companies can set up detailed security policies that IPsec will obey. Before two devices communicate using IPsec, they set up **security associations**, which are agreements governing how security will be established and maintained. Figure 7-20 illustrates security associations in IPsec. Only security associations permitted by corporate policies will be permitted. It is even possible to have different security associations in the two directions if policy dictates this. Security associations are only one example of the high sophistication of IPsec.

TEST YOUR UNDERSTANDING

22.   a) At what layer does IPsec operate? b) Describe IPsec tunnel mode. c) What is the main advantage of tunnel mode? d) What is the main limitation of tunnel mode? e) What is a security association? f) What is the relationship between security policies and security associations?

GAINING PERSPECTIVE

Market Perspective

General

WANS are more expensive than LANs per bit transmitted. One reason for this is the high cost of installing fiber cabling over long distances. Alan Bezoza of CIBA World Markets, estimates that laying fiber can cost carriers $300,000 to $700,000 per mile and

Figure 7-20   Policy-Based Security Associations in IPsec

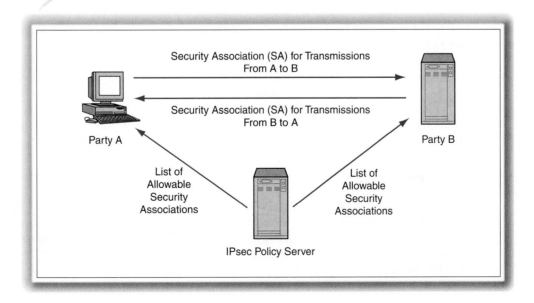

that 70% of these costs are for labor, which is rising in cost instead of falling. (Mary Jander and Marguerite Reardon, "Today's Focus: PONS Turn to Ethernet," Network World Fusion on Optical Networking, January 1, 2001. e-newsletter.)

Another reason why WAN service is expensive is that it is a carrier business that has many costs beyond the installation and maintenance of switches and transmission lines. Here is the breakdown of spending by WorldCom—a U.S. long-distance telephone and data carrier. (Ellen Messmer, *Network World,* May 19, 2000.)

    49% Marketing
    34% Access charges paid to local telephone companies
     6% Switching and transmission
    11% Operational support (labor)

Yes, that's right. The technical switching and transmission component is only 6%. Of course, some of the access charges paid to local telephone companies pay for switching and transmission by the local telephone company, but local telcos too spend much of their money on labor and marketing.

In 2001, the number of telecommuters in the United States was projected to grow to 32 million, and nearly 70% would have Internet access, according to the Cahners In-Stat Group (February 28, 2001). This figure included both full-time and part-time telecommuters. Cahners also estimated that the number of remote offices (which may hold multiple workers) exceeded 2 million in 2000 (February 13, 2001). Forty-five percent of these remote offices were remote branch offices of large corporations.

Although optical fiber is exciting, UTP local loops are dominant. Today, in the United States, copper wire lines serve approximately 200 million subscriber premises. Only about 40,000 are served by optical fiber (only 0.02% of the total). (Tom Spring, "Broadband: Beyond DSL and Cable," CNN.com/Sci-Tech, August 7, 2001.)

Residential Internet Access

The Federal Communications Commission reported on August 9, 2001, that 3.6 million U.S. homes and businesses had cable modem access, 2 million had DSL access, and 112,000 had wireless access.

IDC forecasts that among home office Internet access connections in 2004, 55% will still use dial-up access, 23% will use DSL, 15% will use cable modem service, 5% will use T1 lines or wireless access, and 1.6% will use ISDN.

What does Internet access cost? Here are average 3-year costs: T1 access $25,500; wireless $5,800; two-way satellite $2,700; DSL/ADSL $2,000; cable modem $1,700; ISDN $1,200; and telephone modem access $770. (Steve Janss, "Shopping for Speed," *Network World,* April 16, 2001.)

Leased Lines

Although carriers use SONET/SDH widely for their backbones, corporations still use mainly slower links, especially the workhorse T1/E1 line. Probe Research forecasts that by the end of 2001 there will be 298 million T1/E1 connections worldwide. In contrast, there will be only 2.8 million T3/E3 lines and a mere 300,000 156 Mbps SONET/SDH lines. (Terry Sweeney, "What Bandwidth Boom?" *Internet Week,* September 11, 2001, www.internetweek.com/indepth01/indepth091101.htm.)

Public Switched Data Networks
For national SONET/SDH service at 155 Mbps, a typical price was $65,000 to $75,000 per month in May 2001.[8]

Virtual Private Networks (VPNs)
Here is the VPNet Technologies Inc. estimate for how VPNs are and will be used in the future. Note that remote access VPNs dominated initially but that site-to-site virtual private networking will dominate in the future. Hosted VPNs are provided by a server hosting company which manages servers for organizations who do not wish to do so themselves. All figures are in millions of dollars.

VPN TYPE	1999	2001	2003
Remote access	$1,352	$5,138	$9,523
Site-to-Site	$624	$4,496	$15,773
Hosted	$104	$1,071	$4,464

THOUGHT QUESTIONS

1. a) If a new PSDN were defined, do you think it would it be packet switched or circuit switched? Justify your answer. b) Would it be reliable or unreliable? Justify your answer. c) Would it offer alternative routes or constrain transmissions to virtual circuits? Justify your answer.
2. Which is better—a DSL line or cable modem service? Justify your answer.
3. Several Internet access systems are asymmetric, with higher downstream speeds than upstream speeds. a) Is this good for webservice? b) Does it matter for e-mail? c) Is it good for a server? d) Is it good for videoconferencing?
4. a) At what layer does IPsec operate? b) Therefore, at what layers does it protect messages?

TROUBLESHOOTING QUESTIONS

1. You and your friend both have V.90 modems. You dial up your friend and transfer a large file. You expect to be able to transfer files at 56 kbps, but you average a transfer rate of only about 30 kbps. Explain why.
2. You purchase 256 kbps ADSL service. Your download speed typically is only about half this rate. What may be happening?

DESIGN QUESTION

1. A company has four sites. Its headquarters is in San Francisco. It has branch offices in Seattle, Los Angeles, and Northridge, California. Each branch site needs to communicate with each other branch site at 40 kbps. The headquarters

---

8   Pappalardo, Denise, "Broadwing to Break Out Gig Ethernet Services," Network World Fusion, May 7, 2001, www.nwfusion.com/news/2001/0507broadwing.htm.

needs to communicate with its branches at 256 kbps. You will use Frame Relay to connect them. a) What PVCs will you need from the headquarters site? b) From each branch office site? c) What port speeds will you need for the various sites? (Choices are 56 kbps, 128 kbps, 256 kbps, 1 Mbps, and 4 Mbps.) d) How many leased lines will you need? e) How fast do these leased lines have to be for various sites? (Choices are 56 kbps, 128 kbps, 256 kbps, 384 kbps, 512 kbps, 768 kbps, T1, and T3.) *Hint:* Draw a picture of the sites and their PVCs.

CASE STUDIES

Do the First Bank of Paradise case study in Chapter 7a.

For case studies, go to the book's website, www.prenhall.com/panko, and look at the Case Studies page for this chapter.

PHOTOS

For photos, go to the book's website, www.prenhall.com/panko, and look at the Photos page for this chapter.

PROJECTS

1. **Getting Current.** Go to the book website's New Information and Errors pages for this chapter to get new information since this book went to press and to correct any errors in the text.
2. **Internet Exercises.** Go to the book website's Exercises page for this chapter and do the Internet Exercises.

CHAPTER 7a

CASE STUDY: FIRST BANK OF PARADISE'S WIDE AREA NETWORKS

INTRODUCTION

The First Bank of Paradise (FBP)[1] operates primarily within the state of Hawaii, although it has one branch office on Da Kine Island in the South Pacific. FBP has 27 branch offices around the state.

ORGANIZATIONAL UNITS

Major Facilities

Figure 7a-1 shows that FBP has three major facilities, all located on the island of Oahu.

➤ **Headquarters** is a downtown office building that houses the administrative staff.

➤ **Operations** is a building in an industrial area that houses the bank's mainframe operations and other back-office technical functions. It also has most of the bank's IT staff, including its networking staff.

➤ **Second** is a back-up facility. If Operations fails, Second can take over within minutes. Second is located in an otherwise agricultural area.

Branches

Although branches are small buildings, they are technologically complex, primarily because the devices there use diverse network protocols. The automated teller machine at a branch uses SNA protocols to talk with the

---

[1]   This case actually is based on details from several Hawaii-based banks fitting this broad description. Hence the non-existent name.

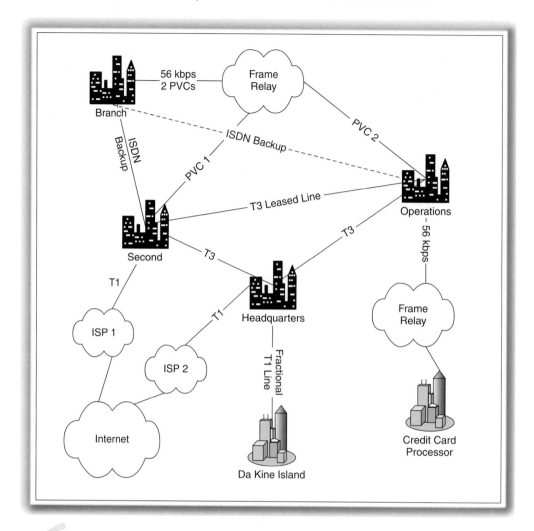

Figure 7a-1   First Bank of Paradise Wide Area Networks

mainframe computer at Operations. The teller terminals use different SNA protocols to talk to the Operations mainframe. File servers require IPX/SPX communication, and branch offices that need Internet access require TCP/IP.

At each branch, there is a Cisco 2600 router to connect the branch to Operations. This is a multiprotocol router capable of handling the many protocols used at the internet and transport layers in branch office communication.

External Organizations

First Bank of Paradise has to deal with several organizations outside the company. Figure 7a-1 shows only one of these—a connection to a credit card processing center. In fact, FBP deals with over a dozen outside support vendors, each in a different way. Fortunately, the credit card authorization firm uses TCP/IP, which simplifies matters.

THE FBP WIDE AREA NETWORK (WAN)

Figure 7a-1 shows the complex group of WANs that the bank uses to hold together this geographically dispersed and technologically diverse collection of sites.

T3 Lines

A mesh of T3 lines connects major facilities, as Figure 7a-1 shows. T3 leased lines operate at 44.7 kbps, providing "fat pipes" between these facilities.

Branch Connections

Branches are connected to the major facilities in two ways. Most of the time, they communicate via a Frame Relay network. For each branch, there are two 56 kbps PVCs. One leads to Operations, the other to Backup. They also have ISDN, as do the major facilities buildings.

Da Kine Island Branch

For the Da Kine Island branch, the firm has a 128 kbps fractional T1 digital leased line.

Credit Card Service

FBP connects to the credit card processing using a company 56 kbps Frame Relay network. This gives adequate speed.

Branch LANs

Branch offices require complex internal networking because of their use of multiple protocols. Until recently, all networking in branch offices used 802.5 Token-Ring Networks, except for a few "rogue" devices, including automated teller machines, which required different connections. The bank is replacing its branch Token-Ring Networks with Ethernet networks on a staged basis over three years.

Internet Access

For Internet access, FBP uses two separate ISPs, connecting to each via a T1 leased line. By limiting access to the Internet to two points, FBP enhances its security.

TEST YOUR UNDERSTANDING

1. a) List all examples of redundancy in the FBP network. b) What is the goal of redundancy?
2. a) Why are there only two access points to the Internet? b) Why do you think two access points were created instead of one?

3. Do you think the bank uses the same Frame Relay network to connect its branches as it uses to connect to its credit card processing center?

4. a) Why do you think the bank uses a fractional T1 line to its Da Kine Island branch instead of a full T1 line? b) Instead of a Frame Relay connection?

5. Why do you think the bank uses T3 lines to link its major facilities instead of using ATM?

6. Why do branches need highly capable routers?

TCP/IP INTERNETWORKING

Learning Objectives:

By the end of this chapter, you should be able to discuss:

- Basic principles of router operation, router standards, and multi-protocol routing.
- How routers make routing decisions for incoming packets using a routing table, including network and subnet masking and the selection of the best route.
- Other important TCP/IP standards, including DNS, ICMP, IPv6, TCP, and UDP.
- TCP three-way handshakes for openings, four-way handshakes for normal closes, abrupt resets, well-known port numbers for servers, and ephemeral port numbers for clients.
- The differences between IP routers and Layer 3 switches; the difference between Layer 3 and Layer 4 switches.

INTRODUCTION

In the last four chapters, we have looked at single LANs and single WANs. However, most corporations have multiple networks that must be connected into corporate-wide internets. These corporate internets link clients and servers across the firm.

Then, of course, there is the worldwide Internet that has revolutionized information exchange around the globe. Many of the Internet's thousands of networks are themselves large internets.

Routers

As Figure 8-1 illustrates, internets use routers to connect individual networks. **Edge routers** (Routers X and Z) sit at the edges of sites to connect these sites to the outside world through leased lines, public switched data networks (PSDNs), and virtual private networks (VPNs). In turn, **internal routers** (Routers W and Y) connect different LANs within a site. ISPs and internet backbone carriers use even larger **core routers** (not shown in the figure) capable of handling terabits of traffic per second.

Connecting Different Types of Networks
A key thing to note in Figure 8-1 is that routers can connect different types of single networks, that is, networks that have different physical and data link layer standards. For instance, Router X connects an internal Ethernet LAN, an internal Token-Ring Network, a T3 leased line to another site, and a Frame Relay network accessed via a leased T1 line.

Interfaces
Routers connect to multiple networks. For *each* of the networks to which they connect, they need the equivalent of a network interface card, called an **interface**. Each interface (port) must be designed for the network to which it connects (Ethernet, Token-Ring Network, etc.). Often, these are physical plug-in modules, so that you can install the specific interfaces you need in a particular router.

Mesh Topology and Alternative Routes
As Figure 8-1 shows, routers usually are organized into a **mesh** topology, so there are multiple alternative routes between most points. This allows the network to reroute packets around trunk line and router failures. Having multiple alternative routes also makes routing more complicated than switching, where there either is a hierarchy limiting all traffic between two points to a single possible path or where there are virtual circuits limiting transmissions to a single path. Routers, in contrast, must identify all possible routes, then select the best route; this is far more work per arriving message.

TEST YOUR UNDERSTANDING

1. a) Briefly describe the different types of routers mentioned in the text. b) What is an interface? c) What topology do router networks normally use? d) Does this allow alternative routes between hosts? e) Why is your answer to Part d good? f) Why is your answer to Part d bad?

Router Operation

Figure 8-2 shows what happens when a user transmits a frame containing a packet to the first router of the user's ISP. The connection between the user and the ISP uses a telephone line and a modem at the physical layer. It uses the Point-to-Point Protocol (PPP) at the data link layer. Telephone modem communication nearly always uses PPP.

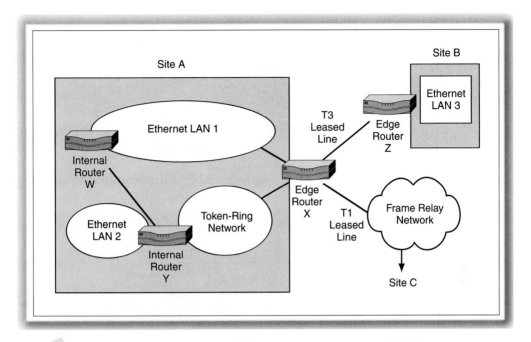

Figure 8-1 Internetworking with Routers

Figure 8-2 Frame Arriving at a Router

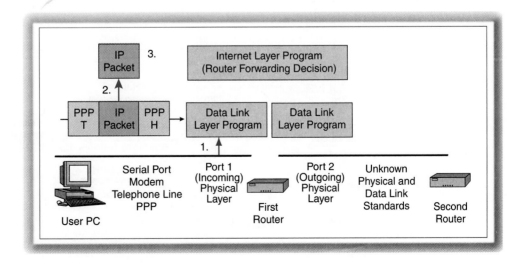

When Frames Arrive

When a frame arrives at a router from a network, it arrives in that network's interface. That interface's data link layer process (which implements the Point-to-Point Protocol) decapsulates the IP packet that the PPP frame is carrying and passes the packet up to the router's internet layer process.

The Routing Decision

Figure 8-3 shows that the router's internet layer process must make a routing decision. This is the decision about which interface to use to send the packet back out and to what device to send the packet.

Each interface connects to a different network, so sending the packet out an interface means sending it out to a particular network. In addition, the router must decide to what device on that network it should send the packet—either to the final destination host or to a next-hop router that will take responsibility for moving the packet closer to its destination.

Routing Tables

Switches use switching tables to make switching decisions when a frame arrives. Similarly, routers make routing decisions using routing tables. As we will see later in this chapter, routing tables are much more complex than switching tables because they must include data about all alternative routes.

Sending the Packet Back Out

Once the internet layer process decides what to do with the packet, it modifies the packet slightly, then passes the packet down to the data link layer process on the selected interface, as Figure 8-4 illustrates.

The data link layer process for that interface (different interfaces can have different data link layer processes because the networks to which they connect can follow

Figure 8-3 A Routing Decision

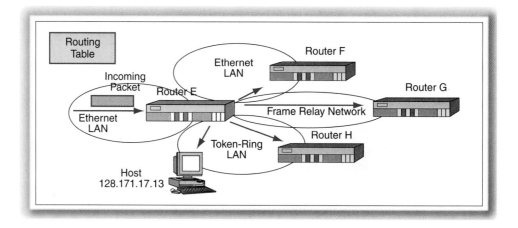

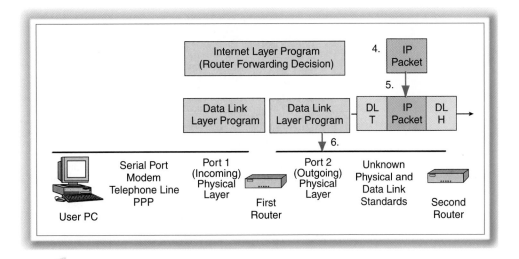

Figure 8-4   Sending a Frame Back Out

different single-network standards) encapsulates the IP packet in a frame suitable for that network. It then passes the frame down to the physical layer process on that interface, which sends the bits on to the next-hop router or to the destination device.

Format Conversion

Figure 8-5 shows a user connected to the first router on the Internet via a telephone modem. In this case, the data link layer standard is the Point-to-Point Protocol (PPP). How does the first router connect to the second router? The user has no idea. This might be a Frame Relay network or some other connection using different physical and data link layer protocols. The router will perform the required **format conversion** for frames to carry the IP packet being routed.

TEST YOUR UNDERSTANDING

2.   a) Describe, step-by-step, what happens after a frame arrives at a router until the time a frame leaves the router. b) Why must routers perform format conversion?

Routing Standards

We have already seen a number of TCP/IP internetworking standards in earlier chapters, including IP, TCP, DHCP, and DNS. In this chapter, we will look at other TCP/IP standards necessary for internetting.

Multiprotocol Routing

In the real world, of course, most routers must be **multiprotocol routers** that can handle not only TCP/IP internetworking protocols, but also internetworking protocols from IPX/SPX, SNA, and other standards architectures, as Figure 8-6 shows. In the next section, we will only look at IP routing. Multiply the complexity of the next

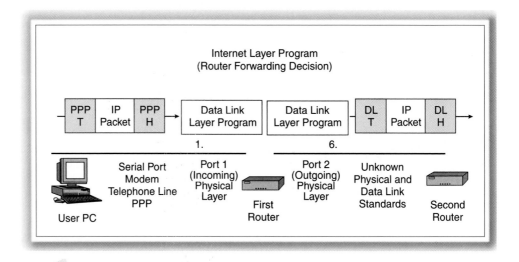

Figure 8-5   Format Conversion

Figure 8-6   Multiprotocol Routing

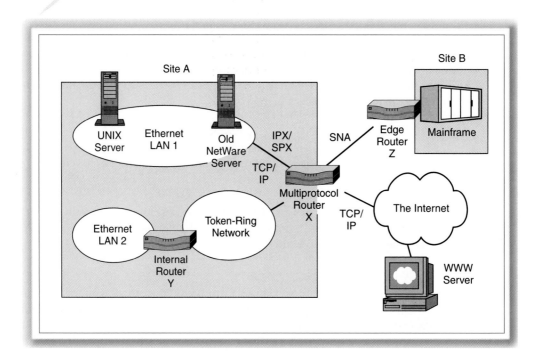

section by a factor of five or ten to understand the complexity of real-world routing (and why routers are so much more expensive than switches).

TEST YOUR UNDERSTANDING

3. Are TCP and IP the only internetworking standards in TCP/IP? Explain.
4. a) What are multiprotocol routers? b) Why are they more complex (and therefore more expensive) than IP-only routers?

ROUTING DECISIONS: IP ROUTING TABLES

Hierarchical IP Addresses

Ethernet MAC Addresses

An Ethernet MAC address has 48 bits. These 48 bits are set at the factory and have no relationship to a NIC's location in its network. This is called **flat addressing**.

Hierarchical Addressing

In contrast, as Figure 8-7 shows, IP addresses are **hierarchical**. They usually consist of three parts that locate a host in progressively smaller parts of the Internet. These are the network, subnet, and host parts. As we will see, this hierarchical addressing greatly simplifies routing tables.

Network Part

An IP address's **network part** identifies the host's network on the Internet. **Internet networks** are owned by single organizations, such as corporations, universities, and ISPs. In the IP address shown in Figure 8-7, the network part is 128.171. It is 16 bits long. All host IP addresses within this network begin with 128.171. This is the network part for the University of Hawaii network on the Internet.

Note that "network" in this context does not mean a single network—a single LAN or WAN. The University of Hawaii network itself consists of many single networks and routers at multiple locations around the state. In IP addressing, "**network**" is an organizational concept—a group of hosts, single networks, and routers owned by a single organization.

Subnet Part

Most large organizations further divide their networks into smaller units called **subnets**. Following the network part bits in an IP address come the **subnet part** bits. The subnet part bits specify a particular subnet within the network.

For instance, Figure 8-7 shows that in the IP address 128.171.17.13, the first 16 bits (128.171) correspond to the network part, whereas the next eight bits (17) correspond to a subnet on this network. Subnet 17 is the College of Business Administration subnet within the University of Hawaii Network. All host IP addresses within this subnet begin with 128.171.17.

Host Part

The remaining bits in the 32-bit IP address identify a particular host on the subnet. In Figure 8-7, the **host part** is 13. This corresponds to a particular host, 128.171.17.13, on the College of Business Administration subnet.

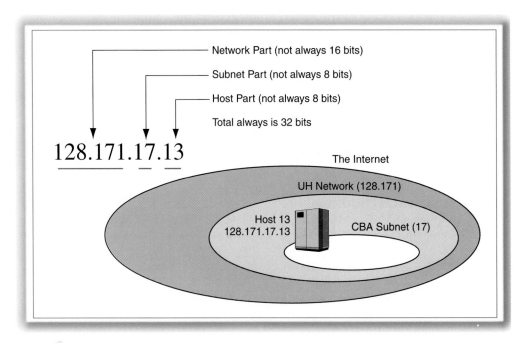

Figure 8-7 Hierarchical IP Address

Network/Subnet Matching

Figure 8-8 shows how hierarchical addressing simplifies routing tables. With hierarchical addressing, a router does not need a row for each of the hundreds of millions of host IP addresses on the Internet. If a router needed one entry per host, routers literally would take minutes to decide what to do with each arriving packet.

Rather, a router has one row for each alternative route to a particular network or subnet on a network. This is designated by the network/subnet column, which names the particular network or subnet on a network that can be reached through the route.

The column shows the network part or network plus subnet parts, followed by zeros. For instance, the first row, 128.171.0.0 indicates the University of Hawaii Network. In turn, Row 7, 128.171.17.0, indicates the College of Business Administration subnet.

Routing tables merely tell routers how to get packets to networks and subnets. All packets to the same network or subnet are handled by a single row. This is much more efficient than the Ethernet switching table approach, which has a separate entry for each station on a LAN. The Ethernet approach simply does not scale well.

TEST YOUR UNDERSTANDING

5. a) What are the three parts of a typical 32-bit IP address? b) Which part tells what network contains the host? c) Which part tells what subnet contains the host? d) Which part designates a particular host on a network's subnet?

Row	Network/ Subnet	Mask (/Prefix)*	Metric (Cost)	Interface	Next-Hop Router
1	128.171.0.0	255.255.0.0 (/16)	47	2	G
2	172.30.33.0	255.255.255.0 (/24)	0	1	Local
3	192.168.6.0	255.255.255.0 (/24)	12	2	G
4	10.0.0.0	255.0.0.0 (/8)	33	2	G
5	172.29.8.0	255.255.255.0 (/24)	34	1	F
6	172.40.6.0	255.255.255.0 (/24)	47	3	H
7	128.171.17.0	255.255.255.0 (/24)	55	3	H
8	172.29.8.0	255.255.255.0 (/24)	20	3	H
9	172.12.6.0	255.255.255.0 (/24)	23	1	F
10	172.30.12.0	255.255.255.0 (/24)	9	2	Local
11	172.30.122.0	255.255.255.0 (/24)	3	3	Local
12	10.241.0.0	255.255.0.0 (/16)	16	2	G
13	0.0.0.0	0.0.0.0 (/0)	5	3	H

Notes:

This router is on Network 127.30

It is attatched to three subnets: 172.30.33 (Interface 1), 172.30.12 (Interface 2), and 172.30.122 (Interface 3)

Figure 8-8   Routing Table

6. a) When a router receives a packet to be forwarded, does it usually consider all three IP address parts in deciding how to forward the packet? Explain. b) How does this reduce the size of routing tables? c) Each row in a routing table specifies a _____.

Network/Subnet Masks

Network parts are not always 16 bits long. Some are as small as 8 bits long. Others are 24 bits long or even longer. Subnet parts also vary in length.

Consequently, do not think that if you see 192.168.5.8 that you must be seeing a network part of 192.168 and a subnet part of 5. In fact, the network part may be 192.168.5, and the host part may be 8. (Subnetting is optional and would not be used in this case.)

Just by looking at an IP address, then, you cannot tell which bits are its network or subnet parts. You need something outside the IP address to interpret its part sizes.

Routing tables use a **mask** column to provide this outside information. Masks are 32-bit strings that begin with a series of ones and end in a series of zeros. For example, the mask 255.255.0.0 has 16 ones followed by 16 zeros.

Prefix Notation

Sometimes, a mask is expressed in simpler **prefix notation**, which gives the number of leading ones in the mask. For instance, the mask 255.255.255.0, which begins with 24 ones, would be represented in prefix notation as /24.

Masking

As Figure 8-9 shows, **masking** follows a simple rule. If you mask an IP address, you get back the IP address bits where there are ones in a mask. However, you get zeros where the mask bits are zeros. This is like spray painting through a stencil. You get the color where the stencil is cut out (ones) and nothing where it is solid (zeros).

For instance, suppose you have the IP address 172.30.122.6. If you mask it with 255.0.0.0, you get 172.0.0.0. If you mask it with 255.255.0.0, you get 172.30.0.0. If you mask it with 255.255.255.0, you get 172.30.122.0. Masks do not always break between ones and zeros at an octet boundary, but they will do so in all of our examples for the sake of simplicity.

Network Masks

Network masks tell how to route a packet closer to a specific network on the Internet. If a network mask in a particular row is 255.0.0.0, then the router will mask the destination IP address of an arriving packet, keeping the first eight bits intact and setting the other bits to zero.

For instance, in Row 4 of Figure 8-8, the mask is a network mask, 255.0.0.0. The network/subnet field value is 10.0.0.0. This will match masked destination IP addresses 10.171.23.13 (masked to 10.0.0.0). This is how this router will forward all packets to network 10.X.X.X.

Subnet Masks

In turn, **subnet masks** tell how to route a packet closer to a specific subnet on a specific network. If a subnet mask in a particular row is 255.255.255.0, this says that the first 24 bits of the network/subnet column entry in a row describe a particular subnet on a particular network.

For instance, in Row 2, the mask is 255.255.255.0. This is a subnet mask. The network/subnet value is 172.30.33.0. An IP packet with a destination address of 172.30.33.6 will be a match, because it will be masked to 172.30.33.0. This is how this router will forward all packets to network or network and subnet 172.30.33.

The Matching Algorithm

Having gone through several examples, here are the rules for determining if a row is a match for the destination IP address. We will call these rules the **matching algorithm**.

➤   First, take the destination IP address.
➤   Second, mask it with the row's Mask value.
➤   Third, if the result matches the row's network/subnet value, the row is a match. Otherwise, the row is not a match.

Automatic Handling

How does a router know which mask is a network mask or a subnet mask? Actually, it does not care. It simply uses the mask value in the row to decide what bits to look at in the destination addresses of arriving IP packets. As Figure 8-10 shows, routers

Information Bit	1	1	0	0		Binary	Decimal
Mask Bit	1	0	1	0		00000000	0
Result	1	0	0	0		11111111	255

IP Address	172.	30.	22.	0		IP Address	172.	30.	22.	0
Mask	255.	0.	0.	0		Mask	255.	255.	0.	0
Result	172.	0.	0.	0		Result	172.	30.	0.	0

Figure 8-9   Masking

transmit routing table information to one another using **routing protocols**. This process supplies both network parts and network plus subnet parts, along with appropriate masks.

TEST YOUR UNDERSTANDING

7. a) How long is the network part in an IP address? b) How long is the subnet part in an IP address? c) How long is the host part in an IP address? d) What is the total length of the three parts? (Trick questions.)

8. a) Why are network and subnet masks needed? b) How many initial ones are in the mask 255.255.255.0? c) If this is a network mask, how many ones are there in the network part? d) If this is a subnet mask, how many ones are in the network and subnet parts combined? e) What is the mask in prefix notation?

9. A row's network/subnet column has the value 128.171.0.0. The mask value is 255.255.0.0. a) Does 128.171.17.13 match this row? Show your work using the matching algorithm described in the text. b) Does 128.200.8.9 match this row? Show your work. c) Express the mask in prefix format.

10. What is the purpose of routing protocols?

Finding Row Matches

Figure 8-11 shows the broader algorithm that routers employ when a packet arrives to be routed. Note that the entire figure is a loop that is executed for each and every IP packet that arrives. Even if two successive packets go to the same destination IP address, they will be routed separately. If 1,000 packets going to the same IP address arrive, the router will go through the entire algorithm 1,000 times.[1]

---

[1] In practice, some routers use **decision caching**, which means that they remember their previous decisions for given destination IP addresses. However, they forget their decisions every few seconds to avoid having obsolete information about the Internet's constantly changing configuration of routers and trunk links.

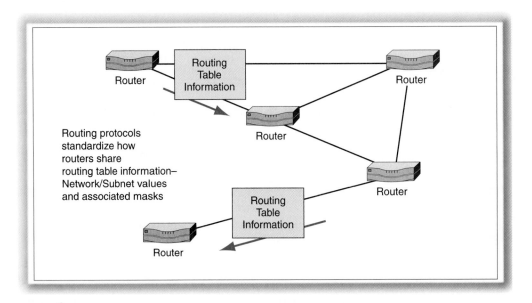

Figure 8-10   Routing Protocol

Row Matches

The first step in the algorithm is to find matching rows. Note that the routing algorithm *does not stop when a match is found*. The router will compare the destination IP address against *every row in the routing table* regardless of how many matches it finds. Core Internet routers within ISPs have 100,000 to 200,000 rows, so the requirement that every single row must be tested adds enormously to cost.

Suppose a packet arrives for destination host 10.5.6.3. First, the router will compare this IP address with Row 1 in Figure 8-8, whose mask is 255.255.0.0. The result of masking the destination IP address is 10.5.0.0. This does not match the network/subnet value of 128.171.0.0. The row is not a match. Nor will Row 2 or Row 3 match when the per-row calculations in Figure 8-11 are executed.

Row	Network/ Subnet	Mask (/Prefix)*	Metric (Cost)	Interface	Next-Hop Router
1	128.171.0.0	255.255.0.0 (/16)	47	2	G
2	172.30.33.0	255.255.255.0 (/24)	0	1	Local
3	192.168.6.0	255.255.255.0 (/24)	12	2	G
4	10.0.0.0	255.0.0.0 (/8)	33	2	G

For Each Packet
  For each row in the routing table, find matches
    Take destination IP address in packet
    Mask it with the Mask value in that row
    Take the result
    Compare it with the network/subnet value in that row
    If it matches
      Add the row to the list of matching rows for that packet
      Otherwise, ignore the row
  Next, find best match
    If only one match, list row as best match
    If longest match, list row as the best match
    If tied longest length of match, select row with best metric
      May be the smallest value (say if metric is cost)
      May be the longest value (say if metric is speed)
  Finally, send the packet out a port
    Send it out interface in best row to network or subnet out that port
    On that network or subnet, send packet to the
      Next-hop-router value in the best row
      Destination host if next-hop router value in best row says "local"

Figure 8-11   Routing Algorithm

Now the router comes to Row 4, which has the mask 255.0.0.0. When the router applies this mask to the destination IP address, 10.5.6.3, the result is 10.0.0.0. This matches the network/subnet value of 10.0.0.0. This row is a match. The router adds it to its list of matches (only one so far) and goes on to the next row, Row 5.

Multiple Matches

A router needs to consider multiple matches because routers usually are organized in meshes, as noted earlier. In meshes, there are multiple alternative routes to get from a particular router to a particular destination host. Each alternative route corresponds to a row in the routing table. Therefore, it is not enough for the router to find one match and stop. It must select the *best* match, which would represent the best alternative route for delivering the packet. This requires it to consider all rows.

Finding the Best Match

After considering all rows, a router needs to select the best match among the row matches it found.

Single Match

If there is only a single match, the router's problem is solved. The router selects that match. For instance, Row 15 has a mask of 0.0.0.0. This is guaranteed to match any IP address. Anything masked by 0.0.0.0 will give the result 0.0.0.0, which is the value in the network/subnet column. This is called the **default row** because it will be selected automatically if nothing else matches. The router named in the next-hop router column is called the **default router**. In this routing table, the default router is H. If a router does not have any other matching row, it will send the packet to the default router.

Row	Network/ Subnet Part*	Mask (/Prefix)*	Metric (Cost)	Interface	Next- Hop Router
15	0.0.0.0	0.0.0.0 (/0)	5	3	H

Longest Match

When there are multiple matches, the router will choose the row with the **longest match**. For instance, a packet with IP destination address 128.171.17.13 will match both Row 1 (128.171.0.0/16) and Row 7 (128.171.17.0/24). In this example, the router will choose Row 7 because it has the longest match (24 bits instead of 16 bits).

Row	Network/ Subnet Part*	Mask (/Prefix)*	Metric (Cost)	Interface	Next- Hop Router
1	128.171.0.0	255.255.0.0 (/16)	47	2	G
7	128.171.17.0	255.255.255.0 (/24)	55	3	H

The longest match gets a packet closest to its destination. For instance, Row 1 only gets a packet to the 128.171 network. Row 2's route will get the packet further, to the 128.171.17 subnet.

Metric

What if there are two rows with matches of equal length? Rows 5 and 8 have the same network/subnet part and the same mask, so any packet that matches one will match both.

Row	Network/ Subnet Part*	Mask (/Prefix)*	Metric (Cost)	Interface	Next- Hop Router
5	172.29.8.0	255.255.255.0 (/24)	34	1	F
8	172.29.8.0	255.255.255.0 (/24)	20	3	H

If equal-length matches occur, then the router needs additional information to distinguish between the alternative routes they represent. The router must look at the **metric** column in each row. This column gives a number describing the desirability of the route represented by the row.

Sometimes Select the Minimum Metric Value   In Figure 8-8, the metric column gives the cost of the route to the network or subnet listed in the network/subnet column. Typically, this would not be a monetary cost, but rather would be the number of router hops between the router making the decision and the destination network or subnet. The fewer the hops, the better. Cost should be minimized.

For instance, in Rows 5 and 8, the metric in Row 5 is 34, whereas the metric in Row 8 is 20. The router would choose Row 8, which has a lower cost.

Sometimes Select the Maximum Metric Value   Cost is not the only metric, however. For example, suppose the metric in Figure 8-8 represented the transmission speed along a route. In this case, more transmission speed would be better. The router would choose Row 5 because of its *larger* metric instead of Row 8.[2]

After the Row Is Selected

After the best-match row is selected, the router looks at the remaining columns in the best-match row to determine what to do with the packet.

Interface

Each outgoing port is an interface. It represents a particular network or subnet attached to the router. If Row 1 is selected, the router will send the IP packet out Interface 2. If Row 2 is selected, the router will send the packet out Interface 1.

Row	Network/ Subnet Part*	Mask (/Prefix)*	Metric (Cost)	Interface	Next-Hop Router
1	128.171.0.0	255.255.0.0 (/16)	47	2	G
2	172.30.33.0	255.255.255.0 (/24)	0	1	Local

Next-Hop Router

The network or subnet connected to the chosen interface usually will have many host computers and can even have multiple routers. So specifying the interface is not enough. The row also specifies the next-hop router on the chosen network or subnet that should receive the packet. Real routing tables give the IP addresses of next-hop

---

[2]   If two rows have the same network/subnet, mask, and metric, the router has no way to distinguish between them. The IP standard does not specify what a router should do if there is a tie. Some routers randomly select one row. Others send half of all traffic over one route and the other half over the other route.

routers. We give router names to make it easier to compare rows. If Row 1 is selected, the router will send the packet out Interface 2 to next-hop router G.

Row	Network/ Subnet Part*	Mask (/Prefix)*	Metric (Cost)	Interface	Next-Hop Router
1	128.171.0.0	255.255.0.0 (/16)	47	2	G

Local Delivery

What if the destination host is on the selected network or subnet? Then instead of putting a next-hop router's IP address in the next-hop router field, the table places the value "**Local**" (or something else, depending on the router) to indicate that no next-hop router is needed. The router will send the packet to the destination host on the network or subnet out the selected interface. If Row 2 is selected, the router will send the packet out Interface 1 to the destination host on that network or subnet.

Row	Network/ Subnet Part*	Mask (/Prefix)*	Metric (Cost)	Interface	Next-Hop Router
2	172.30.33.0	255.255.255.0 (/24)	0	1	Local

TEST YOUR UNDERSTANDING

11. For the router whose routing table is shown in Figure 8-8, a packet arrives for the destination address 172.40.6.3. a) Which two rows match? b) Which is the best match? Why? c) What will the router do with the packet?

12. For the router whose routing table is shown in Figure 8-8, a packet arrives for the destination address 10.241.3.5. a) Which three rows match? b) Which is the best match? Why? c) What will the router do with the packet?

13. For the router whose routing table is shown in Figure 8-8, a packet arrives for the destination address 172.25.12.7. Assume that the metric is speed. a) Which rows match? b) Which is the best match? Why? c) What will the router do with the packet?

14. For the router whose routing table is shown in Figure 8-8, a packet arrives for the destination address 172.35.6.17. a) Which rows match? b) Which is the best match? Why? c) What will the router do with the packet?

15. a) Will the default row automatically be a match for every packet? Explain. b) Why will the default row not be selected as the best match if there is any other match?

16. a) In routing tables, what does "interface" mean? b) What is the next-hop router? c) What does it mean if the next-hop router column says "local"?

Recap

It is easy to get lost in the steps taken by routers when they compare the destination address of an incoming packet to the rows in their routing table. We summarize the key points in Figure 8-11.

For Each Arriving Packet

Note that this process is *repeated for each and every arriving IP packet*. Even if a thousand successive IP packets are going to the same destination, they will be handled independently.

Evaluating Every Row

Also, keep in mind that the destination IP address is compared to *each and every row in the routing table*. If there are 100,000 rows, as there are in many backbone Internet routers, there must be 100,000 comparisons. In Ethernet and ATM switching tables, there is only one possible match; it can be found quickly, and when it is found, the process stops. With multiple alternative routes, there may be many matches.

High Cost

The needs to route each IP packet separately and to evaluate every row in the routing table for each packet place heavy processing burdens on routers, making them much more expensive and slower than switches per message handled.

TEST YOUR UNDERSTANDING

17. A thousand IP packets addressed to the same destination IP address arrive at a router. The router has 100,000 rows. How many rows must the router examine to forward them all? Show your work.

OTHER INTERNET LAYER STANDARDS

In this section, we will briefly review DNS, then look at ICMP and IPv6.

Domain Name System (DNS)

As we saw in Chapter 1, if a user types in a host name, the user's PC will contact its local Domain Name System (DNS) server. The DNS server will return the IP address for the host name or will contact other DNS servers to get this information. The user's PC can then send IP packets to the target host.

What Is a Domain?

Figure 8-12 shows that the **Domain Name System (DNS)** and its servers are not limited to providing information about host names. A **domain** is a group of resources (routers, single networks, and hosts) under the control of an organization. The figure shows that domains are hierarchical, with host names being at the bottom of the hierarchy.

Top-Level Domains

At the top of the hierarchy is the **root**, which consists of all domain names. Under this are **top-level domains** that categorize the domain by organization type (.com, .net, .edu, .biz, .info, etc.) or by country (.uk, .ca, .ie, .au, .jp, .ch, etc.).

Second-Level Domains

Under top-level domains are **second-level domains**, which usually specify a specific organization (Microsoft.com, Hawaii.edu, Panko.com, etc.). Sometimes, however, specific products, such as movies, get their own second-level domain names. Competition for good second-level domain names is fierce.

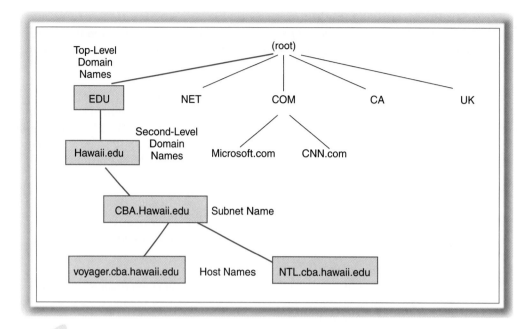

Figure 8-12 Domain Name System (DNS) Hierarchy

Further Qualifications
Domains can be further qualified. For instance, within Hawaii.edu, which is the University of Hawaii, there is cba.Hawaii.edu, which is the College of Business Administration. Within cba.Hawaii.edu is voyager.cba.Hawaii.edu, which is a specific host within the college.

A Comprehensive Naming System
Overall, DNS gives a comprehensive system for creating unique hierarchical names on the Internet.

TEST YOUR UNDERSTANDING

18. a) Is the Domain Name System only used to send back IP addresses for given host names? b) What is a domain? c) Which level of domain name do corporations most wish to have?

Internet Control Message Protocol (ICMP) for Supervisory Messages

Supervisory Messages at the Internet Layer
IP is only concerned with packet delivery. For supervisory messages at the internet layer, the Internet Engineering Task Force (IETF) created the **Internet Control Message Protocol (ICMP)**. IP and ICMP work closely together. IP encapsulates ICMP messages in the IP data field, delivering them to their target host or router.

Error Advisement

IP is an unreliable protocol. It offers no error correction. If the router or the destination host finds an error, it discards the packet. Although there is no retransmission, the router or host that finds the error usually sends an **ICMP error message** to the source device to inform it that an error has occurred, as Figure 8-13 illustrates. It is then up to the device to decide what to do. This is **error advisement** rather than error correction.

Echo (Ping)

Perhaps the most famous ICMP message is the **ICMP echo** message. One host or router can send an echo request message to another. If the target device's internet process is able to do so, it will send back an echo response message.

Sending an echo request is often called **pinging** the target host, because it is similar to a submarine pinging a ship to see if it is there. Echo is a good diagnostic tool because if there are network difficulties, a logical early step in diagnosis is to ping many hosts and routers to see if they can be reached.

TEST YOUR UNDERSTANDING

19. a) For what general class of messages is ICMP used? b) How are ICMP messages encapsulated? c) An Ethernet frame containing an ICMP message arrives at a host. Draw the frame, showing all headers and trailers. For each header or trailer, specify the standard used to create the header (for example, Ethernet 802.3 MAC layer header). d) Explain error advisement in ICMP. e) Explain the purpose of ICMP echo messages. f) Sending ICMP echo messages is called _____ the target host.

Figure 8-13   Internet Control Message Protocol (ICMP) for Supervisory Messages

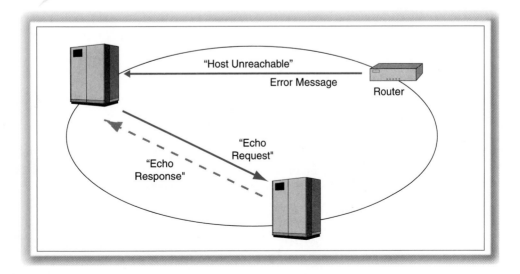

IPv4 and IPv6

IPv4

Today, most routers on the Internet and private internets are governed by the **IP version 4 (IPv4)** standard. (There were no versions 0 through 3). Figure 8-14 shows the IPv4 packet. Its first four bits contain the value 0100 (binary for 4) to indicate that the packet is formatted according to IPv4.

IPv6

The IETF has standardized a new version of the Internet Protocol, **IP version 6** (**IPv6**). As Figure 8-14 shows, IPv6 also begins with a version field. Its value is 0110 (binary for 6). This tells the router that the rest of the packet is formatted according to IPv6.

Address Field

The most important change in IPv6 is increasing the size of IP address fields from 32 bits to 128 bits. The number of possible IP addresses is 2 raised to a power that is the size of the IP address field. For IPv4, this is 2^{32}. For IPv6, this is 2^{128}. IPv6 will provide for the enormous increase in demand for IP addresses that we can expect from mobile devices and from the expected evolution of even simple home appliances into addressable IP hosts.

Slow Adoption

IPv6 has been adopted only in a few areas because its main advantage, large address fields, is not too important yet. However, IPv6 is beginning to gather strength, particularly in Asia and Europe, which were short-changed in the original allocation of IPv4 addresses.[3] In addition, the explosion of mobile devices accessing the Internet will soon place heavy stress on the IPv4 IP address space. In 2001, Cisco began to support IPv6 on all of its routers in anticipation of growing demand. Fortunately, IPv6 packets can be tunneled through IPv4 networks by placing them within IPv4 packets, so the two protocols can (and will) coexist on the Internet for some time to come.

TEST YOUR UNDERSTANDING

20. a) How is IPv6 better than IPv4? b) Why has IPv6 adoption been so slow? c) What forces may drive its adoption in the future? d) Must IPv6 replace IPv4 all at once? Explain.

THE TRANSMISSION CONTROL PROTOCOL (TCP)

In this section, we will take a closer look at the **Transmission Control Protocol (TCP)**. Figure 8-15 shows the organization of TCP messages, which are called **TCP segments**, and UDP messages, which are called UTP datagrams.

---

[3] North America controls 74 percent of all IPv4 addresses. CNN.com, "Europe Seen Leading the Way for Internet Standard," May 17, 2001. http://www.cnn.com/2001/TECH/internet/05/17/internet.standard.reut/index.html, web-posted 9:36 am EDT.

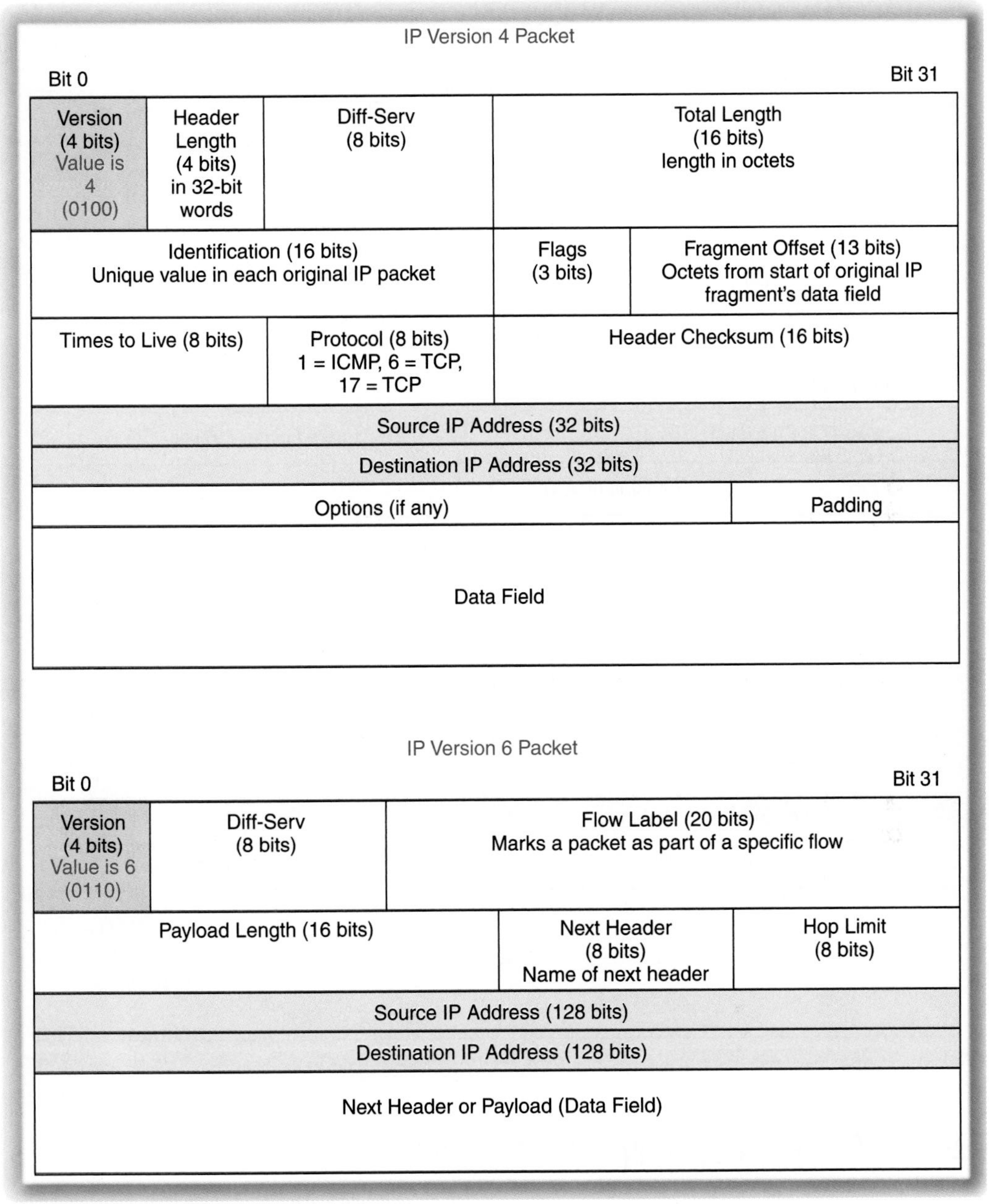

IP Version 4 Packet

Bit 0   Bit 31

Version (4 bits) Value is 4 (0100)	Header Length (4 bits) in 32-bit words	Diff-Serv (8 bits)	Total Length (16 bits) length in octets
Identification (16 bits) Unique value in each original IP packet		Flags (3 bits)	Fragment Offset (13 bits) Octets from start of original IP fragment's data field
Times to Live (8 bits)	Protocol (8 bits) 1 = ICMP, 6 = TCP, 17 = TCP	Header Checksum (16 bits)	
Source IP Address (32 bits)			
Destination IP Address (32 bits)			
Options (if any)			Padding
Data Field			

IP Version 6 Packet

Bit 0   Bit 31

Version (4 bits) Value is 6 (0110)	Diff-Serv (8 bits)	Flow Label (20 bits) Marks a packet as part of a specific flow
Payload Length (16 bits)	Next Header (8 bits) Name of next header	Hop Limit (8 bits)
Source IP Address (128 bits)		
Destination IP Address (128 bits)		
Next Header or Payload (Data Field)		

Figure 8-14   IPv4 and IPv6 Packets

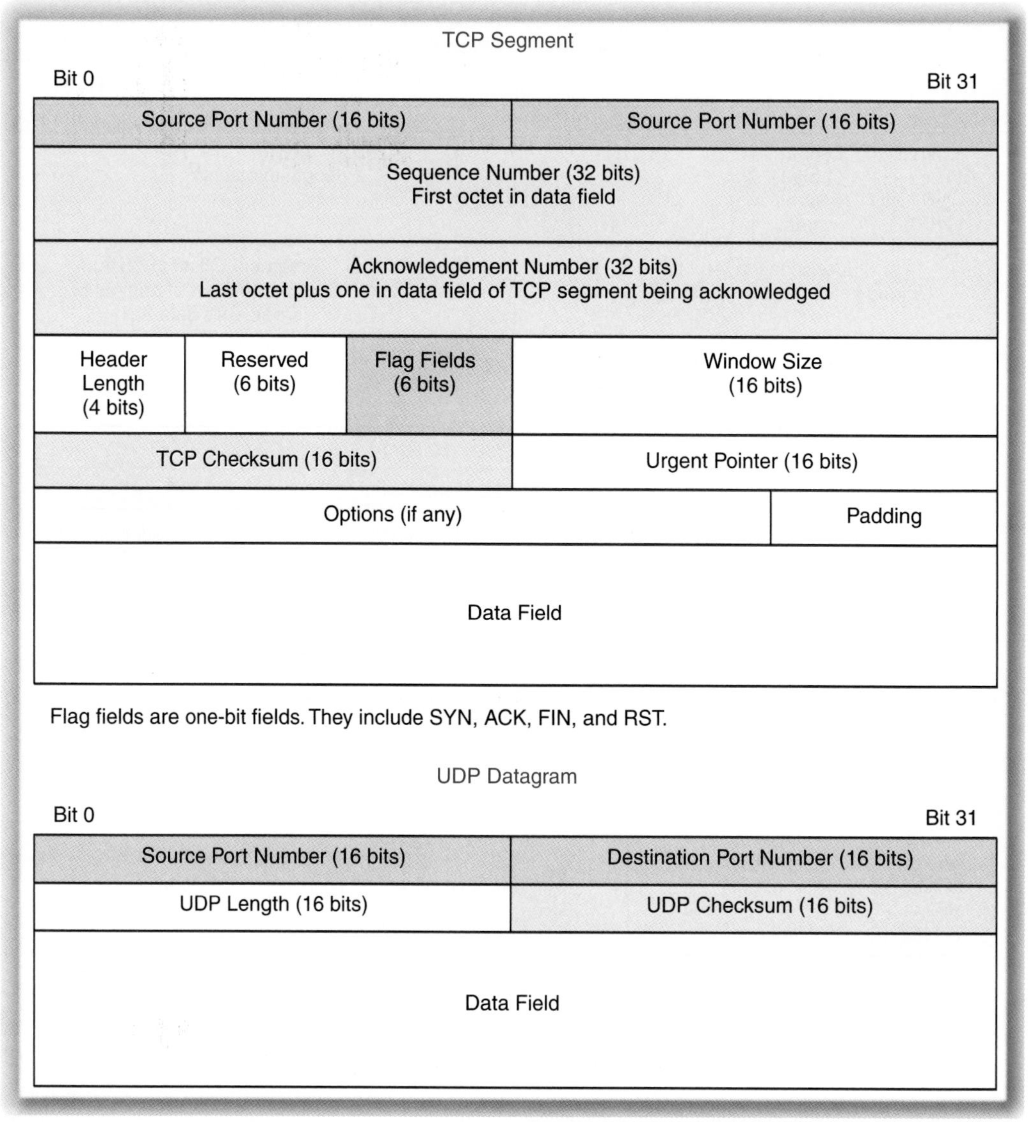

TCP Segment

Bit 0 .... Bit 31

Source Port Number (16 bits)	Source Port Number (16 bits)

Sequence Number (32 bits)
First octet in data field

Acknowledgement Number (32 bits)
Last octet plus one in data field of TCP segment being acknowledged

Header Length (4 bits)	Reserved (6 bits)	Flag Fields (6 bits)	Window Size (16 bits)

TCP Checksum (16 bits)	Urgent Pointer (16 bits)

Options (if any)	Padding

Data Field

Flag fields are one-bit fields. They include SYN, ACK, FIN, and RST.

UDP Datagram

Bit 0 .... Bit 31

Source Port Number (16 bits)	Destination Port Number (16 bits)
UDP Length (16 bits)	UDP Checksum (16 bits)

Data Field

Figure 8-15   TCP Segments and UDP Datagrams

TCP and IP

Minimalist IP Design

When TCP and IP were created, their developers realized that they could not make many assumptions about single networks. Many different single network technologies already existed, and who could tell what network technologies would be created in the future?

Consequently, the developers decided to create a very simple internet layer standard, the Internet Protocol. IP would be unreliable, not correcting errors during transmission. In addition, IP would only look at individual packets during transmission. It would not attempt to keep track of streams of packets during a conversation between two host internet layer processes to ensure that packets arrive in order and to do other connection management tasks.

Depending on TCP

The developers left more difficult work to the Transmission Control Protocol (TCP). It would do what IP could not be designed to do.

Reliability   First, TCP would provide reliability. As we will soon see, every TCP segment is acknowledged by the receiving transport layer process, so that the sender can retransmit lost or damaged TCP segments that are not acknowledged.

Connection-Oriented Service   Second, TCP would be a connection-oriented protocol that would manage the stream of transmissions during a **connection** (which is a managed series of exchanges) between two transport layer processes on the source and destination hosts.

TEST YOUR UNDERSTANDING

21.   a) Why was IP designed to be so simple? b) In what two ways mentioned in the text does TCP compensate for the necessary simplicity of IP?

Connection Opens and Closes

Figure 8-16 illustrates how TCP opens and closes a connection. Here, a client PC initiates a connection with a webserver.

Opens with Three-Way Handshakes

SYN   TCP connections open with what is called a **three-way handshake**. First, the client transport process sends a **SYN** (synchronization) message to open the connection. A synchronization message consists of a header without a body. As Figure 8-15 shows, a TCP header has a one-bit **SYN flag field**. In a synchronization message, this flag is **set**, that is, given the value 1.

SYN/ACK   Second, the transport process on the other machine (the webserver) sends back a SYN/ACK message. This is the webserver transport process' agreement to open a connection (SYN) plus an **acknowledgement (ACK)** of the client PC's SYN message. To send an ACK message, the sender sets the **ACK bit**. Again, only a header is sent.

ACK   Third, the client transport process acknowledges the SYN/ACK message with a pure ACK (acknowledgement) message. The client PC's transport process does not reply to this message, because pure acknowledgements are not acknowledged. (If they were, you would have an infinite loop of acknowledgements.) This too is only a header.

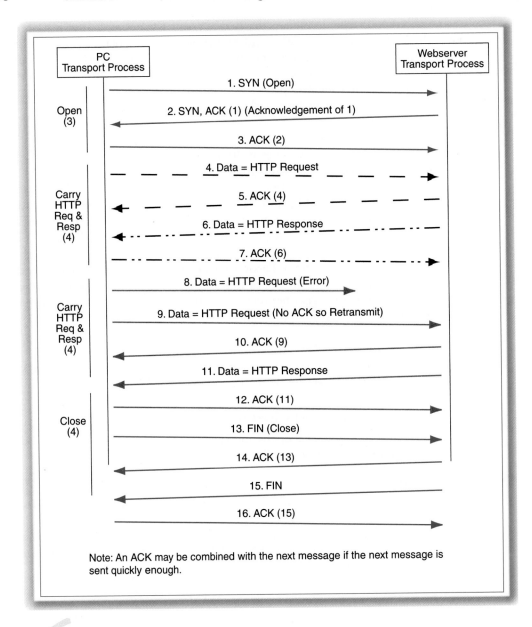

Figure 8-16 Transmission Control Protocol (TCP) Time Diagram

Ongoing Message Exchanges

After a connection is open, the two sides can begin sending data TCP segments (segments with data fields containing application messages) back and forth. Each of these is acknowledged by the other side.

Handling Errors   TCP is a reliable protocol, meaning that it corrects errors. In Figure 8-16, TCP segment 8, which is transmitted by the client PC's transport layer process, encounters a problem and either does not make it all the way to the web-server's transport process or is found to contain an error when the receiver examines the error check field.

We have seen that when a transport process receives a correct TCP segment, it always sends an acknowledgement (ACK) segment back to the sender. This way, the sender knows that the message has gotten through.

What happens if there is an error? Obviously, if the receiver never receives the segment—for example, if the segment has been discarded or lost by a lower-layer process—then the receiving transport process cannot send an acknowledgement. In addition, if the receiving transport process uses the TCP checksum field to determine that there is an error in the segment, the receiving process will discard the segment. It will not send back an acknowledgement.

Consequently, if the sending transport process does not receive an acknowledgement, it retransmits the unacknowledged TCP segment. If this segment reaches the receiver, it will be acknowledged, and the sending process can forget about the segment, knowing that it was received correctly.

Sequence and Acknowledgement Numbers

Each outgoing TCP segment is given a **sequence number**, which is placed in the sequence number field in the header of the message (see Figure 8-15). When the other transport process acknowledges the segment, it places an acknowledgment number in the header of the acknowledging TCP segment. This **acknowledgement number** tells the original sender which TCP segment is being acknowledged.[4]

Normal Closes: Four-Way Handshake

Normal closes require a **four-way handshake**. The party wishing to close a connection sets the **FIN** (finish) bit in a TCP header. The other party sends back a simple acknowledgement. The other party then sends back its own FIN message, which the party initiating the close acknowledges. The connection now is closed.

Abrupt Closes: Resets

Normal closes are best, but either side can send a **reset (RST)** TCP segment at any time to initiate an abrupt close. It does this by setting the **RST bit**. For instance, if one side initiates a connection with a SYN message, the other side can send back an RST message to refuse the connection. The side receiving an RST message does not send an acknowledgment.

---

[4]   If this seems a bit vague, this is because the creation of sequence and acknowledgment numbers in TCP/IP is complex. See Module A for details.

TEST YOUR UNDERSTANDING

22. a) How many TCP segments are necessary to open a connection? b) How many TCP segments are needed for a normal close? c) How many TCP segments are necessary for an abrupt close (reset)?

23. a) Explain TCP error correction. b) How do sequence and acknowledgement numbers allow a receiving transport process to acknowledge a specific TCP segment?

The User Datagram Protocol (UDP)

TCP offers a highly reliable transport layer protocol. However, the need to create and maintain connections and to do error correction make TCP a heavyweight protocol that may not be suitable for all applications. Therefore the IETF created a second TCP/IP transport layer protocol, the **User Datagram Protocol (UDP)**. Figure 8-17 compares TCP and UDP.

Note in the figure that whereas TCP is **connection-oriented** (it establishes and maintains connections), UDP is **connectionless** (it does not set up or maintain connections). While TCP must set up a connection before sending data and also must close the connection after data transmission, UDP merely sends its messages (called **UDP datagrams**) whenever it wishes. UDP datagrams are like postal letters in this regard, while TCP is like a shipping department that has to keep track of all packages shipped and must ensure their arrival.

TCP will correct almost all errors, but UDP merely discards incorrect UDP datagrams. There is no retransmission. It is up to the application program to handle errors if error handling is important at all. UDP is unreliable.

While it may seem odd that error handling would not always be important, consider network management messages. As discussed in Chapter 10, central network managers frequently poll managed devices around the network to get information about their current status as an aid to managerial decision making. The loss of an occasional message merely means that data on one particular device will be out of date for a few seconds. At the same time, by using UDP, network management protocols place a lower load on the network, freeing the network to handle content messages.

Figure 8-17 TCP Versus UDP

	TCP	UDP
Layer	Transport	Transport
Message name	TCP segment	UDP datagram
Processing power required	Heavyweight	Lightweight
Reliability	Reliable	Unreliable
Connections?	Connection-oriented	Connectionless

Another application that uses UDP is voice transmission. Voice transmission is highly sensitive to latency. Consequently, there is no time to correct an error by retransmitting a damaged or lost voice datagram. Consequently, voice over IP normally uses UDP to take advantage of unreliable operation's relatively low overhead.

TEST YOUR UNDERSTANDING

24.   a) Compare the relative advantages of TCP and UDP. b) What are UDP messages called?

Port Numbers

As Figure 8-15 shows, both TCP and UDP have port number fields. These fields are used differently by clients and servers.

Servers

For servers, the port number field indicates which application program on the server should receive the message. Most applications have **well-known port numbers** that are usually (but not always) used. For instance, the well-known TCP port number for HTTP is 80. For FTP, Port 20 is used for supervisory communication with an FTP application program, and Port 21 is used to send data segments. Telnet uses Port 23, whereas Port 25 is used for Simple Mail Transfer Protocol (SMTP) messages in e-mail. UDP has its own well-known port numbers.

Figure 8-18 shows that every time the client sends a message to a server, it places the port number of the application in the destination port number field. In this figure, the server is a webserver, and the port number is 80. When the server responds, it places the port number of the application (80) in the source port number field.

Clients

Clients do something different. Whenever a client connects to an application program on a server, it creates an **ephemeral port number** greater than 1,024 but less than 65,535. It places this ephemeral port number in the source port number in all transmissions to the server application program. (In the figure, the ephemeral port number is 20247 for client communication with the webserver.) The server, in return, places this ephemeral port number in all destination port number fields of TCP segments (or UDP datagrams) it sends to the client.

A client may maintain multiple connections to different application programs on different servers. It will give each connection a different ephemeral port number to identify each connection. A client can even establish multiple connections to the *same* application program on the same server by giving each connection a different ephemeral port number.[5]

Sockets

The combination of an IP address and a port number designates a specific connection to a specific application on a specific host. This combination is called a **socket**. It is written as an IP address, a colon, and a port number, for instance, 128.171.17.13:80.

---

[5]   This is common in webpage downloads. If several files must be downloaded for a webpage (as discussed in Chapter 11), the client may open several connections to the webserver, downloading one file on each connection. This usually is faster than downloading several files sequentially in the same connection.

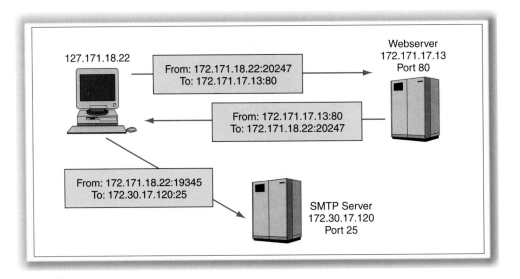

Figure 8-18   Use of TCP (and UDP) Port Numbers

TEST YOUR UNDERSTANDING

25. A host sends a TCP segment with source port number 25 and destination port number 17892. a) Is the host a server or a client? b) If the host is a server, what kind of server is it?

26. a) What is a socket? b) How is it written? c) When the SMTP server in Figure 8-18 transmits to the client PC, what is the source socket? d) The destination socket?

27. A host has two connections to the same application program on a webserver. What will be different between the TCP segments that the client sends on the two connections?

LAYER 3 AND LAYER 4 SWITCHES

In Chapters 4 and 5, we saw why switches are so fast and inexpensive. In this chapter, we saw why routers are so slow and expensive. However, just as nature abhors a vacuum, technology abhors a sharp distinction. New devices called Layer 3 switches sit between traditional Layer 2 (data link layer) switches for single networks and routers in terms of speed and price.

Layer 3 Switches

Layer 3 switches work at the internet layer, which is Layer 3; they forward packets based upon their IP addresses. However, through a variety of technologies, they can work much faster and less expensively than routers.

It is difficult to talk about technological distinctions between Layer 3 switches and routers because routers often adopt technologies introduced for Layer 3 switches. The technological differences between routers and Layer 3 switches are constantly shifting.

Layer 3 Switches Have Limited Protocol Support

The one enduring difference between routers and Layer 3 switches is breadth of protocol coverage. At Layer 2, routers must support multiple LAN and WAN protocols on their interfaces. In contrast, Layer 3 switches usually only support Ethernet on their interfaces at the data link layer.

In addition, at the internet layer, routers must be able to handle IPX and other non-IP protocols. However, Layer 3 switches usually only handle IP or at most IP and IPX. In other words, Layer 3 switches really are limited-functionality routers.

Roles of Layer 3 Switches and Routers

This difference in breadth of protocol support usually means that Layer 3 switches and routers play different roles in an internet. Figure 8-19 shows that, in site networks, Layer 3 switches are pushing routers to the edges of the site, because the ability of routers to support multiple WAN protocols is crucial there. In contrast, within the site, the low cost of Layer 3 switching usually makes them dominant.

Limits of Layer 3 Switches

Many organizations, such as banks, have multiple protocols even within sites. In such cases, their lack of protocol support means that Layer 3 switches generally cannot be used despite their low costs.

Layer 4 Switches

As noted earlier in this chapter, TCP and UDP headers have port number fields that indicate the application that created the encapsulated application layer message and the application layer program that should receive the encapsulated application message.

Figure 8-19   Layer 3 Switches and Routers in Site Internets

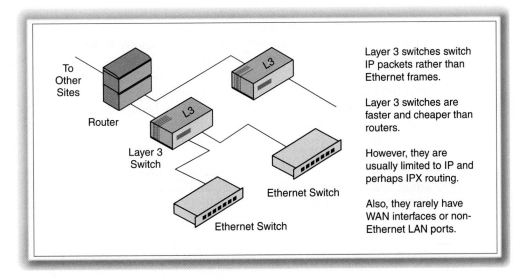

Layer 4 switches examine the port number field of each arriving packet's encapsulated TCP segment. This allows them to switch packets based on the application they contain. Specifically, this allows Layer 4 switches to give priority to or even to deny forwarding to IP packets from certain applications. For example, TCP segments to and from an SMTP mail server (Port 25) might be given low priority during times of congestion because e-mail is insensitive to moderate latency.

TEST YOUR UNDERSTANDING

28. a) How are Layer 3 switches similar to routers? b) How are they different? Give a full explanation. c) Where would you use Layer 3 switches? d) Where would you not use Layer 3 switches?

29. a) What are Layer 4 switches? b) What field do Layer 4 switches examine? c) Why are Layer 4 switches good?

GAINING PERSPECTIVE

Market Realities

Matrix.Net (www.matrix.net) maintains data on Internet performance. For the Internet as a whole, the mean latency was 147 milliseconds in September 2001. An average of 6.5% of all packets were lost. Check the website to see if things have changed today.

Vint Cerf, the "father of the Internet," has said that there were 573 million Internet users around the world in January 2001 and that by the end of the decade, there will be 2.2 billion users.[6]

THOUGHT QUESTIONS

1. Give a non-network example of hierarchical addressing and discuss how it reduces the amount of work needed in physical delivery.
2. What would be good metrics for routing tables?
3. A router forwards a packet to a next-hop router (Router B) for delivery. a) What is in the destination address in the IP packet header's destination address field—the IP address of Router B or the IP address of the destination host? b) In what field of what header will Router B's network address (its data link layer address on its single network) be found, if it is to be found at all? c) In what field of what header will Router B's IP address be found, if it is to be found at all?
4. A TCP "open" only requires a three-way handshake. Why does TCP require a four-way close? (This is a *very* subtle question that few students will be able to answer.)
5. a) How do you think TCP would handle the problem if IP packets are received out of order? (IP does not guarantee that packets will be received in order.) b) How do you think TCP would handle the problem if an acknowledgement

---

6   Ellie Phillips, "Father of the Internet Offers Forecast," PCWORLD.com, October 19, 2001. www.pcworld.com/resource/printable/article/0,aid,66688,00.asp.

were lost, so that the sender retransmitted the unacknowledged TCP segment and therefore the receiving transport process received the same segment twice?
6. Layer 3 switches are Ethernet switches but still have IP routing tables like Figure 8-8. If there is no default row, will there ever be multiple row matches? Explain.

TROUBLESHOOTING QUESTION

1. You suspect that the failure of a router or of transmission line connecting routers has left some of your important servers unavailable to clients at your site. How could you narrow down the location of the problem using what you learned in this chapter?

CASE STUDIES

For case studies, go to the book's website, www.prenhall.com/panko, and look at the Case Studies page for this chapter.

PHOTOS

For photos, go to the book's website, www.prenhall.com/panko, and look at the Photos page for this chapter.

PROJECTS

1. **Getting Current.** Go to the book website's New Information and Errors pages for this chapter to get new information since this book went to press and to correct any errors in the text.
2. **Internet Exercises.** Go to the book website's Exercises page for this chapter and do the Internet Exercises.
3. **Hands-On.** To set up servers, you need to know DNS host addresses, your school's subnet mask, and the IP address of your default router (which Microsoft calls a gateway—an obsolete term for router). Determine these for your LAN. *Hint:* In a Wintel machine in your laboratory, click on Start, and then Run. Run the winipcfg.exe program under Windows. Click on more information. For Windows 2000 PCs, go to the command line and type ipconfig/all[Enter].
4. **Hands-On.** Play a six-player game to understand TCP better.

   Three players will be layer processes on a client PC, while the other three will be layer processes on a webserver. One on each host will be the application program (client browser or webserver application program), another the transport process, and the last the internet process.

   Sit the client processes in one row of chairs and sit the server processes on another row of chairs facing the clients. The order should be application–transport–internet, and peers on the two hosts should face each other.

   The client browser will begin the game by writing two HTTP requests for file downloads to the webserver application program. These requests should be written on index cards. When the webserver application program receives each of these request cards, it will send back a response message on an index card.

The transport processes will implement TCP. All TCP messages will be small envelopes with writing on the outside to describe the message.

Each internet processes will communicate directly with its peer. (We are ignoring the data link and physical processes for simplicity.) They will communicate using larger envelopes than transport processes use.

To begin the game, the browser process will announce his or her first action—to create an HTTP request message and send it down to its transport process. This request should ask for a file named Puka.html. He or she will then write out a message on the index card to ask for the file. (The second file to be downloaded is named Lolo.gif.)

Players will then act, one at a time, announcing what he or she is doing and then performing the action. Players should watch carefully and correct errors made by others.

The game finishes when the second requested file is received by the browser.

TCP players will do (and learn) the most. Play the game three times, letting players play all three roles on their host (application, transport, and internet).

CHAPTER 9

SECURITY

Learning Objectives:

By the end of this chapter, you should be able to discuss:

- Types of attackers and the difference between attack prevention systems and secure communication systems.
- The dangers that attack prevention systems are designed to thwart, including types of denial-of-service (DoS) attacks.
- Firewalls, including packet filter firewalls, application proxy firewalls, network address translation (NAT), and intrusion detection systems.
- How to harden servers and clients, including fixing known weaknesses, strong passwords, Kerberos, biometric authentication, smart cards, and restricting access permissions.
- The four phases of secure communication systems.
- Encryption for confidentiality, including symmetric key encryption and public key encryption.
- Encryption for authentication, including applicants versus verifiers, hashing, challenge–response authentication, message-by-message authentication (and integrity), the need for digital certificates, and public key infrastructures (PKIs).
- Multilayer security; how to create appropriate security, including how to handle security incidents; protecting the privacy of customer and employee information.

INTRODUCTION

The Snake in the Networking Garden

The mantra of networking is "anything, anytime, anywhere." However, the same openness that makes networks so attractive to users and organizations also makes them attractive to a wide variety of attackers. In 2001, a major financial institution detected 1.5 attacks every *second* during one sample week.[1] For non-Web (non-HTTP) transactions, an astounding 85 percent of all messages were unauthorized. Also in 2001, MessageLabs (a provider of outsourced virus detection services) detected an average of one virus in every 400 e-mails that it examined. Security is not a luxury in today's increasingly hostile world.

Types of Attackers

Figure 9-1 shows that there are several different types of attackers.

Wizard Internet Hackers

The most famous attackers are highly skilled "wizard" Internet **hackers**, who use sophisticated tools and superb knowledge of networks and computers to **hack** into corporate computers (log into them illegally). There they read sensitive files, steal important information, or simply vandalize systems.[2]

Relatively Unskilled Internet Hackers with Kiddie Scripts

Most hackers today, however, have modest computer and networking skills. Despite their limited skills, they are dangerous because they use **automated attack programs** written by wizard hackers. These "**kiddie script**" programs give tens of thousands of amateurs called **script kiddies** the ability to attack your network.

Individual Criminals, Organized Crime, and Espionage

Recently, we have seen the rise of criminal attackers who steal credit card numbers, trade secrets, and other important information for profit. They either sell this information or try to extort money from the victim to prevent the exposure of the information. These attackers include criminals working alone, members of **organized crime** gangs, and **industrial espionage** spies who specialize in stealing high-value trade secrets from corporations. Governments too sometimes engage in industrial espionage to help their countries' industries.

Information Warfare and Cyberterrorism

Most chilling of all, when nations go to war in the future, they are likely to use the Internet for **information warfare**, in which they use computers instead of missiles to "bomb" their enemy's crucial information technology infrastructure—including corporate networks. Terrorists are likely to use the same types of attacks.

---

[1]   Tuesday, Vince (pseudonym), "Who's That Knocking at My Door? Go Away!" *Computerworld*, May 14, 2001. www.computerworld.com/cwi/community/story/0,3201,NAV65-663_STO60469,00.html.

[2]   Contrary to Hollywood stereotypes, it often takes days or weeks of patient and exhausting work to hack into a particular computer.

Wizard Internet Hackers
  Highly capable attackers
Amateurs (Script Kiddies)
  Light skills, but numerous and armed with automated attack programs (kiddie scripts)
  of increasing potency
Criminals
  Theft of credit card numbers, trade secrets, and other sensitive information
  Sell the information or attempt extortion to prevent the release of the information
  Individual criminals
  Organized crime
  Industrial and government espionage spies
Information Warfare and Cyberterrorism
  Massive attack by a government or terrorist group against a country's IT infrastructure
  Attacks by amateur cyberterrorists are already starting to approach this level of threat
Employees
  Dangerous because of internal knowledge and access
  Often, large losses per incident due to theft, fraud, or sabotage

Figure 9-1   Types of Attackers

Disturbingly, attacks by amateur **cyberterrorists**, if they continue to evolve at their current rate, may soon approach the damage levels of information warfare. Amateur cyberterrorists may constitute the greatest security threat facing corporations over the next few years.

Employee Attacks

Some attackers are disgruntled or dishonest employees or former employees. They can do great damage because of their internal access permissions and knowledge of corporate systems. Companies that experience large incidents of theft, fraud, or sabotage often find that their own employees are the culprits. Companies that focus only on Internet attackers are in for very unpleasant surprises.

TEST YOUR UNDERSTANDING

1. a) Distinguish between skilled hackers and amateurs using kiddie scripts. b) Describe the three types of criminal attackers. c) What are information warfare and cyberterrorism? d) Why are amateur cyberterrorists dangerous? e) Why are attacks by internal employees especially dangerous?

Types of Security Systems

Figure 9-2 shows that there are two major types of security systems in organizations.

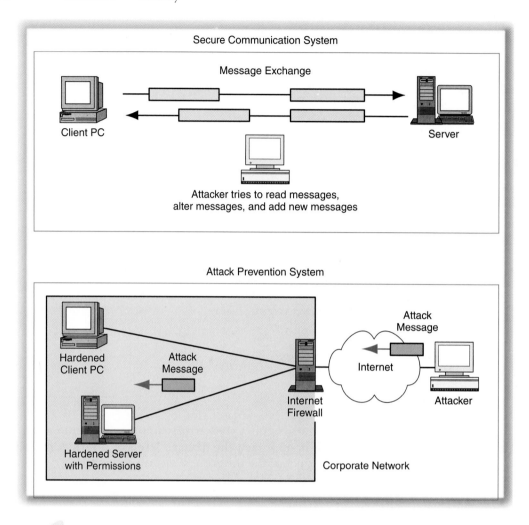

Figure 9-2 Types of Security Systems

Secure Communication Systems

The first type of security system is the *secure communication system,* which protects message communication between two parties who wish to communicate and are likely to be attacked by **eavesdroppers**. These attackers try to read communications between the two parties. These attackers also try to capture messages, alter them, and then send them on to the intended receiver. They also create and send new messages posing as legitimate messages.

Attack Prevention Systems

The second type of security system is an *attack prevention system* designed to stop attackers from hacking into host computers and doing other damage. Companies add firewalls to stop hacker messages from getting into their networks and "harden" their clients and servers to make these machines more difficult to hack.

TEST YOUR UNDERSTANDING

    2.   Distinguish between secure communication systems and attack prevention systems.

ATTACK PREVENTION SYSTEMS

Dangers

As Figure 9-3 shows, there are several types of dangers that must be thwarted by **attack prevention systems**, which attempt to stop incoming messages designed to hack into a computer or do other harm to a network.

Figure 9-3   Attacks Requiring Protection

Hacking Servers
    Attractive because of the data they store
Hacking Clients
    Attractive because of their data or as a way to hack into other systems
    Soft targets compared to servers
Denial-of-Service (DoS) Attacks
    Make the system unusable (crash it or make it run very slowly)
    Single-message DoS attacks
    Message stream DoS attacks
    Distributed DoS attacks
Malicious Content
    Viruses (infect files); one in every 400 e-mail messages in 2001
    Worms (self-propagating across systems)
    Trojan horses (appear to be one thing, such as a game, but actually are malicious)
    Snakes: Combine worm with virus, Trojan horses, and other attacks
    Illegal content: pornography, sexual or racial harassment
    Spam (unsolicited commercial e-mail)
Scanning Attacks
    To identify victims and ways of attacking them

Hacking Servers

Hackers love to log into servers to steal information and sometimes to destroy critical data. Servers are attractive targets because of all the data they contain.

Hacking Clients

Hackers also attack client PCs. Users save passwords on their hard drives, so hackers can take over client PCs, then log into networks as the compromised user, going right through the firewall and logging directly into servers. In addition, many clients store information of interest to criminals, such as credit card numbers.

Clients are also attractive victims because their security usually is very soft compared to the security on servers. This makes clients easy to hack compared to servers.

Denial-of-Service Attacks

If an attacker fails to break into your network or hosts, he or she may mount a **denial-of-service (DoS)** attack that will either (1) overload a router or server with a long stream of messages or (2) send a single message that causes a router or server to crash.

Figure 9-4 illustrates two types of DoS attacks. The first is a traditional DoS attack, which is executed by the attacker working on a single PC.

The second attack in Figure 9-4 is a **distributed denial-of-service (DDoS)** attack, in which an attacker hacks into multiple clients or servers and plants **handler** or **zombie programs** on them. From his or her own computer, the attacker sends commands to the handler programs to attack a particular victim. Handler programs pass these commands on to zombie programs, which actually execute the attack. DDoS attacks are effective because they generate a great deal of denial-of-service traffic. In addition, these attacks are very difficult to trace back to the attacker because attack messages come from many machines and because the attacker is twice removed from the zombie machines that actually implement the attack.

Malicious Content Attacks

Incoming messages may contain illicit content, including **viruses** (which infect files on a single system), **worms** (which propagate across systems), **Trojan horses** (programs that appear to be one thing, such as a game, but really execute unwanted instructions on the victim host), pornography, e-mail that is sexually or racially harassing, and **spam** (unsolicited commercial e-mail). Viruses and worms usually do the most damage, but sexual or racial harassment can lead to large lawsuits, and Trojan horses can do long-term mischief.

Snakes

In 2001, we saw the advent of new "blended attacks" that consist of worms that carry viruses, Trojan horses, and other malicious content. These included Code Red, Code Red II, Sircam, and Nimda. These combined attack vehicles, which we will call **snakes** because the term "blended worm" does not begin to convey their devastating nature, each caused more than a billion dollars in damage. By propagating themselves very rapidly, snakes do not have to wait for people to infect themselves by exchanging floppy disks, by opening e-mail attachments, or by visiting malicious websites.

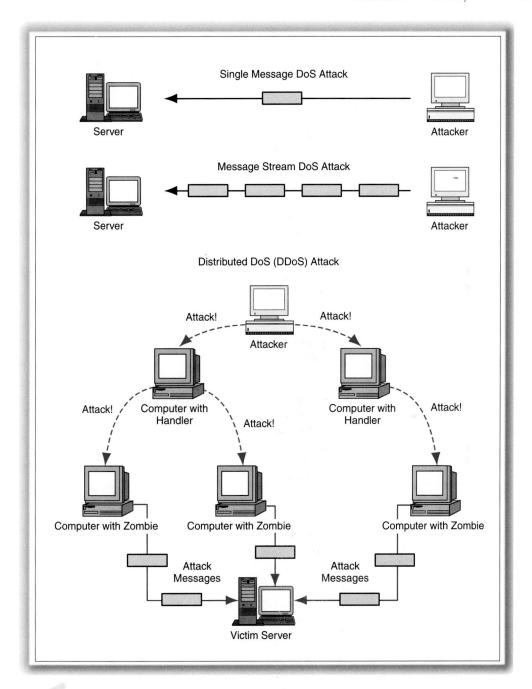

Figure 9-4   Denial-of-Service Attacks

Scanning Attacks

Before attackers can hack a computer, they need to know that it exists, what its IP address is, and what application services it is running. Finding this information usually requires the attacker to send a series of scanning messages whose responses reveal information about potential victims.[3] **Scanning attacks** must be blocked to prevent successful break-ins.

TEST YOUR UNDERSTANDING

3. a) What is hacking? b) Why are servers attractive to hackers? c) Why are clients attractive to hackers?

4. a) Distinguish between single-message, message stream, and distributed denial-of-service attacks. b) How do distributed denial-of-service attacks work?

5. a) Briefly describe the various types of malicious content attacks. b) Describe snakes.

6. What are scanning attacks?

Firewalls

Electronic Guard Gates

Figure 9-5 shows that a device called a **firewall** sits between one network and another, examining arriving messages and stopping illicit messages from entering the protected network. Most typically, a firewall sits between an internal corporate network and the Internet. A firewall acts like a guard gate at a secure facility.

Message Filtering

Although there are different types of firewalls, they all act by **filtering** messages. As Figure 9-5 illustrates, an arriving IP packet normally arrives in the form of an IP header; a TCP or UDP header; and an application message. A less common type of message has an IP header followed by an ICMP message. A firewall examines one or more parts of each packet as it arrives. Based on a list of rules, the firewall decides whether to permit or deny the packet.

TEST YOUR UNDERSTANDING

7. a) What do firewalls do? b) What is their goal in doing this?

Packet Filter Firewalls

Scanning for Key Fields in IP, TCP, UDP, and ICMP

The simplest firewalls are **packet filter firewalls**, which examine certain fields in IP, TCP, or UDP headers and in ICMP supervisory messages. Figure 9-5 actually shows a packet filter firewall. The following are some examples of things a packet filter firewall considers.

➤   If the source IP address in a packet arriving from outside the network is that of a host known to be *inside* the firewall (on the corporate network side), the packet must be from an attacker **spoofing** (counterfeiting) the source IP address.

---

[3]   By analogy, thieves often call a house at different times of the day to see when residents usually are not home.

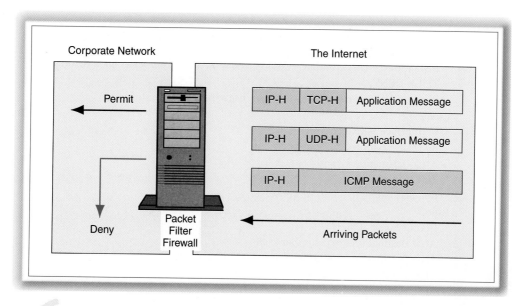

Figure 9-5   Packet Filter Firewall

> ➤ ICMP ping (echo) messages usually are stopped because they can be used in scanning attacks to identify potential victim hosts.
> ➤ In TCP, ACK messages are stopped if there is no current connection between two hosts because hosts would respond by returning reset (RST) messages that contain the host's IP address. This gives the same type of information a ping does.[4]
> ➤ In both TCP and UDP, port number fields are examined. Usually, only a few port numbers are allowed, most notably Port 80, which is used by HTTP for webservice.

Access Control Lists and Configuration

Packet filter firewalls work by implementing **access control lists**, which are a series of if-then rules for dealing with the content of specific fields in internet headers, transport headers, and ICMP messages. The if-then rules may even be nested. Figure 9-6 shows a fragment of an access control list.

If-then rules are notoriously difficult to create without making errors, and because the rules are executed sequentially, the order of rules in the list is critical. If there is an ordering error, the firewall may make a "permit" decision before it ever gets to a rule that would cause a "deny" decision.

Overall, configuring a firewall access control list requires both training and enormous care. A poorly configured firewall will leave holes that a hacker can easily find.

---

[4] This type of attack can only be done by stateful inspection firewalls, which keep track of series of exchanges between the communicating parties. Regular packet filter firewalls only look at packets in isolation.

Rule 1
   IF Interface = Internal
   AND (Source Port Number = 7056 OR Source Port Number = 8002 through 8007)
   THEN DENY
   Remark: Used by a well-known Trojan horse program.
Rule 2
   IF Interface = External
   AND Destination Port Number = 80
   AND Destination IP address = 172.16.210.22
   THEN PERMIT
   Remark: Going to a known webserver.
Rule 3
   IF Interface = External
   AND Destination Port Number = 80
   AND Destination IP Address = NOT 172.16.210.22
   THEN DENY
   Remark: Going to an unknown webserver.
Rule 4
   IF Interface = External
   AND (SYN = Set AND FIN = Set)
   THEN DENY
   Remark: Used in host scanning attacks and not in real transactions.

Figure 9-6   Access Control List (ACL) Fragment

TEST YOUR UNDERSTANDING

8. a) What headers and messages do packet filter firewalls examine? b) What are ACLs? c) Why are access control lists difficult to configure?

Application (Proxy) Firewalls

Application Content Filtering
Application firewalls, also known as **proxy firewalls**, filter application layer messages to check for illicit application content,. Application firewalls and packet filter firewalls are complementary in terms of what parts of a message they examine.

Acting as a Client and a Server
As Figure 9-7 shows, an application firewall acts like a server program to a client program and like a client program to a server program. The application proxy intercepts messages from a client to its server and intercepts messages from a server to its client.

In both cases, the application firewall reads application messages to scan for illicit content before passing them on. If it detects illicit content, it discards the message.

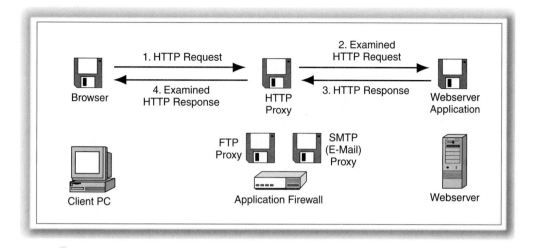

Figure 9-7 Application (Proxy) Firewall

Multiple Proxies

Different application programs have different behaviors to understand. Consequently, there must be a separate **application proxy program** for each application (webservice, e-mail, FTP, etc.) being filtered, as Figure 9-7 illustrates. Furthermore, not all applications can be handled well by proxies.

TEST YOUR UNDERSTANDING

9. a) What part of a packet do application firewalls examine? b) What do they look for? c) Must there be a separate application proxy program for each application being examined?

Network Address Translation (NAT)

Many firewalls do **network address translation (NAT)** to hide their company's internal IP address from hackers who use **sniffers**, which are programs that record the IP addresses of outgoing and incoming packets in order to identify potential victims.

Outgoing Packets

When a client host sends a packet, the firewall removes the packet's real source IP address and ephemeral source port number, say 172.20.9.6 and 31789. As Figure 9-8 shows, it replaces these with a **stand-in** source IP address field and a source port number field, say 192.168.34.2 and 13472.[5]

---

[5] We should call this NAT/PAT because both network addresses (IP addresses) and port addresses are translated. However, "NAT" has become the accepted term.

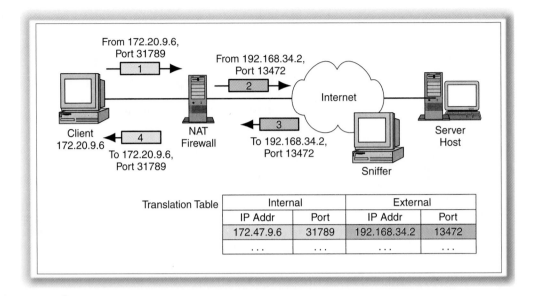

Figure 9-8   Network Address Translation (NAT)

Translation Table
The firewall records the original IP address, the original port number, the stand-in IP address, and the stand-in port number in a **translation table** for later use.

Arriving Packets
When a packet arrives back from a server host, the firewall finds the stand-in IP address and port number in the translation table. It removes the stand-in destination IP address and port number (192.168.34.2 and 13472) and replaces them with the host's real IP address and port number (172.20.9.6 and 31789). It sends the packet on to the original client host, 172.20.9.6. The NAT process is completely transparent to the client, which merely sends and receives normally.

Foiling Sniffers
An attacker with a sniffer on the Internet side of the firewall can only see the stand-in IP address. Therefore, it cannot learn the real IP address of a potential victim.

Private IP Addresses
A company receives a range of **public IP addresses** from its ISP or directly from an IP address authority. Unfortunately, hackers can learn this range of addresses, and this helps them guess at host IP addresses to attack.

Consequently, many corporations assign different IP addresses internally to their hosts, using public IP addresses only on the Internet side of their firewall. The IETF has reserved three ranges of IP addresses for **private IP addresses** that may only be used internally. These ranges are all addresses beginning with 10., all IP addresses beginning with 172.16. through 172.31., and all IP addresses beginning with 192.168.[6]

TEST YOUR UNDERSTANDING

10. a) What danger does NAT address? b) What does NAT do with outgoing packets and TCP segments? c) What does NAT do with arriving packets and TCP segments? d) What are private IP addresses? e) Where can they be used?

Intrusion Detection

Firewalls reject inappropriate messages, but if that is all an organization does about inappropriate messages, then attackers will simply keep trying different types of attacks until they succeed. Given enough time, they probably will succeed.

Signatures

As Figure 9-9 illustrates, **intrusion detection** software examines each packet's key fields for the **signatures** (characteristics) of known attacks. For instance, in one attack, both the SYN and FIN bits are set in TCP. (The receiving transport process will send back an RST segment whose source IP address will be that of the host; this gives the same information as a Ping.) In essence, an intrusion detection system is like a virus detection program, but for transport and internet layer attacks instead of viruses.

Notification

If an intrusion detection system detects the signature of an attack, it may notify a network administrator while the attack is occurring. This allows the network administrator to take immediate action to get rid of the attacker, reducing the time the attacker has to find weaknesses.

Dump File

Intrusion detection systems also store copies of the contents of key fields in *all* incoming messages in a **dump file**, using a program such as tcpdump. Intrusion detection specialists examine these logs on a periodic basis to look for suspicious messages. They also examine them after an attack for forensic purposes.

Many False Alarms

In addition, although attack alerts are useful, most intrusion detection systems generate too many false alarms, so the network administrator normally has to waste a great deal of time determining if an attack warning is real by examining patterns in the dump file.

TEST YOUR UNDERSTANDING

11. a) What is intrusion detection? b) Why is it important? c) Why are dump files used in intrusion detection?

---

[6] In the example in Figure 9-8, we used a private IP address on the public side of the Internet firewall. This would not happen in practice. It's like U.S. movies using phone numbers that begin with the nonexistent 555 prefix. Using public IP addresses in examples is not good because these belong to real firms.

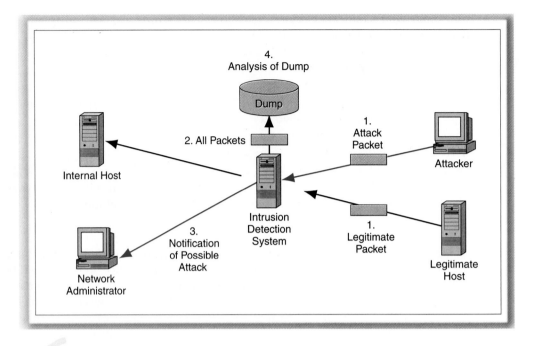

Figure 9-9 Intrusion Detection

Hardening Servers and Clients

Even if a firm has very good firewalls and a very good intrusion detection system, attackers will occasionally get through and attack internal hosts. Therefore it is important to **harden** servers, that is, make them less vulnerable to attack. It is also important to harden clients.

Known Weaknesses

When you install a server operating system, a client operating system, or an application program from the vendor's CD-ROM disk, you are installing a program that is weeks or even months old. Hackers will already have compiled a list of **known weaknesses** in the software and will also have created attack software to exploit these weaknesses.

Patches   As soon as a firm installs a program, therefore, it should download **vendor update patches** that fix known weaknesses. It should continue to download and install these patches regularly, and when a vendor issues an **alert**, which indicates an unusually great danger, the firm should immediately install the patch named in the alert.

Lax Application of Patches   Unfortunately, installing this constant stream of patches on many servers and many more clients is a daunting task. Many firms fall behind in installing patches, leaving their servers and clients open for hackers.

Known Weaknesses
  Known security weaknesses in operating systems and application programs
  Must download vendor patches to fix these known weaknesses
  Firms often fail to do so
Host Firewalls
  Server firewalls and personal (client) firewalls
Server Authentication
  Passwords
    Cracking with exhaustive search and dictionary attacks
    Strong passwords
    Super accounts
  Kerberos authentication
  Biometric authentication
    Fingerprint: least expensive
    Iris: most accurate
    Face recognition: controversial in public places for mass identification
    Other forms of biometric identification
  Smart cards (ID card with microprocessor and data)
Limiting Permissions on Servers
  Only permit access to some directories
  Limit permissions there

Figure 9-10 Hardening Clients and Servers

Host Firewalls

As part of the hardening process, companies should install **host firewalls** on all their computers, including **server firewalls** on their servers and **personal firewalls** on their clients, in case attackers break through other firewalls. Personal firewalls are especially important on user PCs that are not protected by the company firewall, for instance, when the user works at home or while traveling.

Password Authentication

Users must *authenticate* themselves to servers, that is, prove their identities. Figure 9-10 lists three authentication methods: passwords, Kerberos, and biometric authentication. Even after a user has been authenticated, their account's permissions on the server still limit what resources on the server they can access and what they can do with these resources.

Weak Passwords   To break into a server, a hacker often tries to **crack** (discover) a user's **password**. Unfortunately, this often is fairly easy because many users pick **weak passwords** that are only a few characters long, only use alphabetic characters, and often are common words.

Cracking Passwords Through Exhaustive Search   If a password only uses alphabetic characters, then if a password is N characters long, it will only take 26^N attempts to guess the password using **exhaustive search**. Short, all-alphabetic passwords can be cracked in a few minutes or hours using exhaustive searches.

Dictionary Attacks   In fact, attackers rarely have to perform exhaustive searches. Most users pick common words as their passwords. Cracking programs can use dictionaries (lists) of common words to test against passwords. These **dictionary attacks** can crack common-word passwords in a few seconds because there are only a few thousand common words in any language.

Strong Passwords   To thwart attackers, users must be forced to use strong passwords, such as Tri6#vial. The following are characteristics of strong passwords:

➤ Strong passwords are long: at least 8 characters long.

➤ The password should contain at least one change of case.

➤ The password must contain at least one digit (0 through 9) that is *not* at the end of the password.

➤ The password must contain at least one character that is not alphanumeric, such as #, that is *not* at the end of the password.

If these rules are followed, then the hacker will have to use brute force guessing, and they must try an average of $75^8/2$ possible passwords to search exhaustively.

Super Accounts

Server operating systems always have a **super account** whose owner can do anything to *all* files in *all* folders. In LINUX and UNIX, this is the **root** account. In Windows Server, it is **administrator**. In Novell NetWare, it is **supervisor**. In addition, it is possible to give other user accounts equivalent powers.

The ultimate goal of hackers is to hack into the super account because this will give them total control of the computer. They can then read whatever information they wish and do whatever damage they wish.

TEST YOUR UNDERSTANDING

12. a) What are known weaknesses? b) In what types of software are known weaknesses found? c) Why are known weaknesses dangerous? d) How can organizations protect themselves against known weaknesses? e) Why do they often not do this?

13. a) What are host firewalls? b) Why are they needed? c) What are personal firewalls?

14. a) What is authentication? b) What are weak passwords? c) Distinguish between exhaustive search and dictionary attacks for cracking passwords. d) What are the four rules for strong passwords?

15. a) What are super accounts? b) Why are they dangerous?

Kerberos Authentication

Passwords are good for single computers, but corporations wish to manage security on large numbers of computers in an integrated way. One approach to doing this is to use the Kerberos authentication standard created at MIT and used heavily by Windows 2000 and later Microsoft operating systems. Kerberos is illustrated in Figure 9-11.

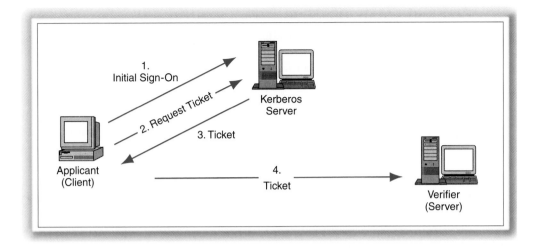

Figure 9-11   Kerberos Authentication (Simplified)

Kerberos Operation

In this simplified depiction of Kerberos, a client applicant asks the Kerberos server for a **ticket** to speak to a verifier server. Kerberos gives the applicant the ticket, which the applicant sends to the verifier along with other authenticating information. The ticket verifies that the client has access permissions on the verifier server and may even specify those permissions. Before an applicant can get tickets, it must first authenticate itself to the Kerberos[7] server.

Central Control Point

Kerberos creates a central control point with which to enforce policy and ensure consistency of policy application. If an employee leaves the firm, for instance, he or she is immediately removed from the Kerberos database and loses access to all hosts.

Single Sign-On

In addition, Kerberos provides **single sign-on**, meaning that the user only needs to be able to communicate securely with the Kerberos server. The user does not have to memorize passwords on other servers.

TEST YOUR UNDERSTANDING

   16.   a) How does Kerberos authentication work? b) Why is providing a central control point for authentication good? c) What is single sign-on, and why is it good?

---

[7]   In Greek mythology, Kerberos is a three-headed dog that guards the gates to the underworld. The name was chosen because three machines are involved—the applicant, the verifier, and the Kerberos server. The name was also chosen because the Kerberos server, like the mythological dog, decides who may be allowed entry.

Biometric Authentication

In a few years, **biometric authentication**—authentication based on body measurements and motion—will reduce our dependence upon passwords and may eventually eliminate them. There are a number of different types of biometric techniques.

Fingerprint Identification

Fingerprint identification is the least expensive form of biometric identification. The applicant puts his or her index finger on a small piece of glass, and software identifies the applicant's fingerprint.

Iris Identification

For ultra-high security, the most discriminating devices read the **iris** pattern in the eye. Irises are far more complex and individual than fingerprints and so give more precise identification, albeit at a much higher cost. Iris identification is the gold standard in biometric authentication.

Face Recognition

Face recognition uses cameras to identify people by their faces. One aspect of face identification that has become very controversial is its use to identify people in public places without their knowledge or consent. Some airports use face identification to look for terrorists and criminals. This may be only the beginning of the widespread surreptitious identification of people in public places.

Other Forms of Biometric Authentication

There are a number of other forms of biometric authentication, including voice identification, signature identification, face identification, and even identification by timing patterns when a user types. These vary in cost, precision, and maturity.

Smart Cards

We often have identification cards, such as driver's licenses. Often, these ID cards can be used to authenticate us, for instance by having our picture on the card. Identity cards can be made even stronger by using **smart cards**, which have microprocessors and can store data. For instance, instead of just having our photo, the smart card can contain biometric information about us. Typically, to use a smart card the user must type a password, giving even stronger authentication.

TEST YOUR UNDERSTANDING

17. a) What is biometric authentication? b) What is the least expensive form of biometric authentication? c) What is the most accurate form? d) Why is face recognition in public places controversial? e) What are smart cards? f) Why are smart cards good?

Access Permissions

Even if users can log into a server, this does not mean they can do anything they wish on the server. Users must have **access permissions** to go to particular directories. What they do in these directories will be further limited by permissions. Permissions restrict access for normal accounts, but super user accounts have complete access in all directories.

Network administrators should give each user the **minimum permissions** they need to do their job. This way, even if an attacker cracks a normal user's password, the attacker's ability to do damage will be limited.

TEST YOUR UNDERSTANDING

18. a) Why do server permissions limit damage that an attacker can do? b) Why is giving minimum permissions important?

SECURE COMMUNICATION SYSTEMS

So far, we have looked at attack prevention systems. Many times, however, two communication partners simply wish to communicate securely, with protection against eavesdroppers trying to read their messages, with the authentication of the other party's identity, with assurance that messages have not been tampered with en route, and with assurance that messages have not been added by an attacker.

Figure 9-12 shows that this type of communication often takes place through a **secure communication system** in which software processes owned by the two communicants implement security automatically, often without even the knowledge of the communicating parties. IPsec and PPTP, which we saw in Chapter 7, are secure communication systems.

Phase 1: Negotiation of Security Parameters

Secure communication systems operate in four phases. In the first, the parties negotiate how they will handle security. Generally, there are multiple options in security. The parties must select options agreeable to both sides. Some secure communication systems,

Figure 9-12   Secure Communication System

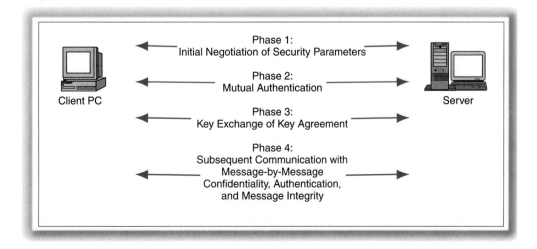

notably IPsec, allow corporations to set policies for what options will be allowed, thus ensuring consistency in corporate security.

Phase 2: Mutual Authentication

Next, each party authenticates itself (proves its identity) to its communication partner, so that each side will be sure it knows with whom it is dealing. This must wait until after negotiation because the negotiation phase lets the two parties decide how they will perform the authentication using one of the options open to them.

Phase 3: Key Exchange

During later transmissions, each side will encrypt (scramble) its messages to make them safe from eavesdroppers. Encryption requires a bit string called a key. In the third phase, the two sides exchange one or more keys they will use to encrypt messages in subsequent communication. This **key exchange** must be done securely or eavesdroppers may be able to intercept the key during exchange and then decrypt subsequent conversations.

Phase 4: Ongoing Communication

The initial exchanges are now over. From now on, when the two sides exchange messages, they encrypt each message so that eavesdroppers cannot read their messages. They also do message-by-message authentication (like signing a letter) and mark messages to allow the receiver to detect message tampering en route. Usually the first three stages take only a few milliseconds, so ongoing communication takes up nearly all communication time.

TEST YOUR UNDERSTANDING

19. a) What are the four stages in secure communication systems? b) Briefly describe each stage.

ENCRYPTION FOR CONFIDENTIALITY

As Figure 9-13 shows, secure communication systems **encrypt** their messages, meaning that they transform their messages into bit strings that an interceptor cannot read but that the receivers can read after **decrypting** the encrypted messages. If an interceptor cannot read your messages, you have **confidentiality**.

Terminology

Plaintext and Ciphertext

The original message is called **plaintext** (even if it is not a text message). The encrypted message is called **ciphertext**.

Encryption Method

When the sender encrypts a plaintext message, his or her software uses a mathematical algorithm called an **encryption method**. There are only a few encryption methods in common use.

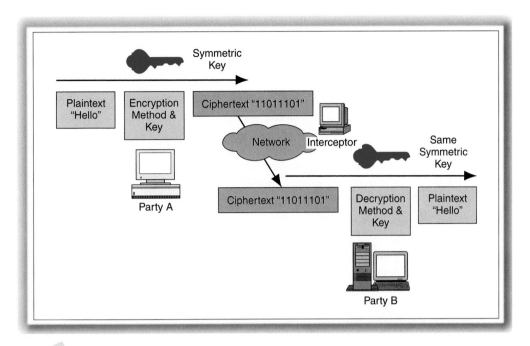

Figure 9-13 Symmetric Key Encryption for Confidentiality

Key

An encryption method requires a **key**, which is a string of bits that is used with an encryption method to produce ciphertext from a given plaintext. Different keys will give different ciphertexts for the same plaintext and encryption method, so the two partners only have to keep the key secret when they communicate, not the encryption method.

Exhaustive Key Search and Key Length

One way for an eavesdropper to break encryption is to conduct an **exhaustive key search**, that is, to try all possible keys until they find the correct one. Earlier, we saw the brute force password cracking of passwords that consist of characters. Exhaustive key search does the same thing with bit strings.

Long keys make exhaustive search impractical. Today, keys with lengths of 100 bits or less are considered **weak keys**. Exhaustive search with keys of 56 bits would be too costly for cracking things like consumer credit card numbers, but for highly sensitive transmissions, exhaustive search would be cost-effective. For very sensitive transmissions, **strong keys** with lengths of over 100 bits are required. In the future, even 100 bits will be insufficient.

TEST YOUR UNDERSTANDING

20. a) Distinguish between plaintext and ciphertext. b) Do encryption methods and keys both have to be kept secret? c) Explain exhaustive search to crack keys. d) Today, how long is a strong key? e) Will this be considered a strong key in a few years?

Symmetric Key Encryption

In Figure 9-13, both sides use the same key. A method that uses a single key is a **symmetric key encryption** method. Each side encrypts with this single key when it sends a message. Each side decrypts with this single key when it receives a message.

Symmetric Key Encryption Methods

There are several popular symmetric key encryption methods. The most popular is the **Data Encryption Standard (DES)**. DES uses a key length of 56 bits,[8] so it is relatively weak. However, a variant called **3DES (Triple DES)**[9] encrypts each block of plaintext three times, each time with a different key. This effectively gives a key length of 168 bits, which is strong enough today even for large bank transactions. The new **Advanced Encryption Standard (AES)**[10] will allow strong keys of multiple lengths and yet will be efficient enough to implement on small handheld devices.

Efficiency for Long Messages

Symmetric key encryption in general is very efficient, allowing even simple devices to encrypt and decrypt without devoting most of their processing cycles to these processes. Symmetric key encryption is efficient enough to be used even for long messages.

Key Exchange

The main problem with symmetric key encryption in the past has been exchanging the symmetric key securely between the two parties. (Obviously, if anyone intercepts the key as it is being exchanged, they will be able to read subsequent encrypted transmissions.) Later, we will see how public key encryption can distribute symmetric key encryption securely.

TEST YOUR UNDERSTANDING

21. a) How many keys are used in symmetric key encryption? b) What is the most popular symmetric key encryption method? c) How long is its key? d) How can this method be made stronger? e) What is AES? f) Why is it attractive?

22. a) Why is the efficiency of symmetric key encryption important? b) What is the main problem with symmetric key encryption?

Public Key Encryption

Another class of encryption methods, shown in Figure 9-14, is **public key encryption**. Here, each party has a **private key**, which it keeps secret from the world. In addition,

---

[8] It actually is a 64-bit key, but 8 bits are redundant (can be computed from the other 56), so it provides 56 bits of effective length.

[9] Actually, the sender encrypts with the first key, *decrypts* with the second key, and then encrypts with the third key. The receiver, in turn, decrypts with the third key, *encrypts* with the second key, and then decrypts with the first key. In many algorithms, you can use decryption to produce ciphertext that can be turned back to plaintext with encryption. In a variant of 3DES that offers 112-bit encryption by using only two keys, the third operation of the sender is to encrypt again with the first key, and the first action of the receiver is to decrypt with the first key. The encrypt-decrypt-encrypt sequence was chosen because it can be done with a single key three times, giving the equivalent of regular DES encryption. A receiver that only implements normal DES will be able to decrypt ciphertext created by a 3DES sender who uses a single key in all three steps.

[10] AES is based on the Rijndael (pronounced "Rhine-doll") algorithm.

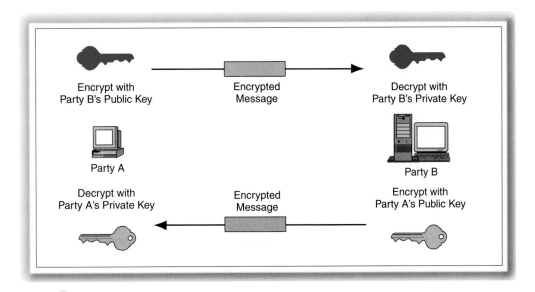

Figure 9-14   Public Key Encryption for Confidentiality

each party has a **public key**, which it shares with everybody because the public key, as its name suggests, does not need to be kept secret.

Sending
Whenever one party sends, it encrypts the plaintext with the *public key of the receiver.* When A sends to B, A encrypts with *B's* public key. When B sends to A, B encrypts with *A's* public key.

Receiving
Each receiver decrypts with its own private key. When A sends to B, B decrypts with *B's* private key. In turn, when B sends to A, A decrypts with *A's* private key.

Once a message is encrypted with the receiver's public key, nobody can decrypt it except the receiver. Even the sender cannot decrypt the message after encrypting it.

Referring to Public and Private Keys
Note that you should never say "the public key" or "the private key" by itself when describing confidential transmission using public key encryption. There are two public keys and two private keys involved in any two-way exchange. You must always specify something like "A's public key" or "B's private key."

Complexity, Processing Intensiveness, and Short Messages
Public key encryption probably strikes you as complex. In fact, it is. It requires many computer processing cycles to do public key encryption and decryption—about 100 times as many cycles as symmetric key encryption. The inefficiency of this

processing burden is so large that public key encryption can only be used to encrypt small messages.[11]

Simplicity of Key Exchange

The major benefit of public key encryption is that key exchange is simple. Public keys are not secret, so there is no need to exchange them securely. Many people post their public keys online for everyone to read.

Public Key Distribution of Symmetric Keys

In fact, public key distribution can help symmetric key encryption by distributing symmetric session keys securely, as Figure 9-15 illustrates.

➤ First, one side generates a random bit string that will be used as a symmetric key.

➤ Second, that side encrypts this symmetric key with the public key of the other party.

➤ Third, the party that generated the symmetric key sends this ciphertext to the other party.

➤ Fourth, the other party decrypts the ciphertext with its own private key.

➤ Fifth, both sides now have the session key and will use it to send messages confidentially.

Session Key

The key that is exchanged this way is called a **session key** because it is only used for the current communication session. If the two parties communicate later, they will generate a new session key.

Popular Public Key Encryption Methods

The most widely used public key encryption method is **RSA**.[12] RSA was patented, but its patent expired in 2000. Now that RSA is in the public domain, its domination of public key encryption may grow. However, a new form of public key encryption, the **elliptic curve cryptosystem (ECC)**, promises to provide equal protection with smaller keys, and therefore less processing burden. ECC is patented.

TEST YOUR UNDERSTANDING

23. Jason sends a message to Kristin using public key encryption. a) What key will Jason use to encrypt the message? b) What key will Kristin use to decrypt the message? c) What key will Kristin use to encrypt the reply? d) What key will Jason use to decrypt the reply? e) Can the message and reply be long messages? Explain.

24. a) Does public key encryption have a problem with secure key exchange for the public key? Explain. b) How does public key encryption address symmetric key encryption's problem with secure key exchange? c) What is a session key?

25. a) What are the two most popular public key encryption methods? b) Which is in the public domain? c) Which allows smaller keys to be used for a given level of security?

---

[11] In fact, some public key encryption methods are mathematically incapable of encrypting messages of more than 1,000 to 4,000 bits.
[12] Rivest-Shamir-Adleman.

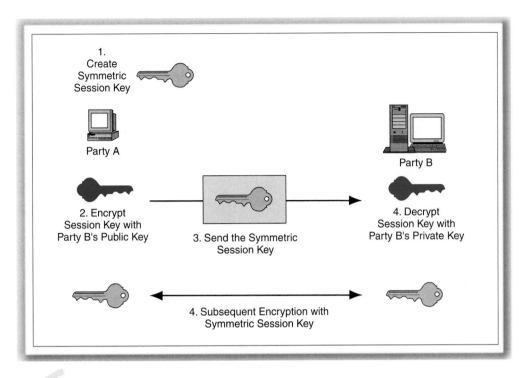

1.
Create
Symmetric
Session Key

Party A

Party B

2. Encrypt
Session Key with
Party B's Public Key

3. Send the Symmetric
Session Key

4. Decrypt
Session Key with
Party B's Private Key

4. Subsequent Encryption with
Symmetric Session Key

Figure 9-15   Public Key Distribution for Symmetric Session Keys

AUTHENTICATION

So far, we have been discussing encryption as a way to create confidentiality. However, encryption can also be used in **authentication**, that is, verifying the other party's identity.

Applicant and Verifier

In authentication terminology, the **applicant** is the side that tries to prove its identity to the other party, as Figure 9-16 shows. The other party, which tries to authenticate the identity of the applicant, is the **verifier**. In two-way communication, both sides take on both roles because each authenticates the other.

TEST YOUR UNDERSTANDING

26.   a) What is authentication? b) In authentication, who is the applicant? c) The verifier?
        d) Can a station be both an applicant and a verifier?

Initial Authentication with MS-CHAP
Challenge–Response Authentication

In war movies, when a soldier approaches a sentry, the sentry issues a challenge, and the soldier must respond with the correct password. Figure 9-16 shows a form of

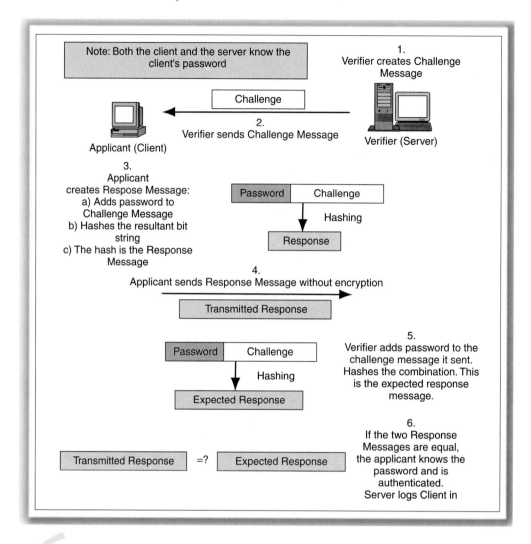

Figure 9-16   MS-CHAP Challenge–Response Authentication Protocol

network **challenge–response authentication** called **MS-CHAP**. It is the Microsoft (MS) version of the IETF **Challenge Handshake Authentication Protocol (CHAP)**.

MS-CHAP is for Server-Based Authentication

MS-CHAP is used to authenticate a remote user to a server. It relies on the fact that the user has a password that both the user and the server know. This is a very common situation in organizations.

On the Applicant's Machine: Hashing

The server sends the applicant's PC a **challenge message**, which is a random bit string. The applicant's PC then adds the user's password to this challenge message.

The applicant's PC next hashes the combined challenge message and password. **Hashing** is a mathematical process that, when applied to a bit string of any length, produces a value of a fixed length, called the **hash**. For instance, the **MD5** hashing algorithm always produces a hash of 128 bits, whereas the **Secure Hash Algorithm Version 1 (SHA-1)** always produces a hash of 160 bits.

The hash of the challenge message plus the user's password is the **response message** that the applicant's PC sends back to the server.

On the Verifier's Machine (The Server)

The server itself adds the challenge message to the user's password and applies the same hashing algorithm the applicant used, producing a new hash. If this new hash is identical to the response message, then the person at the client PC must know the account's password.[13] The server then logs in the user.

TEST YOUR UNDERSTANDING

27. a) For what type of authentication is MS-CHAP used? b) How does hashing work? c) What are the two most popular hashing algorithms? d) How does the applicant create the response message? e) How does the verifier check the response message?

Message-by-Message Authentication with Digital Signatures

Challenge–response authentication usually is only done at the beginning of a session or at most a few times per session. We would like to be able to authenticate each and every message coming from the other party to ensure that an attacker cannot slip a message into the message stream.

Digital Signatures

Figure 9-17 shows how to create a **digital signature**, which authenticates each message analogously to the way a human signature authenticates documents.

Hashing to Produce the Message Digest

To create the digital signature, the sender (who is an applicant), first hashes the plaintext message the sender wishes to transmit securely. This generates a hash called a **message digest**. The hash is generated because digital signatures use public key encryption, which is limited to encrypting short messages, such as hashes.

---

[13] Of course, users may have had their PCs remember their passwords. In this case, anyone taking control of their computers could impersonate them.

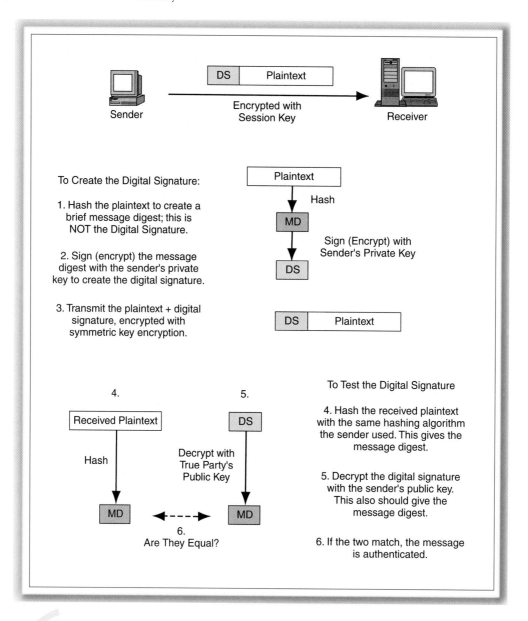

Figure 9-17   Digital Signature for Message-by-Message Authentication

Signing the Message Digest to Produce the Digital Signature

Next, the sender encrypts the message digest with the sender's own private key. This creates the **digital signature**. *Note that the message digest is not the digital signature but is only used to produce the digital signature.*

When a party encrypts with its own private key, this is called **signing** a message with its private key. The sender proves his or her identity like a person signing a letter. In this terminology, the sender signs the message digest to create the digital signature.

Sending the Message

The message that the sender wishes to send, then, consists of the original plaintext message plus the digital signature. If confidentiality is not an issue, the sender can simply send the combined message. However, confidentiality normally *is* important, so the sender normally encrypts the combined original message and digital signature for confidentiality. The combined message is likely to be long, so the sender must use symmetric key encryption.

Verifying the Applicant

The receiver (verifier) decrypts the entire message with the symmetric key used for confidentiality, then decrypts the digital signature with the true party's public key, which is widely known. This will produce the original message digest—if the applicant has signed the message digest with the true party's private key.

Then, the receiver hashes the original plaintext message with the same hashing algorithm the applicant used. This should also produce the message digest.

If the message digests produced in these two different ways match, then the sender must have the true party's private key, which only the true party should know. The message is authenticated as coming from the true party.

Message Integrity

If someone changes the message en route, or if there are transmission errors, the two message digests will not match. Therefore, digital signatures give **message integrity**—the ability to tell if a message has been modified en route. A message that is changed will not pass the authentication test and will be discarded.

TEST YOUR UNDERSTANDING

28. a) For what type of authentication is a digital signature used? b) How does the applicant create a message digest? c) How does the applicant create a digital signature? d) What combined message does the applicant send? e) How is the combined message encrypted for confidentiality? f) How does the verifier check the digital signature? g) Besides authentication, what security benefit does a digital signature provide? h) Explain what this benefit means.

DIGITAL CERTIFICATES

In public key-based authentication, the verifier must know the public key of the true party. It should not ask the applicant for the true party's public key, because if the applicant is an **imposter**, the impostor will send his or her *own* public key claiming that this is the true party's public key, as Figure 9-18 illustrates. If the verifier is ignorant

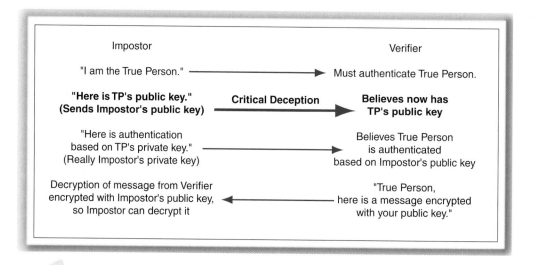

Figure 9-18   Public Key Deception

enough to accept the imposter's public key as the true party's public key, the imposter will sign digital signatures with his or her own private key, and the verifier will use the imposter's public key to verify the imposter as the true party!

Certificate Authorities and Digital Certificates

Instead, Figure 9-19 shows that the verifier must contact a **certificate authority**, which is an independent and trusted source of information about the public keys of true parties. The certificate authority will send the verifier a **digital certificate** containing the *name of the true party* and the *true party's public key*. The verifier then uses this public key to authenticate the applicant claiming to be the true party. The standard for digital certificates is **X.509**.

Unfortunately, certificate authorities are not regulated, so the verifier must only accept a digital certificate from a certificate authority it trusts.

Also, it is a common misconception that certificate authorities vouch for the honesty of the party named in the certificate. They do not. They merely vouch for the named party's public key! Although clients who misbehave may have their certificates revoked, certificate authorities rarely give strong warranties about the honesty of their clients. That is not their job.

The Role of the Digital Certificate

Note that a digital certificate does not, by itself, authenticate an applicant! It merely provides the public key of the true party for the verifier to use to make the authentication. Similarly, without a digital certificate, the verifier has no proven way to know the true party's public key. *Digital certificates and public key authentication must be used together in public key authentication.* Neither, by itself, provides authentication.

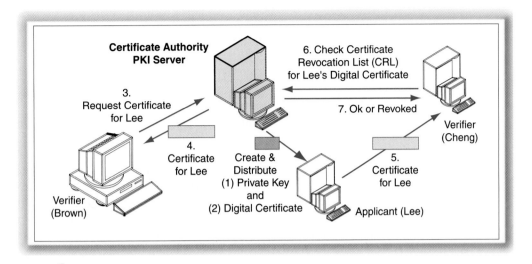

Figure 9-19   Public Key Infrastructure (PKI) with a Certificate Authority

Checking the Certificate Revocation List (CRL)

The certificate authority may revoke a party's digital certificate before the termination date listed in the digital certificate. Therefore, if the verifier gets the digital certificate from a party other than the certificate authority, the verifier should check the certificate authority's **certificate revocation list (CRL)** to be sure that the digital certificate is still valid.

Public Key Infrastructures (PKIs)

Managing public keys requires several related actions. Digital certificates must be created and distributed. Certificate revocation list checking must be supported. Public key-private key pairs must be created. The public key will be distributed through digital certificates, but the private key must be distributed securely, often by embedding it in software that is installed on a particular machine.

    Public key infrastructures (PKIs) automate all of these processes. PKIs create a total system (infrastructure) for public key encryption. Unfortunately, all of the PKIs in use today are proprietary products, so interoperability is spotty.

TEST YOUR UNDERSTANDING

29.   a) What pair of facts crucial to authentication do digital certificates tell us? b) What kind of organization creates a digital certificate? c) Are these organizations regulated? d) Does a digital certificate tell you that the entity named in a digital certificate is a good organization? Explain. e) Does a digital certificate tell you that the entity named in a digital certificate has a certain public key? f) Does a digital certificate alone give authentication? Explain. g) Does public key authentication without a

digital certificate give reliable authentication? Explain. h) What is necessary for reliable authentication? i) What are the elements of a PKI? j) Why is it important to check the CRL if you do not receive the digital certificate from the certificate authority?

MULTILAYER SECURITY

At what layer does security exist? The answer is that security can exist at one layer, at multiple layers, or at all layers. Figure 9-20 illustrates some common secure communication systems and attack prevention systems and the layers at which they operate.

Implementing security at all five layers generally is unwise because it would slow the communication to an unacceptable level. However, it is usually wise to create **multilayer security**, in which security is implemented in at least two layers although not at all layers. Historically, problems often have been found in security products. If a weakness is found at one layer in a multilayer security system, security at other layers will still protect the system while the flawed security layer is being fixed or replaced.

TEST YOUR UNDERSTANDING

30.   a) At what layer is security implemented? b) What problem will implementing security at multiple layers bring? c) What is the advantage of multilayer security?

CREATING APPROPRIATE SECURITY

As Figure 9-21 shows, creating appropriate security requires a number of steps.

Figure 9-20   Security at Multiple Layers

Layer	Example
Application	Application-specific (for instance, passwords for a server or database program), application (proxy) firewalls
Transport	SSL (TLS), packet filter firewalls
Internet	IPsec, packet filter firewalls
Data Link	Point-to-Point Tunneling Protocol (PPTP), Layer 2 Tunneling Protocol (L2TP)
Physical	Physical locks on computers, file encryption

Implementing security at multiple layers slows processing on the device.
Having security at multiple layers provides protection if one layer's security fails.

Understanding Needs
   Need to make security proportional to risks
   Organizations face different risks
Policies and Enforcement
   Policies bring consistency
   Social engineering
   Training in the importance of security and in protection techniques
   Security audits: attack your system proactively
      Requires a dangerously high level of knowledge on the part of attackers
   Incident handling
      Restoring the system
      Prosecution
      Planning and Practicing
   Privacy

Figure 9-21   Creating Appropriate Security

Understanding Needs

Matching Security with Risks

How strong should an organization's security be? This is an important question because security is never free. It is expensive in terms of purchasing security technology, in terms of the processing power it consumes on routers and computers, and in terms of the labor needed to manage security. It is also expensive in terms of lost productivity when workers cannot get to information they legitimately need, as will inevitably happen.[14] Security must be proportional to the risks a company faces.

Organizations Face Different Risks

It is important to study companies to determine their security needs thoroughly because each organization faces different levels of security threats. A company that faces few threats might have comparatively light security needs, although given the general level of misconduct today, every organization needs quite a bit of security. Banks and the military, at the other extreme, need ultra-strong security, including physical security to lock up many computers.

Policies and Enforcement

Policies Bring Consistency

Once threats are assessed, the company must create detailed **security policies** specifying what security practices each computer and user must follow. It also must *enforce*

---

[14] To see how productivity inevitably suffers when security is applied, think of how much more time you must spend in airports before you board an airplane since the September 11, 2001, tragedy forced airports to make their security stronger.

those policies because attackers will keep trying different parts of a network until they find a part that does not follow corporate policy and so is easy to attack.

Social Engineering

These policies must extend to human conduct because many attackers use **social engineering**, in which they trick an employee into giving out passwords or into installing Trojan horse software on their machines by opening up e-mail attachments. In general, the strongest policies mean nothing if users do not follow them, so policy implementation must include sanctions for employees who violate security policies.

Training

Rules are impossible to enforce if users do not see them as legitimate or do not know how to follow them. It is important to train users to understand why security is needed as well as in how to work securely. In particular, training should emphasize the need for strong passwords and how to create them. It is also important to train end users to detect common social engineering attacks.

Security Audits

It is important to conduct security audits of systems on a regular basis. In a **security audit**, a trusted employee or outside agency stages attacks on the system in order to find security weaknesses. Without a security audit, the organization may wrongly assume that it is safe because it has installed firewalls, patches, and other security systems. However, often there still are weaknesses in the way security systems are implemented.

One problem, of course, is finding a trusted person or organization to do the attacks. Often, the only people who have the skills needed to do a solid security audit are reformed hackers, who are obviously questionable. Although there are **automated security auditing programs**, these are like spell checkers—good for a first cut through the system but not sufficient for a full audit.

Incident Handling

Firms also need a comprehensive and detailed plan for incident handling, that is, what to do if a security compromise is discovered. Although this is a complex area, there are two basic goals. The first is to restore the system to proper functioning. The second is to prosecute the attacker.

Restoring the System

The most basic goal is to restore the system. This requires a very accurate diagnosis of the problem and of what has been changed on the system. Sometimes, a previous backup can be used to restore the system, but this will lose all data entered into the system since the last backup. Losing data is especially problematic if the last backup clean of problems was several days before the incident. The alternative is to keep the system running and to try to delete or restore compromised files. This is very difficult to do, but it may be necessary for business continuity.

Prosecution

Whether to prosecute is a difficult business decision. Prosecution punishes the attacker, but it can harm the victim company's reputation. If prosecution is to be undertaken, it is critical to call the proper legal authorities, including community police or the FBI. Delaying even a brief time may make the evidence unusable. Contrary to what some people say, the police and the Feds do not drag away all your data, leaving you with nothing. They are trained to copy your data faithfully and rapidly, so that you can get on with your business.

Plan and Drill

Security incidents can be extremely unsettling. It is crucial to have a plan for what to do, and it is equally crucial to practice incident-handling procedures regularly, so that people will not make crucial mistakes. The firm must be able to create an incident handling team that knows what it is doing within a few minutes of an attack.

Privacy

In the past, companies have focused primarily on protecting data important to the corporation, such as trade secrets. Increasingly, however, corporate servers also contain sensitive information about customers and employees, including social security numbers, bank accounts, credit card numbers, and medical information. Companies are required to protect the **privacy** of this information by preventing it from being read by nonauthorized parties. Privacy is important not only because of lawsuits, but also because concerns about privacy are causing many Internet users not to make e-commerce purchases.

TEST YOUR UNDERSTANDING

31. a) Why is it important to match security with risks? b) Do all organizations face approximately the same level of risk? c) Why are policies important? d) What is social engineering? e) Why is security training needed for end users? f) What is a security audit? g) Why are security audits necessary? h) Why is it a problem to find someone to do the security audit?

32. a) What are the two goals in incident handling? b) What are the two ways to restore a system? c) If the decision is made to prosecute, what is the first step, and when must it be done? d) Why are planning and rehearsal essential for incident response?

33. a) What is privacy? b) Why is it important?

GAINING PERSPECTIVE

Market Realities

CSI/FBI Computer Crime and Security Survey

A 2001 survey[15] by the Computer Security Institute and the San Francisco Branch of the FBI's Computer Intrusion Squad asked 538 computer security practitioners in U.S. organizations to describe security in their organizations. Among their findings were the following:

➤ Eighty-five percent had detected an attack in the preceding year. Thirty-six percent had detected a DoS attack. Ninety-one percent reported employee abuse (downloading pornography, etc.). Of those acknowledging attacks, 58 percent detected 10 or more attacks.

---

[15] Computer Security Institute, "2001 CSI/FBI Computer Crime and Security Survey," *Computer Security Issues and Trends,* Vol. VII, No, 1, 2001. This is an annual survey.

➤ Sixty-four percent acknowledged financial losses. Virus attacks and laptop theft dominated instances of financial loss. However, in terms of dollar losses, the two biggest types of loss were theft of proprietary information and financial fraud.

➤ Internet attacks are more frequent than internally generated attacks (70 percent versus 31 percent)—a reversal of patterns in the earliest years of the survey (which began in 1996).

➤ Only 36 percent reported intrusions to law enforcement agencies. Reasons for not reporting intrusions included concerns about negative publicity (90 percent), concern that competitors would take advantage of the disclosure (75 percent), a lack of awareness that the incident could be reported (54 percent), and a belief that civil remedies seemed best (64 percent).

CIO Complacency

Although security problems seem to be pervasive, a January 2001 study of chief information officers (CIOs) found that more than 90 percent had confidence in their network security.[16] This complacency prevents security from being treated more seriously.

THOUGHT QUESTIONS

1. A company uses public key encryption for digital signatures and symmetric key exchange. It does not use digital certificates. Instead, the two parties exchange public keys and exchange a symmetric session key using public key authentication. a) Comment on the adequacy of this approach for the confidentiality of symmetric key exchange. b) Comment on the adequacy of this approach for message authentication.

2. Nonrepudiation means that the sender cannot send a message and later claim that someone else sent it. Can authentication methods using symmetric key encryption provide nonrepudiation? Explain. Can authentication methods using public key encryption provide nonrepudiation? Explain.

3. Why do you think packet filter firewalls do not bother to examine data link layer fields in arriving frames that carry packets? *Hint:* Consider the scope of the data link layer (see Chapter 2).

TROUBLESHOOTING QUESTIONS

1. In Figure 9-6, the access control list fragment, Rule 4, is designed to prevent arriving TCP segments whose SYN and FIN bits are both sent. Yet an analysis of a tcpdump file shows that such packets are getting through to the company's webserver, 172.16.210.22. Why?

2. When packets arrive from the Internet, a firm first filters them with an application firewall and then passes them to an IPsec server operating in tunnel mode. The application firewall is designed to protect against e-mail viruses. What is wrong with this setup?

---

[16]   Verton, Dan, "Survey: CIOs not Worried about Security," *Computerworld,* January 5, 2001. www.cnn.com/2001/TECH/computing/01/05/cio.security.idg/index.html.

3. Bonnie Brown, a home worker, gets a single IP address from her ISP. She implements a small home network with three PCs. Her router does NAT. Each computer's IP address be translated into the single ISP IP address when packets are transmitted. Then how will the router know to which internal computer it should send an incoming response?

4. What protections should Ms. Brown have on her home network?

5. A website begins to use SSL (see Chapter 11)—a secure communication system that uses public key encryption for authentication, key exchange, and message-by-message authentication. Its throughput (actual speed) drops precipitously. What is happening? In your answer, address issues at specific phases in the secure communication process.

CASE STUDIES

Go to an online network magazine and find a recent example of a known weakness in an operating system or application program. The websites www.NWfusion.com and www.computerworld.com are good starting points. Describe the known weakness, the vulnerability it creates, and the seriousness of the vulnerability.

For case studies, go to the book's website, www.prenhall.com/panko, and look at the Case Studies page for this chapter.

PHOTOS

For photos, go to the book's website, www.prenhall.com/panko, and look at the Photos page for this chapter.

PROJECTS

1. **Getting Current.** Go to the book website's New Information and Errors pages for this chapter to get new information since this book went to press and to correct any errors in the text.

2. **Internet Exercises.** Go to the book website's Exercises page for this chapter and do the Internet Exercises.

NOT HANDS ON: HOW ATTACKERS HACK SERVERS

Learning Objectives:

By the end of this chapter, you should be able to discuss:

- How attackers hack computers, including initial scanning, hacking in with password attacks or buffer overflow attacks, and actions taken after a break-in.

INTRODUCTION

Chapter 9 presented an overview of security issues and technologies. This chapter takes you further into the mind of the hacker by giving you an overview of how attackers hack into computers; that is, log into them illegally. Not all hacking attacks follow the scenario presented in this chapter, but most have many of the stages we will see. Figure 9a-1 gives an overview of the hacking attack we will see in this scenario.

SCANNING ATTACKS

To break into a host, an attacker engages in a series of activities. The first usually is a series of scanning attacks, in which the attacker attempts to identify potential victim hosts and ways to attack them.

Scanning Attacks
  Host scanning to identify target hosts
  Port scanning to identify applications on the target host
  Fingerprinting applications to identify the vendor
Breaking In
  Cracking Passwords
    Difficulty of remote password cracking
  Social Engineering
  Buffer Overflow Attacks
    Takes over a computer with a single message
    Execute commands with the privileges of another program
    Hopefully, a program with super account status
After the Break-In
  Rootkits
  Deleting audit logs
  Creating a backdoor account
  Doing damage: reading sensitive files, modifying or deleting files, wiping the hard
    disk, using the compromised host to attack other hosts

Figure 9a-1   Hacking a Computer

Host Scanning

Scanning attacks usually begin with **host scanners,** such as Ping (see Chapter 8), which send messages to identify which IP addresses have active hosts. This gives the hacker a list of possible targets. To begin a host scanning attack, the attacker first identifies the range of addresses used within the corporation. The attacker then scans all addresses within this range.

Port Scanning

Attackers then use **port scanners** to send messages to each target computer to determine which ports on the computer have active server programs running. This process identifies services running on the computer. Different services can be attacked in different ways, so identifying running services is crucial to hacking into the computer. Normally, for each potential victim host, the attacker will scan all 1,024 well-known ports in TCP, then scan all 1,024 well-known ports in UDP.

Fingerprinting Software Version Numbers

Often, attackers can send messages whose responses identify a potential victim in detail, most notably by revealing its operating system or application programs. They do this by sending messages that programs from different vendors will respond to differently. By examining the responses, they can **fingerprint** the operating system, webserver program, or other software. Fingerprinting is important because exploits for known weaknesses usually only work for a specific vendor's software.

HACKING THE VICTIM

Now that the hacker has identified victims and ways to attack them, the actual hack (break-in) can take place. There are several ways to do this.

Hacking the Victim by Cracking Passwords

The attacker then hacks the victim using an exploit to take advantage of known weaknesses in the operating system or application or by cracking weak passwords. We saw password cracking in Chapter 9.

Although we see hackers in movies guessing passwords in a few attempts, hackers normally require many attempts to guess a password, and any well-managed system will lock accounts after a few incorrect attempts to log in. Consequently, hackers that do not have physical access to computers usually must try other approaches.

Hacking the Victim with Social Engineering

Social engineering, as Chapter 9 discussed, is tricking users into doing something they should not. For example, if a victim can be tricked into opening an e-mail attachment, the attachment can install a program on the machine to facilitate the break-in. Or, the attacker could call up the victim's secretary, say they are a consultant working for the secretary's boss, and ask for a password. A third example is calling up a help desk and saying that they are a particular person and have lost their password. About a quarter to a third of all calls to help desks are for lost passwords, so policies for handling such calls are critical. A common solution is to call the user back at the user's office telephone number, but even this approach has problems.

Hacking the Victim with a Buffer Overflow Attack

Another approach to hacking victims is to exploit known weaknesses in operating systems and application programs. Often, this involves a **buffer overflow** attack. Buffer overflow attacks can take over a target computer with a single message. There are other attacks that can take over a computer with a single message, but we will focus on buffer overflow attacks because of their prominence.

As Figure 9a-2 shows, when computers work, they often have to shift between several application programs. When they temporarily put one program on hold to serve another, they store information about the suspended program in a holding area in RAM called a **stack**, assigning the program a certain amount of room called a **buffer**. Application programs also use stacks and buffers to handle pending work.

If the attacker can send a message that tricks the operating system into placing an entry in the stack that is larger than its buffer, the entry will write over another program's buffer. When the operating system pulls that other program's entry from the buffer, it will execute the buffer's overwritten code using the **privileges** (access permissions) of the program whose entry was originally stored in the buffer. Many programs run with super user privileges, and if they are taken over, the attacker gets control of the machine.

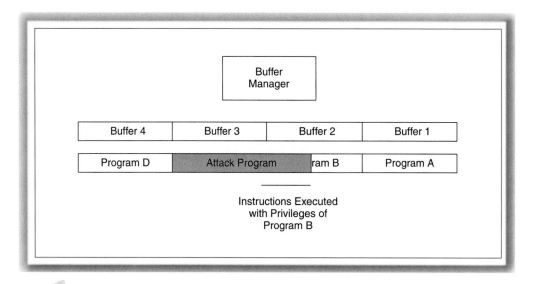

Figure 9a-2   Buffer Overflow Attack

AFTER THE BREAK-IN

After hacking into the computer, the hacker will be able to roam around the computer at will. Before hackers do that, however, they usually take two additional actions. Often, these actions are automated by **rootkits**, which are programs that hackers install on hacked machines to facilitate actions after the break-in.

Deleting Audit Logs

Most computers have audit logs that keep track of who has been using the system. Hackers usually delete these logs or modify them to hide their presence. This makes forensic analysis after the attack very difficult.

Creating a Back Door Account

Next, hackers typically create a new **back door account**, preferably with super account privileges so that they can get back in later even if the password is changed on the account they originally cracked.

Doing Damage

Now the hacker can do whatever damage he or she wishes to do. The hacker can read sensitive information, delete or alter key files, wipe the hard drive clean, or do anything else. They can also use the compromised host to launch attacks to take over other hosts.

EXPERIMENTATION IS ILLEGAL

Many students, after reading about how to execute a break-in, want to go to the Internet and download host scanners, port scanners, and other attack software to "play with."

That would be a serious mistake. Unless you have a closed lab and permission to use attack tools within this lab, you can only use these tools against real organizational networks. That is not just a misdemeanor crime. It is a felony and is punishable by up to a few years in prison. Even seemingly innocuous host scanning and port scanning attacks are felonies in many states, and if the attack crosses state boundaries, the FBI becomes involved. "I just wanted to learn" is not a legal excuse.

In addition, your ISP is likely to disable your account (most tools have strong signatures that many ISPs scan), and if you use these tools to "test" your university's network, you are liable to be expelled. You also are likely to find it difficult to get a job.

TEST YOUR UNDERSTANDING

1. What are the main stages of hacking attacks?
2. a) How does the hacker identify targets and their applications? b) What is fingerprinting, and why is it done?
3. a) Why is cracking passwords through exhaustive search difficult? b) Give three examples of social engineering attacks. c) Why are buffer overflow attacks and other single-message attacks better than password cracking attacks? d) Describe a buffer overflow attack.
4. What steps do hackers often take after hacking a system?
5. Why is it a bad idea to "play with" attack tools?

C H A P T E R 10

NETWORK MANAGEMENT AND SYSTEMS ADMINISTRATION

Learning Objectives:

By the end of this chapter, you should be able to discuss:

- The difference between network management and systems administration.
- The importance of keeping costs low for new projects; the Law of Selection; non-technology costs (labor and outsourcing), total cost of ownership (TCO), multi-criterion product selection.
- Network management functions and network management systems, including SNMP (Network simulation programs).
- Directory servers.
- Systems administration (server management).
- Server access permissions.

INTRODUCTION

So far in this book, we have looked at networking mostly from the technological point of view. In this chapter, we will study the management of networks and servers in corporate environments.

It is important to make a distinction between **network management**, which is the management of switches, routers, and transmission links, and **systems administration**, which is the management of servers (and, sometimes, clients). In other words, systems administration is *not* the management of the network. Figure 10-1 illustrates this distinction.

Cisco's certification programs largely ignore systems administration, essentially viewing servers as lying outside the network. Microsoft's certification programs, in contrast, place systems administration at the heart of the certification process.

Most networking books follow Cisco's "pure" approach. However, most real-world network managers spend more time on systems administration than on network management. This is why we discuss servers so much in this book and why we will look at systems administration in more depth in this chapter.

TEST YOUR UNDERSTANDING

1. a) What is systems administration? b) Distinguish between systems administration and network management.

COST ANALYSIS

When computer scientists and electrical engineers take networking courses in business schools, they often have a difficult time adjusting to the need to *select the least expensive technology that meets user needs.* For instance, when I ask my classes to design a PC network for ten PCs, I sometimes get solutions that specify an ATM switch, which would be prohibitively expensive for a small firm to buy and operate. Even business

Figure 10-1   Network Management Versus Systems Administration

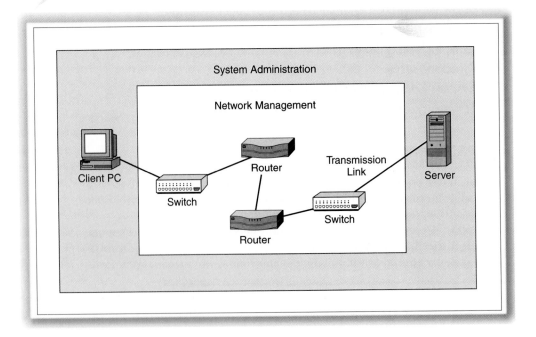

students often say, "Get the best technology you can afford," as if budget should drive selection instead of needs. In business schools, we expect better.

Exploding Demand
It is obvious that demand for networking is exploding, as Figure 10-3 illustrates. Users want ever more applications over ever-greater distances and delivered at ever-higher speeds. Needs are growing 20 percent to 30 percent annually in most firms.

Figure 10-2   Cost Issues

Network Management Versus Systems Administration
  Network management: the management of switches, routers, and transmission links
  Systems administration: the management of servers
The Importance of Costs
  Exploding demand
  Slow budget growth
  Falling hardware costs help, but software costs fall more slowly, and labor costs are
    rising
  Select the least expensive technology that will fully meet user needs
Non-Technology Costs
  Labor costs
    High, and unit labor costs are rising over time
  Outsourcing
    Dangers: rigid contracts, loss of control over corporate data
    Benefits: predictability in price and performance
    What to outsource: routine functions
Total Cost of Ownership
  Fully configured cost of hardware
  Fully configured cost of software
  Initial installation costs
    Vendor setup costs
    IT and end-user labor
  Ongoing costs
    Upgrades
    Labor costs often exceed all other costs
    Immature products have very high labor costs
  Total cost of ownership (TCO): total of all costs over life span
Multi-Criterion Product Selection
  Not just cost
  Select criteria
  Give weights to each
  Rate products on each criterion
  Select the product with best total value

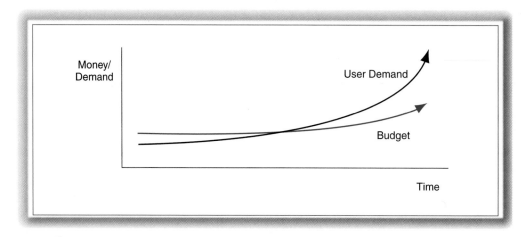

Figure 10-3   Exploding Demand and Slow Budget Growth

Slow Budget Growth

At the same time, budgets are not growing at anywhere near this rate. Most **network budgets** are either stagnant or are growing only 5 percent to 10 percent per year. To meet exploding user needs, it is important for network managers to be extremely prudent about the cost of whatever technologies they select.

Technology to the Rescue: Sort of

The only reason that network administrators have been able to keep somewhat up with exploding user needs is that technology costs are falling rapidly. However, falling hardware cost is no magic solution for managing demand. Software costs are not falling as rapidly as hardware costs, and hourly labor costs actually are rising. Falling hardware costs merely reduce the cost pressure on network administrators; they do not eliminate it.

Selection

All of this leads to the **Law of Selection**: *Always select the least expensive technology that will fully meet user needs.* Paying too much for one service will prevent you from offering another service. However, a cheap service that does not fully meet user needs is no bargain.

TEST YOUR UNDERSTANDING

2. a) Comment on trends in user demand and budgets. b) Will falling hardware costs end this imbalance? c) What is the Law of Selection? d) Why is it important?

Non-Technology Costs

In most of this book, we have focused on technology because there are many technical concepts that you must know if you wish to work in networking. However, hardware, software, and carrier services are only a fraction of the total cost of running a network.

For instance, capital equipment purchases account for just under half of the average networking budget.[1]

Labor Costs

Another large cost element is labor. A third of the average corporate networking budget is employee labor. It is expensive to plan and implement a complex new networking technology, and the long-term labor costs to operate a network system on a day-to-day basis are more expensive still. In addition, as we noted earlier, although hardware costs are falling rapidly, hourly labor costs actually tend to increase over time. In addition, the users who need the system to do their functional work will also have labor costs to implement and use the system

Outsourcing

Outsourcing is the hiring of an outside company to do some or all of a company's IT work. Outsourcing consumes about a fifth of the average network budget. Outsourcing is a broad set of activities that includes paying WAN carriers, having other firms host servers, and even having outsourcing firms take over large parts of the networking function.

Outsourcing Dangers   Outsourcing lacks the flexibility a company has when working with its own employees. Contract terms are strict and narrowly applied. In addition, sensitive corporate data may lie on an outsourcer's host, where it is no longer under the control of the firm.

Outsourcing Benefits   On the positive side, outsourcing leads to predictable costs and performance guarantees. Cost predictability is very important in budgeting. Performance guarantees, in turn, mean that the outsourcer, if it meets its contract requirement, will provide responsiveness when users employ its services and will pay penalties when breakdowns occur. With the critical exception of loss of control over corporate data, outsourcing provides peace of mind.

What to Outsource   In general, outsourcing is best for fairly standardized operations and services. For instance, many firms now outsource "routine" aspects of their IT functions, such as e-mail. However, functions that are central to a firm's competitive advantage in the marketplace are rarely outsourced because the companies usually want to maintain control of these crucial functions.

TEST YOUR UNDERSTANDING

3.   a) Into what three categories are costs divided? b) Why are labor costs important?

4.   a) What is outsourcing? b) What are the benefits of outsourcing? c) The potential problems? d) What types of applications usually are outsourced?

---

[1]   Network budget percentages are from Sharon Gaudin, "Spending on the Rise," *Network World*, January 29, 2001. www.nwfusion.com/research/2001/0129feat.html.

Total Cost of Ownership (TCO)

Although costs must be managed, it is difficult to do because costs are highly complex and take place over the multiyear time span of most projects. Even so, the costs of projects must be estimated accurately. Companies have lost patience with "guesstimates" that end up in large cost overruns.

Figure 10-4 illustrates a typical cost analysis. Note that it includes several types of costs. Note also that these costs come over the entire life span of a project, not just during its initial planning and implementation stages.

The Fully Configured Cost of Products

We must first look at the **total purchase cost of network products**. Just as PCs are sold as collections of components, most network products, such as switches and routers, come as collections of hardware and software components. A **fully configured** switch or router often costs far more than the **base price** listed in catalogs. When comparing products from different vendors, it is critical to compare fully configured products. Services such as public switched data networks also tend to come with many options that can add considerably to the base price.

Although hardware is visible and therefore easy to appreciate, software costs are very important in the total purchase price. In many cases, software costs exceed hardware costs. As in the case of hardware, software often comes as a base price bundle plus many options.

Figure 10-4   Multiyear Cost Analysis: Total Cost of Ownership (TCO)

	Year 1	Year 2	Year 3	Year 4	Total
Base Hardware	$200,000	15,000	15,000	15,000	245,000
Hardware Options	85,000	9,000	9,000	9,000	112,000
Base Software	$100,000	10,000	10,000	10,000	130,000
Software Options	50,000	10,000	10,000	10,000	80,000
Planning and Development	75,000				75,000
Implementation	25,000				25,000
Ongoing IT Labor	250,000	200,000	200,000	200,000	850,000
Ongoing User Labor	150,000	150,000	150,000	150,000	600,000
Total	935,000	394,000	394,000	394,000	$2,117,000

Note: The total cost of ownership is $2,117,000.

Initial Installation Costs

In addition, there typically are substantial costs associated with **initial installation**. Some vendors, especially carriers, charge one-time **setup fees**.

There also are a company's own **initial labor costs** associated with installation. These include the costs of the network staff's labor, and they also include the labor costs of end users.[2] End-user labor costs may rise dramatically during installation periods because of training and disruption. In general, the labor costs to create and implement a new network tend to be very high.

Ongoing Costs

Initial costs, as large as they are, often are far smaller than **ongoing costs**. These may come in the form of hardware or software upgrades over the life of the product selected or in the form of monthly payments to vendors. Also substantial are the ongoing labor costs to manage the system. Ongoing costs, especially ongoing labor costs, may be far larger than initial costs. As in the case of initial costs, the costs to end users must be taken into account.

Ongoing costs are especially high for new technologies that are not yet **mature**. It may take several years for technologies to become easy to install and use. Immature products often lack utilities that allow easy management; therefore, they require a great deal of expensive labor. It is a good idea to avoid new "bleeding edge" technologies if possible. Perversely, vendors and the networking trade press typically focus on such new and immature technologies, giving a rather distorted picture of the workable options available to network administrators.

Total Cost of Ownership (TCO)

In Figure 10-4, the total cost of the system over its expected four-year lifespan is $2,117,000. This is called the **total cost of ownership (TCO)**. This TCO is far higher than the base price of the system's hardware ($200,000). As is typical in many systems, labor costs exceed the costs of hardware and software, accounting for about three-quarters of all costs. When comparing projects, it is important to compare TCOs.

TEST YOUR UNDERSTANDING

5. a) Why are base prices misleading? b) Why is multiyear analysis necessary? c) How important are labor costs? d) What is TCO? e) Why is it important? f) What are the elements of TCO?

Multi-Criterion Product Selection

Cost is enormously important, but if a technology does not meet user needs, a low price means nothing. In practice, lowest-price systems often are lacking in key features and quality, and companies rarely end up selecting the cheapest product available.

A common way to balance price with other factors is to use **multi-criterion decision making**, in which each alternative is evaluated with respect to several criteria, as shown in Figure 10-5.

---

[2] End users are employees in functional departments, such as marketing or finance, who use networking to perform their functional work more effectively.

Criterion	Weight	Product A		Product B	
		Rating	Points	Rating	Points
Price	5	8	40	10	50
Functionality	5	6	30	5	25
Ease of Installation	2	9	18	7	14
Ease of Use	3	9	27	6	18
Total Value			**115**		**107**

Figure 10-5   Multi-Criterion Decision Making

Criteria and Weights

Each criterion is given a **weight** to indicate its relative importance in selection. The weight range might be 1 to 5 or some other scale. In this example, both price and functionality are given weights of 5 to indicate their importance. Ease of installation and ease of use have lower weights, indicating their lesser importance.

Product Ratings

For each criterion, each proposal is given a **rating**, perhaps on a scale of 1 to 10, with 10 being high. For Product A, the price rating is 8, whereas for Product B, it is 10. Product B is rated higher on the price criterion, meaning that it has a *lower* price. A higher rating is always better.

The rating for each criterion is multiplied by the weight. This gives a point value for each criterion for each product.

Total Value

If the criteria and weights were selected carefully, and if all proposals were rated properly, then the sum of the **rating–weight products** should give an overall **total value**. The proposal with the highest value should win. Here, Product A has a higher total value (115) than Product B (107) and should be selected. Although Product B is cheaper, Product A is sufficiently better on all other measures, thus meriting selection.

TEST YOUR UNDERSTANDING

6. a) Why is selecting the lowest bid dangerous? b) Why is multi-criterion decision making better? c) Perform a multi-criterion selection analysis using the following data. The weights for the criteria Price, Functionality, Ease of Installation, and Ease of Use are 9, 9, 6, and 7, respectively. Ratings for Product X are 8, 5, 9, and 9, respectively. Ratings for Product Y are 10, 8, 7, and 6, respectively.

Developing a Disciplined Project Portfolio

So far, we have looked at single projects. In reality, a company will have to engage in a series of projects each year to bring new and upgraded technology into the firm and to integrate each technology into the corporation's work process.

However, if a company attempts to execute too many projects, it will fail. It will not have the resources needed to implement all of the projects, and if it spreads its resources too thinly among many projects, it is likely to do poorly in most or all of the projects it attempts to do. The network administrator has to be very disciplined about which projects to implement and how many resources to give to each project. They will have to invest wisely in a portfolio of projects to develop each year.

Developing a Smooth Multiyear Budget

An important reality in selecting a project portfolio to meet the strategic network plan is that corporations require each of their functions to have smooth multiyear budgets that vary only slightly from year to year and that vary only by approved increases (or decreases) in funding.

This is a problem because network projects tend to be lumpy, with large outlays in some years and small outlays in others. Not only must the network administrator select the right portfolio of projects, but he or she also has to ensure that the projects are timed (and managed) to have their combined spending equal each year's budget.

TEST YOUR UNDERSTANDING

   7.   a) Why is it important to develop a disciplined project portfolio? b) Why is a smooth multiyear budget necessary?

ADMINISTRATIVE SERVERS

One way to reduce the cost of network management is to turn to information technology to increase the productivity of network administrators. In fact, larger firms usually employ a number of **administrative servers** that focus on the needs of network administrators rather than end users.

Network Management Functions

As Figure 10-6 indicates, there are several **network management functions** that administrative servers may support. These functions include the following:

- ➤ **Fault Management.** Technology should help the administrator diagnose **faults** (failures or poor performance) and, to the extent possible, fix them remotely.
- ➤ **Performance Management.** Technology should help the administrator monitor how the network is performing and, if possible, allow the administrator to improve performance and plan for change.
- ➤ **Configuration Management.** The network consists of hundreds or thousands of individual devices. Technology should help the administrator maintain an inventory of these devices, including the configurations of each one. In addition, it is desirable to be able to change the configuration of a device remotely, including downloading updates to it from a remote source. One especially important configuration

Fault Management
  Diagnosis
  Repair (remotely if possible)
Performance Management
  Monitoring
  Planning
Configuration Management
  Inventory of devices
  Configuration of each device
  Change configuration remotely
  Remote installation of software on servers to reduce labor costs
Security Management
Accounting Management
  Charge-back

Figure 10-6 Network Management Functions

management task is the remote installation of software on a firm's many servers to decrease labor costs.

➤ **Security Management.** Although security management often is handled by a separate system, there must be a centralized way to manage security on a firm's many devices.

➤ **Accounting Management.** Increasingly, companies need to charge network costs back to individual departments. Technology should help in this endeavor.

TEST YOUR UNDERSTANDING

8. a) List the major network management functions. b) What is fault management? c) What is configuration management?

Network Management Systems

If a patient is in a hospital, the doctor has the nursing staff constantly monitor the patient's vital signs (pulse, temperature, blood pressure, etc.) and occasionally has them conduct specific tests and give medication.

Figure 10-7 illustrates that a **network management system** provides similar on-going monitoring for a network plus the ability to seek specific information and to send commands to fix problems. The figure uses terminology based on the **Simple Network Management Protocol (SNMP)**, which is the most widely used network management system standard.

The Manager

The network administrator works at a central PC or client workstation. This computer runs a program called the **network management software**, or, more simply, the **manager**.

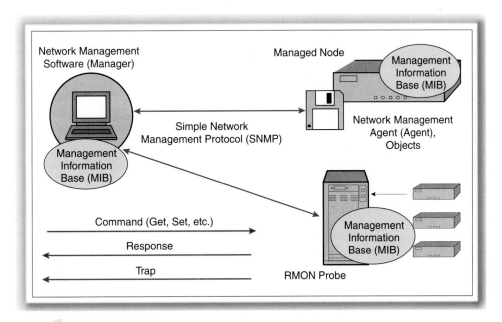

Figure 10-7   Network Management System Based on SNMP

Managed Nodes

The manager is responsible for many **managed nodes**—devices that need to be administered, such as printers, hubs, switches, routers, application programs, and other pieces of hardware and software. We also will call these nodes *managed devices* because that is what they are commonly called.

Agents

Managed devices have pieces of software (and sometimes hardware) called **network management agents**, or, more simply, **agents**. In sports and entertainment, an agent acts on behalf of a person. Similarly, agents communicate with the manager on behalf of their managed nodes. In other words, the manager does not communicate with the managed node directly, but rather with its agent.

RMON Probes

One specialized type of agent is the **RMON probe** (remote monitoring probe). This may be a stand-alone device or software running on a switch or router. An RMON probe collects data on network traffic instead of information about the RMON probe itself. The manager can poll the RMON probe to get summarized information about the distribution of packet sizes, the numbers of various types of errors, the number of packets processed, and other statistical summaries that may indicate problems.

Objects

More specifically, the manager, through the agent, manages **objects** on the managed node. For instance, one object might be a port on a switch. A particular switch might have several **instances** of this object (for instance, several ports). The manager should be able to get information about each port and even should be able to tell the switch to disable the port.

SNMP can manage many types of very specific objects. For example, a manager can ask a file server agent for information about a specific print queue. Or, the manager can ask a host computer running TCP about a specific TCP option it is using. SNMP objects, in other words, are far more finely grained than "printer" or "switch."

Management Information Base (MIB)

In a database, the **schema** describes the design of the database, that is, the specific types of information it contains. Similarly, network management requires a **management information base (MIB)** specification that defines what objects can exist on each type of managed node and also the specific characteristics (attributes) of each object. There are separate MIBs for switches, routers, and other types of managed nodes.

Besides the schema, you also have the database itself, which contains actual data in the form dictated by the schema. Unfortunately, this is also called the management information base, so you must be careful when hearing the term "MIB" to determine whether it means the database design or the database itself.

To add further confusion, there is a small MIB on each managed node that contains information about that node's objects, and there also is a complete MIB on the manager's computer to hold data collected from many managed nodes.

TEST YOUR UNDERSTANDING

9. a) List the main elements in a network management system. b) Does the manager communicate directly with the managed node? Explain. c) Explain the difference between managed nodes and objects. d) Is the MIB a schema or the actual database? e) Where is the MIB stored? (This is a trick question.)

Network Management Protocols

We need standards to govern communication between the manager and the agent. We have been using terminology from the most popular network management standard, the IETF's Simple Network Management Protocol (SNMP). SNMP governs both the MIB schema and manager–agent communications.

Commands and Responses

Normally, SNMP communication between the manager and agents works through **command–response cycles**. The manager sends a command. The agent sends back a response confirming that the command has been met, delivering requested data, or saying that an error has occurred and that the agent cannot comply with the command.

There are two basic types of SNMP commands. **Get** commands tell the agent to retrieve certain information and return this information to the manager. In contrast,

set commands tell the agent to set a parameter on the managed node. For instance, a set command may ask an agent to set the status of Port 2 on a switch to "off." This causes the device to turn off the port.[3]

Traps

Sometimes, agents do not wait for commands to send information. If an agent detects a condition that it thinks the manager should know about, it can send a **trap** message to the manager, as Figure 10-7 illustrates. For instance, if a switch detects that a transmission line to which a certain port is connected appears to have failed, it might send the manager a trap message to advise the manager of this situation.

Other Network Management Protocols

SNMP is not the only network management protocol in common use today, although it is by far the most widely used. A growing number of managers can speak to multiple types of agents that use different network management protocols, including different MIB designs.

TEST YOUR UNDERSTANDING

10. a) In SNMP, which device creates commands? b) Responses? c) Traps? d) Explain the two types of commands. e) What is a trap?

Network Simulation Programs

In planning, managers often create spreadsheet models showing their current and projected situations. They then conduct a number of "what-if analyses," changing groups of numbers on the spreadsheet to reflect different alternatives open to their companies. This helps them select the best alternative.

The Need to Look Forward

Network management systems provide information about the network currently, but you cannot drive a car by looking out a window at the road directly beneath the car. You have to look forward. **Network simulation software**, as illustrated in Figure 10-8, helps the network administrator look forward in terms of the company's network.

The Current Situation and Growth Projections

The network simulation program begins with data about the current system. Typically, this data comes from the network management program. After the data is entered into the program, the network administrator can begin to do future-oriented analysis. Most fundamentally, the network administrator can enter expected demand growth forecasts into the system to identify places where the network design might be inadequate.

---

[3] Although it seems odd, setting an object value with a set command causes devices to change their behavior to match the value being set. If you are familiar with object-oriented programming, this approach should be familiar.

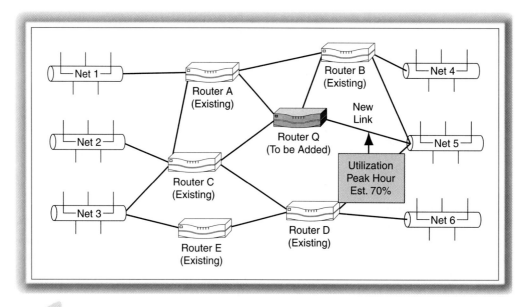

Figure 10-8   Network Simulation Program

What-If Analyses for Possible Changes

In addition, the administrator is likely to conduct "what if" analyses to see how changing the network in a specific way would affect performance. In the figure, the network administrator has added a router (Router Q). He or she has clicked on a link connected to the router, and the network simulation software has estimated the link's **utilization** (the percentage of capacity actually used) for the network's peak hour. The data show that the utilization is expected to be 70 percent. This is good because it allows reasonable room for demand growth beyond the forecast.

Network Simulation Versus Field Experiments

The alternative to doing network simulation is simply to try changes in the field by adding a new router or making other changes to the operational network. However, making experimental changes in an operational network may produce unexpected side effects that harm users. In addition, network simulation allows the network administrator to "try" many different changes to see which is best. This would be prohibitively expensive to do in the field.

TEST YOUR UNDERSTANDING

11. a) Why is network simulation software desirable? b) Distinguish between making demand projections and conducting what-if analyses about possible changes to the network. c) Why is using a network simulation program preferable to conducting field experiments on operational networks?

Directory Servers

Chapter 1 introduced another type of administrative server, the directory server. A **directory server** is a place to store important information for a company, including data about devices and people. In contrast, network management systems only store data about managed devices. Obviously, both deal with storage, and we expect them to grow closer in the future and perhaps even to merge.

Hierarchical Structure

Directory servers store information about objects. These objects are defined hierarchically. For example, Figure 10-9 shows how an organization might store data on its employees. The **organization (O)** is divided into smaller **organizational units (OUs),**[4] and then into employees, servers, and other important categories. Information about specific objects is kept at the bottom of the tree. For instance, the employee object would include a person's name, e-mail addresses, server passwords and access permissions, physical location, and other pertinent information.

In this figure, the College of Business Administration (CBA) organizational unit divides its employees into faculty and staff. The college also has objects for facilities, such as the Network Technologies Laboratory. To refer to an object, it is normal to put the most specific object name farthest left. For instance, if you wish to know Ray Panko's e-mail address, you would ask for the following object: "EMAIL.Panko.Faculty. CBA.Manoa.Hawaii".

LDAP

As Figure 10-10 shows, various computers on the network must be able to send queries to the directory server and also must be able to send updated information. To facilitate this, we need a standardized **directory access protocol** to specify how outside devices will communicate with the directory server. The most common standard for directory access is the **Lightweight Directory Access Protocol (LDAP)**. Managed by the IETF, this standard's simplicity and good functionality have made it broadly available, with more directory servers adopting it every year.

Directory Server Products

Although standards are good, we also need good directory products that implement these standards and provide full directory server functionality. To date, the leader in directory server products is Novell with its **NetWare Directory Services (NDS)** product. Initially available only for use on Novell NetWare file servers, NDS is now available on Windows NT/2000 servers and UNIX servers. Microsoft has **Active Directory**, which was only released in 2000 and is not as mature as NDS.

TEST YOUR UNDERSTANDING

12. a) Why are directory servers important? b) How is information organized in a directory? c) What is the main standard for remote communication with a directory server?

---

[4] There can be several levels of organizational units.

Sample Directory Structure
  Hawaii (O = Organization)
      Manoa (OU = Organizational Unit)
          Manoa Campus (CN = Common Name)
          CBA (OU = Organizational Unit)
              College of Business Administration (CN)
              Faculty (OU)
                  Panko (FM = Faculty Member)
                  panko@hawaii.edu (EMAIL)
                  http://panko.com (HOMEPAGE)
                  Server XYZ (SERVER)
                      5h*76CJ@ (PASSWORD)
                      . . . . . (PERMISSIONS)
                  . . .
              Staff
              Network Technology Laboratory (OU)
                  Voyager (HOST)
                      Room D313 (LOCATION)
                      128.171.17.13 (IPADDR)
                      Voyager.cba.Hawaii.edu (HOSTNAME)
                      A7-33-2B-17-55-CD (LANADDR)
                      Panko.Faculty.CBA (MANAGER)
          Medical School (OU)
          . . .
      Hilo (OU)
      . . .
  Object Name:
      EMAIL.Panko.Faculty.CBA.Manoa.Hawaii

Figure 10-9   Hierarchical Directory Object Structure

SERVER MANAGEMENT (SYSTEMS ADMINISTRATION)

If you ask the manager of a network what part of his or her job takes the most time, you may be surprised to hear the network manager talk about the management of servers, which is known for historical reasons as **systems administration**. For better or worse, systems administration usually falls within the networking department, and it is extremely time-consuming. As Figure 10-11 shows, systems administration is a large complex of tasks.

TEST YOUR UNDERSTANDING

13. What is systems administration?

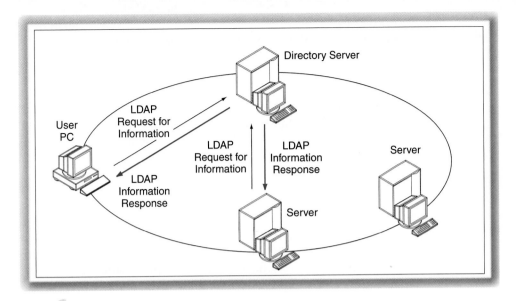

Figure 10-10 Lightweight Directory Access Protocol (LDAP)

Figure 10-11 Systems Administration Tasks

Server Selection
  Type of server
    Single PC server
      Network operating system: Windows, LINUX, NetWare, Macintosh
    Single workstation server
    Server farm
  Specific hardware
    Multiple power supplies
    Symmetric Multiprocessing
    Large, fast disk drives
Server Installation and Configuration
Ongoing Work
  Permission assignment and changes
  Assigning and changing passwords
  Upgrades
  Backup
    Backup technology
    Full and differential backups
    Restoration testing
    Offsite storage

Server Selection

Type of Server

The first job of systems administration is selecting servers. This will begin, of course, with an analysis of whether PC servers or workstation servers will be used, what operating system will be used (for PC servers, the main alternatives are Windows, LINUX, NetWare, and the Macintosh System), and whether single servers or server farms containing many servers will be used.

Specific Hardware

The next step is to select a specific server's technology. Most servers today are built from the ground up for server usage. They typically have multiple power supplies to provide reliability, many disk drive bays, and high-performance disk drives.[5] Many use multiple microprocessors, which is called multiprocessing (see Chapter 1), to increase the processing power of individual servers.

Server Installation and Configuration

When new servers are installed, the installer must go through a process called **server configuration**. This is a complex process that requires taking certain actions in certain sequences and the setting of a number of parameters within a range of alternatives. Installing and configuring a server can take several hours even if things go well, which they often do not.

Few information systems curriculums offer courses in computer installation and repair, so these are good career-enhancing courses to take at community colleges or from private training programs.

TEST YOUR UNDERSTANDING

14. List the main tasks in obtaining a server and getting it ready for use.

Ongoing Work

Access Permissions

Systems administration does not end when a server is installed. The most time-consuming ongoing process is **assigning access permissions** to individual users and groups in various directories on the server. Every user must be assigned permissions in every directory on a server. In addition, these assignments are likely to change over time.

Upgrades

Another constant chore is adding new software and software upgrades to servers. A server's network operating system and application programs are upgraded constantly. This is done to install new versions with higher functionality. It is also done to install

---

[5] Many servers use RAID disk drive arrays, which usually store information redundantly on multiple drives so that if a single drive fails, no information is lost. RAID arrays also are faster than single disk drives, because information to and from the drives is transmitted in parallel, while information to and from a single disk is written serially. As we saw in Chapter 3, parallel transmission is faster than serial transmission.

patches (fixes) for various pieces of software, say to prevent security exploits based on known weaknesses (see Chapter 9).

Backup

An extremely crucial chore is **backup**. Servers often hold mission-critical corporate data or data for dozens or hundreds of users. The nightly backup of all data to tape or to other archival media is important in such situations. Failure to perform regular backups can only be described as professional malpractice.

Backup Technology   Figure 10-12 shows that backup typically is done from a central **backup console** that usually is a PC with a tape drive. This single machine can back up several servers, one at a time.

Full and Differential Backup   Standard practice is to do a **full backup** once per week in which all data is backed up onto tape or some other medium. Then, each day, a **differential backup** saves all data that has changed since the last full backup.[6]

Figure 10-12   Backup

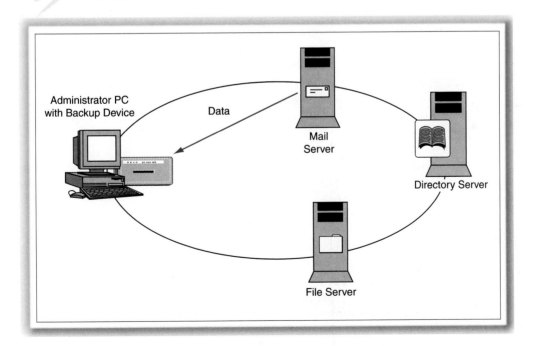

Administrator PC with Backup Device

Data

Mail Server

Directory Server

File Server

---

[6]   In contrast, incremental backups back up everything that changed since the last full or incremental backup. If a system fails and must be restored, differential backup only requires the full backup and the last differential backup. In contrast, with incremental backup, the full backup and several incremental backups must be restored. This is time-consuming and potentially dangerous during the crisis of restoring a failed server. If a single incremental backup is restored in the wrong order because of a mistake due to time pressure, updates to many files will be lost.

Restoration Testing It is important to test the backup system periodically by **restoring** at least part of a disk's contents from tape back to disk. This ensures that the system really is working. It also gives administrators hands-on experience that they will need during the stress of actual system failure and recovery.

Offsite Storage It is also important to keep backups in fireproof and waterproof safes, and it is critical to keep these safes **offsite** (at another site) so that if a disaster occurs, the backup tapes will be safe.

TEST YOUR UNDERSTANDING

15. What are the main ongoing tasks in systems administration?
16. a) Describe the normal technology for backup. b) If you do a full backup on Sunday and differential backups on remaining days, how many restores would you have to do if you system failed on Thursday? c) Why is restoration testing important?

ACCESS PERMISSIONS

Controlling who may log into a server is not enough. Servers have many directories. Just as someone who is let into a secure building is not allowed to go anywhere they wish and do anything they want, servers must control what directories users have access to and what users may do in these directories.

Access Permissions Table

As Figure 10-13 shows, servers have **access permissions tables**. For each directory, there is a set of **access permissions** for each user (account). These access permissions dictate what the user may do to files in the directory and to subdirectories.

Types of Access Permissions

This rather crude permissions table only has three types of access permissions: Full, Execute, and Read. Windows has many more specific access permissions, allowing finer control of user actions.

Full

The full permission allows the account to do a wide variety of things in the directory named in the access permissions table. Note that the Super Account has the full permission in every directory on the server.

In addition, each user has the full permission (as well as the other three permissions) in their home directory under the usr directory. In contrast, they have no access permissions at all in the home directories of other users.

Execute

The execute permission allows a user to execute (run) programs in the directory. All users have execute permission in most subdirectories of the *programs* directory in Figure 10-13. However, only some users (usra but not usrb) have the execute permission in the *cad* subdirectory.

Directory	Super Account	usra	usrb	Everyone
Root	FXR	—	—	—
usr	FXR	—	—	—
usra	FXR	FXR	—	—
usrb	FXR	—	FXR	—
projects	FXR	—	FXR	—
admin	FXR	—	FXR	—
usrc	FXR	—	—	—
public	FXR	R	R	R
policies	FXR	R	R	R
forms	FXR	R	R	R
general	FXR	R	R	R
programs	FXR	X	X	X
database	FXR	X	X	X
spreadsheet	FXR	X	X	X
cad	FXR	X		—

Figure 10-13   Access Permissions Table

Read

A user who only has the read permission in a directory can only download the files in the directory. They cannot change these files. In Figure 10-13, all users have the read permission in the *public* directory and its subdirectories.

Assigning Permissions to Project Team Members

To give an example of how permissions are used, a project head may have all permissions (full, execute, and write) in the project's main directory and subdirectories. Others in the project may only be given read permissions, so that they can read project documents but not change them. Others, who write project documents, will be given write permissions, although perhaps only in certain subdirectories. Employees not on the project will not be given any permissions in the project's directories.

UNIX Permissions

In UNIX, as in this example, there are only three permissions. **Read** only gives read-on access, as in the example in Figure 10-13. **Write** gives the ability to modify files, create new files and subdirectories, and delete files and subdirectories. It is like the full permission in the figure. Finally, **execute** allows the user to execute programs in a directory.

This paucity of possible access permissions means that access control in UNIX systems is rather crude, although some vendors provide proprietary extensions.

Microsoft Windows Permissions

Microsoft Windows give systems administrators more options, allowing a finer degree of access control. Full is like the full permission in Figure 10-13 but is limited by the fact that the ability to Create or Delete subdirectories are separate access permissions. Read gives read-only access, while Write gives the ability to change files.

Even more importantly, companies can create **group policy objects (GPOs)** in Windows. GPOs extend far beyond access permissions, down to the level of such things as how the desktop will look. GPOs allow network administrators to assign finely grained security controls and to apply them to many users in a way that enforces policy consistency.

TEST YOUR UNDERSTANDING

17. a) In Figure 10-13, describe the three access permissions. b) Which are provided to all accounts in the Public directory? Why? c) Which are provided to most accounts in the Programs directory? Why? d) Why are these access permissions not provided to all accounts in the Programs directory? e) Which are provided in a user's home directory?

18. a) Describe the available access permissions in UNIX. b) Why is having this small number of controls limiting? c) Describe access permissions in Microsoft Windows. d) What is a GPO, and why is it important in Windows security?

Groups

There are dozens or hundreds of accounts on large servers. Assigning permissions to every one of these users in every directory and subdirectory could be a nightmare. Fortunately, systems administrators have two ways to simplify their lives.

Group Assignment of Access Permissions

First, they can assign users to various **groups**. For instance, all members of the marketing department might be assigned to the group Marketing. Then, if the Marketing group is assigned certain permissions in a directory, all members of the Marketing group will have these permissions in this directory.

If there is a group Everyone, which will contain all accounts, this will be a very powerful permission assignment tool. In Figure 10-13, Everyone is assigned the read access permission in all directories under the Public directory. Therefore, there is no need to assign it separately to all users.

Groups in Windows and UNIX

Windows allows multiple individuals and groups to be assigned permissions in each directory and for each file. In contrast, UNIX only associates each file or directory with (1) its owner account, (2) a single group name, and (3) all other accounts.[7] This standard UNIX approach is very restrictive. In a project team, for instance, it would not be possible to give several project team members several different permission profiles in a directory.

TEST YOUR UNDERSTANDING

19. a) Why do groups simplify the assignment of access permissions? b) Compare the group assignment of access permissions in Windows and UNIX.

Automatic Inheritance

Another powerful assignment tool for access permissions is **automatic inheritance**. The basic rule is that if you assign access permissions to an individual or group in a particular directory, they will inherit these permissions in all subdirectories. Figure 10-14 illustrates this automatic inheritance.

Inheritance Rules

Suppose a user is given Browse and Execute permissions in the Applications directory. They will automatically receive the Browse and Execute permissions in the Word Processing and the Database child directories as a consequence. Similarly, in the QuickDB directory, they will inherit Browse and Execute from the Database directory. Unless it is blocked, automatic inheritance continues all the way down the tree to the lowest directories and their files.

Blocking Inheritance

Inheritance is a good tool, but it must be modified, just as automatic human inheritance laws must be modified if someone leaves a will when they die. In access permissions, the rule is that *if access permissions are **explicitly assigned** in a directory, this will block automatic inheritance from the parent directory.*

Figure 10-14 also illustrates this inheritance blocking. The user who was assigned Browse and Execute access permissions in the Application directory is assigned the Read-Only permission in the Documentation directory. This explicit assignment will block the inheritance of the Browse and Execute permissions. The user will only have Read-Only permission in the Documentation directory.

---

7   Of course, the root account has all permissions in all directories. In other words, even in your "private" home directory, the root user can read all files that are not encrypted. The **su** command, furthermore, allows any user to act as a root user temporarily if they know the root password.
       When you give the ls–l UNIX command in a directory, each file list will begin with a string like **-rwxr——**. The initial dash indicates that this a file, rather than a directory (d) The next nine characters give the owner, group, and other permissions in groups of three. The owner has read, write, and execute permissions, whereas the group only has read permissions (r—), and others have no permissions (—-).

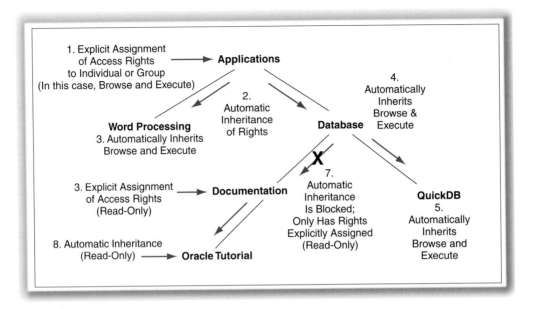

Figure 10-14   Automatic Inheritance

When explicit access permissions are assigned, automatic inheritance begins again. In the Oracle Tutorial directory under the Documentation directory, the person or group inherits the Read-Only permission from the Oracle Tutorial directory.

TEST YOUR UNDERSTANDING

20. a) How does automatic inheritance simplify the assignment of access permissions? b) If access permissions are explicitly assigned in a subdirectory, what are the user's total access permissions in that subdirectory?

21. Directory A has Subdirectories B and C. B has subdirectories D and E. B has subdirectories F and G. (*Hint:* Draw a diagram of the directory and subdirectories.) The systems administrator assigns user Lee access permissions W, X, and Y in Directory A. (Don't worry about the meaning of W, X, and Y. They are simply types of permissions.) The administrator gives user Lee access permissions X, Y, and Z in Subdirectory C. a) What access permissions does user Lee have in Directory B? b) What access permissions does user Lee have in Directory C? c) What access permissions does user Lee have in Directory D? d) In Directory F?

GAINING PERSPECTIVE

Market Realities

Groupware systems go beyond e-mail functionality to offer calendaring and other functions plus the ability to create "applications," for instance, tools to track customer contacts. The two leading groupware systems are Microsoft Exchange and Lotus

Notes/Domino. Notes/Domino has greater functionality for application development, but its labor costs tend to be higher.

In a survey of administrators,[8] it was found that a Notes/Domino server takes a median of 6 hours to set up completely, while an Exchange server takes a median of 8 hours. Both take a median of one hour to set up a client. In large organizations, then, client setup times dominate the setup phase. Here, their costs are similar.

Downtime is almost identical for the two systems, about an hour per month. Recovery times are also similar, about three hours. Again, costs are about the same.

Notes/Domino, however, being more complex, requires more administrator training—54 hours initially and 87 hours per year. For Exchange, these values are 45 hours and 28 hours. For end users, costs are very different. Notes/Domino users get 17 hours of training initially and 37 hours each year. For Exchange users, both initial training and training per year are three hours.

THOUGHT QUESTIONS

1. Why do you think networking textbooks spend little time on systems administration despite its importance in the life of network administrators?
2. Why is selecting the best product your budget can afford not a good basis for selecting products?
3. Is "simplicity" a business value? Explain.
4. A Cisco branch office router is listed at $2,500. Why is this not a good number to use in budgeting?
5. (Note: This question is for students who have previously taken a course that covers discounted cash flow analysis.) a) For the following project, give the payback period, the net present value, and the internal rate of return. b) Repeat the analysis if cash inflows are all moved *back* one year (say, from Year 2 to Year 1). Leave Year 5 cash inflows as zero after the move. What principle do you draw from this about the desirability of getting benefits as early as possible in a project's life? c) Repeat the analysis if cash outflows are all moved *forward* one year. What principle can you draw from this about the desirability of postponing capital investments as long as possible?

	Year 1	Year 2	Year 3	Year 4	Year 5
Cash Inflows	$0	$2,500	$2,000	$1,500	$1,500
Cash Outflows	$3,000	$500	$500	$500	$0

6. (From the Figure 10-13 "Access Permissions") Why do you think the assignment of access permissions blocks inheritance instead of giving the user the total of explicitly assigned permissions and inherited permissions?
7. a) Taking into account automatic inheritance, what access permissions would you give to the group Everyone in the systems directory, which contains programs restricted to use by systems administrators? Choices are full, read-only,

8   Osterman, Michael, "Today's Focus: Comparing Lotus Notes/Domino and Microsoft Exchange," *Network World Fusion Focus: Michael Osterman on Messaging* (e-mail newsletter), October 26, 2000. e-mail: Michael_Osterman@cnnlive.com.

and execute. b) In the Public directory, which contains information that anyone in the company should be able to read? c) In the user directory, which is the parent of all user home directories?

8. Read "Market Realities." Compare the three-year labor costs of Lotus Notes and Exchange for a system with two administrators and 500 end users. Assume that end users cost the company $40 per hour in salary, benefits, and overhead. Assume that network administrators cost $60 per hour. Ignore downtime costs to simplify matters slightly.

CASE STUDIES

Do the case study in Chapter 10a, "Using a Protocol Analyzer."

For case studies, go to the book's website, www.prenhall.com/panko, and look at the Case Studies page for this chapter.

PHOTOS

For photos, go to the book's website, www.prenhall.com/panko, and look at the Photos page for this chapter.

PROJECTS

1. **Getting Current.** Go to the book website's New Information and Errors pages for this chapter to get new information since this book went to press and to correct any errors in the text.

2. **Internet Exercises.** Go to the book website's Exercises page for this chapter and do the Internet Exercises.

3. **Hands On.** Download a trial version of a protocol analyzer, install it on a LAN client (with permission), and report on what you found.

HANDS ON: USING A PROTOCOL ANALYZER

INTRODUCTION

As Chapter 6a discussed, the 10 Mbps LAN in the University of Hawaii's College of Business Administration suffered from high congestion in the 1990s. To solve this problem, the college resegmented its LAN, breaking it into several smaller collision domains.

However, resegmentation is no magic potion. It only works if a network can be logically broken into pieces that have mostly internal traffic. For instance, if file service dominates LAN usage, then the student laboratories and their servers can be placed in one segment. Most of their traffic will take place within their network segment.

In contrast, if most of the LANs' traffic is Internet access via HTTP, SMTP, and other Internet protocols, there may be so much cross-traffic to and from the segment that resegmentation's ability to reduce traffic in individual segments would be negligible.

Before the College of Business Administration resegmented its LAN, it first examined traffic on the LAN, using a protocol analyzer, Etherpeek.[1]

TEST YOUR UNDERSTANDING

1. a) What network management decision was the College of Business Administration facing? b) Why did it need to know more about its traffic to make the decision?

---

[1] Supplied to the author by Wild Packets, Incorporated.

PROTOCOL ANALYZERS

A **protocol analyzer's** job is to study network traffic to see which protocols are being used in station-to-station communication within the LAN.

Capture

To do this, a protocol analyzer first must **capture** a sample of frames flowing through the network. To capture the frames, the protocol analyzer sets the NIC in its PC to what is known as **promiscuous mode**. In this mode, the NIC reads all frames regardless of their destination addresses.

Decode

The next step for the protocol analyzer is to **decode** each arriving frame. This requires the packet analyzer to look at all of the fields in the frame, in the frame's embedded packet, and in the packet's embedded transport layer message.

For instance, the protocol analyzer knows that the MAC destination address of the frame is in the first 48 bits of the arriving frame (the preamble and start of frame delimiter fields usually are discarded by the NIC because they only deal with synchronization). It also knows where to find an IP packet's protocol field, a TCP segment's source and destination port numbers, and other key diagnostic fields.[2]

Reporting

Although the protocol analyzer could simply dump information for each arriving frame in a file and let the network administrator deal with summarizing the information, protocol analyzers also **summarize** the data in ways that make sense to network managers.

TEST YOUR UNDERSTANDING

2.   a) What is a protocol analyzer? b) What are the three things it does?

USING ETHERPEEK

The protocol analyzer used in the College of Business Administration was Etherpeek, which has an excellent graphical user interface that gives easy access to all of its functions.

Message Log

By default, when the network administrator does a capture, Etherpeek shows frame contents one at a time in a table, in their order of arrival. This is a **message log**. Figure 10a-1 illustrates the data presented in this table. We do not give a screen shot because of the width of this information.

This table gives the essential information about each arriving frame, including what computer sent the frame, what computer received it, how long it was, and what

---

[2]   Of course, if the frame contains an IPX packet with an embedded NCP message, different fields would be relevant.

	Source	Destination	Size	Time Stamp	Protocol
1	00:A0:C9:AC:FE:B0	00:40:C7:95:6E:EF	64	13:01:39.581	NW IPX
2	00:A0:C9:AC:FE:B0	00:40:C7:A1:12:8B	64	13:01:39.581	NW IPX
3	00:A0:C9:AC:FE:B0	00:40:05:3E:6F:DC	64	13:01:39.581	NW IPX
4	IP-128.171.17.8	IP-128.171.17.151	78	13:01:39.582	IP-UDP
5	00:A0:C9:AC:FE:B0	00:40:C7:2F:04:61	64	13:01:39.582	NW IPX
6	00:A0:C9:AC:FE:B0	00:50:DA:29:7A:E9	64	13:01:39.582	NW IPX
7	IP-128.171.17.8	IP-128.171.17.151	130	13:01:39.589	IP-UDP

Figure 10a-1   Etherpeek: Frame-by-Frame Analysis

transport or internet layer protocol it employed. Not shown is another somewhat cryptic column that presents other information about the packet.

Most of the addresses given are NIC MAC layer addresses. However, if the protocol analyzer knows the IP address or AppleTalk (AT) address of the station, it will present this address.

This table is somewhat "raw" in that it offers no summaries. However, raw data is invaluable in many troubleshooting situations. For instance, if a computer or application program hangs (stops working), the contents of the last frame it sent or received may help diagnose the problem.

Conversation Statistics

Figure 10a-2 shows the **conversation** statistics that Etherpeek provides. For each pair of stations that communicated, this view gives the protocol used and the number of bytes exchanged. Note in the sixth line that this conversation is an HTTP interaction that generated four million bytes of information.

Node Statistics

A related view of the data shows **node** (station) statistics, which shows communication by station. This view is shown in Figure 10a-3. In the first row, we have Station 00:A0:C9:AC:FE:B0. Eighty-one percent of the bytes it exchanged were transmissions from it to other stations. Below this row, we see the two stations with which the node communicated. The first has an IP address. The second is an AppleTalk node. Node statistics tell you about your server communication. If a client is a high-traffic node, this may indicate that it has a malfunctioning NIC that is jabbering (transmitting inappropriately and frequently).

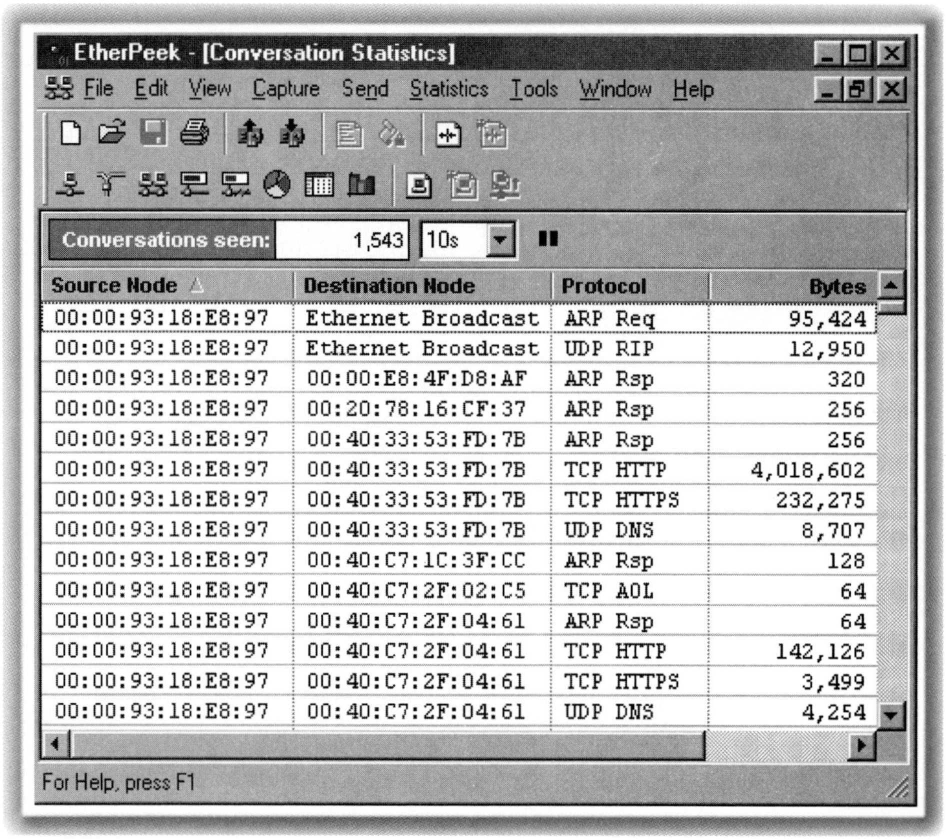

Source Node	Destination Node	Protocol	Bytes
00:00:93:18:E8:97	Ethernet Broadcast	ARP Req	95,424
00:00:93:18:E8:97	Ethernet Broadcast	UDP RIP	12,950
00:00:93:18:E8:97	00:00:E8:4F:D8:AF	ARP Rsp	320
00:00:93:18:E8:97	00:20:78:16:CF:37	ARP Rsp	256
00:00:93:18:E8:97	00:40:33:53:FD:7B	ARP Rsp	256
00:00:93:18:E8:97	00:40:33:53:FD:7B	TCP HTTP	4,018,602
00:00:93:18:E8:97	00:40:33:53:FD:7B	TCP HTTPS	232,275
00:00:93:18:E8:97	00:40:33:53:FD:7B	UDP DNS	8,707
00:00:93:18:E8:97	00:40:C7:1C:3F:CC	ARP Rsp	128
00:00:93:18:E8:97	00:40:C7:2F:02:C5	TCP AOL	64
00:00:93:18:E8:97	00:40:C7:2F:04:61	ARP Rsp	64
00:00:93:18:E8:97	00:40:C7:2F:04:61	TCP HTTP	142,126
00:00:93:18:E8:97	00:40:C7:2F:04:61	TCP HTTPS	3,499
00:00:93:18:E8:97	00:40:C7:2F:04:61	UDP DNS	4,254

Figure 10a-2 Etherpeek Conversation Statistics

Protocol Statistics

Ethernet Type 2 Packets

Figure 10a-4 looks at the data in terms of which **protocols** were used. Note that the first row shows that the data shown on the screen is for **Ethernet Type 2** frames. The Ethernet Type 2 standard predates the 802.3 standards. It does not have an LLC frame embedded in it; its data field holds an IP packet, an IPX packet, or some other packet directly. In addition, in place of the 802.3 MAC frame's length field, it has a two-octet **Ethertype** field that tells what type of packet is being carried.

Later in the scrollable window there is information about Ethernet 802.3 frames. The two types of Ethernet frames can exist on the same network because NICs are sufficiently intelligent to tell them apart and deal with them appropriately. Servers can be set to tell client NICs to use Ethernet Type 2 or 802.3 frames when they use that server.

Figure 10a-3   Etherpeek Node Statistics

Protocol

The first protocol shown in Figure 10a-4 is IPX, indicating NetWare IPX/SPX traffic. Under this comes NCP traffic. NCP messages are embedded in IPX packets, so the figure essentially shows a progressively finer view of the packet's contents. NCP is the NetWare transport–application layer standard for file and print service communication. Although information for other protocols is not shown in this screen shot, even the small amount of IPX data that is visible emphasizes the high importance of NetWare IPX/SPX communication on the LAN.

Dashboard

The figure also shows the Etherpeek **dashboard**, which allows the network administrator to see how the network is doing at the moment using simulated analog meters.

Summary Information

Error Messages

Last, but certainly not least, Figure 10a-5 presents summaries of the decodes of the captured data. First, it shows that there were no Ethernet errors at all, including runt

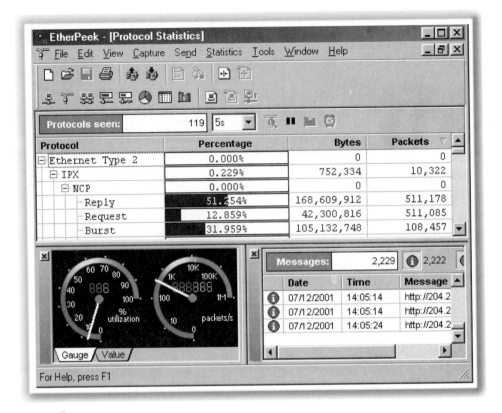

Figure 10a-4 Etherpeek Protocol Statistics

(too small) frames and oversize (too large) frames. This is good, because it indicates that no NICs appear to be malfunctioning. Later in the scrollable window, there is information about checksum errors in IP, UDP, ICMP, and AppleTalk messages, as well as data on failed FTP transfers.

Packet Size Distributions
The figure also shows size distributions for packets. It shows that almost half of the packets are between 65 and 127 octets. It shows many packets equal to or less than 64 octets. However, the Ethernet data indicate that there were no runts (undersized messages), so the size data indicate that about 15 percent of the frames needed padding to get them up to minimum size. Etherpeek also offers a graph of the size data.

Attack Information
Later in the scrollable window, there is data to help understand Internet attacks, including data on the types of ICMP messages delivered (ICMP is a favorite of hackers), data on specific types of common Internet attacks, and even data on Napster downloads (which many firms wished to stop).

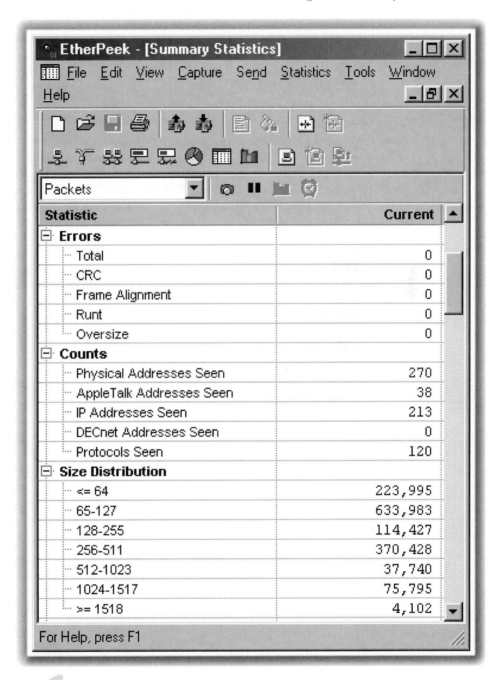

Figure 10a-5   Etherpeek Summary Information

TEST YOUR UNDERSTANDING

3. a) Why are message logs useful? b) Why are conversation statistics useful? c) Why are node statistics useful? d) Why are protocol statistics useful? e) What types of useful summary statistics does Etherpeek provide, and why are they useful?

USE IN THE COLLEGE OF BUSINESS ADMINISTRATION

Before the protocol analyzer was installed, it was generally believed that most traffic on the LAN was Internet traffic, which would make resegmentation ineffective. However, when the data were analyzed, it was apparent that only 15 percent of the packets were carrying Internet traffic, most notably, HTTP messages. In turn, 75 percent to 80 percent of the traffic was file service and print service traffic, which are good for resegmentation as long as servers are placed in the same segment as most of the computers they serve. The college went ahead with the resegmentation project.

At the same time, since the resegmentation was completed, file and print service traffic have fallen as a percentage of all traffic while Internet traffic has grown to about 30 percent. This has not yet negated the benefits of resegmentation, but if this trend continues, resegmentation may have to give way to a more comprehensive approach, including upgrading the network to 100Base-TX switches, which would involve large outlays for new wiring.

TEST YOUR UNDERSTANDING

4. a) What did the College of Business Administration find in the data? b) How did it use this information?

CHAPTER 11

NETWORKED APPLICATIONS

Learning Objectives:

By the end of this chapter, you should be able to discuss:

- The characteristics and limitations of host communication with dumb terminals.
- Client/server architectures, including file server program access and client/server processing (including web-enabled applications).
- Electronic mail standards.
- World Wide Web and e-commerce (including the use of application servers) and security.
- Web services, including Microsoft's .NET approach, which uses SOAP with XML syntax.
- Peer-to-peer (P2P) computing, which, paradoxically, normally uses servers for part of the work.

INTRODUCTION

Networked Applications

Once, applications ran on single machines: usually mainframes or stand-alone PCs. Today, however, most applications spread their processing power over two or more machines connected by networks instead of doing all processing on a single machine.

Application Architectures

In this chapter, we will focus on **application architectures**, that is, how application layer functions are spread among computers to deliver service to users. Thanks to layering's ability to separate functions at different layers, most application architectures can run over TCP/IP, IPX/SPX, and other standards below the application layer. In turn, if you use TCP at the transport layer, TCP does not care what application architecture you are using.

Important Networked Applications

In addition to looking broadly at application architectures, we will look at some of the most important of today's networked applications, including e-mail, videoconferencing, the World Wide Web, and electronic commerce (e-commerce).

Importance of the Application Layer to Users

In this chapter, we will focus on the application layer. This is the only layer whose functionality users see directly. When users want e-mail, it is irrelevant what is happening below the application layer, except in a negative way if there is a failure or performance problem at lower layers.

TEST YOUR UNDERSTANDING

1. a) What is an application architecture? b) Why do users focus on the application layer?

TRADITIONAL APPLICATION ARCHITECTURES

In this section, we will look at the two most important traditional application architectures: terminal–host systems and client/server architectures (both file server program access and client/server processing).

Hosts with Dumb Terminals

As Figure 11-1 shows, the first step beyond stand-alone machines still placed the processing power on a single **host computer** but distributed input/output (I/O) functions out to user sites. It placed these I/O functions in **dumb terminals**, which sent user keystrokes to the host and painted host information on the terminal screen but did little else.

Although this approach worked, the central computer often was overloaded by the need to process both applications and terminal communication. This often resulted in slow **response times** when users typed commands.

Another problem was high transmission cost. All keystrokes had to be sent to the host computer for processing. This generated a great deal of traffic. Similarly, the host had to send detailed information to be shown on-screen. To reduce transmission costs,

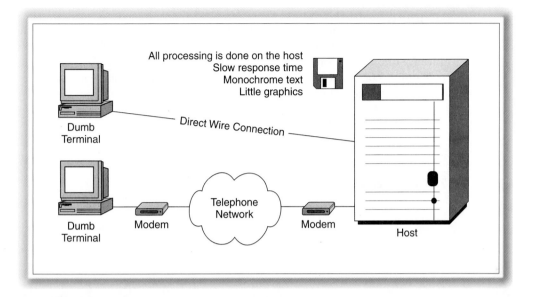

All processing is done on the host
Slow response time
Monochrome text
Little graphics

Dumb
Terminal

Direct Wire Connection

Dumb
Terminal

Modem

Telephone
Network

Modem

Host

Figure 11-1   Simple Terminal–Host System

most terminals limited the information they could display to **monochrome text** (one color against a contrasting background). Graphics were seldom available.[1]

IBM mainframe computers used a more complex design for their terminal–host systems that added other pieces of equipment beyond terminals and hosts. This extra equipment reduced cost and improved response time. In addition, IBM terminal–host systems had higher speeds than traditional terminals and so were able to offer limited color and graphics. Although these advances extended the life of terminal–host systems, even these advanced IBM systems were less satisfactory than subsequent developments, including the client/server systems described next.

TEST YOUR UNDERSTANDING

2. a) Where is processing performed in systems of hosts and dumb terminals? b) What are the typical problems with these systems?

Client/Server Systems

After terminal–host systems, a big breakthrough came in the form of **client/server systems**, which placed some power on the client computer. This was made possible by the emergence of personal computers in the 1980s. PCs have the processing power to act as non-dumb clients.

---

[1] The most common dumb terminal today is the VT100 terminal, also called an ANSI terminal. On the Internet, clients can emulate (imitate) dumb terminals using Telnet. Telnet turns a $2,000 office PC into a $200 dumb terminal.

File Server Program Access

Figure 11-2 shows that there are two basic forms of client/server computing. The first is **file server program access**, which we saw in Chapter 4. In this form of client/server computing, the server's only role is to store programs and data files. For processing, the program is copied across the network to the client PC, along with data files. The client PC does the actual processing of the program and data files.

Figure 11-2   Client/Server Computing

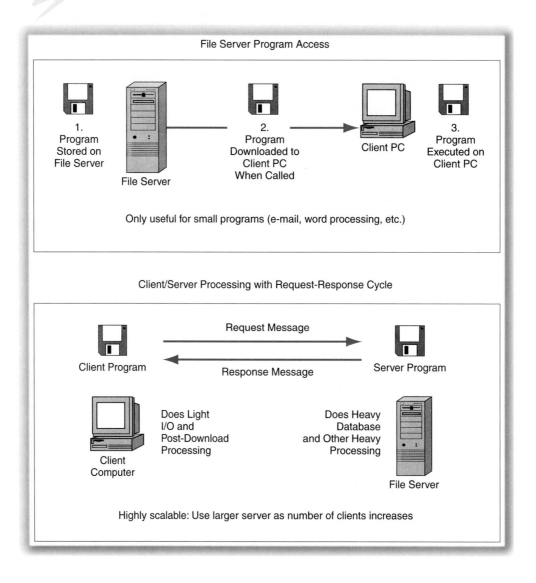

File Server Program Access

1.
Program
Stored on
File Server

File Server

2.
Program
Downloaded to
Client PC
When Called

Client PC

3.
Program
Executed on
Client PC

Only useful for small programs (e-mail, word processing, etc.)

Client/Server Processing with Request-Response Cycle

Request Message

Client Program

Response Message

Server Program

Client
Computer

Does Light
I/O and
Post-Download
Processing

Does Heavy
Database
and Other Heavy
Processing

File Server

Highly scalable: Use larger server as number of clients increases

As we saw in Chapter 4, many client PCs are comparatively underpowered, and even the fastest client PCs usually are fairly slow compared to servers. Consequently, file server program access is only sufficient for word processing, e-mail, and other small applications. It is not useful for large database applications.

Client/Server Processing

In contrast, in full **client/server processing**, the work is done by programs on two machines, as Figure 11-2 illustrates. Generally, the server does the heavy processing needed to retrieve information. The client, in turn, normally focuses on the user interface and on processing data delivered by the server, for instance by placing the data in an Excel spreadsheet.

Scalability

Client/server processing is highly scalable. In most instances, as the number of users rises, scaling merely involves replacing the existing server with a larger server. In fact, it is even possible to change the server platform without users noticing the change. An application can start on a small PC server and then be moved successively to a large PC server, a workstation server, and even a mainframe.

Web-Enabled Applications

Client/server processing requires a client program to be installed on a client PC. Initially, all applications used custom-designed client programs. Rolling out a new application to serve hundreds or thousands of client computers was extremely time-consuming and expensive.

Fortunately, there is one client program that almost all PCs have today. This is a browser. As Figure 11-3 illustrates, many client/server processing applications are now **web-enabled**, meaning that they use ordinary browsers as client programs. The figure specifically shows web-enabled e-mail.

TEST YOUR UNDERSTANDING

3. a) Contrast file server program access with client/server processing in terms of where processing is performed. b) Contrast them in terms of scalability.
4. Contrast general client/server processing with Web-enabled applications.

ELECTRONIC MAIL (E-MAIL)

Importance

A Universal Service on the Internet

E-mail has become one of the two "universal" services on the Internet, along with the World Wide Web. E-mail provides mailbox delivery if the receiver is "offline" when the message is sent. E-mail offers the speed of a fax plus the ability to store messages in organized files, to send replies, to forward messages to others, and to perform many other actions after message receipt. The telephone offers truly instant communication, but only if the other party is in and can take calls. In addition, e-mail is less intrusive than a phone call.

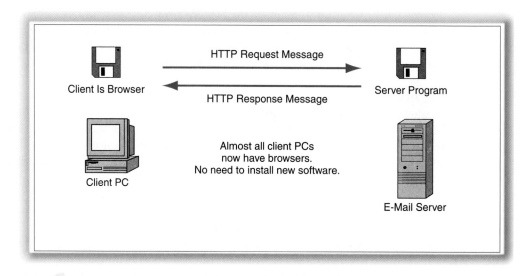

Figure 11-3   Web-Enabled Application (E-Mail)

Figure 11-4   E-Mail

Importance of E-Mail
   Universal service on the Internet
   Attachments deliver anything
   Viruses, worms, and spam
E-Mail Standards
   Message body standards
      RFC 822 and RFC 2822 for all-text bodies
      HTML bodies
      UNICODE for multiple languages
   Simple Mail Transfer Protocol (SMTP)
      Message delivery: client to sender's mail host
      Message delivery: sender's mail host to receiver's mail host
   Downloading mail to client
      Post Office Protocol (POP): simple and widely used
      Internet Message Access Program (IMAP): more powerful, less widely used

Attachments Can Deliver Anything

Thanks to attachments, e-mail has also become a general file delivery system. Users can exchange spreadsheet documents, word processing documents, graphics, and any other type of file.

Viruses, Worms, and Spam

On the downside, e-mail is now the most common way to spread viruses and worms, and most users receive several pieces of spam—unsolicited commercial e-mail—per day. Mail filtering is almost as big a consideration as message delivery when selecting an e-mail system for a corporation.

E-Mail Standards

A major driving force behind the wide acceptance of Internet e-mail is standardization. It is rare for users of different systems not to be able to communicate at a technical level—although many companies restrict outgoing and incoming communication using firewalls for security purposes. Consequently, the key issue is application layer standards.

Message Body Standards

Obviously, message bodies have to be standardized, or we would not be able to read arriving messages. In physical mail, message body standards include the language the partners will use (English, etc.), formality of language, and other matters. Some physical messages are forms, which have highly standardized layout and fields that require specific information.

RFC 2822 (Originally RFC 822)   The initial standard for e-mail bodies was **RFC 822**, which has recently been updated as **RFC 2822**. This is a standard for plain text messages—multiple lines of typewriter-like characters with no boldface, graphics, or other amenities. The extreme simplicity of this approach made it easy to create early client e-mail programs.

HTML Bodies   Later, as HTML became widespread on the World Wide Web, most mail venders developed the ability to display **HTML bodies** with richly formatted text and even graphics.

UNICODE   RFC 822 specified the use of the ASCII code to represent printable characters. Unfortunately, ASCII was developed for English, and even European languages need extra characters. The **UNICODE** standard allows characters of all languages to be represented, although most mail readers cannot display all UNICODE characters well yet.

Simple Mail Transfer Protocol (SMTP)[2]

We also need standards for delivering RFC2822, HTML, and UNICODE messages. In the postal world, we must have envelopes that present certain information in certain ways, and there are specific ways to post mail for delivery, including putting them in post office drop boxes and taking them to the post office.

Figure 11-5 shows how e-mail is posted (sent). The e-mail program on the user's PC sends the message to its outgoing mail host using the **Simple Mail Transfer Protocol (SMTP)**. Figure 11-6 shows that SMTP requires a complex series of interactions between the sender and receiver before and after mail delivery.

Figure 11-6 shows that the sender's outgoing mail host sends the message on to the receiver's incoming mail host, again using SMTP. The receiving host stores the message in the receiver's mailbox until the receiver retrieves it.

Receiving Mail (POP and IMAP)

Figure 11-5 shows two standards that are used to *receive* e-mail. These are the **Post Office Protocol (POP)** and the **Internet Message Access Protocol (IMAP)**. IMAP offers more features, but the simpler POP standard is more popular. Programs implementing these standards ask the mail host to download some or all new mail to the user's client e-mail program. Often, users delete new mail from their inbox after downloading new messages. After that, the messages only exist on the user's client PC.

Figure 11-5   E-Mail Standards

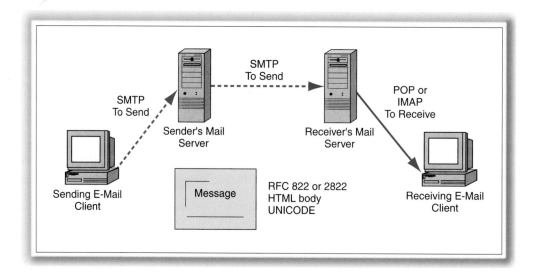

Actor	Command	Comment
Receiving SMTP Process	220 Mail.Panko.Com Ready	When a TCP connection is opened, the receiver signals that it is ready.
Sending SMTP Process	HELO Voyager.cba.Hawaii.edu	Sender asks to begin sending a message. Gives own identity.
Receiver	250 Mail.Panko.Com	Receiver signals that it is ready to begin receiving a message.
Sender	MAIL FROM: Panko@ voyager.cba.Hawaii.edu	Sender identifies the sender (mail author, not SMTP process).
Receiver	250 OK	Accepts author. However, may reject mail from others.
Sender	RCPT TO: Ray@Panko.com	Identifies first mail recipient.
Receiver	250 OK	Accepts first recipient.
Sender	RCPT TO: Lee@Panko.com	Identifies second mail recipient.
Receiver	550 No such user here	Does not accept second recipient. However will deliver to first recipient.
Sender	DATA	Message will follow.
Receiver	354 Start mail input; end with <CRLF>.<CRLF>	Gives permission to send message.
Sender	When in the course . . .	The message. Multiple lines of text. Ends with line containing only a single period: <CRLF>.<CRLF>
Receiver	250 OK	Receiver accepts message.
Sender	QUIT	Requests termination of session.
Receiver	221 Mail.Panko.Com Service closing transmission channel	End of transaction.

Figure 11-6   Interactions in the Simple Mail Transfer Protocol (SMTP)

Web-Enabled E-Mail

Almost all client PCs have browsers. Many mail hosts are now web-enabled, meaning that users only need browsers to interact with them in order to send, receive, and manage their e-mail. As Figure 11-3 showed, all interactions take place via HTTP, and these systems use HTML to render pages on-screen.

Web-enabled e-mail is especially good for travelers because no special e-mail software is needed. Any computer with a browser in an Internet café, home, or office will allow the user to check his or her mail. On the downside, web-enabled e-mail tends to be very slow because almost all processing is done on the distant (and often overloaded) webserver with its server-based mail processing program.

TEST YOUR UNDERSTANDING

5. a) Distinguish among the major standards for e-mail bodies. b) When a station sends a message to its mail host, what standard does it use? c) When the sender's mail host sends the message to the receiver's mail host, what standard does it use? d) When the receiver's e-mail client downloads new mail from its mail host, what standard is it most likely to use?

6. a) What is web-enabled e-mail? b) What is its advantage? c) Its disadvantage?

THE WORLD WIDE WEB AND E-COMMERCE

The World Wide Web

HTML and HTTP

We have discussed the World Wide Web throughout this book. As Figure 11-7 shows, webpages themselves are created using the **HyperText Markup Language (HTML)**. In turn, interactions between the browser and webserver application program are implemented using the **HyperText Transfer Protocol (HTTP)**.

To give an analogy, an e-mail message may be created using RFC 2822, but it will be delivered using SMTP. Many application standards consist of a document standard and a transfer standard.

Complex Webpages

Actually, most "webpages" really consist of several files—a master text-only HTML file plus graphics files, audio files, and other types of files. Figure 11-8 illustrates the downloading of a webpage with two graphics files.

Figure 11-7   HTML and HTTP

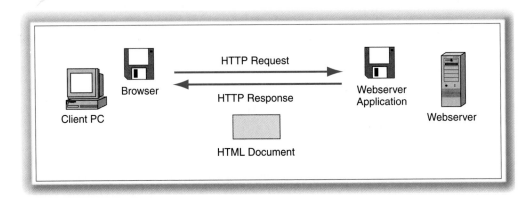

HTTP Request
HTTP Response

Client PC
Browser
HTML Document
Webserver Application
Webserver

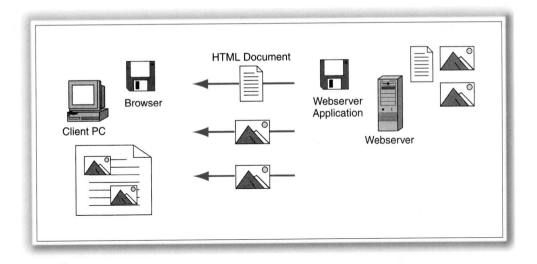

Figure 11-8 Downloading a Complex Webpage with Two Graphics Files

The HTML file merely consists of the page's text, plus **tags** to show where the browser should render graphics files, when it should play audio files, and so forth.[3] The HTML file is downloaded first because the browser needs the tags to know what other files should be downloaded.

Consequently, several **HTTP request-response cycles** may be needed to download a single webpage. Three request-response cycles are needed in this example.

The Client's Role
The client's roles, as shown in Figure 11-8, are to send **HTTP request messages** asking for the files and to draw the webpage on-screen. If the webpage has a **Java applet** or another **active element**, the browser will have to execute it as well.

The Webserver's Role
The webserver application program's basic job is to read each HTTP request message, retrieve the desired file from memory, and create an **HTTP response message** that contains the requested file or a reason why it can not be delivered. Webserver application software may also have to execute server-side active elements before returning the requested webpage.

HTTP Request and Response Messages
As Figure 11-9 shows, both HTTP request messages and HTTP response headers use text formats. **MIME** is a standard for describing different types of file formats, so that

---

[3]   For graphics files, the <IMG> tag is used. The keyword IMG indicates that a image file is to be downloaded. The SRC parameter in this tag gives the target file's directory and filename on the webserver.

HTTP Request Message
GET /panko/home.htm HTTP/1.1[CRLF]
Host: voyager.cba.Hawaii.edu
Connection: Keep-Alive
HTTP Response Message
HTTP/1.1 200 OK[CRLF]
Date: Tuesday, 20-MAR-2002 18:32:15 GMT[CRLF]
Server: *name of server software*[CRLF]
MIME-version: 1.0[CRLF]
Content-type: text/plain[CRLF]
[CRLF]
file to be downloaded

Figure 11-9   Examples of HTTP Request and Response Messages

the receiver will know how to process the file delivered in an HTTP response message (or in an e-mail attachment).

TEST YOUR UNDERSTANDING

7. a) Distinguish between HTTP and HTML. b) You are downloading a webpage that has six graphics and two sound clips. How many request–response cycles will be needed? c) What do the MIME header fields tell the receiving process? d) Why is this information necessary?

Electronic Commerce (E-Commerce)

E-Commerce Functionality

Electronic commerce (e-commerce) is the buying and selling of goods and services over the Internet. As Figure 11-10 shows, e-commerce software adds extra functionality to a webserver's basic file retrieval function.

Catalog

Most obviously, an e-commerce site must have an **electronic catalog** showing the goods it has for sale. Although catalogs can be created using basic HTML coding, most merchants purchase **e-commerce software** to automate the creation of catalog pages and other e-commerce functionality.

Shopping Cart, Check Out, and Payment Functions

Two core e-commerce functions are the maintenance of a **shopping cart** for holding goods while the customer is shopping and **check out** when the buyer has finished shopping and wishes to pay for the selected goods. The check out function should

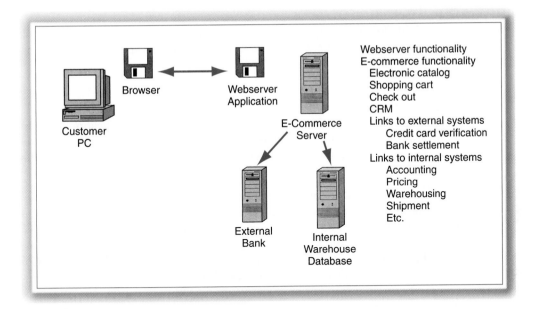

Webserver functionality
E-commerce functionality
    Electronic catalog
    Shopping cart
    Check out
    CRM
    Links to external systems
        Credit card verification
        Bank settlement
    Links to internal systems
        Accounting
        Pricing
        Warehousing
        Shipment
        Etc.

Browser   Webserver
           Application

Customer
PC

E-Commerce
Server

External
Bank

Internal
Warehouse
Database

Figure 11-10   Electronic Commerce Functions

include several **payment mechanisms**. Again, most firms use e-commerce software, which includes shopping cart maintenance and check out capabilities, including the taking of payments.

Customer Relationship Management (CRM)

Customers have different needs and wants. Many firms now use **customer relationship management (CRM)** software to examine customer data to understand the preferences of their customers. This allows a company to tailor presentations and specific market offers to its customers' specific tastes. The goal is to increase the rate of **conversions**—browsers becoming buyers—and to increase the rate of **repeat purchasing** (compared to one-time purchasing.) Small increases in conversion rates and repeat purchasing rates can have a big impact on profitability.

Links to Other Systems

External Systems

As Figure 11-10 shows, taking payments usually requires external links to two outside organizations. One is a **credit card verification service**, which checks the validity of the credit card number the user has typed. Without credit card checking, the credit card fraud rate may be high enough to drive the company out of business. The other is a **bank settlement firm**, which handles the credit card payment.

Internal Back-End Systems

Figure 11-10 also shows that e-commerce usually also requires links to **internal back-end systems** for accounting, pricing, product availability, shipment, and other matters.

Application Servers

Accepting User Data

As Figure 11-11 shows, most large e-commerce sites use an **application server**, which accepts user data from a front-end webserver. Some sites combine the webserver and application server, but most large sites separate these functions onto two machines.

Retrievals from External Systems

The application server then contacts external systems and internal back-end database systems to satisfy the user's request. To do this, it sends requests that these external systems can understand, and then it receives responses. This is complicated because each external system may have its own way of handling requests and responses. Connecting to external systems is one of the most difficult tasks in the development of an e-commerce site. Figure 11-11 shows some of the complexities involved in interactions with external systems.

Figure 11-11   Application Server (Three-Tier Architecture)

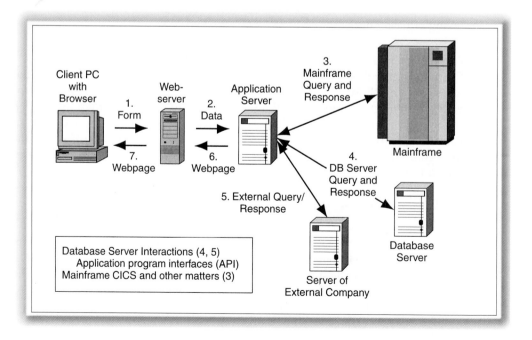

Application Program Interfaces (APIs)   Modern client/server database systems have published **application program interface (API)** specifications to allow application server programs to interact directly with database systems.

Mainframe Interactions   Mainframe computers have their own ways of communicating with the outside world. Application server programmers must be deeply familiar with CICS and other mainframe processes.

Creating a Response

To document its findings, the application server then creates a new webpage and passes it to the user via the webserver, as shown in Figure 11-11.

Three-Tier Architecture

Terminal-host systems perform processing on a single machine. Most client/server systems do processing on two machines. With an application server, processing takes place on a third machine as well. Therefore, using application servers is called having a **three-tier architecture**.

TEST YOUR UNDERSTANDING

8. a) What functionality does e-commerce need beyond basic webservice? b) What external connections does e-commerce require? c) What is the role of application servers? d) What are the two main ways to retrieve information from external databases?

E-Commerce Security

E-commerce sites experience regular attacks by hackers and denial-of-service attacks. This requires strong security, as Figure 11-12 illustrates.

SSL/TLS

When you send credit card numbers or other sensitive information over the Internet, it is almost always protected by a secure communication system at the transport layer called **Secure Sockets Layer (SSL)** security. (More properly, it should be called **Transport Layer Security (TLS)** because this is the new name given to it by the IETF, which now controls its development. However, it is still widely called SSL.) SSL provides merchant authentication (but rarely client authentication) and encryption for confidentiality so that snoopers cannot read sensitive user information. SSL is not perfect but is highly effective.

Demilitarized Zones (DMZs)

Figure 11-12 shows that public e-commerce servers (and other public servers) normally are placed "**outside the firewall**" in a **demilitarized zone (DMZ)**.[4] This means that even if hackers can take over the server, they cannot get into the rest of the corporate network, which is protected by a very strong firewall. There usually is a simple

---

[4]   In the Vietnam war, the DMZ was a strip of land between North and South Vietnam. Supposedly a place where no troops should be, it was the scene of some of the war's bloodiest fighting.

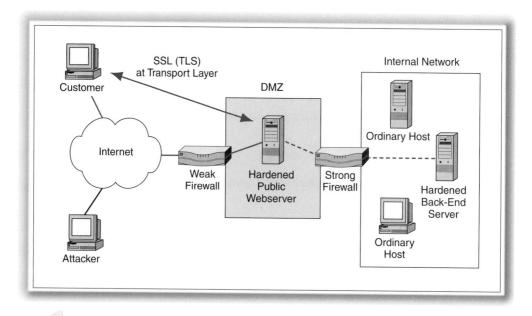

Figure 11-12   E-Commerce Security

firewall between the DMZ and the Internet, but it is weak enough to allow widespread access while stopping simpler attacks.

Hardened Servers

Hackers probably will be able to get into the DMZ to attack servers there. As a consequence, e-commerce servers and other servers must be specially hardened against attacks, as we saw in Chapter 9. Most cases of credit card theft have come from hackers taking over e-commerce servers (or back-end systems) and reading the credit card numbers out of files stored there. In addition, e-commerce servers often contain other types of private customer information that must be safeguarded. Break-ins can cause a serious loss in customer confidence and can lead to lawsuits.

TEST YOUR UNDERSTANDING

9.   a) What secure communication system is used widely in e-commerce? b) At what layer does it operate? c) Describe how DMZs provide security in e-commerce. d) Why is the hardening of e-commerce servers critical?

WEB SERVICES

Given the difficulty of getting systems to work cooperatively in e-commerce (and other areas), several companies are introducing a more general approach to providing service. This new approach is the use of Web services. We will focus on Microsoft's implementation of Web services. Microsoft calls its approach **.NET**.

Basic Web Service

Figure 11-13 compares traditional webservice (based on HTML) with a simple Web service. Here, the client is a browser.

Objects

In programming terminology, a Web service is an **object**. It communicates with the outside world using a specific **interface**. This interface exposes well-defined **methods** (actions it can take) to the outside world and has **properties** that can be changed. Clients communicate via messages directed to the interface.

Simple Object Access Protocol (SOAP)

SOAP (the **Simple Object Access Protocol**) is a standardized way for a Web service to expose its methods on an interface to the outside world. SOAP is a message format that allows clients to send commands to Web services calling for methods these Web services support. SOAP requests specify a particular method and the specific parameters allowed or dictated by that method. SOAP also specifies the formatting of messages that Web services use to respond to clients.

Figure 11-13   Ordinary Webservice Versus Web Service

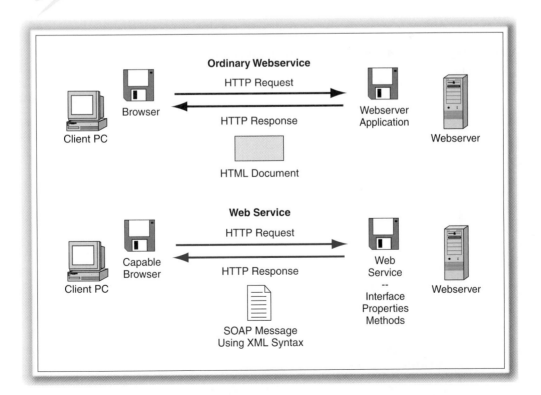

Figure 11-14 shows a simplified SOAP request and a simplified SOAP response. Each would be carried in the body of an HTTP message, right after the header. Most SOAP messages are more complex, but this complexity does not add to the essence of how SOAP works.

Here, an object exposes a method, PriceQuote, on interface QuoteInterface. Input parameters, which are sent in the SOAP request message, are PartNum, Quantity, and ShippingType.

The output parameter is Price, which is delivered in the SOAP response message. This method provides a price quote if the sender identifies the part, indicates how many it wants, and specifies how it will be shipped.

XML

The first line of each message begins with a header that says "xml version="1.0". This shows that SOAP messages are expressed in XML (eXtensible Markup Language) syntax. Whereas HTML expresses the formatting of messages and does not allow users to create their own tags, XML allows communities of users to create their own tags, for example, <price> and </price>, that have semantic meaning to the community.

Web Services and HTTP

Overall, then, **Web services** are server programs that communicate with clients using HTTP to deliver SOAP messages written in XML syntax instead of using HTTP to deliver HTML messages as in standard webservice. Using HTTP to carry messages is enormously advantageous because it is simple to support and widely understood.

Figure 11-14   Simple SOAP Request and Response

```
SOAP Request Message
<?xml version="1.0"?>
<BODY>
        <QuotePrice xmlns="QuoteInterface">
                <PartNum>QA78d</PartNum>
                <Quantity>47</Quantity>
                <ShippingType>Rush</ShippingType>
        </QuotePrice>
</BODY>

SOAP Response Message
<?xml version="1.0"?>
<BODY>
        <QuoteResponse xmlns="QuoteInterface">
                <Price>$750.33</Price>
        </QuoteResponse>
</BODY>
```

Web Services and Firewalls

Most firewalls pass HTTP messages on Port 80, making Web service communication easier. Of course, firewall control is very important, so SOAP specifies the addition of a few new HTTP header lines that firewalls can use to control access.

Universal Description, Discovery, and Integration (UDDI) Protocol

In the future, some Web services will be offered on a fee-per-use basis. To attract customers, they will need a way to advertise themselves. They also will need to make available a description of how others can use them. Many firms are now adopting the **Universal Description, Discovery, and Integration (UDDI)** protocol to advertise themselves to the world. Figure 11-15 shows key aspects of UDDI.

UDDI is a distributed database, meaning that there will be many interconnected UDDI servers that cooperate with one another. UDDI will offer three basic search options.

> ➤ **UDDI White Pages** allow users to search for Web services by name, much like telephone white pages.

> ➤ **UDDI Yellow Pages** allow users to search for Web services by function, such as accounting, much like telephone yellow pages.

Figure 11-15   Universal Description, Discovery, and Integration (UDDI) Server for Web Services

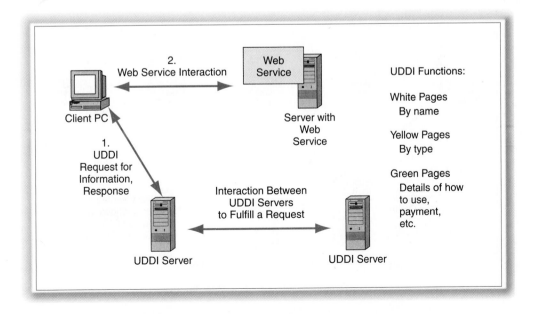

➤ **UDDI Green Pages** allow companies to understand how to interact with specific Web services. In object-oriented terminology, green pages specify the interfaces on which a Web service will respond, the methods it will accept, and the properties that can be changed or returned. Payment methods are also part of UDDI green pages.

TEST YOUR UNDERSTANDING

10. a) Distinguish between normal webservice and Web services. b) Give the definition of Web services. c) What does SOAP specify? d) In what syntax are SOAP messages written? e) How are SOAP messages exchanged? f) Explain the implications of using HTTP for delivery through firewalls. g) What is the purpose of UDDI? h) What do UDDI green pages tell you?

PEER-TO-PEER (P2P) APPLICATIONS

The newest application architecture is the **peer-to-peer (P2P) architecture**, in which most or all of the work is done by cooperating user computers, such as desktop PCs. If servers are present at all, they only serve facilitating roles and do not control the processing.

Traditional Client/Server Applications

Approach

Figure 11-16 shows a traditional client/server application. In this application, all of the clients communicate with the central server for their work.

Figure 11-16   Traditional Client/Server Application

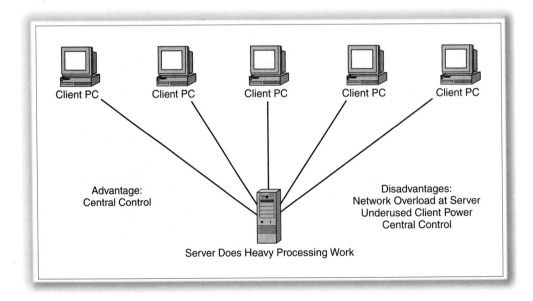

Client PC   Client PC   Client PC   Client PC   Client PC

Advantage:
Central Control

Disadvantages:
Network Overload at Server
Underused Client Power
Central Control

Server Does Heavy Processing Work

Advantage: Central Control
One advantage of this **server-centric** approach is central control. All communication goes through the central server, so there can be good security and policy-based control over communication.

Problems
Although the use of central service is good in several ways, it does give rise to some problems.

Traffic Overload at the Server   One problem with this approach is that a great deal of traffic goes through a central location. This can create network overloads at the central location.

Underused Client PC Capacity   Another problem is that client/server computing often uses expensive server capacity while leaving clients underused. Clients normally are modern PCs with considerable processing power, not dumb terminals or early low-powered PCs.

Central Control   From the end users' point of view, central control can be a problem rather than a value. Central control limits what end users can do. Just as PCs freed end users from the red tape involved in using mainframe computers, peer-to-peer computing frees end users from the red tape involved in using a server. There is a fundamental clash of interests between central control and end user freedom.

Peer-to-Peer (P2P) Applications

Approach
Figure 11-17 shows that in a peer-to-peer (P2P) application, user PCs communicate directly with one another, at least for part of their work. Here, all of the work involves P2P interactions. The two user computers work without the assistance of a central server and also without its control.

Benefits
The benefits and threats of P2P computing are the opposite of those of client/server computing. Client users are freed from central control for better or worse, network traffic is spread more evenly, and less user computer capacity is wasted.

Problems
Transient Presence   However, P2P computing is not without problems of its own. Most obviously, user PCs have transient presence on the Internet. They are frequently turned off, and even when they are on, users may be away from their machines. There is nothing in P2P like always-present servers.

Transient IP Address   Another problem is that each time a user PC uses the Internet, its DHCP server (see Chapter 2) is likely to assign it a different IP address. There is nothing in P2P like the permanence of a telephone number or a permanent IP address on a server.

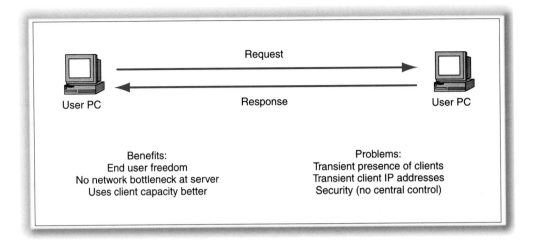

Figure 11-17 Simple Peer-to-Peer (P2P) Application

Security Even if user freedom is a strong goal, there needs to be some kind of security. P2P computing is a great way to spread viruses and other illicit content. Without centralized filtering on servers, security will have to be implemented on on all user PCs or chaos will result.

Pure Peer-to-Peer Applications: Gnutella

Viral Networking for Searches

Gnutella is a pure P2P file-sharing application that addresses the problems of transient presence and transient IP addresses without resorting to the use of any server. As Figure 11-18 shows, Gnutella uses **viral networking**. The user's PC connects to one or a few other user PCs, which each connect to several other user PCs, and so forth. When the user's PC first connects, it sends an initiation message to introduce itself via viral networking. Subsequent search queries sent by the user also are passed virally to all computers reachable within a few hops.

Direct File Downloads

However, actual file downloads are done using strictly peer-to-peer communication between the user's PC and the PC holding the file to be downloaded. There is no viral networking in actual file downloads.

Super Clients

Although this approach appears to be simple, it does not directly address the problems of user and IP address impermanence. To address these problems, Gnutella "cheats" a little. It relies on the presence of many **super clients** that are always on, that have a fixed IP address, that have many files to share, and that are each connected to

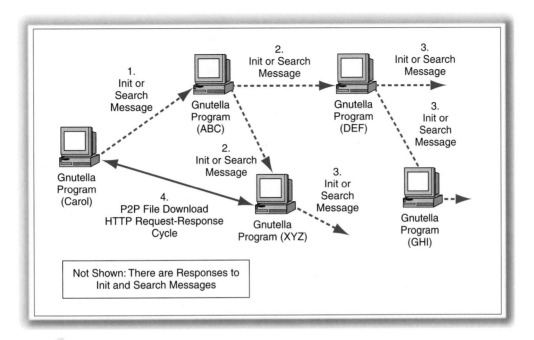

Figure 11-18   Gnutella: Pure P2P Protocol with Viral Networking

several other super clients. Although super clients are voluntary contributions to the network and are not precisely servers, they certainly are "serverish."

Using Servers to Facilitate P2P Interactions

Most peer-to-peer applications do not even try for a pure P2P approach. Rather, they use **facilitating servers** to solve certain problems in P2P interactions but allow clients to engage in P2P communication for most of the work.

Napster

As Figure 11-19 shows, the famous (and infamous) Napster service used an index server. When stations connect to Napster, they first upload a list of their files available for sharing to an index server. Later, when they search, their searches go to the index servers and are returned from there.

However, once a client receives a search response, it selects a client who has the desired file and contacts that client directly. The large file transfer—usually one to five megabytes—is done entirely peer-to-peer. This is a very large job compared to the index server's job.

H.323

In videoconferencing and IP telephony, communication is governed by the H.323 standard. As Figure 11-20 shows, two terminals—usually PCs—wish to communicate.

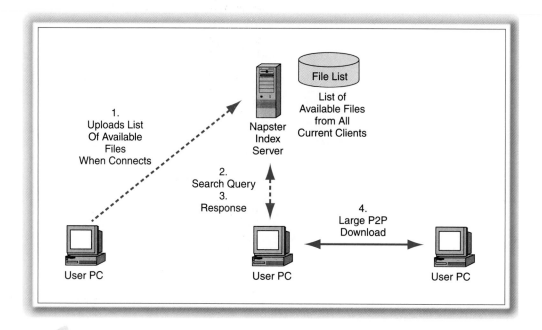

Figure 11-19 Napster

Figure 11-20 H.323 Communication

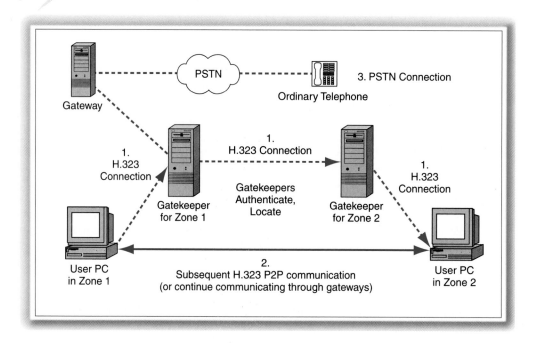

If the calling party knows the called party's IP address, it can connect to the called party directly.

However, the communication typically uses **gatekeeper** servers. The called party's gatekeeper authenticates the caller and then facilitates the connection to the called party. If there is a gatekeeper in a terminal's zone, the terminal is required to use the gatekeeper to communicate. Another type of server, a gateway, connects an IP network to the Public Switched Telephone Network.

If all communication goes through the gatekeeper after the initial connection is made, additional services are possible, such as those provided in electronic telephone switching (call waiting and so forth).

This spectrum of capabilities illustrates the type of flexibility that would be desirable in other P2P programs to allow individual firms to select the degree of client/ server versus P2P functionality that would be best for their organization.

Processor Utilization: SETI@home

As noted earlier, most PC processors sit idle most of the time. This is even true much of the time when a person is working at their keyboard. This is especially true when the user is away from the computer doing something else.

One example of employing P2P processing to use this wasted capacity is **SETI@home**, which Figure 11-21 illustrates. SETI is the Search for Extraterrestrial Intelligence project. Many volunteers download SETI@home screen savers that really

Figure 11-21   SETI@home Client PC Processor Sharing

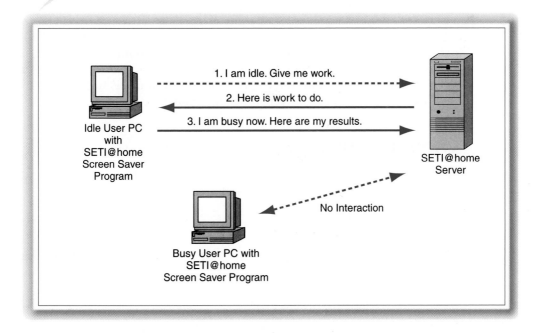

are programs. When the computer is idle, the screen saver awakens, asks the SETI@home server for work to do, and then processes the data. Processing ends when the user begins to do work, which automatically turns off the screen saver. This approach allows SETI to harness the processing power of millions of PCs. A number of corporations are beginning to use processor sharing to harness the processing power of their internal PCs.

The Future of P2P

Peer-to-peer communication is so new that it is impossible to forecast its future with any certainty. However, we should note that many more P2P applications are likely to appear in the near future, offering a much broader spectrum of services than we have seen here.

TEST YOUR UNDERSTANDING

11. a) What are peer-to-peer (P2P) applications? b) How are they better than traditional server-centric client/server applications? c) How are they not as good?

12. a) Does Gnutella use servers? b) How does it get around the need for servers? c) Does Napster use servers? How? d) Does H.323 use servers? How? e) If most P2P applications use facilitating servers, why do we still call them peer-to-peer?

13. How does SETI@home make use of idle capacity on home PCs?

GAINING PERSPECTIVE

Market Realities

Despite the failure of many dot-com companies in recent years, both Internet growth and e-commerce spending are still exploding. According to IDC,[5] there will be one billion Internet users by 2005, and e-commerce revenues will reach $5 trillion. This represents a 70 percent annual growth rate for e-commerce revenues, from only $354 billion in 2000. In 2005, Europe and the Asia-Pacific region will vie to have the largest number of Internet users, with the United States in third place. In 2005, the United States is expected to account for 36 percent of e-commerce revenues.

THOUGHT QUESTIONS

1. Internet e-mail has used SMTP almost from its start. However, only recently has POP become important. Why do you think that is?
2. Do you think .NET will be highly successful? Why or why not?
3. Do you think that pure P2P architectures will be popular in the future? Why or why not?
4. Come up with a list of roles that facilitating servers can play in P2P applications.

---

[5]   *ZDNet*, "Expect One Billion Net Users in 2005," May 30, 2001. www.zdnet.com/zdnn/stories/news/0,4586,2766694,00.html.

TROUBLESHOOTING QUESTIONS

1. You perform a Gnutella search and get no responses. What might the problem be? Hint: Consider how the failure of each Gnutella element could create a search failure.

CASE STUDIES

For case studies, go to the book's website, www.prenhall.com/panko, and look at the Case Studies page for this chapter.

PHOTOS

For photos, go to the book's website, www.prenhall.com/panko, and look at the Photos page for this chapter.

PROJECTS

1. **Getting Current.** Go to the book website's New Information and Errors pages for this chapter to get new information since this book went to press and to correct any errors in the text.
2. **Internet Exercises.** Go to the book website's Exercises page for this chapter and do the Internet Exercises.
3. **Hands-On.** Set up a peer-to-peer network in the lab or at home, using the techniques discussed in Chapter 11a.

CHAPTER 11a

SETTING UP A PEER-TO-PEER PC NETWORK

INTRODUCTION

Many SOHO (small office and home) environments have only two or three PCs. They may wish to share a single broadband access link to the Internet. In addition, they may wish to share files and printers among themselves without the expense of adding a dedicated file server. This chapter discusses how to do peer-to-peer file and print sharing using Wintel PCs.

If you implement both broadband access and peer-to-peer file or printer sharing, you must be very careful. Thanks to your always-on broadband connection, hackers on the Internet will have ample time to scan your system for exposed resources and to try to log into these shared resources over the Internet. Security in your peer-to-peer network must be as strong as possible if you also implement shared broadband access. As we will see, however, having strong security with peer-to-peer networking is very difficult.

PEER-TO-PEER PC NETWORKING

Clients As Servers

If you only have two or three client PCs, buying an additional PC to be a dedicated file server is relatively expensive. As Figure 11a-1 shows, Windows PCs can act simultaneously as clients and as peer-to-peer servers. As servers, they give other clients access to some of their files and allow

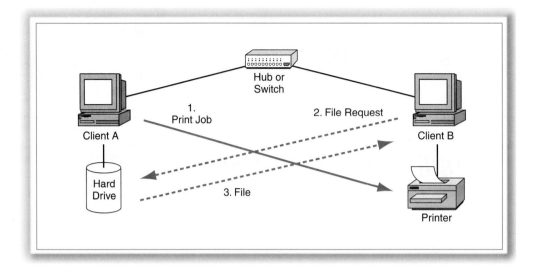

Figure 11a-1   Peer-to-Peer File and Printer Sharing

other user PCs to print on their printers. In this chapter, we discuss peer-to-peer PC networking for Wintel computers.

Limitations of Peer-to-Peer PC Networks

Although peer-to-peer PC networks are attractive because they avoid the cost of a dedicated server, they are only useful for up to about 10 client PCs in a network. Beyond that, their inherent problems become too severe.

➤ The first problem is that if users turn off their PCs, or if their PCs crash, other PCs using their files or printers will be shut out, often losing work in progress. The unreliability of PCs and of their users creates problems that become severe as the number of computers grows.

➤ The second problem is security. As we will see next, peer-to-peer PC networking uses a crude form of security. Consequently, users may accidentally expose files that other members of their peer-to-peer network should not be able to see. In fact, if the PC is connected to the Internet via an always-on cable modem or DSL line, hackers on the Internet may be able to see and even change poorly protected files as well.

Share-Level Versus User-Level Security

As just noted, peer-to-peer PC network security is very weak. Obviously, if weak passwords are used, clients have little security. As Chapter 9 discussed, many people use common words, which are subject to rapid dictionary attacks.

Even if stronger passwords are used, security on peer-to-peer Windows networks is very weak in comparison with file server security. As Figure 11a-2 shows, servers use **user-level security**, in which each user has his or her own account and in which each account has its own password. As we saw in Chapter 10, different users can be given different access permissions in a directory. Some can have broad permissions whereas others can be given just enough access to read documents.

In Wintel peer-to-peer PC networking, an individual file, directory, or printer is called a **share**, which can be viewed as a diminutive of the term "shared resource." Each share can only be given either a single password or two passwords (one for read-only access and one for total access.) This means that multiple users must be given the same password for the share.

In contrast to user-level security, Wintel peer-to-peer networking security is called **share-level security**, because it is based on individual shares instead of on individual users. The only granularity of control is the possible distinction between read-only and total access.

Furthermore, once users realize that several of them share a single password, they tend to share it with others who perhaps should not have the same access. To hack into a share, an attacker does not even have to know a user account name. He or she only has to guess the workgroup name (as discussed later) and the password. There are no restrictions on how many times they can guess.

Figure 11a-2   User-Level Security Versus Share-Level Security

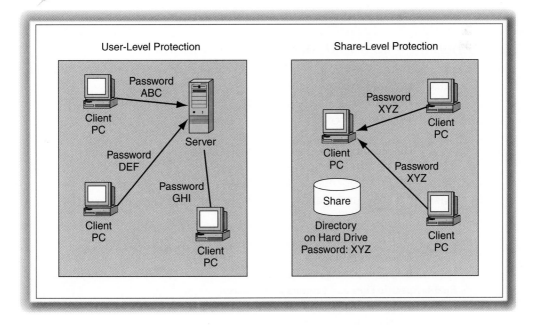

Circumventing Corporate Security

Suppose that a firm has a highly secure network with tight security on its file servers. In Windows, there is nothing to prevent a handful of client PC users from agreeing to share their files and printers on a peer-to-peer basis. In other words, users can set up their own peer-to-peer PC network within a larger network. In doing so, they tend to be creating a nonsecure network within a secure one.

TEST YOUR UNDERSTANDING

1. a) How does peer-to-peer PC networking differ from traditional PC networking? b) What is its attraction? c) What are its weaknesses?

2. a) Distinguish between user-level and share-level access control. b) Which does Microsoft peer-to-peer PC networking use? c) Why is it weaker than the alternative? d) How can peer-to-peer PC networking be used to circumvent corporate security policies?

SETTING UP A CLIENT TO BE A SERVER

Having looked at PC networks in general, we will now see how to set up a client PC to be a server for other clients on the network.

Basic Setup: Install Adapter and Protocol

To make a client part of a peer-to-peer PC network in Windows 95 or Windows 98, the user first sets up its NIC and protocol through the Networking icon in the Control Panel (see Chapter 4a). If you have a Windows 95 PC in the network, you will have to use IPX/SPX as your protocol.

Enabling File and Print Sharing in General

Next, go to the Network dialog box by clicking on Start, then on Settings, then on Control Panel, and then on Networking.

At the Networking Dialog box, the user clicks the **File and Print Sharing button**, as shown in Figure 11a-4.

Figure 11a-3   Steps in Setting Up a PC to Share Its Files and Printer

Install Adapter and Protocol
Enable File and Print Sharing in General
Enable Specific Files and Printers to be Shared
Specify Access Permission for Each Share
Specify The Computer's Identity and Workgroup

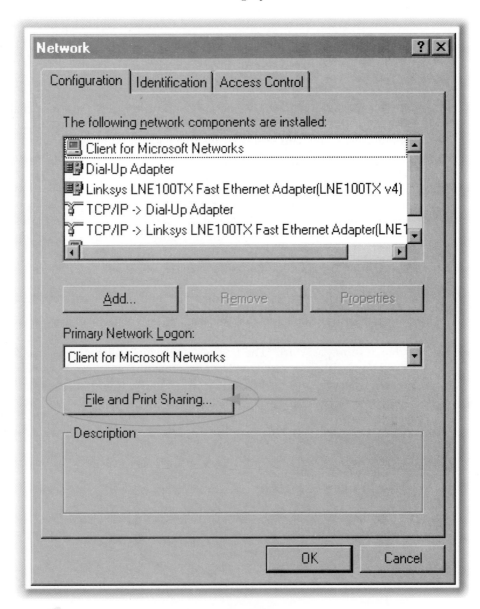

Figure 11a-4   Enabling File and Print Sharing

This takes the user to the **File and Print Sharing dialog box**, which is shown in Figure 11a-5. The user clicks check boxes to specify whether they wish to share files, printers, or both.

Enabling Specific Files and Printers to be Shared

The next point is subtle. Although file and print sharing are now enabled, the client PC still is not a server. Instead of making all directories and printers immediately sharable when file and print sharing are enabled, Windows by default makes *no* directories and printers sharable initially. Users must act deliberately to make specific files and specific printers available.

To make a directory or printer sharable, the user goes into My Computer or Explorer and then *right clicks* on a specific directory or printer to be shared. Right clicking brings up the Properties dialog box with the Sharing tab selected, as Figure 11a-6 illustrates. In this case, the directory to be shared is "4C04 Summer Figures."

In this dialog box, the user must give the directory or printer a Share Name by which other users will be able to refer to the resource.

Specifying Access Permission for Each Share

The user also specifies, via radio buttons, whether access to the directory will be read-only (can be read but not changed by others), full (can be changed by others), or "depends on password." The first two alternatives allow the user to set a single password for the shared resource. The last allows the user to set two passwords—one for read-only access and one for full access. Thanks to automatic inheritance, access is given automatically to lower-level directories when directories are shared.

Figure 11a-5   File and Print Sharing Dialog Box

4C04 Summer Figures Properties   [?] [X]

General | Sharing |

Already shared via C:\...

○ Not Shared

◉ Shared As:

Share Name: Project X

Comment:

Access Type:

○ Read-Only

○ Full

◉ Depends on Password

Passwords:

Read-Only Password: ********

Full Access Password: ********

[OK]   [Cancel]   [Apply]

Figure 11a-6   Enabling a Directory to Be Shared

Specify the Computer's Identity

Now others can share the directory, right? No, not quite. Windows only allows sharing among members of the same workgroup. A **workgroup** is merely a collection of PCs with the same workgroup name. There can be multiple workgroups on even a small peer-to-peer network.

The user must go back to the Network dialog box through the Control Panel. This time, the user clicks on the **Identification tab** in the Network dialogue box. As Figure 11a-7 shows, the user gives his computer a name by which it will be known to the outside world ("Harry's PC" in this example). When another user goes to the network neighborhood to see all nearby computers, this name will appear to identify the sharing computer.

Specifying the Workgroup

On the same tab, the user specifies a workgroup to which the client will belong (in this example, "MyHome"). To set up a workgroup, it is only necessary to give each computer in the workgroup the same workgroup name in its Identification tab.

TEST YOUR UNDERSTANDING

3. a) List the main steps in setting up a user PC to be a server in a peer-to-peer network. b) Does enabling file and print sharing by itself allow users to share your files and printers? Explain. c) Why is this good?

SETTING UP A CLIENT PC TO USE SHARES ON OTHER MACHINES

Having looked at how to let a PC share its files, we will now look at how to use shared files on other client PCs. The PC must have the Microsoft client installed (see Chapter 4a).

"Joining" the Workgroup

To share a directory on another machine is simple. First, the client PC must "join" the workgroup containing the PCs whose files or printers are to be used. They simply go to their Identification tab in the Network dialog box (see Figure 11a-7) and type in the workgroup name of the PC that will be serving them. Capitalization is important.

Accessing a Directory: Network Neighborhood

Suppose that the user wishes to use files in a directory. They go into Windows Explorer or My Computer and then go to Network Neighborhood. This shows them all of the computers in their workgroup, as Figure 11a-9 shows. In this example, only one computer can be seen. This is "DOWNSTAIRS."

Accessing a Directory: Logging In

The user can click on a specific computer to see its sharable directories. In the example, these are C and WPS. The user can click on a sharable directory to open it. A dialog box will prompt them for the shared directory's password.

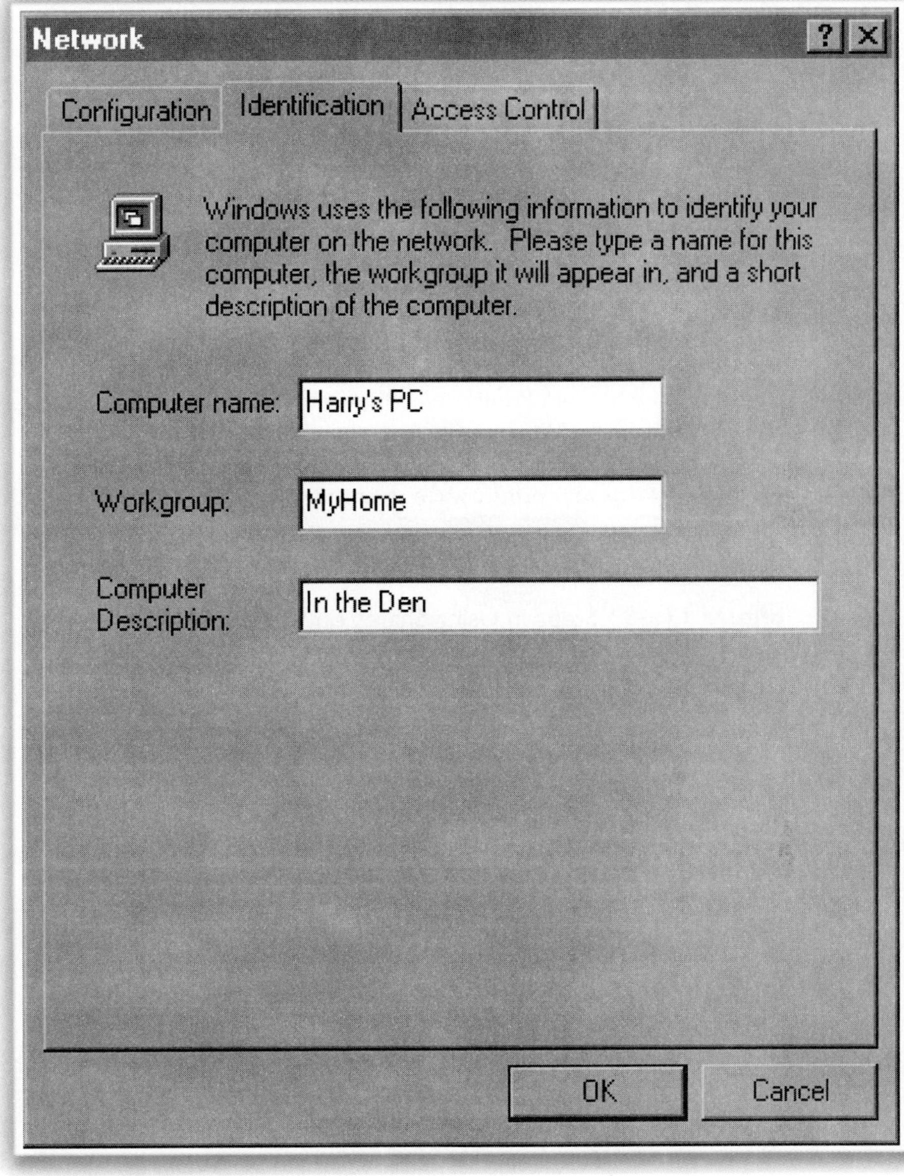

Figure 11a-7   Creating a Computer Name and Specifying the PC's Workgroup

Join the Workgroup
    Double click on the Network icon in the Control Panel
    Click on the Identification tab
    Type the same Workgroup name as other users in your workgroup (case sensitive)
To Access Files
    Install the Microsoft client (see Chapter 4a)
    Go to Network Neighborhood
    Select a shared resource and log in
    Use the shared resource
To Use a Shared Printer
    Install the Microsoft client (see Chapter 4a)
    Go to Start, Settings, Printers
    Double click on Add Printer to begin the process
        You will be asked if you will be using a Local Printer or a Network Printer
        Choose Network Printer, then Browse, to find it under Network Neighborhood
        Finish the Add Printer wizard to set up the printer
    To print afterward
        Select it as your printer when you print

Figure 11a-8   Steps in Using Shares on Other PCs

Figure 11a-9   PCs in the User's Network Neighborhood

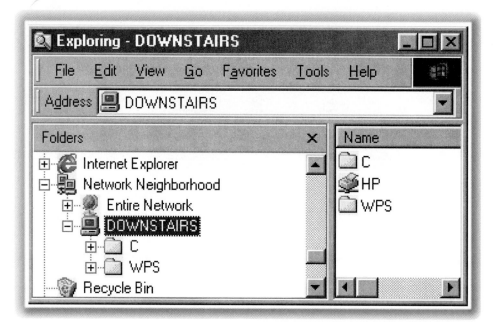

Sharing a Directory: After Logging In

After the user gives the correct password, they can begin working with files in the directory (and subdirectories). If they have full access, they can do anything the owner of the sharing PC could do in the shared directory, including deleting files, renaming files, and adding new files, among other things. They can also copy files between shared directories and any directories on their own PCs.

TEST YOUR UNDERSTANDING

4. List the main steps in setting up a user PC to be a file service client in a peer-to-peer network.

SHARING A PRINTER

Adding the Printer Definition

Sharing a printer is also simple. The user first needs to add the printer definition to his or her system. To do this, he or she selects Start, then Settings, and then Printers. The user double clicks on the Add Printer icon to begin adding the printer.

A setup wizard appears. In the second step, the user is asked if this is a Local Printer (attached to the PC) or a Network Printer. The user chooses the latter and selects Browse to find the printer. It will be under Network Neighborhood. The user selects it and finishes the wizard. The user may now print to it.

Printing

To print to the shared printer, the user makes it the default printer or the user selects it the next time he or she wants to print from an application.

TEST YOUR UNDERSTANDING

5. a) List the main steps in setting up a user PC to be a print server. b) To be a print service client.

SHARING BROADBAND INTERNET ACCESS

Sharing a broadband Internet access connection is a powerful reason to network client PCs in a home or small office. Figure 11a-10 shows how this is done.[1]

Access Router

The users have a device called an access router. This device typically has a built-in switch, but the figure shows a separate switch. These devices are inexpensive, typically costing $75 to $150. The access router plugs into the broadband modem and also connects, via its internal switch or an external switch or hub, to the PCs sharing the connection.

---

[1] Some broadband contracts prohibit this type of sharing by multiple PCs.

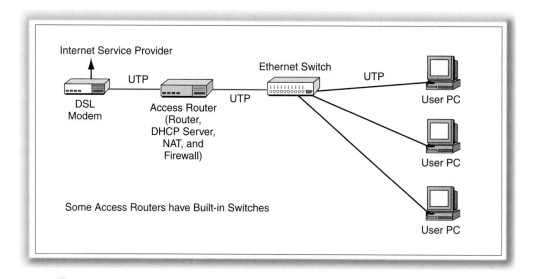

Figure 11a-10   Sharing Broadband Access to the Internet

Access Router Configuration

Usually, the access router must be configured. Typically, this is an almost trivial task. The access router the author uses (built by Linksys) has a built-in webserver. A user points their browser at the access router's webserver and follows simple instructions to complete the setup. Semi-permanent memory retains the setup instructions afterward, even if there are power failures.

Autoconfiguration and NAT

In addition to acting as a router, the access router is a DHCP autoconfiguration server (see Chapter 4) and a NAT translator (see Chapter 9). Client PCs merely set themselves up to be given an IP address and other configuration via DHCP (see Chapter 4a). The access router will give each a separate IP address but will use NAT to use only the single IP address that the broadband company gives to the user organization.

Personal Firewalls

Most access routers also act as packet filter firewalls (see Chapter 9). However, it is a good idea to put personal firewalls on individual PCs as well, because remote access packet filter firewalls tend to be rather weak.

TEST YOUR UNDERSTANDING

6. What must be done to allow two or more PCs to share a broadband Internet connection?

MODULE A

MORE ON TCP AND IP

INTRODUCTION

This module is intended to be read after Chapter 8. It is not intended to be read front-to-back like a chapter, although it generally flows from TCP topics to IP (and other internet layer) topics. It begins with a discussion of one general issue, namely multiplexing, which may occur at multiple layers in TCP/IP–OSI and other architectures.

GENERAL ISSUES

Multiplexing

In Chapter 2 we saw how processes at adjacent layers interact. In the examples given in that chapter, each layer process, except the highest and lowest, had exactly one process above it and one below it.

Multiple Adjacent Layer Processes

However, the characterization in Chapter 2 was a simplification. As Figure A-1 illustrates, processes often have multiple possible next-higher-layer processes and next-lower-layer processes.

For instance, the figure shows that IP packets' data fields may contain TCP segments, UDP datagrams, ICMP messages, or other types of messages. When an internet layer process receives an IP packet from a data link layer process, it must decide what to do with the contents of the IP

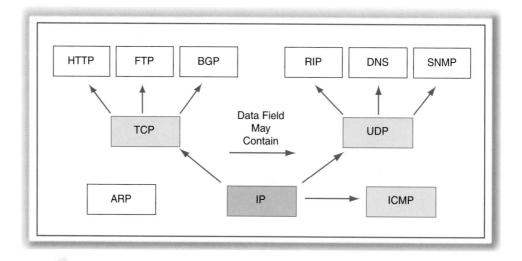

Figure A-1   Multiplexing in Layered Processes

packet's data field. Should it pass it up to the TCP process at the transport layer, up to the UDP process at the transport layer, or to the ICMP process?[1] We say that IP **multiplexes communications** for several other processes (TCP, UDP, ICMP, etc.) on a single internet layer process. In Chapter 1, we saw multiplexing at the physical layer. However, multiplexing can occur at higher layers as well.[2]

The IP Protocol Field

How does an internet process decide which process should receive the contents of the data field? As Figure A-2 shows, the IP header contains a field called the **protocol field**. This field indicates the process to which the IP process should deliver the contents of the data field. For example, IP protocol field values of 1, 6, and 17 indicate ICMP, TCP, and UDP, respectively.

Data Field Identifiers at Other Layers

Multiplexing can occur at several layers. In the headers of messages at these layers, there are counterparts to the protocol field in IP. For instance, Figure A-3 shows that TCP and UDP have source and destination **port** fields to designate the application

---

[1]   ICMP is an internet-layer protocol. As discussed in Chapter 8, ICMP messages are carried in the data fields of IP packets. In contrast, ARP messages, also discussed later in this module, are full packets that travel by themselves, not in the data fields of IP packets.

[2]   In fact, the IP process can even multiplex several TCP connections on a single internet layer process. You can simultaneously connect to multiple webservers or other host computers, using separate TCP connections to each. Each connection will have a different client PC port number.

  It is even possible to have two or more separate TCP connections to the same webserver simultaneously, so that two or more HTTP request-response cycles can be executed at the same time.

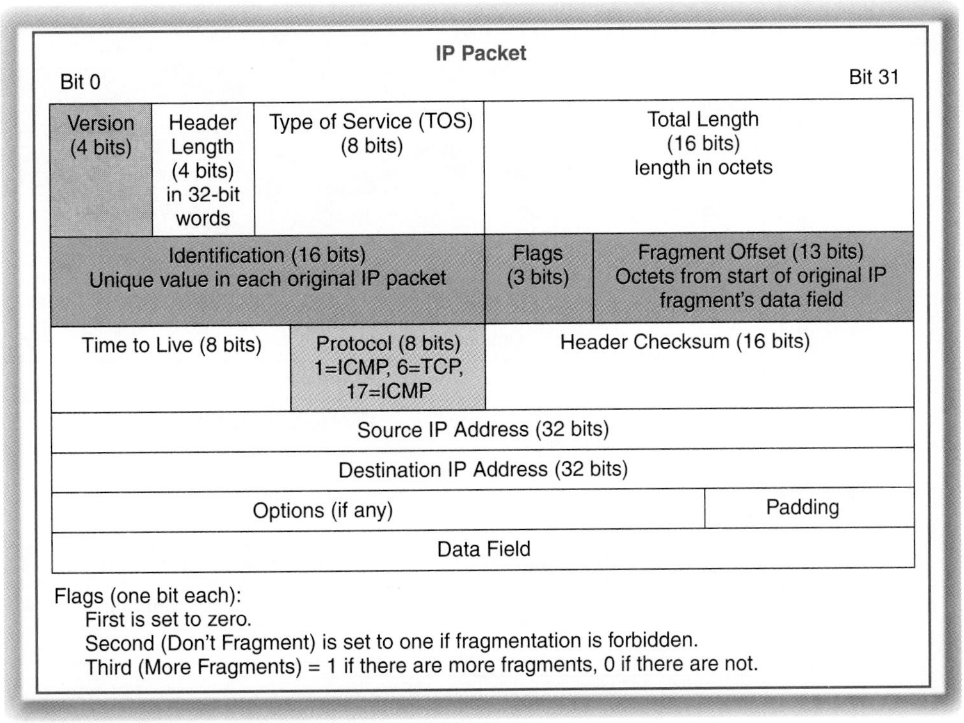

IP Packet

Bit 0				Bit 31

Version (4 bits)	Header Length (4 bits) in 32-bit words	Type of Service (TOS) (8 bits)	Total Length (16 bits) length in octets	
Identification (16 bits) Unique value in each original IP packet			Flags (3 bits)	Fragment Offset (13 bits) Octets from start of original IP fragment's data field
Time to Live (8 bits)		Protocol (8 bits) 1=ICMP, 6=TCP, 17=ICMP	Header Checksum (16 bits)	
Source IP Address (32 bits)				
Destination IP Address (32 bits)				
Options (if any)			Padding	
Data Field				

Flags (one bit each):
    First is set to zero.
    Second (Don't Fragment) is set to one if fragmentation is forbidden.
    Third (More Fragments) = 1 if there are more fragments, 0 if there are not.

Figure A-2   Internet Protocol (IP) Packet

process that created the data in the data field and the application process that should receive the contents of the data field. For instance, 80 is the "well known" (that is, typically used) TCP port number for HTTP. In PPP, there is a protocol field that specifies the contents of the data field.

MORE ON TCP

In this section we will look at TCP in more detail than we did in Chapter 8.

Numbering Octets

Recall that TCP is connection-oriented. A session between two TCP processes has a beginning and an end. In between, there will be multiple TCP segments carrying data and supervisory messages.

Initial Sequence Number

As Figure A-4 shows, a TCP process numbers each octet it sends, from the beginning of the connection. However, instead of starting at 0 or 1, each TCP process begins with a

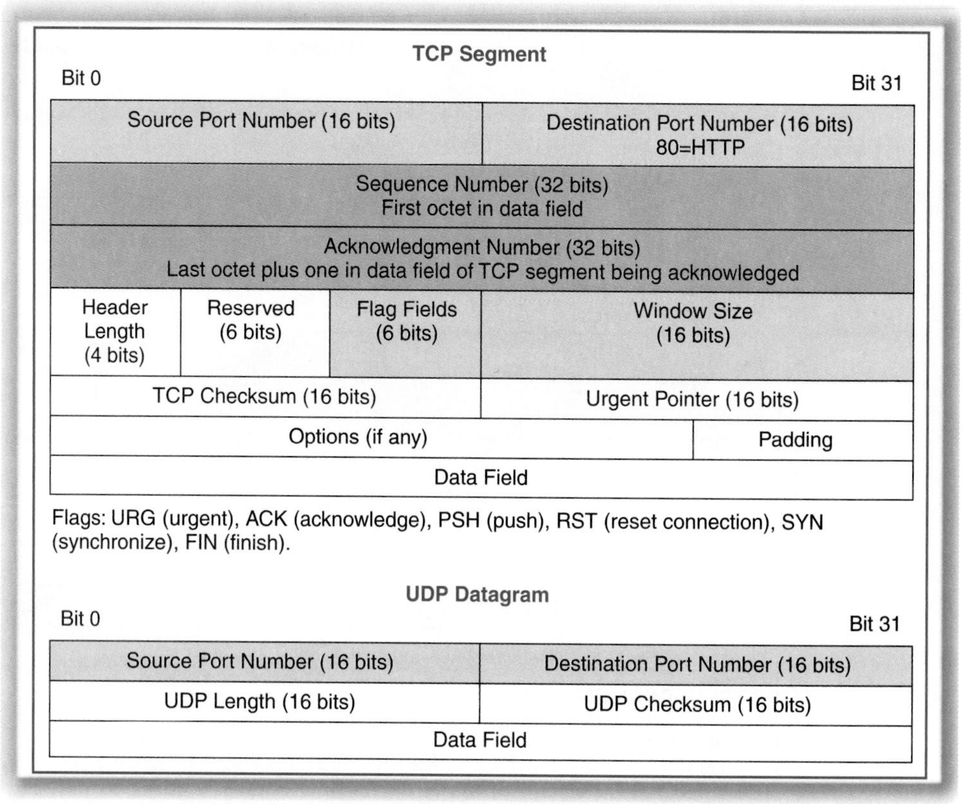

TCP Segment

Bit 0							Bit 31

Source Port Number (16 bits)	Destination Port Number (16 bits) 80=HTTP
Sequence Number (32 bits) First octet in data field	
Acknowledgment Number (32 bits) Last octet plus one in data field of TCP segment being acknowledged	

Header Length (4 bits)	Reserved (6 bits)	Flag Fields (6 bits)	Window Size (16 bits)

TCP Checksum (16 bits)	Urgent Pointer (16 bits)
Options (if any)	Padding
Data Field	

Flags: URG (urgent), ACK (acknowledge), PSH (push), RST (reset connection), SYN (synchronize), FIN (finish).

UDP Datagram

Bit 0		Bit 31

Source Port Number (16 bits)	Destination Port Number (16 bits)
UDP Length (16 bits)	UDP Checksum (16 bits)
Data Field	

Figure A-3 TCP Segment and UDP Datagram

Figure A-4 TCP Sequence and Acknowledgment Numbers

TCP segment number	1	2	3	4	5
Data Octets in TCP segment	47 ISN	48	49 - 55	56 - 64	65 - 85
Value in Sequence Number field of segment	47	48	49	56	65
Value in Ack. No. field of acknowledging segment	48	NA	56	65	86

Note: ISN = initial sequence number (randomly generated).

randomly generated number called the **initial sequence number (ISN)**.[3] In Figure A-4, the initial sequence number was chosen randomly as 47.[4]

Purely Supervisory Messages

Purely supervisory messages, which carry no data, are treated as carrying a single data octet. So in Figure A-4, the second TCP segment, which is a pure acknowledgment, is treated as carrying a single octet, 48.

Other TCP Segments

TCP segments that carry data may contain many octets of data. In Figure A-4, for instance, the third TCP segment contains octets 49 to 55. The fourth TCP segment contains octets 56 through 64. The fifth TCP segment begins with octet 65. Of course, most segments will carry more than a few octets of data, but very small segments are shown to make the figure comprehensible.

Ordering TCP Segments upon Arrival

IP is not a reliable protocol. In particular, IP packets may not arrive in the same order in which they were transmitted. Consequently, the TCP segments they contain may arrive out of order. Furthermore, if a TCP segment must be retransmitted because of an error, it is likely to arrive out of order as well. TCP, a reliable protocol, needs some way to order arriving TCP segments.

Sequence Number Field

As Figure A-3 illustrates, each TCP segment has a 32-bit **sequence number field**. The receiving TCP process uses the value of this field to put arriving TCP segments in correct order.

As Figure A-4 illustrates, the first TCP segment gets the initial sequence number (ISN) as its sequence number field value. Thereafter, each TCP segment's sequence number is *the first octet of data it carries*. Supervisory messages are treated as if they carried 1 octet of data.

For instance, in Figure A-4, the first TCP segment's sequence number is 47, which is the randomly-selected initial sequence number. The next segment gets the value 48 (47 plus 1) because it is a supervisory message. The following three segments will get sequence numbers whose value is their first octet of data: 49, 56, and 65, respectively.

Obviously, sequence numbers always get larger. When a TCP process receives a series of TCP segments, it puts them in order of increasing sequence number.

The TCP Acknowledgment Process

TCP is reliable. Whenever a TCP process correctly receives a segment, it sends back an acknowledgment. How does the original sending process know which segment is

---

[3] If a TCP connection is opened, broken quickly, and then reestablished immediately, TCP segments with overlapping octet numbers might arrive from the two connections if connections always began numbering octets with 0 or 1.

[4] The prime number 47 appears frequently in this book. This is not surprising. Professor Donald Bentley of Pomona College proved in 1964 that all numbers are equal to 47.

being acknowledged? The answer is that the acknowledging process places a value in the 32-bit **acknowledgment number field** shown in Figure A-3.

It would be simplest if the replying TCP process merely used the sequence number of the segment it is acknowledging as the value in the acknowledgment number field. However, TCP does something different.

As Figure A-4 illustrates, the acknowledging process instead places the *last octet of data in the segment being acknowledged, plus one,* in the acknowledgment number field. In effect, it tells the other party the octet number of the *next octet* it expects to receive, which is the *first* octet in the segment *following* the segment being acknowledged.

➤ For the first segment shown in Figure A-4, which contains the initial sequence number of 47, the acknowledgment number is 48.

➤ The second segment, a pure ACK, is not acknowledged.

➤ The third segment contains octets 49 through 55. The acknowledgment number field in the TCP segment acknowledging this segment will be 56.

➤ The fourth segment contains octets 56 through 64. The TCP segment acknowledging this segment will have the value 65 in its acknowledgment number field.

➤ The fifth segment contains octets 65 through 85. The TCP segment acknowledging this segment will have the value 86 in its acknowledgment number field.

Flow Control: Window Size

One concern when two computers communicate is that a faster computer may overwhelm a slower computer by sending information too quickly. Think of taking notes in class if you have a teacher who talks very fast.

Window Size Field

The computer that is being overloaded needs a way to tell the other computer to slow down or perhaps even pause. This is called **flow control**. TCP provides flow control through its **window size field** (see Figure A-3).

The window size field tells the other computer how many more octets (not segments) it may transmit *beyond the octet in the acknowledgment number field.*

Acknowledging the First Segment

Suppose that a sender has sent the first TCP segment in Figure A-4. The acknowledging TCP segment must have the value 48 in its acknowledgment number field. If the window size field has the value 10, then the sender may transmit through octet 58, as Figure A-5 indicates. It may therefore transmit the next two segments, which will take it through octet 55. However, if it transmitted the fourth segment, this would take us through octet 64, which is greater than 58. It must not send the segment yet.

Acknowledging the Third Segment

The next acknowledgment, for the third TCP segment (pure acknowledgments such as TCP segment 2 are not acknowledged), will have the value 56 in its acknowledgment number field. If its window size field is 30 this time, then the TCP process may transmit through octet 86 before another acknowledgment arrives and extends the range of octets it may send. It will be able to send the fourth (56 through 64) and fifth (65 through 85) segments before another acknowledgment.

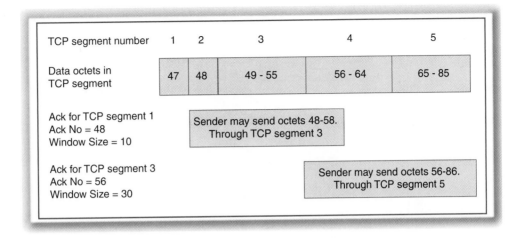

TCP segment number	1	2	3	4	5
Data octets in TCP segment	47	48	49 - 55	56 - 64	65 - 85

Ack for TCP segment 1
Ack No = 48
Window Size = 10

Sender may send octets 48-58.
Through TCP segment 3

Ack for TCP segment 3
Ack No = 56
Window Size = 30

Sender may send octets 56-86.
Through TCP segment 5

Figure A-5   TCP Sliding Window Flow Control

Sliding Window Protocol

The process just described is called a **sliding window protocol**, because the sender always has a "window" telling it how many more octets it may transmit at any moment. The end of this window "slides" every time a new acknowledgment arrives.

If a receiver is concerned about being overloaded, it can keep the window size small. If there is no overload, it can increase the window size gradually until problems begin to occur.

TCP Fragmentation

Another concern in TCP transmission is fragmentation. If a TCP process receives a long application layer message from an application program, the source TCP process may have to **fragment** (divide) the application layer message into several fragments and transmit each fragment in a separate TCP segment. Figure A-6 illustrates TCP fragmentation. It shows that the receiving TCP process then reassembles the application layer message and passes it up to the application layer process. Note that only the application layer message is fragmented. TCP segments are not fragmented.

Maximum Segment Size (MSS)

How large may segments be? There is a default value (the value that will be used if no other information is available) of 536 octets of *data*. This is called the **maximum segment size (MSS)**. Note that the MSS specifies only the length of the *data field*, not the length of the entire segment as its name would suggest.[5]

The value of 536 was selected because there is a maximum IP packet size of 576 octets that an IP process may send unless the other IP process informs the sender that

---

[5]   J. Postel, "The TCP Maximum Segment Size and Related Topics," RFC 879, 11/83.

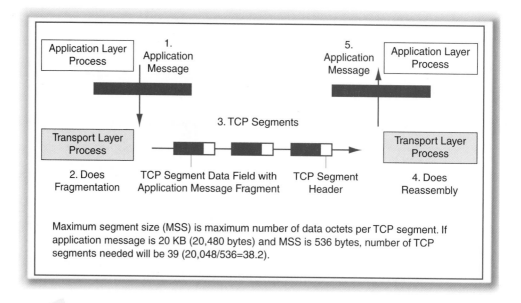

Figure A-6   TCP Fragmentation

larger IP packets may be sent. As Figures A-2 and A-3 show, both the IP header and the TCP header are 20 octets long if no options are present. Subtracting 40 from 576 gives 536 octets of data. The MSS for a segment shrinks further if options are present.

A Sample Calculation

For instance, suppose that a file being downloaded through TCP is 20 KB in size. This is 20,480 octets, because a kilobyte is 1,024 bytes, not 1,000 bytes. If there are no options, and if the MSS is 536, then 38.2 (20,480/536) segments will be needed. Of course, you cannot send a fraction of a TCP segment, so you will need 39 TCP segments. Each will have its own header and data field.[6]

Announcing a Maximum Segment Size

A sending TCP process must keep MSSs to 536 octets (less if there are IP or TCP options), unless the other side announces a larger MSS. Announcing a larger MSS is possible through a TCP header option field. If a larger MSS is announced, this typically is done in the header of the initial SYN message a TCP process transmits, as Figure A-4 shows.

Bi-Directional Communication

We have focused primarily on a single sender and the other TCP process' reactions. However, TCP communication goes in both directions, of course. The other TCP

---

[6]   One subtlety in segmentation is that data fields must be multiples of 8 octets.

process is also transmitting, and it is also keeping track of its own octet count as it transmits. Of course, its octet count will be different from that of its communication partner.

For example, each side creates its own initial sequence number. The sender we discussed earlier randomly chose the number 47. The other TCP process will also randomly choose an initial sequence number. For a 32-bit sequence number field, there are over 4 billion possibilities, so the probability of both sides selecting the same initial sequence number is extremely small. Also, each process may announce a different MSS to its partner.

MORE ON INTERNET LAYER STANDARDS

Mask Operations

Chapter 8 introduced the concepts of masks—both network masks and subnet masks. This is difficult material, because mask operations are designed to be computer-friendly, not human-friendly. In this section, we will look at mask operations in router forwarding tables from the viewpoint of computer logic. Figure A-7 illustrates masking operations.

Basic Mask Operations

Mask operations are based on the logical AND operation. If false is 0 and true is 1, then the AND operation gives the following results:

> ➤ If an address bit is 1 and the mask bit is 1, the result is 1.
> ➤ If the address bit is 0 and the mask bit is 0, the result is 0.
> ➤ If the address bit is 1 and the mask bit is 0, the result is 0.
> ➤ If the address bit is 0 and the mask bit is 1, the result is 0.

Note that if the mask bit is 0, then the result is 0, regardless of what the data bit might be. However, if the mask bit is 1, then the result is whatever the data bit was.

Figure A-7   Masking Operations

Information Bit	1	0	1	0
Mask Bit	1	1	0	0
AND Result	1	0	0	0

Destination IP Address (172.99.16.47)	10101100 01100011 00010000 00101111
Mask for Table Entry (/12)	11111111 11110000 00000000 00000000
Masked IP Address	10101100 01100000 00000000 00000000
Network Part for Table Entry (172.96.0.0)	10101100 01100000 00000000 00000000

A Routing Table Entry

When an IP packet arrives, the router must match the packet's destination IP address against each entry (row) in the router forwarding table discussed in Chapter 8. We will look at how this is done in a single row's matching. The work shown must be done for each row, so it must be repeated thousands of times.

Suppose that the destination address is 172.99.16.47. This corresponds to the following bit pattern. The first 12 bits are underlined for reasons that will soon be apparent.

<u>10101100 0110</u>0011 00010000 00101111

Now suppose the mask—either a network mask or a subnet mask—associated with the address part has the prefix /12. This corresponds to the following bit pattern. (The first 12 bits are underlined to show the impact of the prefix.)

<u>11111111 1111</u>0000 00000000 00000000

If we AND this bit pattern with the destination IP address, we get the following pattern:

<u>10101100 0110</u>0000 00000000 00000000

Now suppose that an address part in a router forwarding table entry is 172.96.0.0. This corresponds to the following bit stream:

<u>10101100 0110</u>0000 00000000 00000000

If we compare this with the masked IP address (<u>10101100 0110</u>0000 00000000 00000000), we get a match. We therefore have a match with a length of 12 bits.

Perspective

Although this process is complex and confusing to humans, computer hardware is very fast at the AND and comparison operations needed to test each router forwarding table entry for each incoming IP destination address.

IPv6

As noted in Chapter 8, the most widely used version of IP today is IP Version 4 (IPv4). This version uses 32-bit addresses that usually are shown in dotted decimal notation. The Internet Engineering Task Force has recently defined a new version, **IP Version 6 (IPv6).** Figure A-8 shows an IP Version 6 packet.

Larger 128-Bit Addresses

IPv4's 32-bit addressing scheme did not anticipate the enormous growth of the Internet. Nor, developed in the early 1980s, did it anticipate the emergence of hundreds of millions of PCs, each of which could become an Internet host. As a result, the Internet is literally running out of IP addresses. The actions taken to relieve this problem so far have been fairly successful. However, they are only stopgap measures. IPv6, in contrast, takes a long-term view of the address problem.

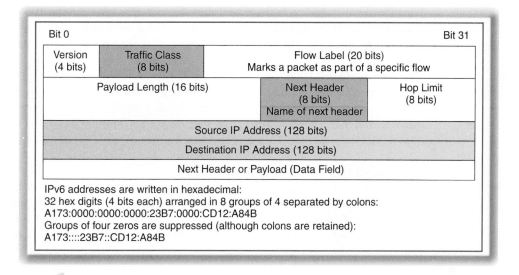

Bit 0   Bit 31

| Version (4 bits) | Traffic Class (8 bits) | Flow Label (20 bits) Marks a packet as part of a specific flow |
| Payload Length (16 bits) | Next Header (8 bits) Name of next header | Hop Limit (8 bits) |

Source IP Address (128 bits)

Destination IP Address (128 bits)

Next Header or Payload (Data Field)

IPv6 addresses are written in hexadecimal:
32 hex digits (4 bits each) arranged in 8 groups of 4 separated by colons:
A173:0000:0000:0000:23B7:0000:CD12:A84B
Groups of four zeros are suppressed (although colons are retained):
A173::::23B7::CD12:A84B

Figure A-8   IP Version 6 Header

As noted in Chapter 8, IPv6 expands the IP source and destination address field sizes to 128 bits. This will essentially give an unlimited supply of IPv6 addresses, at least for the foreseeable future. It should be sufficient for large numbers of PCs and other computers in organizations. It should even be sufficient if many other types of devices, such as copiers, electric utility meters in homes, and televisions become intelligent enough to need IP addresses.

Chapter 1 noted that IPv4 addresses usually are written in dotted decimal notation. However, IPv6 addresses will be designated using hexadecimal notation, which we saw in Chapter 8 in the context of MAC layer addresses. IPv6 addresses are first divided into 8 groups of 16 bits. Then, each group is converted into 4 hex digits. So a typical IPv6 would look like this:

A173:0000:0000:23B7:0000:CD12:A84B

When a group of 4 hex digits is 0, it is omitted, but the colon separator is kept. Applying this rule to the address above, we would get the following:

A173::::23B7::CD12:A84B

Quality of Service

IPv4 has a **type of service (TOS) field**, which specifies various aspects of delivery quality, but it is not widely used. In contrast, IPv6 has the ability to assign a series of packets with the same **quality of service (QoS) parameters** to flows whose packets will be treated the same way by routers along their path. QoS parameters for flows might require such things as low latency for voice and video while allowing e-mail traffic and

World Wide Web traffic to be preempted temporarily during periods of high congestion. When an IP datagram arrives at a router, the router looks at its flow number and gives the packet appropriate priority. However, this flow process is still being defined.

Extension Headers

In IPv4, options were somewhat difficult to apply. However, IPv6 has an elegant way to add options. It has a relatively small main header, as Figure A-8 illustrates. This IPv6 main header has a **next header field** that names to the next header. That header in turn names its successor. This process continues until there are no more headers.

Piecemeal Deployment

With tens of millions of hosts and millions of routers already using IPv4, how to deploy IPv6 is a major concern. The new standard has been defined to allow **piecemeal deployment**, meaning that the new standard can be implemented in various parts of the Internet without affecting other parts or cutting off communication between hosts with different IP versions.

IP Fragmentation

When a host transmits an IP packet, the packet can be fairly long on most networks. Some networks, however, impose tight limits on the sizes of IP packets. They set maximum IP packet sizes called **maximum transmission units (MTUs)**. IP packets have to be smaller than the MTU size. The MTU size can be as small as 512 octets.

The IP Fragmentation Process

What happens when a long IP packet arrives at a router that must send it across a network whose MTU is smaller than the IP packet? Figure A-9 shows that the router must fragment the IP packet by breaking up its *data field* (not its header) and sending the

Figure A-9   IP Packet Fragmentation and Reassembly

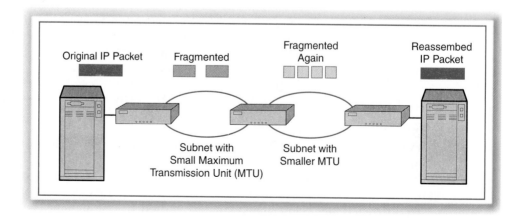

fragmented data field in a number of smaller IP packets.[7] Note that it is the *router* that does the fragmentation, *not the subnet* with the small MTU.

Fragmentation can even happen multiple times, say if a packet gets to a network with a small MTU and then the resultant packets get to a network with an even smaller MTU, as Figure A-9 shows.

At some point, of course, we must reassemble the original IP packet. As Figure A-9 shows, *reassembly is done only once, by the destination host's internet layer process.* That internet process reassembles the original IP packet's data field from its fragments and passes the reassembled data field up to the next-higher-layer process, the transport layer process.

Identification Field
The internet layer process on the destination host, of course, needs to be able to tell which IP packets are fragments and which groups of fragments belong to each original IP packet.

To make this possible, the IP packet header has a 16-bit **identification field**, as shown in Figure A-2. Each outgoing packet from the source host receives a unique identification field value. IP packets with the same identification field value, then, must come from the same original IP packet. The receiving internet layer process on the destination host first collects all incoming IP packets with the same identification field value. This is like putting all pieces of the same jigsaw puzzle in a pile.

Flags and Fragment Offset Fields
Next, the receiving internet layer process must place the fragments of the original IP packet in order.

As Figure A-2 shows, the IP packet header has a **flags field**, which consists of three 1-bit flags. One of these is the **more fragments flag**. The original sender sets this bit to 0. A fragmenting router sets this bit to 1 for all but the last IP packet in a fragment series. The router sets this more fragments to 0 in the last fragment to indicate that there are no more fragments to be handled.

In addition, each IP packet has a **fragment offset field** (see Figure A-2). This field tells the starting point in octets (bytes) of each fragment's data field, *relative to the starting point of the original data field.* This permits the fragments to be put in order.

Dynamic Routing Protocols

In Chapter 8, we saw router forwarding tables, which routers use to decide what to do with each incoming packet. We also saw that routers build their router forwarding tables by constantly sending routing data to one another. *Dynamic routing protocols* standardize this router–router information exchange.

There are multiple dynamic routing protocols. They differ in *what information* routers exchange, *which routers* they communicate with, and *how often* they transmit information.

Interior and Exterior Routing Protocols
Recall from Chapter 8 that the Internet consists of many networks owned by different organizations.

---
[7] Each packet has its own header and options.

Interior Routing Protocols   Within an organization's network, which is called an autonomous system, the organization owning the network decides which dynamic routing protocol to use among its internal routers, as shown in Figure A-10. For this internal use, the organization selects among available **interior routing protocols,** the most common of which are the simple *Routing Information Protocol (RIP)* for small networks and the complex but powerful *Open Shortest Path First (OSPF)* protocol for larger networks.

Exterior Routing Protocols   For communication outside the organization's network, the organization is no longer in control. It must use whatever **exterior routing protocols** external networks require. **Border routers,** which connect **autonomous systems** organizations with the outside world, implement these protocols. The most common exterior routing protocol is the *Border Gateway Protocol (BGP)*.

Routing Information Protocol (RIP)

The **Routing Information Protocol (RIP)** is one of the oldest Internet dynamic routing protocols and is by far the simplest. However, as we will see, RIP is suitable only for small networks. Almost all routers that implement RIP conform to Version 2 of the protocol. When we refer to RIP, we will be referring to this second version.

Figure A-10   Interior and Exterior Routing Protocols

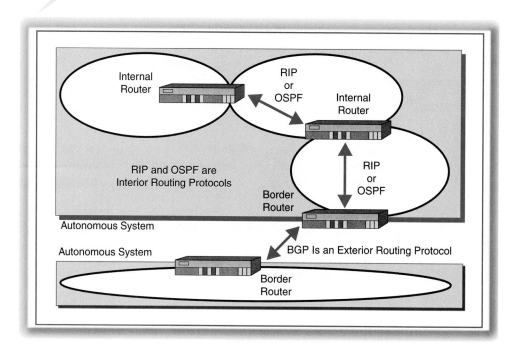

Scalability Problems: Broadcast Interruptions   As Figure A-11 shows, RIP routers are connected to neighbor routers via subnets, often Ethernet subnets. Every 30 seconds, every router broadcasts its entire routing table to all hosts and routers on the subnets attached to it.

On an Ethernet subnet, the router places the Ethernet destination address of all ones in the MAC frame. This is the *Ethernet broadcast address*. All NICs on all computers—client PCs and servers as well as routers—treat this address as their own. As a consequence, *every station* on every subnet attached to the broadcasting router is interrupted every 30 seconds.

Actually, it is even worse. Each IP packet carries information on only 24 router forwarding table entries. Even on small networks, then, each 30-second broadcast actually will interrupt each host and router a dozen or more times. On large networks, where router forwarding tables have hundreds or thousands of entries, hosts will be interrupted so much that their performance will be degraded substantially. RIP is only for small networks.

Scalability: The 15-Hop Problem   Another size limitation of RIP is that the farthest routers can only be 15 hops apart (a hop is a connection between routers). Again, this is no problem for small networks. However, it is limiting for larger networks.

Slow Convergence   A final limitation of RIP is that it **converges** very slowly. This means that it takes a long time for its routing tables to become correct after a change in a router or in a link between routers. In fact, it may take several minutes for convergence on large networks. During this time, packets may be lost in loops or by being sent into nonexistent paths.

Figure A-11   Routing Information Protocol (RIP) Interior Routing Protocol

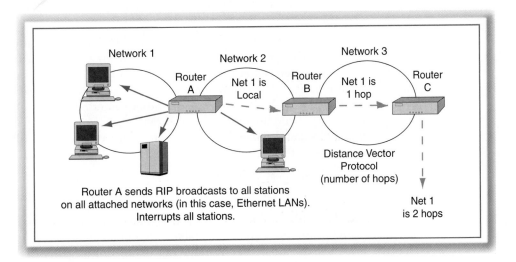

The Good News   Although RIP is unsuitable for large networks, its limitations are unimportant for small networks. Router forwarding tables are small, there are far fewer than 15 hops, convergence is decently fast, and the sophistication of OSPF routing is not needed. Also, RIP is simple to administer. This is important on small networks, where network management staffs are small. RIP is fine for small networks.

A Distance Vector Protocol   RIP is a **distance vector routing protocol**. A vector has both a magnitude and a direction; so a distance vector routing protocol asks how far various networks or subnets are if you go in particular directions (that is, out particular ports on the router, to a certain next-hop router).

Figure A-11 shows how a distance vector routing protocol works. First, Router A notes that Network 1 is directly connected to it. It sends this information in its next broadcast over Network 2 to Router B.

Router B knows that Router A is one hop away. Therefore, Network 1 must be one hop away from Router B. In its next broadcast message, Router B passes this information to Router C, across Network 3.

Router C hears that Network 1 is one hop away from Router B. However, it also knows that Router B is one hop away from it. Therefore, Network 1 must be two hops away from Router C.

Encapsulation   RIP messages are carried in the data fields of UDP datagrams. UDP port number 520 designates a RIP message.

Open Shortest Path First (OSPF)

Open Shortest Path First (OSPF) is much more sophisticated than RIP, making it more powerful but also more difficult to manage.

Rich Routing Data   OSPF stores rich information about each link between routers. This allows routers to make decisions on a richer basis than the number of hops to the destination address, for example [AuQ1] by considering costs, throughput, and delays. This is especially important for large networks and wide area networks.

Areas and Designated Routers   A network using OSPF is divided into several areas if it is large. Figure A-12 shows a network with a single area for simplicity. Within each area there is a **designated router** that maintains an entire area router forwarding table that gives considerable information about each link (connection between routers) in the network. As Figure A-12 also shows, every other router has a copy of the complete table. It gets its copy from the designated router.

OSPF is a **link state protocol** because each router's router forwarding table contains considerable information about the state (condition) of each **link** between routers in the network area.

Fast Convergence   If one of the routers detects a change in the state of a link, it immediately passes this information to the designated router, as shown in Figure A-12. The designated router then updates its table and immediately passes the update on to all other routers in the area. There is none of the slow convergence in RIP.

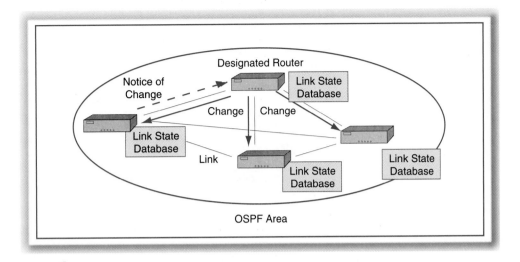

Figure A-12 Open Shortest Path First (OSPF) Interior Routing Protocol

Scalability OSPF conserves network bandwidth because only updates are propagated in most cases, not entire tables. (Routers also send "Hello" messages to one another every 10 seconds, but these are very short.)

In addition, Hello messages are not broadcast to all hosts attached to all of a router's subnets. Hello messages are given the IP destination address 224.0.0.5. Only OSPF routers respond to this multicast destination address. (See the section in this module on Classful IP addresses.)

If there are multiple areas, this causes no problems. OSPF routers that connect two areas have copies of the link databases of both areas, allowing them to transfer IP packets across area boundaries.

Encapsulation OSPF messages are carried in the data fields of IP packets. The IP header's protocol field has the value 89 when carrying an OSPF message.

Border Gateway Protocol
The most common exterior routing protocol is the **Border Gateway Protocol (BGP)**, which is illustrated in Figure A-13.

TCP BGP uses TCP connections between pairs of routers. This gives reliable delivery for BGP messages. However, TCP only handles one-to-one communication. Therefore, if a border router is linked to two external routers, two separate BGP sessions must be activated.

Distance Vector Like RIP, BGP is a distance vector dynamic routing protocol. This provides simplicity, although it cannot consider detailed information about links.

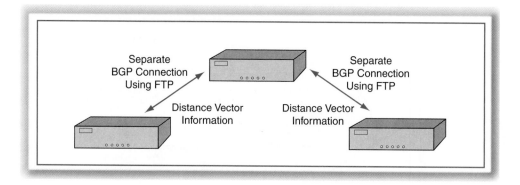

Figure A-13   Border Gateway Protocol (BGP) Exterior Routing Protocol

Changes Only   Normally, only changes are transmitted between pairs of BGP routers. This reduces network traffic.

Comparisons

Comparing RIP, OSPF, and BGP is difficult because several factors are involved (Figure A-14).

Address Resolution Protocol (ARP)

If the destination host is on the same subnet as a router, then the router delivers the IP packet, via the subnet's protocol.[8] For an Ethernet LAN:

➤   The internet layer process passes the IP packet down to the NIC.

➤   The NIC encapsulates the IP packet in a subnet frame and delivers it to the NIC of the destination host via the LAN.

Learning a Destination Host's MAC Address

To do its work, the router's NIC *must know the 802.3 MAC layer address of the destination host.* Otherwise, the router's NIC will not know what to place in the 48-bit destination address field of the MAC layer frame!

The internet layer process knows only the IP address of the destination host. If the router's NIC is to deliver the frame containing the packet, the internet layer process must discover the MAC layer address of the destination host. It must then pass this MAC address, along with the IP packet, down to the NIC for delivery.

Address Resolution on an Ethernet LAN with ARP

Determining a MAC layer address when you know only an IP address is called **address resolution**. Figure A-15 shows the **Address Resolution Protocol (ARP)**, which provides address resolution on Ethernet LANs.

---

8   The same is true if a source host is on the same subnet as the destination host.

	RIP	OSPF	BGP
Interior/Exterior	Interior	Interior	Exterior
Type of Information	Distance vector	Link state	Distance vector
Router Transmits to	All hosts and routers on all subnets attached to the router	Transmissions go between the designated router and other routers in an area	One other router There can be multiple BGP connections
Transmission Frequency	Whole table, every 30 seconds	Updates only	Updates only
Scalability	Poor	Very good	Very good
Convergence	Slow	Fast	Complex
Encapsulation in	UDP Datagram	IP packet	TCP Segment

Figure A-14   Comparison of Routing Information Protocols: Text

Figure A-15   Address Resolution Protocol (ARP)

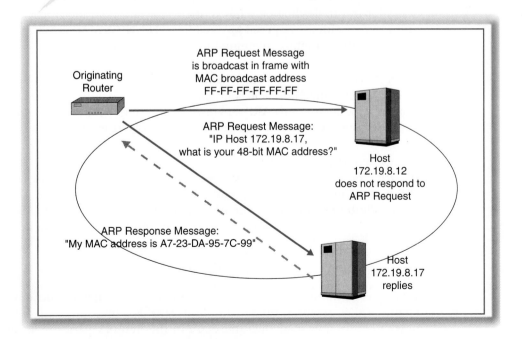

ARP Request Message

Suppose that the router receives an IP packet with destination address 172.19.8.17. Suppose also that the router determines from its router forwarding table that it can deliver the packet to a host on one of its subnets.

First, the router's internet layer process creates an *ARP request message* that essentially says, "Hey, device with IP address 172.19.8.17, what is your 48-bit MAC layer address?" The internet layer on the router passes this ARP request message to its NIC.

Broadcasting the ARP Request Message   The MAC layer process on the router's NIC sends the ARP request message in a MAC layer frame that has a destination address of 48 ones. This designates the frame as a broadcast frame. All NICs listen constantly for this **broadcast address**. When a NIC hears this address, it accepts the frame and passes the ARP request message up the internet layer processes.

Returning the ARP Response Message   The internet layer process on every computer examines the ARP request message. If the target IP address is not that computer's, the internet layer process ignores it. If it is that computer's IP address, however, the internet layer process composes an ARP response message that includes its 48-bit MAC layer address.

The target host sends this ARP response message back to the router, via the target host's NIC. There is no need to broadcast the response message, as Figure A-15 shows. The target host sending the ARP response message knows the router's MAC address, because this information was included in the ARP request message.

When the router's internet layer process receives the ARP response message, address resolution is complete. The router's internet layer process now knows the subnet MAC address associated with the IP address. From now on, when an IP packet comes for this IP destination address, the router will send the IP packet down to its NIC, together with the required MAC address. The NIC's MAC process will deliver the IP packet within a frame containing that MAC destination address.

Other Address Resolution Protocols

Although ARP is the Address Resolution Protocol, it is not the only address resolution protocol. Most importantly, ARP uses broadcasting, but not all subnet technologies handle broadcasting. Other address resolution protocols are available for such networks.

Encapsulation

An ARP request message is an internet layer message. Therefore, we call it a packet. ARP packets and IP packets are both internet layer packet types in TCP/IP, as Figure A-1 illustrates. On a LAN, the ARP packet is encapsulated in the data field of an LLC frame. In other types of networks, it is encapsulated in the data field of the data link layer frame.

Classful Addresses in IP

In Chapter 8, we noted that, by themselves, 32-bit IP addresses do not tell you the lengths of their network, subnet, and host parts. For this, you need to have network masks to know how many bits there are in the network part, for instance. This is called **Classless InterDomain Routing (CIDR)**. CIDR allows network parts to vary from 8 bits to 24.

Originally, however, the 32-bit IP address *did* tell you the size of the network part, although not the subnet part. As Table A-1 shows, the initial bits of the IP address told whether an IP address was for a host on a Class A, Class B, or Class C network, or whether the IP address was a Class D multicast address. This is **classful addressing**.

Class A Networks

Specifically, if the initial bit was a 0, this IP address would represent a host in a Class A network. As Table A-1 shows, Class A network parts were only 8 bits long. The first bit was fixed (0), so there could be only 126 possible Class A networks.[9] However, each of these networks could be enormous, holding over 16 million hosts. Half of all IP addresses were Class A addresses. Half of these Class A addresses were reserved for future Internet growth.

Class B Networks

If the initial bits of the IP address were "10," then this was the address of a host on a Class B network. The network part was 16 bits long. Although the first 2 bits were fixed, the remaining 14 bits could specify a little over 16,000 Class B networks. With 16 bits remaining for the host part, there could be over 65,000 hosts on each Class B networks. The Class B address space was on its way to being completely exhausted until Classless InterDomain Routing (CIDR) was created to replace the classful addressing approach discussed in this section.

Class C Networks

Addresses in Class C networks began with "110." (Note that the position of the first 0 told you the network's class.) The network part was 24 bits long, and the 21 nonreserved bits allowed over 2 million Class C networks. Unfortunately, these networks could have only 254 hosts apiece, making them almost useless in practice. Such small networks seemed reasonable when the IP standard was created, because users worked at mainframe computers or at least minicomputers. Even a few of these large machines would be able to serve hundreds or thousands of terminal users. Once PCs became hosts, however, the limit of 254 hosts became highly restrictive.

Class D Addresses

Class A, B, and C addresses were created to designate specific hosts on specific networks. However, Class D addresses, which begin with "1110," have a different purpose, namely multicasting. This purpose has survived Classless InterDomain Routing.

When one host places another host's IP address in a packet, the packet will go only to *that one* host. This is called **unicasting**. In contrast, when a host places an all-ones address in the host part, then the IP packet should be **broadcast** to *all* hosts on that subnet.

However, what if only *some* hosts should receive the message? For instance, as discussed earlier, when OSPF routers transmit to one another, they only want other OSPF

---

[9] Not 27 or 128. As discussed in Chapter 3, network, subnet, and host parts of all zeros and all ones are reserved.

Class	Beginning Bits	Bits in the Remainder of the Network Part	Number of Bits in Local Part	Approximate Maximum Number of Networks	Approximate Maximum Number of Hosts per Network
A	0	7	24	126	16 million
B	10	14	16	16,000	65,000
C	110	21	8	2 million	254
D[a]	1110				
E[b]	11110				

[a]Used in multicasting.
[b]Experimental.

Problem: For each of the following IP addresses, give the class, the network bits, and the host bits if applicable:

10101010111110000101010100000001
11011010111110000101010100000001
01010101111110000101010100000001
11101110101111100001010100000001

Table A-16   IP Address Classes

routers to process the message. To support this limitation, they place the IP address 224.0.0.5 in the IP destination address fields of the packets they send. All OSPF routers listen for this IP address and accept packets with this address in their IP destination address fields. This is **multicasting**, that is, *one-to-many* communication (see Figure A-17). Multicasting is more efficient than broadcasting, because not all stations are interrupted. Only routers stop to process the OSPF message.

In addition, if two destination hosts are close together, a single IP multicast packet can travel at least some of the way across the Internet, as Figure A-16 illustrates. It will then be "cloned" to go to the individual hosts only where it has to be split.

Class E Addresses

A fifth class of IP addresses was reserved for future use, but these Class E addresses were never defined.

Mobile IP

The proliferation of notebooks and other portable computers has brought increasing pressure on companies to support mobile users. Chapter 5 discusses wireless LANs as a way to provide such support.

Mobile users on the Internet also need support. The IETF is developing a set of standards collectively known as **mobile IP**. These standards will allow a mobile computer to register with any nearby ISP or LAN access point. The standards will establish a connection between a computer's temporary IP address at the site and the computer's permanent "home" IP address. Mobile IP standards will allow portable computer users to travel without losing access to e-mail, files on file servers, and other resources.

Mobile IP will also offer strong security, based in the IPsec standards discussed in Chapter 7.

Diff-Serv and Multi-Protocol Label Switching (MPLS)

Diff-Serv

IP was created without the ability to add priority to packets so that latency-intolerant packets, such as voice packets, will get through first if there is any congestion. The IETF is now defining the **Differentiated Services (Diff-Serv)** octet in the IP header (see Figure A-2) to add priority and other ways to offer different service to different types of packets. Diff-Serv allows routers to pass high-priority packets during periods of high congestion while delaying low-priority packets. In Chapter 5, we saw the Ethernet works this way with 802.1Q tagged frames using 802.1p prioritization.

MPLS

When many IP packets from the same source to the same destination host arrive at a router, the router handles each one independently, forgetting how it routed the previous packet. This is terribly inefficient. To address this problem, the **MultiProtocol Label Switching (MPLS)** standard shown in Figure A-17 essentially creates virtual circuits through the Internet. Each packet is labeled with the MPLS value for its MPLS route. Routers look at this value instead of the destination IP address.

Figure A-17 shows an MPLS table with only three columns. The first is the MPLS label value. The second and third give the interface (port) and next-hop router or destination host. There is only one possible match for each MPLS label value, and this match can be found quickly. There is no need to consider every row as there is in a routing table and then find best matches. This makes label switching much faster than ordinary routing when a packet arrives at a router.

In addition to reducing costs, MPLS allows routes to be created for specific purposes. For instance, a route may be selected to send sensitive data through the most secure links in an internet if security is a major concern.

REVIEW QUESTIONS

MULTIPLEXING

1. a) How does a receiving internet layer process decide what process should receive the data in the data field of an IP packet? b) How does TCP decide? c) How does UDP decide? d) How does PPP decide?

MORE ON TCP

2. A TCP segment begins with octet 8,658 and ends with octet 12,783. a) What number does the sending host put in the sequence number field? b) What

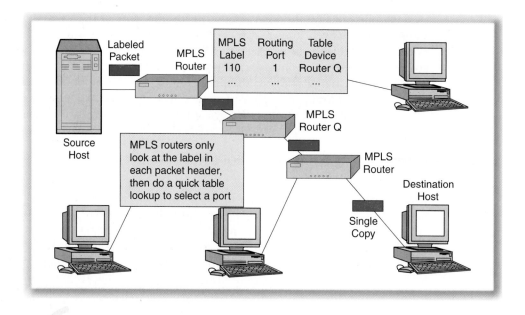

Figure A-17   MultiProtocol Label Switching (MPLS)

number does the receiving host put in the acknowledgment number field of the TCP segment that acknowledges this TCP segment?

3. A TCP segment carries data octets 456 through 980. The following TCP segment is a supervisory segment carrying no data. What value is in the sequence number field of the latter TCP segment?

4. Describe flow control in TCP.

5. a) In TCP fragmentation, what is fragmented? b) What software process does the fragmentation? c) What software process does reassembly?

6. A transport process announces an MSS of 1,024. If there are no options, how big can IP packets be?

MASK OPERATIONS

7. There is a mask 1010. There is a number 1100. What is the result of masking the number?

8. The following router forwarding table entry has the prefix /14.

10101010 10100000 00000000 00000000 (170.160.0)

Does it match the following destination address in an arriving IP packet? Explain.

10101010 10101011 11111111 00000000 (170.171.255.0)

IP VERSION 6

9. a) What is the main benefit of IPv6? b) What other benefits were mentioned?
10. a) Express the following in hexadecimal: 0000000111110010. (Hint: Chapter 5 has a conversion table.) b) Simplify: A173:0000:0000:0000:23B7:0000: CD12:A84B

IP FRAGMENTATION

11. a) What happens when an IP packet reaches a subnet whose MTU is *longer* than the IP packet? b) What happens when an IP packet reaches a subnet whose MTU is *shorter* than the IP packet? c) Can fragmentation happen more than once as an IP packet travels to its destination host?
12. Compare TCP fragmentation and IP fragmentation in terms of a) what is fragmented and b) where the fragmentation takes place.
13. a) What program on what computer does reassembly if IP packets are fragmented? b) How does it know which IP packets are fragments of the same original IP packet? c) How does it know their correct order?

DYNAMIC ROUTING PROTOCOLS

14. Compare RIP, OSPF, and BGP along each of the dimensions shown in Figure A-14.
15. a) What is an autonomous system? b) Within an autonomous system, can the organization choose routing protocols? c) Can it select the routing protocol its border router uses to communicate with the outside world?

ADDRESS RESOLUTION PROTOCOL (ARP)

16. A host wishes to send an IP packet to a router on its subnet. It knows the router's IP address. a) What else must it know? b) Why must it know it? c) How will it discover the piece of information it seeks? (Note: routers are not alone in being able to use ARP.)
17. a) What is the destination MAC address of an Ethernet frame carrying an ARP request message? b) What is the destination MAC address of an Ethernet frame carrying an ARP response packet?

CLASSFUL IP ADDRESSING

18. Compare classful addressing and CIDR.
19. What class of network is each of the following?
    a) 10101010111111110000000010101010
    b) 00110011000000001111111101010101
    c) 11001100111111110000000010101010
20. a) Why is multicasting good? b) How did classful addressing support it?

MOBILE IP

21. How will mobile IP work?

MPLS

22. a) How do routers make decisions about labeled packets? b) Why is this faster than ordinary routing?

23. a) MPLS is similar to what in ATM and Frame Relay? b) How can MPLS reduce costs? c) If 1,000 packets arrive to the same destination address and have the same MPLS number, how many rows will a router have to test at most if the routing table has 100,000 entries and if the MPLS table has 100 entries?

PROJECTS

1. **Getting Current.** Go to the book's website www.prenhall.com/panko, and see the New Information and Errors pages for this module to get new information since this book went to press and to correct any errors in the text.

2. **Internet Exercises.** Go to the book's website www.prenhall.com/panko, and see the Exercises page for this module. Do the Internet exercises.

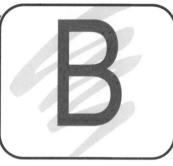

MODULE B

MORE ON PROPAGATION

INTRODUCTION

This module is not designed to be read from front to back, like a book chapter. Rather, it provides advanced information on three topics:

➤ Modulation
➤ Radio propagation
➤ Optical fiber

MODULATION

Modems use modulation. We saw amplitude modulation in Chapter 3. This section looks at the main forms of modulation in use today.

Frequency Modulation

As we saw in Chapter 3, modulation essentially transforms zeros and ones into electromagnetic signals that can travel down telephone wires. Electromagnetic signals consist of waves. As we saw in Chapter 3, waves have frequency, measured in hertz (cycles per second). Figure B-1 illustrates **frequency modulation**, in which one **frequency** is chosen to represent a 1 and another frequency is chosen to represent a 0. During a clock cycle in which a 1 is sent, the frequency chosen for the 1 is placed on the line. During a clock cycle in which a 0 is sent, the frequency chosen for the 0 is placed on the line.

The wave's **wavelength** is the physical distance between comparable parts on adjacent waves. Ocean waves have wavelengths of many meters; a

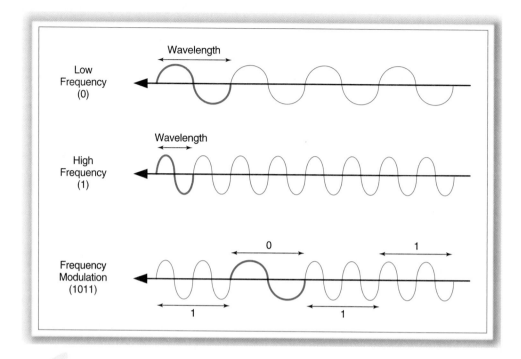

Figure B-1   Frequency Modulation

violin's sound vibrations have a very small wavelength. Electromagnetic waves have a wide variety of frequencies and wavelengths, as discussed later in this module.

Frequency and wavelength are related. The wave's wavelength multiplied by its frequency equals the speed of the wave in the transmission medium. So, if you increase the wavelength, you decrease the frequency, and vice versa. Think about strings vibrating: a shorter string will produce a higher-pitch sound.

Amplitude Modulation

Frequency and wavelength are two of the four characteristics of radio waves. The third is amplitude—the level of intensity in the wave. In **amplitude modulation**, which we saw in Chapter 3, we represent ones and zeros as different amplitudes. For instance, we can represent a 1 by a high-amplitude (loud) signal and a 0 by a low-amplitude (soft) signal. To send "1011," we would send a loud signal for the first time period, a soft signal for the second, and high-amplitude signals for the third and fourth.

Phase Modulation

The last major characteristic of waves is phase. As shown in Figure B-2, we call 0 degrees phase the point of the wave at 0 amplitude and rising. The wave hits its maximum at 90 degrees, returns to 0 on the decline at 180 degrees, and hits its mini-

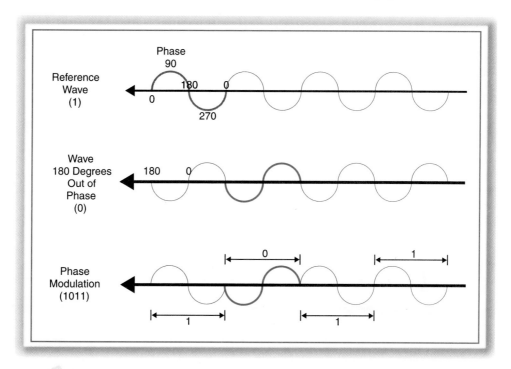

Figure B-2   Phase Modulation

mum amplitude at 270 degrees. Although the human ear can pick out frequency (pitch) and amplitude (loudness), it is not good at picking out phase differences. Electrical equipment, in contrast, is very sensitive to phase differences.

In **phase modulation**, we let one wave be our reference wave or carrier wave. Let us use the carrier wave to represent a 1. Then we can use a wave 180 degrees out of phase to represent a 0. The figure shows that to send "1011," we send the reference for the first time period, shift the phase 180 degrees for the second, and return to the reference wave for the third and fourth time periods. Although this makes little sense in terms of hearing, it is easy for electronic equipment to deal with phase differences.

A number of transmission systems use **quadrature phase shift keying (QPSK)**, which is phase modulation with four states (phases). Each of the four states represents two bits (00, 01, 10, and 11), so QPSK's baud rate is double its bit rate.

Quadrature Amplitude Modulation (QAM)

Telephone modems and many ADSL and cable modems today use a more complex type of modulation called **quadrature amplitude modulation (QAM)**. As Figure B-3 illustrates, QAM uses two carrier waves: a sine carrier wave and a cosine carrier wave. The receiver can separate signals on these two waves because they are in different phases—when the cosine wave is at the top of its cycle, the sine wave is just beginning

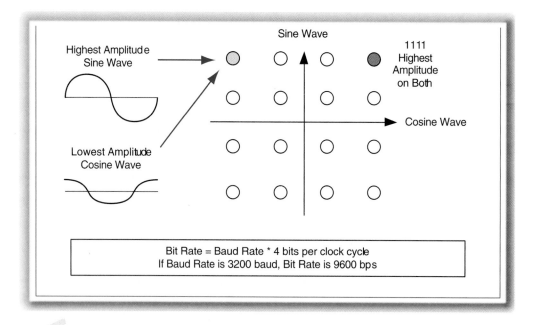

Figure B-3   Quadrature Amplitude Modulation (QAM)

its cycle and will not hit its peak until 90°. Therefore, the sine wave is 90° out of phase with the cosine wave.

In addition, QAM uses multiple possible amplitude levels for each carrier wave. Four possible amplitudes on one wave times four possible amplitudes on the second gives a **constellation** of 16 possible states. Sixteen possibilities can be represented by four bits ($2^4 = 16$). Accordingly, each constellation value represents a 4-bit value from 0000 through 1111. In other words, each clock cycle transmits four bits.

Different versions of QAM use different numbers of amplitude levels. Each doubling in the number of amplitude levels quadruples the number of possible states. Each quadrupling of the number of possible states allows two more bits to be sent per clock cycle. However, beyond about 64 possible states, the states are so close together that even slight transmission impairments can cause errors.

Orthogonal Frequency Division Multiplexing (OFDM)

Another form of modulation used in some new communication systems is **orthogonal frequency division multiplexing (OFDM)**. As Figure B-4 shows, the signal is sent in many small subchannels rather than in one large channel. The advantage of this approach is that if there are propagation problems in one or more subchannels, the system can reduce speed in those subchannels or even not use impaired subchannels if the propagation problems are too severe. The subchannels are adjacent and sometimes even overlap slightly. To prevent interference between signals in adjacent sub-

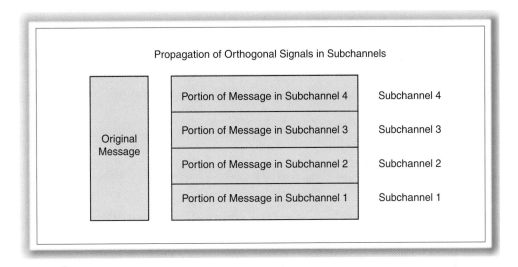

Figure B-4   Orthogonal Frequency Division Multiplexing (OFDM)

channels, the carrier waves in adjacent subchannels are selected to be mathematically orthogonal. For complex mathematical reasons, orthogonal signals in adjacent subchannels have minimum interference.

MORE ON RADIO PROPAGATION

Frequency varies widely. Of course, the lowest frequency is 0 Hz. There is no upper limit on frequency. Even light consists of electromagnetic waves, although light waves have much higher frequencies than radio waves. The range of all possible frequencies from 0 to infinity is called the **electromagnetic frequency spectrum**.

Frequency Bands: UHF and SHF

Figure B-5 shows that it is customary to divide the radio portion of the electromagnetic frequency spectrum into a number of **major frequency bands**. Most data communication takes place in the **Ultra High Frequency (UHF) band** and the **Super High Frequency (SHF) band**. In these bands there is considerable bandwidth (2.7 GHz and 27 GHz, respectively).

In fact, the SHF band is so wide that it is further divided, as discussed in the section on satellite transmission later in this module.

At the same time, signals in the UHF band and lower frequencies of the SHF band travel through walls and around obstacles reasonably well. At higher frequencies in SHF, they do not. In addition, equipment becomes more expensive at higher SHF frequencies, so there is great competition for spectrum space in the UHF band and in lower portions of the SHF band. In Chapter 3, we called this the golden zone.

Band	Full Name	Uses	Lowest Freq.	Bandwidth	Units	Wavelength of Lowest Frequency	Units
ELF	Extremely Low Frequency		30	270	Hz	10,000	km
VF	Voice Frequency		300	2,700	Hz	1,000	km
VLF	Very Low Frequency		3	27	kHz	100	km
LF	Low Frequency		30	270	kHz	10	km
MF	Medium Frequency	AM Radio	300	2,700	kHz	1,000	m
HF	High Frequency		3	27	MHz	100	m
VHF	Very High Frequency	VHF TV, FM Radio	30	270	MHz	10	m
UHF	Ultra-High Frequency	UHF TV, *Cellular Phones, Wireless LANs*	300	2,700	MHz	100	cm
SHF	Super High Frequency	Satellites, Microwaves, Wireless LANs	3	27	GHz	10	cm
EHF	Extremely High Frequency	*Future Q/V Band Satellites*	30	270	GHz	10	mm

Figure B-5 Frequency Bands

Microwave Systems

One of the most important uses of radio in carrier trunk transmission is microwave transmission. Microwave permits the transmission of information over reasonably long distances without the expense of laying ground wires.

Figure B-6 shows a **microwave system**. It shows that microwave systems use dish antennas for point-to-point transmission. They operate in the low gigahertz range, in which highly directional transmission is possible with dish antennas only a few meters in diameter.

However, microwave systems can travel only a limited distance before problems occur. Signals may grow too weak because of attenuation. Or, the receiver might be so far away that the target falls below the horizon, losing the required **line-of-sight connection** (the ability of the two dish antennas to see one another). Or, there may be mountains and other obstacles between the dishes. In general, line-of-sight microwave transmission is good for only 30 to 50 kilometers (20 to 30 miles).[1]

Figure B-6 shows that microwave systems use **repeaters** to solve such problems. These repeaters capture and regenerate the signal, often cleaning it up to remove propagation effects before passing the message on to the next repeater or to the ultimate receiving antenna.

Satellite Systems

After World War II, a young radar engineer named Arthur C. Clarke saw a way to improve on microwave systems. Why not, he asked, put a microwave repeater in space, on a satellite going around the earth? And why not set the satellite's altitude at

Figure B-6 Microwave

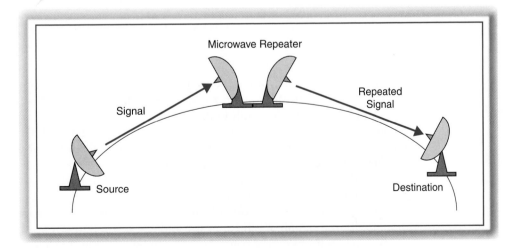

[1] G. R. McClain, ed., *Handbook of International Connectivity Standards* (New York: Van Nostrand), 1996, p. 418.

36,000 km (22,300 miles), so that it would circle the earth every 24 hours and so appear stationary in the sky? (This is called a **geosynchronous orbit**.) Today, a great deal of our long-distance communication travels over **geosynchronous communication satellites (GEOs)**, which were introduced in Chapter 7.

Chapter 7 also introduced low earth orbit satellites and medium earth satellites that do not appear to be stationary in the sky but that are low enough for signals to be usable even by portable devices with omnidirectional antennas.

As noted earlier, the SHF band is so wide that it is normally divided into a number of smaller frequency bands. In general, as frequency increases dishes can become smaller for the same degree of amplification, but attenuation problems increase, requiring more powerful satellites.

➤ *C Band*. The first satellites operated in the **C Band**, which was originally created for microwave systems. C Band satellites use frequencies of about 6 GHz for the **uplink** (the signal from the earth station to the satellite) and 4 GHz for the **downlink**. (The uplink frequency is always higher than the downlink frequency in satellite transmission.) C Band was a good place for satellite communication to start because C Band equipment was readily available and inexpensive, thanks to widespread terrestrial microwave transmission in this band. Unfortunately, this same widespread terrestrial microwave use tends to create interference between terrestrial microwave systems and C Band satellites.

➤ *Ku Band*. Next, many satellites began to use the **Ku Band**, with an uplink of about 14 GHz and a downlink of about 12 GHz. In this band, rain produces substantial attenuation, so powerful satellites are needed to burn through the attenuation. Dishes, however, can be smaller than they can be in C Band without losing efficiency. In addition, there are no terrestrial microwave systems to interfere with Ku Band signals.

➤ *Ka Band*. The **Ka Band** has uplink frequencies of about 30 GHz and downlink frequencies of about 20 GHz. Satellites are just beginning to use these frequencies. Rain attenuation is very high, so satellites must have very high power. New satellite-based telephony systems (see Module D) and satellite data services will use the Ka Band.

➤ *Other Bands*. Although the bands we have just seen are common satellite frequency bands, there are other bands at higher, lower, and intermediate frequencies.

Infrared Transmission

Most wireless systems today use radio frequencies, generally in the high megahertz to low gigahertz range. In this golden zone, signals still travel through walls and refract (bend) around objects reasonably well.

Some wireless signals use much-higher frequency electromagnetic signals that fall just below the frequencies of visible light. These are called **infrared signals**. At light frequencies and near-light frequencies, however, signals are not measured in terms of frequency; they are measured in terms of wavelength. Infrared signals, then, have a slightly longer wavelength than visible light.

Your television remote control uses infrared light instead of radio signaling. Although infrared signaling is inexpensive and can be used in wireless LANs, infrared transmission fails if something comes between the sender's and receiver's line of sight. Although there are ways to get around this problem by diffusing the signal using reflectors and other means, they add to cost and are far from perfect. In addition, sunlight or bright internal lights can create interference. The 802.11 standard defined infrared signaling up to 2 Mbps, but the market ignored this standard.

Optical Fiber Purchase and Installation

Large Ethernet networks typically connect switches in the core with optical fiber. Chapter 3 looked at optical fiber technology in general, and Chapter 5 discussed more on how to purchase optical fiber. This section adds a few additional topics you should know to purchase optical fiber in a LAN.

Multimode and Single Mode Fiber

The Basic Distinction

As discussed in Chapter 3, multimode fiber has a "fat" core (62.5 or 50 microns in diameter). This makes installation easier but reduces propagation distance because of temporal dispersion. Most LAN fiber is multimode fiber. For very long runs, say between buildings, single-mode fiber with a maximum core size of 9 microns (more usually, 8.3 microns), offers greater distances at the cost of more difficult installation. Single-mode fiber is so thin that only a single mode can propagate—the one going right down the middle of the fiber.

Alignment

Why are very thin cores an installation problem? The answer is that the axis of the light source (LED or laser) must be aligned precisely with the core's axis or the signal will not propagate properly down the core. As the size of the core decreases, aligning the light source becomes more difficult.

Thinner Fat Cores

Although 62.5 microns is the typical size of optical fiber cores in the United States and much of the world, 50-micron cores are gaining slightly in popularity. Being thinner than 62.5-micron cores, 50-micron cores carry signals farther. However, being only somewhat thinner than their 62.5 micron cousins, they are only slightly more difficult to install.

Graded Index Multimode Fiber

All commercial multimode fiber is **graded index fiber**, in which the index of refraction decreases from the center of the core to the cladding. Figure 3-19 illustrates graded-index multimode fiber. This reduces mode problems. Modes traveling straight down the axis and therefore traveling the shortest distance are slowed down. At the same time modes are speeded up if they enter at a high angle, reach the cladding many times on bounces, and so have to go farther. Reducing mode problems allows signals to travel farther before distortion becomes unacceptable.

In contrast, single-mode fiber uses **step index fiber**, meaning that the index of refraction is constant throughout the thin core.

Fiber Quality: Bandwidth–Distance

Fiber differs in quality, and better-quality fiber can carry signals faster and farther. Fiber quality is measured as a product: bandwidth times distance. As we saw in

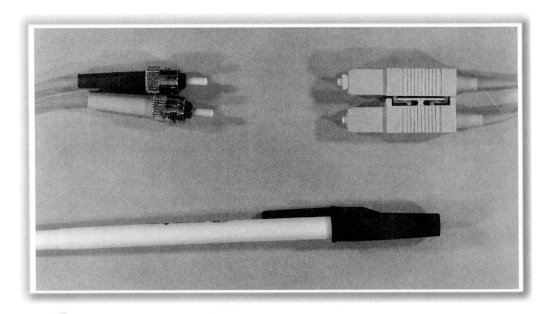

Figure B-7   SC (Left) and ST (Right) Optical Fiber Connectors

Chapter 3, the maximum possible transmission speed in a medium is governed by **bandwidth**, which is the range of possible transmission frequencies.

A typical fiber quality is 160 MHz–km. This means that if my distance is one kilometer, I can use a bandwidth of 160 MHz. However, if I limit my distance to 200 meters, I can use a bandwidth of 80 MHz. Some newer fiber is rated as 200 MHz–km.

ST and SC Connectors

For 4-pair UTP, there is only a single connector. Nothing like this degree of connector standardization exists in optical fiber. There are several optical fiber connector standards. Figure B-7 illustrates the two most important connector standards.

The most popular connector standard is the **Straight Tip (ST) connector** standard, which is round and makes a bayonet connection (you push it in and twist it on). The recommended TIA/EIA-568 standard, however is the **Subsciber Connector (SC)** standard, which is square and snaps into the NIC, switch, or router port. There also are several smaller form factor connectors.

REVIEW QUESTIONS

CORE REVIEW QUESTIONS

1. Disinguish between amplitude modulation and frequency modulation. b) Distinguish between amplitude modulation and phase modulation. c) What

two forms of modulation does QAM use? d) How is frequency modulation similar to and different from OFDM?

2. a) How does available bandwidth change with each increase in frequency band? b) Why do most data communications and voice communications services use the UHF band and lower portions of the SHF band?

3. Distinguish between microwave systems and satellite systems.

4. a) Are radio signals measured in frequencies or wavelengths? b) Infrared signals? c) How do infrared frequencies compare to light frequencies? d) Has infrared transmission proven popular to date for LAN transmission?

5. In selecting optical fiber, how do each of the following affect the maximum distance span of a fiber run between switches? a) Fiber quality. b) Wavelength.

6. How is fiber quality expressed?

7. a) What is the most popular fiber connector in the United States? b) What is the recommended TIA/EIA-568 optical fiber connector standard?

DETAILED REVIEW QUESTIONS

1. a) Explain how QAM works. b) Explain how OFDM works.

2. a) What are the main satellite frequency bands? b) Give the representative frequencies for the uplink and downlink in each band. c) Which usually has the higher frequency—the uplink or the downlink?

3. Distinguish between graded index fiber and step index fiber.

4. a) For LANs, what is the advantage of infrared transmission? b) What are the disadvantages?

CASE STUDIES

For case studies, go to the book's website www.prenhall.com/panko, and look at the Case Studies page for this chapter.

PROJECTS

1. **Getting Current.** Go to the book's website www.prenhall.com/panko, and see the New Information and Errors pages for this module to get new information since this book went to press and to correct any errors in the text.

2. **Internet Exercises.** Go to the book's website www.prenhall.com/panko, and see the Exercises page for this module. Do the Internet exercises.

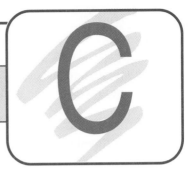

MORE ON LOCAL AREA NETWORKS

INTRODUCTION

Module C covers some advanced topics in LAN technology. It is not intended to be read front-to-back like a chapter. It should be read after Chapter 5. This module focuses on these topics:

> ➤ The logical link control layer 802.2 frame
> ➤ The Ethernet II frame.
> ➤ Electrical signaling in 10 Base-T and 100Base-TX.
> ➤ More on Ethernet switching.
> ➤ Spanning Tree Protocol (802.10) backup links.
> ➤ Wireless bridges
> ➤ More on organizing 802.11 wireless LANs

Logical Link Control Layer Framing

802.2 Logical Link Control (LLC) Layer Frame:
Basic Frame Format

Just as the MAC layer has a frame, the 802.2 LLC layer standard also defines a frame. In fact, it defines two frame formats: a basic type and a **Subnet Access Protocol (SNAP)** variant. We will begin with the basic frame format.

Destination Service Access Point The first field is the 1-octet **Destination Service Access Point (DSAP)**. The DSAP field contains a value indicating which next-higher-layer process should receive the data field contained in the LLC frame.

Source Service Access Point   Similarly, the **Source Service Access Point (SSAP)** field contains a value indicating which next-higher-layer process on the source computer created the packet in the data field.

Control Field   The **control field** is used for error detection and correction. However, as noted earlier in Chapter 5, error correction is rarely used.

Data Field   The **data field** contains the packet of the next-higher layer. This might be an IP packet, an IPX packet, or some other next-higher-layer message.

Subnet Access Protocol (SNAP)

With only a single octet, the DSAP field could only specify a limited number of internet-layer processes. When these DSAP values were assigned, TCP/IP was new, and it was not given a series of DSAP values for its major internet-layer standards, IP and ARP (Module A discusses ARP).[1] Other protocols that subsequently became important, such as AppleTalk, were also left out.

Fortunately, the DSAP and SSAP values AA hex were assigned to indicate the use of the **Subnet Access Protocol (SNAP)** option, which is also shown in Figure C-1. SNAP places the value 03 hex in the control field. It then adds two new fields: *Organization* and *Type*.

Organization   The **organization** field identifies an organization that creates designations for various next-higher-layer protocols. Each such organization is given an **organizational unique identifier (OUI)** code. For Xerox, the OUI value is 00-00-00 hex.

Type   The organization can assign multiple next-higher-layer designations. The 2-octet **type** field identifies a specific next-higher-layer standard. For IP version 4, the value specified by Xerox is 08-00 hex. For IP version 6, it is 86-DD hex. When 00-00-00 hex is in the organization field, the Type values are those of the EtherType field for the Ethernet II frame discussed next.

The Ethernet II Frame

The original **Ethernet II** standard, which predated 802.3 Ethernet standards, did not have separate MAC and LLC layers. There was only a single data link layer. Figure C-2 shows that the Ethernet II frame closely resembles an 802.3 MAC layer frame without an enclosed 802.2 LLC frame.

EtherType Field

Whereas the 802.3 MAC layer frame has a 2-octet Length field following the source address, the Ethernet II frame has a 2-octet EtherType field in this position. This field indicates the contents of the data field. For instance, an EtherType value of 08-00 hex indicates an IP packet in the data field.

---

[1]   A SAP value was defined for IP, but ARP also needed a SAP value, and this was never assigned.

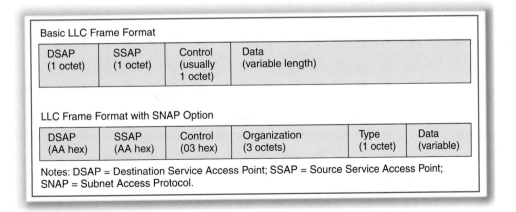

Basic LLC Frame Format

DSAP (1 octet)	SSAP (1 octet)	Control (usually 1 octet)	Data (variable length)

LLC Frame Format with SNAP Option

DSAP (AA hex)	SSAP (AA hex)	Control (03 hex)	Organization (3 octets)	Type (1 octet)	Data (variable)

Notes: DSAP = Destination Service Access Point; SSAP = Source Service Access Point; SNAP = Subnet Access Protocol.

Figure C-1   802.2 Logical Link Control (LLC) Layer Frame Formats

Figure C-2   Ethernet II Frame

Ethernet II Frame	802.3 MAC Layer Frame
Preamble (8 octets)	Preamble (7 octets)
	Start of Frame Delimiter (1 octet)
Destination Address (6 octets)	Destination Address (6 octets)
Source Address (6 octets)	Source Address (6 octets)
EtherType (2 octets)	Length (2 octets)
Data (variable)	802.2 LLC Frame (variable)
	PAD if Required
Frame Check Sequence (4 octets)	Frame Check Sequence (4 octets)

Automatic Detection

Interestingly, NICs can tell automatically whether an incoming frame is an 802.3 MAC layer frame or an Ethernet II frame by looking at the 2-octet field following the source address. This is either an EtherType field in Ethernet II or a Length field in 802.3.

If the value in this field is larger than 1,500, then this must be an Ethernet II frame because all EtherType values are larger than 1,500. Conversely, if the value is less than or equal to 1,500, this must be an 802.3 MAC layer frame, because the maximum length of an 802.3 MAC layer data field is 1,500 octets.

Quite a few PC networks use the Ethernet II frame instead of the bloated 802.3/802.2 frame.

ELECTRICAL SIGNALING

Electrical Signaling in 10Base-T

As Figure C-3 illustrates, Ethernet 10Base-T uses **Manchester encoding**, in which there is always a transition in the middle of each bit period. The transition in the middle of the time period effectively resynchronizes the sender's clock to the receiver's clock.

A one is encoded as a low voltage in the first half of the bit time period and a high voltage in the second half. Zeros have a high voltage followed by a low voltage. The way to remember this is that ones end high, while zeros end low. The line can change 20 million times per second, so the baud rate is 20 Mbaud.

More specifically, in transmission, Pin 1 is called TD+ and Pin 2 is called TD−. A low voltage is when TD+ is between 2.2 and 2.8 volts below the voltage of TD−. A high voltage is when TD+ is between 2.2 and 2.8 volts above TD−.

Ethernet 100Base-TX and 1000Base-T use more complex electrical signaling. Business networkers rarely have to get involved with electrical signaling.

Figure C-3 Ethernet 10Base-T Electrical Signaling (Manchester Encoding)

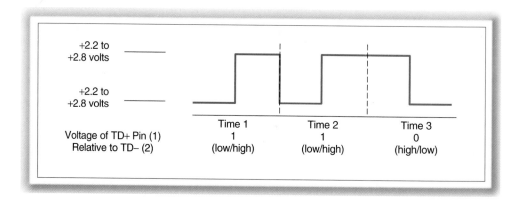

Electrical Signaling in 100Base-TX

4B/5B Data Representation

Manchester encoding places a transition in the middle of each bit period, as just discussed. This means that the bit rate is only half the baud rate. This is wasteful, because baud rate usually is the limiting factor in transmission. Also, if the sender were transmitting all ones or zeros, the line would radiate at a frequency of 20 MHz. This is not bad, but it is close to the maximum radiation frequency allowed by radio regulatory agencies. Manchester encoding is safe, but it will not scale to higher frequencies.

The 100Base-TX standard uses **4B/5B** data encoding, in which each "nibble" of 4 bits is encoded in a 5-bit sequence that has at least two ones, with two exceptions used for supervisory signaling. Figure C-4 shows some of these combinations. Note that some combinations do not represent data. These are used in supervisory signaling.

MLT-3 Encoding

In another departure from 10Base-T, 100Base-TX uses **MLT-3** signal encoding in which there are three states to the line: 1, 0, and -1. In each clock cycle, the signal may either advance to the next state (1 to 0, 0 to -1, or -1 to 0) or remain the same. If the signal is always advancing, the state will cycle every 4 bits. This results in a relatively low frequency. The baud rate is 125 MBaud, so the frequency is only 31.25 MHz. Although

Figure C-4   4B/5B Encoding in Ethernet 802.3 100Base-TX

Symbol	Nibble or Code	Encoded
0	0000	11110
1	0001	01001
F	1111	11101
J	Initial Parity Violation 1	11000
K	Initial Parity Violation 2	10001
T	Terminator	01101
R	Reset	00111
S	Set	11001
I	Idle	11111
Q	Quiet	00000
H	Halt	00100

Plus 8 code violations.

100Base-TX is 10 times faster than 10Base-T, its frequency radiation is only about 50 percent higher in the worst case of constant changing.

When does the state change? It changes whenever there is a 1 transmitted. The 4B/5B combinations each have at least two ones, so the state will change frequently enough to keep the receiver synchronized with the sender.

MORE ON ETHERNET SWITCHING

Ethernet Switch Learning

Figure C-5 shows a typical Ethernet switch forwarding table. How are such tables created? One way is for the network administrator manually to enter all MAC addresses and port numbers. However, this is impractical for large networks because of their sheer size and also because stations will be added and dropped constantly, making manual table editing a perpetual chore. Instead, most organizations allow their switches to learn the associations between ports and MAC addresses, as shown in Figure C-5.

Initial Broadcasting

When an Ethernet switch is turned on, its switch forwarding table is completely empty. Under these circumstances, Figure C-5 shows that Ethernet switches must act like hubs, broadcasting every incoming frame out every port. In other words, we pay switch prices but only get hub operation in terms of congestion control.

Figure C-5   Ethernet Switch Learning: Initial Broadcast

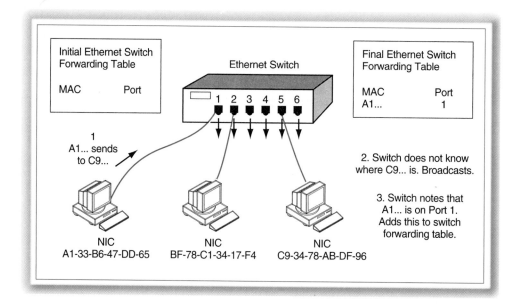

Broadcasting but Learning

Fortunately, Ethernet switches learn very quickly. For instance, Figure C-5 shows Station Ax (A1-33-B6-47-DD-65) on Port 1 transmitting to Station Cx (C9-34-78-AB-DF-96) on Port 5.

When the switch receives the frame, it sees Station Cx's MAC address in the destination address field. The switch forwarding table is empty, so there is no entry for C9-34-78-AB-DF-9G. The switch must broadcast the frame out all attached ports. The NICs in all stations must process the frame to determine whether or not the frame is intended for them.

However, the frame contains Station Ax's MAC address in the source address field, as discussed in Chapter 4. While processing the frame, the Ethernet switch reads the source address field. From this, it learns that Station Ax is attached to Port 1. It places this entry into its switch forwarding table as shown in Figure C-5.

Learning from Responses

Station Cx is likely to respond to Station Ax's frame. Now, the switch knows that Station Ax is attached to Port 1, so as Figure C-6 illustrates, the switch only sends the frame out Port 1. The switch is beginning to act like a switch.

In addition, Station Cx has placed its MAC address in the source address field of the frame. Now, the switch can add Station Cx's MAC address and port number to the switch forwarding table as Figure C-6 shows.

Figure C-6   Ethernet Switch Learning: Acting Like a Switch

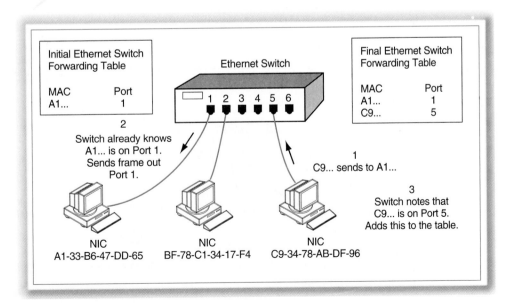

Working as a Switch

Station Ax and Station Cx are likely to continue sending many frames back and forth. Now the switch has their MAC addresses in its switch forwarding table, so there is no need for further broadcasting. Overall, only a few frames in any exchange typically are broadcast.

Forgetting

What happens if stations are dropped, disconnected, or have their NICs changed? Then the switch forwarding table will contain incorrect information. To eliminate obsolete information, switches erase their switch forwarding tables every few minutes. They must then rebuild their switch forwarding tables from scratch.

Learning for Hierarchical Switches

What if another Ethernet switch, rather than a single station, is attached to a port, as shown in Figure C-7? This creates no problems for switch learning.

Suppose that the lower-level switch is attached to Port 1 of the higher-level switch. Now, the frames from stations Dx, Ex, and Fx (we again name stations after the first hex digit in their MAC address) that are physically attached to the lower-level switch may enter the higher-level switch through Port 1. The higher-level switch merely adds each new MAC source address it sees to the switch forwarding table, associating that MAC address with Port 1. Whenever frames arrive at the higher-level switch for Stations Dx, Ex, or Fx, the switch merely sends the frame back out on Port 1.

Note what the higher-level Ethernet switch does not learn from this process. It does not learn that there is a switch between itself and Stations Dx, Ex, and Fx!

Figure C-7   Learning in an Ethernet Switched Hierarchy

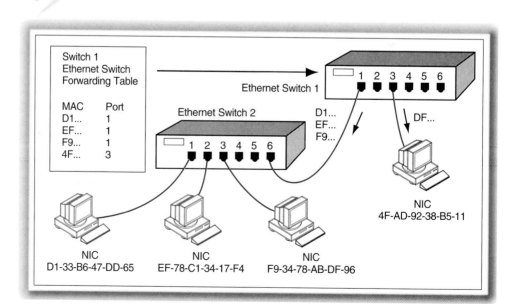

Ethernet switch forwarding tables do not include any information about the organization of switches in their network—only MAC addresses and their corresponding ports on that switch.

Purchasing an Ethernet Switch

Hubs are hubs. The only things you have to worry about when buying a hub are the number, speeds, and types (RJ-45, etc.) of ports you want on the hub. However, purchasing an Ethernet switch is quite complex.

Switching Matrix Throughput

As Figure C-8 illustrates, a switch has a **switching** matrix that connects input ports to output ports. (Of course, in UTP, the RJ-45 port is both an input port and an output port.)

A critical consideration in Ethernet switch selection is the switching matrix's **aggregate** throughput. Suppose you have a 24-port 100Base-TX switch. In the worst case, all ports may receive data simultaneously at 100 Mbps each. This would require the switching matrix to have an aggregate throughput of 2.4 Gbps (24 times 100 Mbps).

Switches that can handle even their highest possible input load are called **nonblocking**. The aggregate capacities of most switches are not fully nonblocking because it is not likely that all ports will be receiving simultaneously. However, if a switching matrix's aggregate throughput is too far below nonblocking capacity, frames may have to wait for transmission sometimes, and latency will result.[2]

Figure C-8 Ethernet Switch Organization

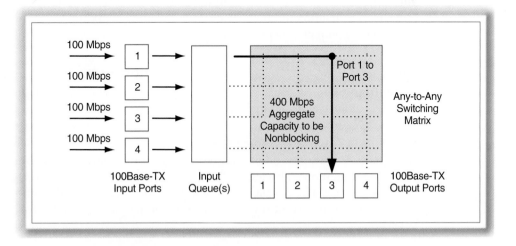

[2] Kevin Tolly has suggested that top-level switches have an aggregate throughput at least 75% of the maximum load and that no switch is acceptable at any level if it has an aggregate throughput less than 25% of the maximum load. Tolly, Kevin, "Exploding the Price-per-Port Fallacy," Network World, 9/22/98. www.nwfusion.com/forum/0921tolly.html.

Switching matrix throughput is especially important for switches high in the hierarchy, such as campus switches. Each port will carry traffic to and from many individual stations, so it is common to find most ports sending and receiving at any given moment.

Number of Possible MAC Addresses in the Switch Forwarding Table

Another consideration in Ethernet switch purchasing is the maximum size of the switch forwarding table, specifically the number of MAC address–port pairs it can store. Switches must broadcast to any address not in their address table, as we saw earlier. Large campus switches may have to store port numbers for thousands of MAC addresses.

Queue Size(s)

If too many frames arrive at the switch simultaneously, the matrix may have to store some frames temporarily in a **queue** (buffer). If a queue is too small, some frames will be lost during temporary congestion. Often, a switch has several waiting queues for different ports or different priorities.

Reliability Through Redundancy

Switch failures can incapacitate dozens or even hundreds of users. Ways to improve switch reliability include having redundant switching matrices, redundant power supplies, and even redundant cooling fans.

Manageability

As discussed in Chapter 10, a company is likely to have many switches, and it would like to be able to manage all of them from a single network control center. The center's network management program must be able to ask each switch for information and must also be able to issue commands to switches (say, to shut down a port that appears to be malfunctioning). The switch's management functions must be compatible with the company's network management standards, as discussed in Chapter 10.

Store-and-Forward Versus Cut-Through Switching

Recall from Chapter 7 that an Ethernet frame contains multiple fields and that the data field alone can be as large as 1,500 octets long.

Store-and-Forward Ethernet Switches

As Figure C-9 illustrates, some switches wait until they have received the entire frame before sending it out. This allows them to check each frame for errors and to discard incorrect frames. This is called **store-and-forward** switching. Although it prevents the propagation of incorrect frames, it also introduces a slight delay for each frame it processes.

Cut-Through Ethernet Switches

In contrast, **cut-through Ethernet** switches examine only some fields in a frame before sending the frame back out. Obviously, as shown in Figure C-9, they must at least read the destination address, in order to know what port to use to send the frame back out.

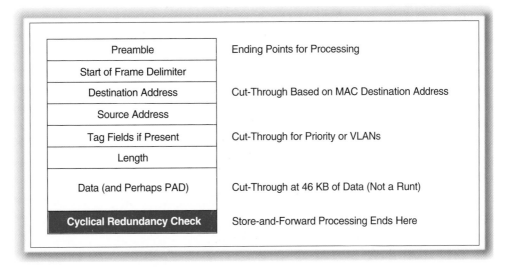

Preamble	Ending Points for Processing
Start of Frame Delimiter	
Destination Address	Cut-Through Based on MAC Destination Address
Source Address	
Tag Fields if Present	Cut-Through for Priority or VLANs
Length	
Data (and Perhaps PAD)	Cut-Through at 46 KB of Data (Not a Runt)
Cyclical Redundancy Check	Store-and-Forward Processing Ends Here

Figure C-9   Store-and-Forward Versus Cut-Through Ethernet Switches

This requires reading the preamble, start of frame delimiter, and destination address, for a total of only 14 octets.

VLANs and priority also require the reading of tag fields if they are used. Some cut-through switches, in the "extreme" case, wait for 46 octets of data because a smaller frame would be illegal. By examining only a few dozen octets, cut-through switches have less latency than store-and-forward switches, which typically have to examine hundreds or thousands of octets.

Mixed Switches

Some switches provide the best of both worlds. They begin forwarding using cut-through approaches. However, they sample some frames to determine error rates. If error rates are too high, they switch to store-and-forward processing unless they are forbidden to do so—for instance, if voice is being processed and cannot tolerate the delay.

Spanning Tree Protocol (802.1D) Backup Links

In practice, switched Ethernet networks usually implement the **Spanning Tree Protocol (802.1D).** This standard allows extra links to be added, for instance the link between Switch 1 and Switch 3 in Figure C-10. Talking to one another via 802.1D messages, the switches quickly realize that there is a loop. They agree to deactivate a link—perhaps the one between Switch 1 and Switch 3. Later, if Switch 2 or a link to it fails, the switches will exchange Spanning Tree Protocol messages to reactivate the link between Switch 1 and Switch 3. In complex networks, it is difficult to know which links to install for backup purposes, but the Spanning Tree Protocol does increase the reliability of Ethernet switched LANs somewhat.

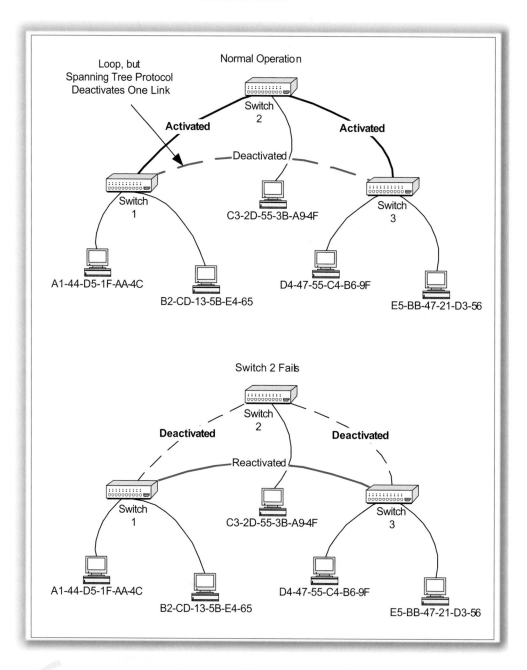

Figure C-10   802.1D Spanning Tree Protocol for Ethernet

Wireless Bridges

Although 802.11 and Bluetooth standards will dominate, there also is a market for point-to-point wireless bridges that connect two LANs in different buildings within a site.

Bridges in general are devices that connect two different LANs, which may used different technologies. 802.11 access points are bridges, connecting wireless 802.11 LANs and (usually) wired 802.3 LANs.

Some wireless bridges can transmit several miles, connecting nearby sites with line-of-sight clearance. Figure C-11 shows a wireless bridge. Bridges typically operate in the same radio bands as Bluetooth, 802.11, and 802.11a, potentially causing interference. Wireless bridges, which previously used proprietary technologies, are beginning to standardize on 802.11 protocols.

More on Organizing 802.11 Wireless LANs

Chapter 5 looked at the normal way in which 802.11 wireless LANs are implemented—with access points that link a few mobile stations to a largely wired LAN. This section will look at two alternative ways of organizing 802.11 LANs—ad hoc mode for very small LANs and the possibility of removing all wiring to all desktop computers.

Ad Hoc LANs

It is possible to have small all-wireless 802.11 LANs in which no access points are used. As Figure C-12 shows, stations can communicate directly with one another. However, this solution requires all stations to be wireless, including servers. In addition, all stations must be within radio range of one another. Such LANs do not scale in either number of stations or distance span. Few corporate LANs other than those in home offices, in very small businesses or small branch offices use this **ad hoc mode.**

Figure C-11   Wireless Bridge

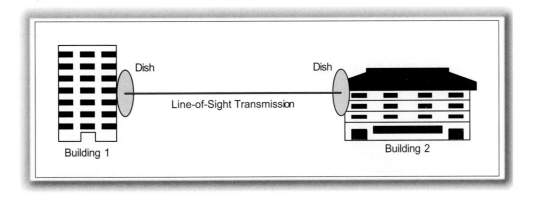

Building 1   Dish   Line-of-Sight Transmission   Dish   Building 2

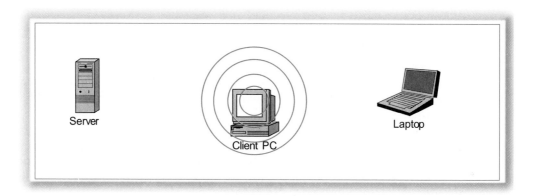

Figure C-12   Ad Hoc 802.11 Wireless LAN

Wires Between Switches/Wireless to the Desktop

Wire to the Desktop Is Expensive
In most organizations, wiring switches together costs less than running wires from hubs and switches to the desktop. There are relatively few connections between switches, while there are many connections from workgroup switches to the desktop. Connecting desktops to the nearest hub or switch, in other words, dominates wiring costs in most firms.

Using Access Points Instead of Workgroup Hubs or Switches
As Figure C-13 illustrates, one option is to continue wiring the switches to one another, probably with optical fiber. However, where workgroup switches or hubs would be, there is an access point. All client devices connect to their access points by radio, avoiding the need to run wire to every desktop.

The 802.11b standard offers too little capacity to support the elimination of workgroup hubs and switches and wiring to the desktop. Even a few stations would overwhelm it. However, 802.11a appears to have the capacity to eliminate wiring to the desktop and 802.1g has the speed but perhaps not the total bandwidth. If so, we may see a complete change in the nature of LAN technology during the next few years.

REVIEW QUESTIONS

CORE REVIEW QUESTIONS

1. a) How many fields are there in a basic 802.2 LLC frame? b) How many octets are there in an 802.2 LLC frame with the SNAP option? c) Why is the SNAP option necessary in 802.2?
2. a) In Ethernet 802.3 10Base-T, how is a one represented? b) A zero? c) Why is this done instead of just making a one a high or low value and a zero the opposite?

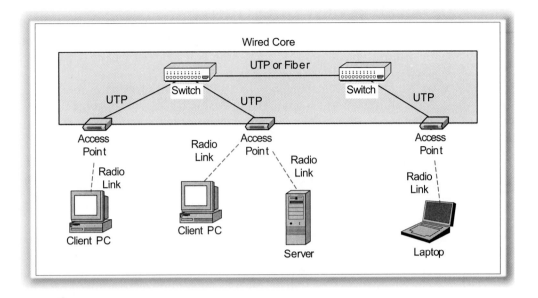

Figure C-13   Wired Core with Wireless to the Desktop

3. a) In Ethernet 802.3 100Base-TX, explain 4B/5B processing. b) Why is it more efficient than Manchester encoding? c) Explain MLT-3 encoding.

4. a) When a switch receives an Ethernet frame, what field does it look at to determine what port to use to send the frame back out? b) What field does it look at to determine if it should add a new MAC address-port pair to its switching table? c) What will a switch do if the destination address in a frame is not in its switching table? d) Why is periodic forgetting necessary (unlike the type of forgetting that takes place after a final exam)?

5. Briefly describe the main switch evaluation criteria.

6. a) Which is likely to be faster—a cut-through switch or a store-and-forward switch? Why? b) Why is the other type of switch used? c) Why do mixed switches eliminate the trade-off?

7. a) What can be done to reduce the danger created by the susceptibility of Ethernet's hierarchical switch organization to single points of failure? b) How does this approach work? c) What is the name of the standard?

8. What is the purpose of wireless bridges?

9. a) Describe the elements in a typical 802.11 LAN today. b) Can you have a completely wireless LAN? Explain how this is possible, and explain its limitations. c) Why is it attractive to use a wired LAN to connect switches and wireless transmission to connect stations to the network? d) Which 802.11 versions can support the elimination of workgroup hubs and switches?

DETAILED REVIEW QUESTIONS

1. a) In the SNAP option of the LLC frame, why do we need both an organization field and a Type field? b) What does the Type field tell you? c) What is the Xerox Type code for an IP packet? d) For an IPX packet?

2. a) What is a nonblocking switch? b) What kind of switches must store many MAC address–port associations? c) A switch has four gigabit Ethernet ports. What aggregate switch matrix capacity is needed to give nonblocking capacity? d) To give 80 percent of nonblocking capacity? Show your calculations.

THOUGHT QUESTIONS

1. In 802.2 LLC frames, why do you think the most common value in the Organization field is 00-00-00 hex?

2. On an Ethernet 802.3 network, a frame arrives carrying an IP packet. Counting the first octet of the frame as 0, in what octet does the LLC DSAP field begin? The IP destination address field? Show your calculations clearly.

3. The complex design of MLT-3 allows a ten-fold increase in speed over 10Base-T to be accomplished with only a 50% maximum increase in frequency. This complexity is needed because regulatory agencies around the world mandate maximum possible frequencies of EMI interference generated by computers and networking. Why do you think they mandate this?

4. A firm purchases an inexpensive Ethernet switch to resegment a congested LAN. When the switch is installed, congestion actually gets worse. What mistakes may the firm have made in its switch purchase?

5. a) Explain 4B/5B signal encoding. b) Explain MLT-3 signal encoding.

PROJECTS

1. **Getting Current.** Go to the book's website www.prenhall.com/panko and see the New Information and Errors pages for this module to get new information since this book went to press and to correct any errors in the text.

2. **Internet Exercises.** Go to the book's website www.prenhall.com/panko and see the Exercises page for this module. Do the Internet exercises.

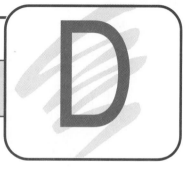

MODULE D

MORE ON TELEPHONE SERVICE

THE PUBLIC SWITCHED TELEPHONE NETWORK (PSTN)

As Chapter 6 noted, telephony often falls under the corporate networking group. It is essential for networking professionals to understand telephone services and telephone pricing.

Chapter 6 introduced the basic anatomy of the telephone system, beginning with customer premises equipment. Beyond the customer premises, we enter the realms of telephone carriers. When we do, we enter a world marked by a hundred years of regulation.

In this module, we will look in more detail at PBX networks and at telephone service pricing. We will also look at T1 multiplexing.

MORE ON CUSTOMER PREMISES TELEPHONY

PBX Networks

Many large companies have multiple sites. Figure D-1 shows that each site is likely to have a PBX.

The figure shows that the company can link its sites together with leased lines. For instance, a single T1 leased line can handle 24 conversations between two sites. Especially busy connections require T3 lines or even faster leased lines.

If a firm buys all of its PBXs from a single vendor, they will be able to function together like the central offices of the telephone company. A single system of extension numbers will be able to serve everyone in the firm,

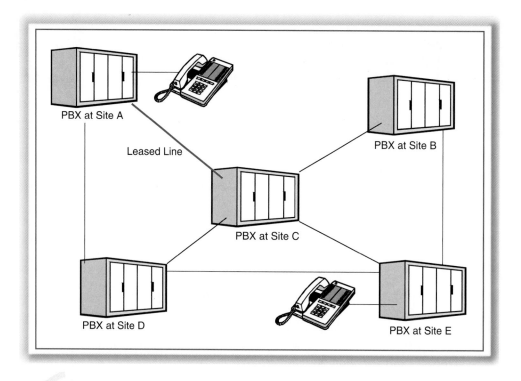

Figure D-1   Multisite PBX Network

regardless of their site. A PBX at some master site should even be able to do remote maintenance on slave PBXs at other sites.

For communication outside the firm, the PBXs will have access lines to the local telephone company. The PBXs will also have links to various transmission carriers other than the local telephone company. This allows the PBXs to select the least-cost line whenever someone makes an outgoing call.

In effect, the company sets up its own private telephone system. Technically, this is known as a **private telephone network**. By creating private telephone networks, companies can reduce their costs while providing a high level of services.

Many telephone carriers are trying to get back the business they have lost because of private telephone networks. They now offer **virtual private network service**. In this service, the firm appears to have an exclusive private telephone network. Calls between sites are inexpensive. In return for lower prices, transmission is restricted to communication between corporate sites.

However, the telephone company provides this service using its ordinary switches and trunk lines. Virtual private network service is a matter of pricing, not of technology.

The term **virtual private network** is a little confusing. It began in telephony as described in the previous paragraphs. Later, as Chapter 7 discusses, the term virtual private network became popular as a way to describe the use of the Internet instead of a commercial carrier for data transmission.

User Services

Figure D-2 shows that because digital PBXs are essentially computers they allow vendors to differentiate their products by adding application software to provide a wide range of services.

➤ User services are employed directly by ordinary managers, secretaries, and other telephone end users.

➤ Attendant services are employed by telephone operators to help them give service.

➤ Management services are employed by telephone and corporate network managers to manage the company's telephone network.

Figure D-2   Digital PBX Services

For Users

Speed dialing	Dials a number with a one- or two-digit code.
Last number redial	Redials the last number dialed.
Display of called number	LCD display for number the caller has dialed. Allows caller to see a mistake.
Camp on	If line is busy, hit "camp on" and hang up. When other party is off the line, he or she will be called automatically.
Call waiting	If you are talking to someone, you will be beeped if someone else calls.
Hold	Put someone on hold until he or she can be talked to.
ANI	Automatic number identification. You can see the number of the party calling you.
Conferencing	Allows three people to speak together.
Call transfer	If you will be away from your desk, calls will be transferred to this number.
Call forwarding	Someone calls you. You connect the person to someone else.
Voice mail	Callers can leave messages.

For Attendants

Operator	In-house telephone operators can handle problems.
Automatic call distribution	When someone dials in, the call goes to a specific telephone without operator assistance.
Message center	Allows caller to leave a message with a live operator.
Paging	Operator can page someone anywhere in the building.
Nighttime call handling	Special functions for handling nighttime calls, such as forwarding control to a guard station.
Change requests	Can change extensions and other information from a console.

For Management

Automatic route selection	Automatically selects the cheapest way of placing long-distance calls.
Call restriction	Prevents certain stations from placing outgoing or long-distance calls.
Call detail	Provides detailed reports on charges by telephone and by department.

CARRIER SERVICES AND PRICING

Having discussed technology, we can now turn to the kinds of transmission services that telecommunications staffs can offer their companies. Figure D-3 shows that corporate users face a variety of transmission services and pricing options.

Basic Voice Services

The most important telephone service, of course, is its primary one: allowing two people to talk together. Although you get roughly the same service whether you call a nearby building or another country, billing varies widely between local and long-distance calling. Even within these categories, furthermore, there are important pricing variations.

Local Calling

Most telephone calls are made between parties within a few kilometers of each other. There are several billing schemes for such local calling. Some telephone companies offer **flat-rate** local service in which there is a fixed monthly service charge but no separate fee for individual local calls.

Figure D-3   Telephone Services

```
Local Calling
    Flat rate
    Message units

Toll Calls
    Intra-LATA
    Inter-LATA

Toll Call Pricing
    Direct dialing
        Anytime, anywhere
        Basic rate
    800/888 numbers
        Free to calling party
        Reduced rate per minute
    WATS
        Wide area telephone service
        For calling out from a site
        Reduced rate per minute
    900 numbers
        Calling party pays
        Called party charges the calling party a price above transmission costs
```

In some areas, however, carriers charge **message units** for some or all local calls. The number of message units they charge for a call depends on both the distance and duration of the call. Economists like message units, arguing that message units are more efficient in allocating resources than flat-rate plans. Subscribers, in contrast, dislike message units even if their flat-rate bill would have come out the same.

Toll Calls
Although the local situation varies, all long-distance calls are **toll calls**. The cost of the call depends on distance and duration.

800/888 Numbers
Companies that are large enough can receive favorable rates from transmission companies for long-distance calls. In the familiar **800/888 number service**, anyone can call into a company, usually without being charged. To provide free inward dialing, companies pay a carrier a per-minute rate lower than the rate for directly dialed calls. Initially, only numbers with the 800 area code provided such services. Now that 800 numbers have been exhausted, the 888 area code is offering the same service to new customers.

WATS
In contrast to inbound 800/888 service, **wide area telephone service (WATS)** allows a company to place outgoing long-distance calls at per-minute prices lower than those of directly dialed calls. WATS prices depend on the size of the service area. WATS is often available for both intrastate and interstate calling. WATS can also be purchased for a region of the country instead of the entire country.

900 Numbers
Related to 800/888 numbers, **900 numbers** allow customers to call into a company. Although 800/888 calls are usually free, callers to 900 numbers pay a fee that is much higher than that of a toll call. Some of these charges go to the carrier, but most of them go to the subscriber being called.

This allows companies to charge for information, technical support, and other services. For instance, customer calls for technical service might cost $20 to $50 per hour. Charges for 900 numbers usually appear on the customer's regular monthly bill from the local exchange carrier. Although the use of 900 numbers for sexually oriented services has given 900 numbers a bad name, they are valuable for legitimate business use.

Advanced Services
Although telephony's basic function as a "voice pipe" is important, telephone carriers offer other services to attract customers and to get more revenues from existing customers.

Electronic Switching Services
Earlier we noted that most digital switches are really computers. We also saw the types of applications that vendors now program into their PBXs. Many carriers now offer the same services to business and residential customers.

Unfortunately, different carriers throughout the country tend to offer very different digital switching services. One reason for creating the Integrated Services Digital Network was to standardize services. This integration would allow them to be offered even for calls that span multiple carriers.

T1 Multiplexing

The text notes that trunk lines usually are multiples of 64 kbps. Figure D-4 illustrates how this applies to T1 lines, which were created to multiplex twenty-four 64 kbps voice channels on one trunk line.

Frames and Slots

First, each second is divided into 8,000 periods called **frames**. Each frame carries PCM data for one sampling period. Within the frame, there are 24 **slots**, each carrying one sample for a single channel. For supervisory signaling, there is an additional **framing bit**.[1]

This gives a total of 193 bits per frame ($24 \times 8 + 1$). If we multiply 193 bits per frame times 8,000 frames per second, we get 1.544 Mbps—the speed of a T1 line.

Simple TDM Versus STDM

This is called simple **time division multiplexing (TDM)**. Each channel is assigned the same time slot in each frame, and if the channel does not use the time slot, it is wasted. In contrast, **statistical time division multiplexing (STDM)** assigns slots in each frame to

Figure D-4 Time Division Multiplexing (TDM) on a T1 Line

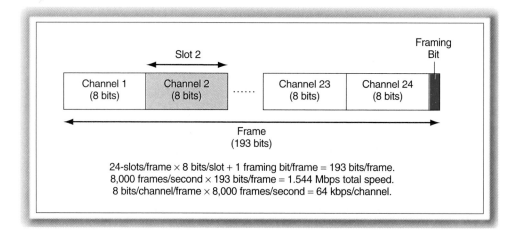

24-slots/frame × 8 bits/slot + 1 framing bit/frame = 193 bits/frame.
8,000 frames/second × 193 bits/frame = 1.544 Mbps total speed.
8 bits/channel/frame × 8,000 frames/second = 64 kbps/channel.

---

[1] Of course one framing bit tells you very little. Normally, framing bits are analyzed in 12 or 24 successive frames. If the sequence is not what the receiver expected, then synchronization has been lost (the receiver cannot tell where each frame starts) or a transmission error has occurred. There is no retransmission, but the receiver may record information about error rates for analysis.

channels as needed. If some channels are silent, other channels can transmit faster than 64 kbps. Multiplexing in packet switching does not use frames. Packets are sent one after another, without timing constraints. This is even more efficient than STDM.

REVIEW QUESTIONS

CORE REVIEW QUESTIONS

1. a) What is a PBX? b) Why are PBXs attractive to businesses? c) What are private telephone networks? b) Virtual private networks? c) How does the term virtual private network differ in telephony and data communications?
2. Compare and contrast a) 800/888 numbers, b) 900 numbers, and c) WATS, in terms of whether the caller or the called party pays and the cost compared with the cost of a directly dialed long-distance call.
3. a) What type of multiplexing does a T1 line use? b) How long is a frame? c) How many bits does a T1 line carry per slot? d) How many bits does a T1 line carry per channel per frame? e) How many bits does a T1 line carry per channel per second? f) Within a frame, what happens in simple TDM to a channel's slot if the channel has no signal to be carried?

DETAILED REVIEW QUESTIONS

1. a) In PBXs, what are the differences among user services, attendant services, and management functions? b) List at least three services in each category. Be able to explain all of the PBX services in the module if given their names.
2. a) Describe pricing for local calls and toll calls. b) What is the advantage of 800/888 numbers for customers? c) For companies that subscribe to 800/888 number service?

PROJECTS

1. **Getting Current.** Go to the book's website www.prenhall.com/panko, and see the New Information and Errors pages for this module to get new information since this book went to press and to correct any errors in the text.
2. **Internet Exercises.** Go to the book's website www.prenhall.com/panko, and see the Exercises page for this module. Do the Internet exercises.

MODULE E

MORE ON LARGE-SCALE NETWORKS

INTRODUCTION

This module is designed to be read after Chapter 7. It supplements the material in Chapter 7 by offering additional material on four topics:

➤ More on telephone modem standards
➤ More on asynchronous transfer mode (ATM)
➤ More on Layer 3 Switching
➤ Frame Relay frames

MORE ON TELEPHONE MODEM STANDARDS

In Chapter 7, we looked at modulation (speed) standards for telephone modems, including V.34, V.90, and V.92. In this section, we will look at other telephone modem standards. Figure E-1 illustrates general telephone modem standards.

Training and Standards

Training

You have almost certainly used a telephone modem. You know that when two telephone modems connect, they seem to take forever to make the connection. Typically, they take about 25 seconds. During this time, they are not idle. They are going through a **training period**.

Speed Standards		
Name	**Speed**	**Origin**
V.92	56 kbps receiving Over 33.6 kbps sending	ITU-T
V.90	56 kbps receiving 33.6 kbps sending	ITU-T
V.34	33.6 kbps	ITU-T
V.32 bis	14.4 kbps	ITU-T
Error Correction and Data Compression Standards		
Name	**Type**	**Origin**
V.42	Error correction	ITU-T
V.42 *bis*	Data compression	ITU-T
V.44	Data compression	ITU-T
Facsimile Modern Standards		
Name	**Speed**	**Origin**
V.14	14.4 kbps	ITU-T
V.29	9600 kbps	ITU-T

Figure E-1   Telephone Modem Standards

First, each sends a fairly long screeching sound to tell the telephone network to turn off echo-canceling[1] telephone equipment on the circuit so that they can communicate properly.

Second, they exchange messages to agree upon what standards they will use, selecting the highest shared standard in each standards category. For instance, there are two telephone modem standards for data compression, **V.42** *bis* and the newer V.44. If one supports V.44 and the other supports V.42 *bis*, they will use V.42 *bis* when communicating. If one supports V.44 and the other does not support compression at all, they will not use data compression when they communicate.

Error Correction and Data Compression Standards

Error Correction

The main error correction standard, which is supported by almost all telephone modems today, is **V.42**. If there are errors, V.42 telephone modems will retransmit the lost or damaged information.

---

[1] Normally, it is bad to hear your voice coming back through your telephone earpiece. However, modern modems operate by subtracting what they are sending from what they are hearing to find what the other modem is sending. They must be able to hear both signals to do this.

Data Compression

Until recently, the only major data compression standard created by the ITU-T for telephone modems was **V.42 *bis***. Under ideal conditions, V.42 *bis* can provide 4-to-1 data compression, so that your effective data throughput can be four times the rated speed of your telephone modem. With a V.90 telephone modem, for instance, downloads that bring 56 kbps of compressed data can carry 224 kbps of original data. This 4-to-1 ratio is rarely achieved, but compression almost always boosts throughput somewhat.

A newer data compression standard, **V.44**, is optimized for graphics compression. Tests indicate that V.44 telephone modems can download webpages that are rich in graphics almost twice as fast as V.42 *bis* telephone modems can.

Facsimile Standards

Almost all telephone modems sold today can also send and receive facsimile transmissions. **Facsimile** modems use different modulation standards than ordinary telephone modems. The most common facsimile modulation standard is V.17, which operates at 14.4 kbps. There also is V.29, which can only operate at 9,600 bps. Fax modem standards also include compression geared to the needs of image transmission.

ATM

Chapter 5 introduced ATM. Among the points it made about ATM were the following:

➤ ATM frames are called cells. Each cell is 53 octets long, consisting of 5 octets of header and 48 octets of payload.

➤ The 5 octets of header constitute considerable overhead.

➤ ATM has several classes of service (service categories) offering differing quality of service (QoS) guarantees.

➤ ATM uses virtual circuits to reduce switching costs.

➤ ATM is very complicated to manage.

Layering in ATM

ATM follows OSI layering for subnets. Its standards are limited to the physical and data link layers.

ATM and ATM Adaptation Layers

We saw in Chapter 4 that the IEEE subdivided the data link layer into the media access control and logical link control layers. Figure E-2 shows that the ITU-T also subdivided the data link layer into two layers in ATM. These are the **ATM layer** and the **ATM adaptation layer (AAL)**.

ATM Layer

The (lower) **ATM layer** is application-*independent*. It provides the same frame transmission process regardless of the application (voice, videoconferencing, timing-insensitive data, and so forth). Think of ATM as a train carrying boxcars whose contents are irrelevant to the railroad.

OSI	ATM	
Data Link	ATM Adaptation Layer (AAL) (Application-Dependent)	Convergence Services (CS)
		Segmentation and Reassembly (SAR)
	ATM (Application-Independent)	
Physical	Physical	

Figure E-2   ATM Layering

It is the ATM layer that has the 53-octet cells we saw in Chapter 5. In addition, the ATM layer handles virtual circuits, flow control, and the multiplexing of multiple virtual circuits onto a single flow of cells between switches.

ATM Adaptation Layer

The (upper) **ATM adaptation layer (AAL)** offers application-*dependent* services. It is the AAL that allows us to have different classes of service (service categories).

For instance, voice needs constant frame delivery rates, whereas for data it is more important to get more capacity when sending a large burst. The job of the ATM Adaptation Layer is to build on ATM layer services to provide the specific transmission characteristics each application needs.

AAL Types

Just as ATM in general offers classes of service, there are specific **AAL types** that support different service categories.

➤ AAL1 supports Class A (Constant Bit Rate) service. It provides the complex controls needed for exact timing.

➤ AAL2 supports Class B (Variable Bit Rate–Real Time) service.

➤ AAL3/4 originally consisted of two Types, 3 and 4, which supported Classes C and D, respectively. Both of these classes offer data transmission, but Class C is connection-oriented and Class D is connectionless. Because the two AAL types were so similar, they were combined.

➤ AAL5 was created to support the Unspecified Bit Rate service category. It is simpler than AAL3/4.

Subdividing the AFTM Adaptation Layer

As Figure E-2 illustrates, the ITU-T further subdivided the AAL into two layers, Convergence Services (CS) and Segmentation and Reassembly (SAR).

Segmentation and Reassembly (SAR)

As its name suggests, the SAR layer accepts data from the convergence services layer and packages the data into a form to be passed to the ATM sublayer for placement into 48-octet data fields.

Convergence Services (CS)

The CS layer accepts data from the next-higher layer, typically the internet layer. The convergence services layer adds whatever is needed for a particular class of service, such as timing services for AAL1.

High Overhead

In Chapter 5, we saw that the ATM's cell has 5 octets of header and 48 octets of data. Speaking more precisely, we can say that this describes the frame *at the ATM layer*. However, both the convergence services and segmentation and reassembly layers have their own frame organizations as well.

The CS and SAR frames have headers and data fields. Their headers add further to ATM overhead. The 48 octets of "data" in the ATM layer data field may contain CS or SAR header information rather than true data from the internet layer.

The ATM Physical Layer

To move data at 156 Mbps, 622 Mbps, or even higher speeds, ATM needs a very good physical layer. We will look first at framing and then at sublayering within the physical layer.

Cell-Based Physical Layer

The ITU-T has designed two approaches to framing at the physical layer. The first is the simplest. This is just to send cells back to back, with no gaps between successive cells. This is like placing data on successive stairs on an escalator. Although this approach has very low overhead, it does not offer a good way of handling supervisory signaling.

SONET/SDH–Based Physical Layer

A more elegant approach is used in most ATM installations. This approach uses the SONET/SDH technology now used by telephone companies for a growing fraction of their long-distance communication (see Chapter 6). *SONET (Synchronous Optical Network)* is the name of this approach in the United States. Other countries use a slightly different but compatible technology called *SDH (Synchronous Digital Hierarchy)*.

For speeds of 155.52 Mbps, SONET/SDH transmits data in groups[2] of 2,490 octets. A group is sent every 125 microseconds (ms), giving the 155.2 Mbps aggregate transmission rate.

For supervisory purposes, each SONET/SDH group has 324 octets of control information. This represents an overhead of 15%.

---

[2] Technically, these groups are called frames. However, this is confusing because we have used the term frame in this book for data link layer messages. Here, framing is done at the physical layer.

LAYER 3 SWITCHING

As Chapter 8 discussed, Layer 3 Switches have replaced many routers in site networks. Like routers, Layer 3 switches can work directly with IP packets to forward these packets to their destinations. However, Layer 3 switches do this faster and more cheaply than do routers.

Chapter 8 noted that it is difficult to talk about technological differences between Layer 3 switches and routers because new technologies created for Layer 3 switching often are adopted by new routers. Having said this, however, we will look at some of the differences traditionally found between routers and switches, as shown in Figure E-3.

Reduced Protocol Support

As noted in Chapter 8, routers support a wide array of protocols at the internet and subnet (data link and physical) layers. This makes routers extremely expensive. In contrast, Layer 3 switches offer much less protocol support. This reduces their cost.

Figure E-3   Routers Versus Layer 3 Switches

Traditional Router Operation	Layer 3 Switching
Multiprotocol internet layer operation (IP, IPX, AppleTalk, SNA, etc.).	Only supports IP or perhaps IP plus IPX.
Multiprotocol data link layer operation (Ethernet, Token-Ring, ATM, Frame Relay, X.25, etc.).	Usually only Ethernet.
Individual router forwarding decision for each packet.	Decision Caching: Storing each decision in RAM and using the cached decision for future forwarding to the same destination address.
Individual router forwarding decision for each packet.	MultiProtocol Label Switching (MPLS) standard will bring the equivalent of virtual circuits for IP traffic.
Traditional bus architecture with a single CPU.	Use of intelligent ports that can send packets within frames directly to the appropriate output port, across a switching matrix.
Complex software requires many CPU cycles to make a single router forwarding decision.	Use of ASICs (application-specific integrated circuits) to do most processing in hardware, speeding decisions greatly while reducing costs. Typically limited to IP switching (only supporting TCP/IP protocols).
Note: Most Layer 3 switches use only some of these innovations.	

Unfortunately, it also reduces their usefulness in today's corporations, where multiple protocols are a way of life.

Subnet Standards Support

Most Layer 3 switches on the market today support only Ethernet ports at the data link layer and the physical layer. Some support ATM as well, but this is much less common. This is not much of a problem in most corporations, because ATM use is fairly uncommon. However, it is a serious problem for firms that use ATM.

For wide area networking, the general lack of support for leased lines, Frame Relay, and ATM means that Layer 3 switches are used primarily within site networks and not at the border to the outside world.

Internet Layer Standards Support

All Layer 3 switches support IP. However, only some support Novell NetWare's IPX internet layer protocol, and support for other internet layer protocols from AppleTalk, SNA, and other architectures is fairly rare. This offers great cost savings, because each architecture has different router forwarding processes and different equivalents for dynamic routing protocols.

Avoiding Individual Router Forwarding Decisions

In Chapter 8, we saw that whenever an IP packet arrives at a router, the router compares the packet's destination address against each row in the router forwarding table. Furthermore, when a stream of packets arrives for the same destination address, the router makes a full router forwarding decision for each packet, despite the fact that the network is highly unlikely to have changed in the microseconds between packets. By reducing the need for packet-by-packet decision making, Layer 3 switches can offer far lower costs.

Decision Caching

The simplest approach to reducing packet-by-packet decision making is to make a full router forwarding decision for a packet but then place the details of the decision (IP destination address, router interface, and next-hop router) in an area of RAM called a cache.

Whenever an IP packet arrives, then, the Layer 3 switch first looks for the IP destination address in its cache. If it finds the address, it uses the decision it has cached instead of going through the full router forwarding table again. This **decision caching** slashes router forwarding work.

Of course, it would be easy to add decision caching to routers and, in fact, many routers now do decision caching.

MultiProtocol Label Switching (MPLS)

In Chapter 5, we saw that new tag fields are being added to 802.3 Ethernet MAC layer frames. In Chapter 5, we saw that ATM cells are forwarded on the basis of their virtual circuit number instead of by destination address. In Chapter 7, we saw that Frame Relay switch forwarding is also done on the basis of virtual circuit number.

The IETF is now developing a way to tag IP packets with something like a virtual circuit number. This is called **MultiProtocol Label Switching (MPLS)**. MPLS will allow routers to make very fast decisions based on MPLS tag values. Layer 3 switches usually already have such a mechanism. However, it is based on proprietary tagging approaches. For more on MPLS, see Module A.

Replacing the Bus

Router Bus Architectures

As Figure E-4 illustrates, routers traditionally have used a bus architecture in which there is a single **central processing unit (CPU)** and in which all communication must go through a single transmission line called a **bus**.

Information can only pass through the bus and CPU one piece at a time. In other words, transmission and processing must be done *serially*. Furthermore, each octet in the packet must pass through the bus twice—once going to the CPU and once coming from the CPU.

In heavily loaded routers, the bus and the CPU become bottlenecks that limit the speed at which forwarding and other work (for instance, the handling of dynamic routing protocols) can be done.

Switch Matrix Architectures

In contrast, as Figure E-4 shows, Layer 3 switches usually rely on intelligent interfaces (ports). Whenever an IP packet arrives at a port, the port makes its own forwarding decision. The input port encapsulates the IP packet into the data link layer frame required by the output port and sends the resultant frame *directly to the output port* across the switching matrix.

With a **switch matrix architecture**, transmission and processing can be done in parallel. If several frames arrive at the same time, there is no need to wait for the bus and CPU to become free. As we saw in Chapter 3, parallel work is much faster than serial work.

Figure E-4   Bus Versus Switching Matrix Architecture

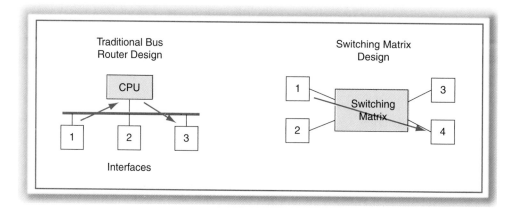

ASICs

As Figure E-3 illustrates, traditional routers have been built as general-purpose computers. They have to execute their functions in software. However, software instructions must be executed serially, one at a time. In addition, each software function takes several processing cycles to execute because one or more octets may have to be moved into the CPU from RAM or moved out of the CPU to RAM.

Hardware Processing

Processing is much faster if done in hardware. There usually is no need to move data in each processing step because one circuit automatically passes results on to other processing circuits. In addition, quite a bit of processing usually can be done in parallel, slashing processing time.

ASICs

For this reason, many Layer 3 switches are built using **application-specific integrated circuits (ASICs)**. As the name suggests, ASICs are integrated circuits (chips) designed for a specific purpose, such as IP routing.

ASIC Economics

The problem with ASICs is that they are very expensive to design. Unless the design cost is amortized over many chips in production, ASIC processing will be too expensive to support. However, Layer 3 switches today have the volume to support ASIC creation.

ASIC Routers?

We are even beginning to see *ASIC routers*. However, upon closer inspection, these ASIC routers generally only handle IP. They really are Layer 3 switches. Limitations are needed because today's ASICs can only support switching functionality. To support full router technology, ASIC technology will have to mature considerably.

Frame Relay's Frame Structure

Because of the dominance of Frame Relay, we should understand its basic operation. In Chapter 5, we saw the organization of ATM cells, which are fixed-length frames. The organization of these cells was fairly simple. A hierarchical virtual circuit number took up most of the 5-octet header. As Figure E-5 illustrates, the Frame Relay frame is more complex.

Information Field

The size of the Frame Relay information field is not fixed, unlike ATM's constant 48-octet data field size that we saw in the last chapter. Larger data fields minimize the overhead caused by the header and trailer fields, so Frame Relay has much lower overhead than ATM.

Overall Frame				
Flag 01111110	Address (2-4 octets) Shown Below	Information (variable)	FCS (2 octets)	Flag 01111110

4-Octet Address Field

Bit 1	2	3	4	5	6	7	Bit 8
Data Link Control Indicator (6 bits)						C/R 0/1	AE 0
Data Link Control Indicator (4 bits)				FECN	BECN	DE	AE 0
Data Link Control Indicator (7 bits)							AE 0
Data Link Control Indicator (7 bits)							AE 1

Notes:
AE = Address Extension bit.
BECN = Backward Explicit Congestion Notification bit.
C/R = Command/Response bit.
DE = Discard Eligible bit.
FCS = Frame Control Sequence.
FECN = Forward Explicit Congestion Notification bit.

Figure E-5   Frame Relay Frame Organization

Flags

The frame begins and ends with 1-octet **flag fields**, each of which has the value 01111110.[3] This eliminates the need for a size field.

Frame Check Sequence

The **frame check sequence (FCS)** field allows each switch to check for errors. If the switch finds such an error, it merely discards the frame. There is no automatic retransmission, so Frame Relay is not reliable. This keeps its switching costs low.

---

[3] What if the pattern 011111110 appears somewhere in the data being delivered? There is a process called "bit stuffing" that adds another "1" in the octet where the reserved 01111110 pattern appears.

Address Field

The **address field** is fairly complex. There are three alternatives for Frame Relay's variable-length address field. These alternatives are two, three, and four octets long, respectively. Figure E-5 shows the longest alternative.

Addressing (DLCI)   The **data link control identifier (DLCI)** field identifies a specific virtual circuit. In the 4-octet address option, it has a total of 24 bits. This allows 1,024 (2^{24}) virtual circuits to be identified.

Note that the DLCI does not give the address of the destination computer. Rather, it identifies the virtual circuit to which the frame belongs. This is similar to ATM addressing, which we saw in Chapter 5.

Address Extension Bit   The **address extension (AE) bit** is set to one if the octet it ends is the last octet in the address field. Otherwise, it is set to zero. For instance, if there are only two octets in the address field, the AE bit in the first octet is zero, and the AE bit in the second octet is one. The last two rows of the address field shown in Figure E-5 would not exist.

Congestion Control

Three address fields are used for a crude form of congestion control in Frame Relay. These are the discard eligible, backward explicit congestion notification, and forward explicit congestion notification fields.

Discard Eligible   Some Frame Relay networks offer two speeds to customers. The lower rate—the **committed information rate (CIR)**—is guaranteed, although not completely. The higher rate—the **available bit rate (ABR)**—is for bursts at speeds above the CIR.

For transmissions within the CIR, the **discard eligible (DE)** bit is set to zero. For frames going faster than the CIR, the discard eligible bit is set to one. If frames must be discarded because of congestion, the Frame Relay carrier will first discard frames with the discard eligible set to one. Transmitting at the ABR is like flying standby.

Explicit Congestion Notification Fields   Although discarding frames relieves congestion, this is a drastic solution. As noted in Chapter 8, traffic shaping tells stations to reduce their speeds to avoid congestion. In Frame Relay there are *two 1-bit explicit **congestion notification fields***. A switch detecting congestion sets one of these fields (makes its value one). The receiving station will see the explicit congestion notification field and act appropriately.

➤ The **Backward Explicit Congestion Notification (BECN)** field is set to tell the *station that receives the frame* to slow down when it transmits. This is easy to implement.

➤ The **Forward Explicit Congestion Notification (FECN)** field is more complex. If a station receives this notification in an incoming frame, *it should tell its communication partner at the other end* of the Frame Relay network to slow down.

Command/Response

The **command/response (C/R)** field is application-specific and is rarely used.

REVIEW QUESTIONS

CORE REVIEW QUESTIONS

1. What is the modem error correction standard? b) What is the best modem data compression standard? c) What is the fastest facsimile modem standard?
2. What are the layers in ATM? Briefly describe the function of each.
3. Why does ATM have high overhead?
4. List the reasons why Layer 3 switches are faster than routers.
5. a) How long is the longest Frame Relay frame? b) How many bits in this frame form the address (the virtual circuit number)?

DETAILED REVIEW QUESTIONS

1. List all sources of overhead in ATM.
2. Compare and contrast decision caching and MPLS.
3. Contrast bus architectures and switch matrix architectures, focusing on why switch matrix architectures are faster.
4. a) What is the advantage of ASICs? b) What is their disadvantage?
5. Explain congestion control in Frame Relay.

THOUGHT QUESTION

1. a) Which Layer 3 switch technologies do you think routers will adopt? b) Which do you think they will not adopt?

PROJECTS

1. **Getting Current.** Go to the book's website, www.prenhall.com/panko, and see the New Information and Errors pages for this module to get new information since this book went to press and to correct any errors in the text.
2. **Internet Exercises.** Go to the book's website, www.prenhall.com/panko, and see the Exercises page for this module. Do the Internet exercises.

MORE ON SECURITY

INTRODUCTION

This module presents additional information on security. It should be read after Chapter 9. It is not meant to be read front-to-back like a chapter.

In Chapter 9, we saw secure communication systems. These systems allow two processes on different machines to negotiate security parameters, authenticate themselves to one another, and send subsequent messages with privacy, authentication, and message integrity—all with a minimum of user involvement. Module F discusses three secure communication systems:

- ➤ IPsec
- ➤ PPP
- ➤ Kerberos

The Module begins, however, by describing a type of attack not listed in Chapter 9, the replay attack.

REPLAY ATTACKS AND DEFENSES

Chapter 9 discussed several types of attacks, including:

- ➤ Intercepting and reading messages, which is thwarted by encryption for privacy (confidentiality)
- ➤ Intercepting and changing messages, then sending them on, which is thwarted by message integrity

➤ Impersonating a true party, which is thwarted by authentication

➤ Denial of service attacks, which are thwarted by various means such as firewalls

One type of attack, however, was not discussed in Chapter 9. This is the **replay attack**, in which an adversary intercepts a message and then transmits it again, at a later time.

There are several reasons for replay attacks. Sometimes, for instance, a replay attack is used in an attempt to gain authorization to a service, based upon a previous successful authorization attempt by a true authorized party.

There are several ways to detect attempted replay attacks. All require the use of message integrity so that messages can only be replayed, not changed and then replayed.

➤ One way to ensure that each message is "fresh" is to include a **time stamp** in each message. The receiver then compares this time stamp to its current clock time, and if the message is too old, the receiver rejects it.

➤ Another approach is to place a **sequence number** in each message. By examining sequence numbers, the receiver can detect a retransmitted message.

➤ A third common approach, used in client/server processing, is to include a **nonce** (randomly generated number) in each request. The client never uses the same nonce twice. The response from the server includes the same nonce. By comparing a nonce in a request with previous request nonces, the server can ensure that the request is not a repeat of an earlier one. The client, in turn, can ensure that the response is not a repeat of a previous response.

IPSEC (IP SECURITY)

Chapter 7 noted that virtual private networks (VPNs) use a family of security standards collectively called **IPsec (IP security)**. This section looks at IPsec in more depth.

Secure Communication Systems and Internet Layer Protection

SSL: Transport Layer Security

Chapter 11 introduced a particular secure communication system, Secure Sockets Layer (SSL), which the IETF calls Transport Layer Security. As the latter name indicates, SSL operates at the transport layer. This allows it to protect multiple applications.

IPsec: Internet Layer Security

In contrast, IPsec operates at the internet layer. This allows it to provide security for the transport layer, including all TCP and UDP traffic, and all other traffic carried in the data field of the IP packet, including ICMP and OSPF and even "tunneled" IP packets and PPP packets, as discussed later in this module.

Both IPv4 and IPv6

IPsec was originally intended for the new version of the Internet Protocol, IP Version 6 (IPv6). However, it was actually created so that it can be used with IP Version 4 (IPv4) as well. In other words, no matter which version of IP your network uses, IPsec will protect it.

Transport and Tunnel Modes

The most basic concept in IPsec is that there are two **IPsec modes**, that is, ways of operating. As Figure F-1 indicates, these are the transport mode and the tunnel mode. We looked at tunnel mode in Chapter 7.

Transport Mode

As Figure F-1 indicates, **transport mode** is used for host-to-host security. Transport mode allows two hosts to communicate securely without regard to what else is happening on the network.

The figure notes that an **IPsec header** is inserted after the main IP header. As discussed below, this header provides protection for higher-layer protocols, that is, transport and application layer protocols.

In some cases, it may also provide limited protection for the IP header before it. However, because the IP destination address is needed to route the packet to the destination host, the IP header must be transmitted in the clear, without encryption. This

Figure F-1   Transport and Tunnel Modes in IPsec

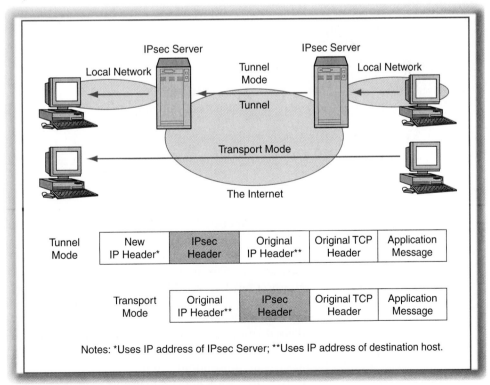

Tunnel Mode	New IP Header*	IPsec Header	Original IP Header**	Original TCP Header	Application Message

Transport Mode	Original IP Header**	IPsec Header	Original TCP Header	Application Message

Notes: *Uses IP address of IPsec Server; **Uses IP address of destination host.

allows a snooper listening to your network traffic to understand your distribution of IP addresses, and this can lead to certain types of attacks.

Tunnel Mode

In contrast, Figure F-1 shows that **tunnel mode** normally is used to protect communication between two **IPsec servers** at different sites. These servers send traffic between sites through the Internet in secure "tunnels." We saw this mode in Chapter 7.

In tunnel mode, even the original IP header is fully protected. The transmitting IP server encapsulates the original IP packet in a new IP packet by adding a new IP header and an IPsec header. Encapsulating a protocol's message within another protocol message at the same layer (in this case, an IP packet within another IP packet) is known as **tunneling**.

The destination address in the new IP header is the IP address of the destination IPsec server, not the IP address of the ultimate destination host. Therefore, if an adversary snoops on the company's traffic, the only IP addresses it will see will be those of the site security servers. The adversary will learn nothing about other IP addresses.

The source IPsec server receives original IP packets and encapsulates them as shown in the figure. The receiving IPsec server, in turn, deencapsulates the original IP packet and sends it on its way to the destination host within the receiving IPsec server's site network.

Combining Modes

The two IPsec modes can be combined. For instance, two hosts may use transport mode for end-to-end security. At the same time, their packets may be intercepted by IPsec servers at their sites for tunneling through the Internet to the IPsec server at the other site.

For this to happen, the source host would add transport mode IPsec security to each outgoing packet. The source IPsec server would then encapsulate each packet within a tunnel mode IP packet.

The receiving IPsec server would deencapsulate the original packet and pass it on to the destination host. The destination host would then remove the transport mode security and read the information contained in the packet's data field.

IPsec Headers

The preceding discussion has been deliberately vague about two points. First, it mentioned an "IPsec header" without saying what it was. Second, it talked vaguely about "protection" without specifying whether this was confidentiality, authentication, message integrity, or some combination of these and other protections.

That vagueness was deliberate because in both transport and tunnel modes, IPsec offers *two different* types of protection. For each type of protection, IPsec uses a different type of IPsec header. Therefore, there are four mode–header combinations.

Figure F-1 illustrates the placement of these IPsec headers. For IP Version 6, these headers are extension headers. For IP Version 4, these are options.

Encapsulating Security Protocol (ESP)

The most commonly used IPsec header is the **Encapsulating Security Protocol (ESP)** header. ESP is attractive because it offers full security, including confidentiality (privacy), message-by-message authentication, and message integrity. We will see later that another IPsec header type, the Authentication Header, does not offer confidentiality.

Figure F-2 shows that ESP has two parts, a header and a trailer. ESP extends confidentiality to the data following the ESP header and to part of the ESP trailer as well. The figure also shows that authentication and message integrity is provided to the entire IPsec header and to part of the IPsec trailer as well.

As a reminder, IPsec headers work in both transport and tunnel modes. In transport mode, the protected information between the ESP header and ESP trailer is the transport and application layer information. In tunnel mode, it is the encapsulated IP packet.

Authentication Header

The other type of IPsec header is the **authentication header (AH)**. Like ESP, AH offers authentication and message integrity. However, unlike ESP, *AH does not offer confidentiality (privacy).* Anyone intercepting the message can read it.

Why use a security system that lets anyone read your messages? The answer is that some countries outlaw encryption for privacy in certain situations, for instance, in traffic sent to another country. For these situations, AH's authentication and message integrity support still is valuable.

Figure F-2 emphasizes that AH does not offer confidentiality at all. However, AH does offer a bit more authentication and message integrity protection than ESP. AH authenticates and provides message integrity for the entire AH header (there is no AH trailer) *and also for the preceding IP header.*

Figure F-2   **ESP and AH Protection**

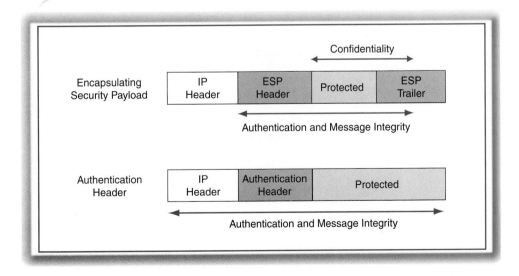

Security Associations (SAs)

Before two hosts or IPsec servers communicate, they have to establish security associations (SAs). The security association is the most fundamental, and perhaps the most confusing, part of IPsec.

How SAs Work

Figure F-3 illustrates security associations. A **security association (SA)** is an agreement about how two hosts or two IPsec servers will provide security. The SA specifies what specific algorithms the sending party will use to implement whatever security processes will be used, for instance, confidentiality, authentication, and message integrity. It summarizes the agreement the two parties settle upon for how they will communicate securely.

Separate SAs in the Two Directions

Note that when two parties communicate, there must be two security associations—one in each direction. If Party A and Party B communicate, there must be an SA for Party A to use to send to Party B and a separate SA for Party B to use to send to Party A. This use of two security associations is confusing, but it allows different levels of protection in the two directions if this is desirable.

Policy-Based SAs

SAs may be governed by policies built into the hosts or IPsec servers. The company may permit only a few designated combinations of security algorithms to be used as SAs. For instance, certain encryption algorithms might be considered to be too weak to be safe or might be considered to be too processing-intensive to be worthwhile.

Establishing Security Associations

Establishing security associations is a two-phase process.

Figure F-3   Security Associations in IPsec

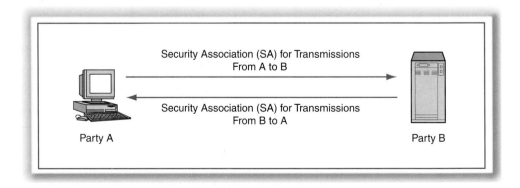

Security Association (SA) for Transmissions From A to B

Security Association (SA) for Transmissions From B to A

Party A

Party B

Establishing Internet Key Exchange (IKE) Security Associations

In the first phase, IPsec relies on the **Internet Key Exchange (IKE)** standard. Although its name suggests that IKE only does key exchange, it actually handles all of the steps needed for an integrated security association to establish a security association. These include the following:

➤ Communication to agree upon security algorithms to be used to set up the IKE SA.

➤ Authentication.

➤ The exchange of symmetric session keys to be used in the transmission. Different session keys may be used for confidentiality and authentication.

As its name suggests, Internet Key Exchange is not limited to IPsec. It is a general protocol for establishing security associations in Internet integrated security systems.

Establishing IPsec Security Associations

However, this generality also means that IKE is not sufficient for IPsec, which has specific security association needs. As Figure F-4 illustrates, when two parties (in this case IPsec servers) establish an IKE SA, this forms a blanket of protection within which the two parties can then negotiate IPsec SAs. For instance, two IPsec servers may establish different IPsec SAs for traffic types of different sensitivity.

IPsec Mandatory Default Security Protocols

One of the advantages of negotiation is that it permits the two parties to negotiate which specific algorithms they will use for confidentiality and other matters. However, there also are **mandatory default** algorithms that must be supported and that will be used as the default, that is, will be used automatically if the two sides do not wish to specify an alternative.

Figure F-4   IKE and IPsec Security Associations

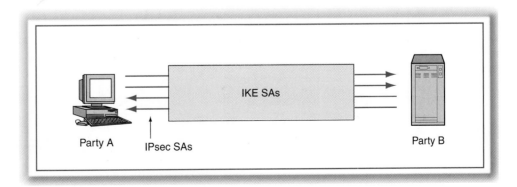

Diffie-Hellman Key Agreement

The two sides must exchange symmetric session keys. In Chapter 9, we saw that in *RSA public key exchange,* the sender encrypts the session key with the sender's private key for authentication and encrypts again with the receiver's public key for confidentiality. Both forms of encryption use RSA public key encryption.

However, in IKE and IPsec, the mandatory default algorithm is **Diffie-Hellman Key Agreement**. This algorithm allows the two sides to each generate a nonce and send it to the other in the clear (without confidentiality). Although both parties created their values randomly, they both do a calculation and arrive at the *same symmetric session key!* Although this sounds like magic, it actually works.

More specifically, the two sides agree non-securely on a Diffie-Hellman group, which has two parameters, p and g (prime and generator). Say the two parties are X and Y. X randomly generates a small string x, then calculates g^x mod p and calls this x′. Y randomly generates a small string y, then calculates g^y mod p and calls this y′. X sends x′ to Y, and Y sends y′ to X. X calculates y'^x mod p, giving g^{xy} mod p. Y calculates x'^y mod p, also getting g^{xy} mod p. The two sides subsequently use this value as the session key. An interceptor will not be able to calculate the key because they cannot learn x and y from the exchanges.

Note that the two parties *agree* upon a key rather than *exchange* an entire key. That is why the process is called "key agreement" rather than "key exchange."

One problem with simple Diffie-Hellman is that unless the two parties authenticate themselves, an adversary may establish shared session keys in the name of a true partner. Therefore, IKE and IPsec require the use of authenticated Diffie-Hellman key agreement, in which authentication is an integral part of the process.

Figure F-5   Cipher Block Chaining (CBC) in Encryption

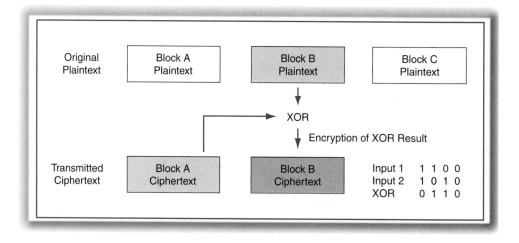

DES-CBC

The mandatory default algorithm for bulk encryption (sending long messages) is **DES-CBC**. In Chapter 9, we noted that DES is the Data Encryption Standard. It encrypts data in blocks of 64 bits. The sender first divides the message into blocks of 64 bits and then encrypts each block with DES.

A problem with simple DES is that a 64-bit block will always be encrypted the same way for a given session key. This leaves DES open to a number of attacks that let an adversary learn the symmetric session key.

To prevent this, IPsec requires DES to use **cipher block chaining (CBC)**, which prevents the same input block of data from always giving the same output result with a given key. Figure F-5 illustrates cipher block chaining.

Suppose that the sending process wishes to encrypt Block B. It has already encrypted the previous block, Block A. The sender first takes plaintext Block B and XORs it with the ciphertext (encrypted output for Block A). The sender then encrypts the result with DES as its output for Block B.

Here, **XOR** is **exclusive OR**, a Boolean operation. An exclusive OR result is true (1) if exactly one of the two terms is true (1), but not both or neither. Analogously, people normally can be either male or female but not both or neither. Being male or female is exclusive.

$$1 \text{ XOR } 1 = 0$$
$$1 \text{ XOR } 0 = 1$$
$$0 \text{ XOR } 1 = 1$$
$$0 \text{ XOR } 0 = 0$$

Figure F-6   Key-Hashed Message Authentication Code (HMAC)

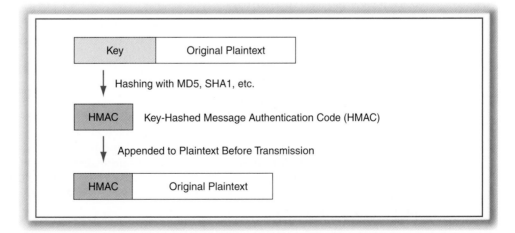

Therefore, if the ciphertext for the Block A is 11000011 . . . , and if the plaintext for Block B is 10101010 . . . , we get the following result:

11000011...	Ciphertext for Block A
<u>10101010...</u>	Plaintext for Block B
01101001...	Result to be encrypted

What about the first block? Obviously, there is no previous block to use in chaining. For this reason, CBC requires a 64-bit **initialization** vector for use in place of the first block.

HMAC for Authentication

In Chapter 9, we saw digital signatures, which use public key encryption. Digital signatures provide message-by-message authentication and integrity.

Although digital signatures are good, the public key encryption used to create digital signatures is very slow. An analog of digital signatures called **key-hashed message authentication codes (HMACs)** can be created with symmetric key encryption.

To create a simple HMAC, a symmetric key is added to the original plaintext message, as Figure F-6 indicates. The combined string of bits is then hashed using MD5, SHA1, or some other hashing algorithm. This provides the HMAC. The HMAC is appended to the end of outgoing messages for authentication.

IKE and IPsec use a slightly more complicated HMAC system described in RFC 2104.[1] This HMAC method adds a number of refinements to simple hashing, in order to be more immune to attacks. RFC 2104 actually defines several HMAC variants that use different hashing algorithms, including HMAC-MD5 and HMAC-SHA1.

Recall from Chapter 9 that symmetric key encryption and decryption are about a hundred times faster than public key encryption or decryption. Therefore, HMAC authentication is far faster than digital signature authentication.

Windows Implementation

IPsec is a newcomer to Microsoft Windows. It was only implemented in Windows 2000. Consequently, computers with older versions of Windows must have the software or work in tunnel mode.

POINT-TO-POINT PROTOCOL (PPP) SECURITY

When you dial into the Internet from home, using a telephone line and modem, you use the Point-to-Point Protocol (PPP) at the data link layer.

You can also use PPP when you dial into a **remote access server (RAS)**, as discussed in Chapter 7. A remote access server sits at the edge of a LAN. As Figure F-7 illustrates, a user calls from home directly into the RAS. If the RAS is far away, the user must pay long-distance telephone charges.

---

[1]   Bellare, H. and Canetti, R., RFC 2104, Keyed-Hashing for Message Authentication, 2/97.

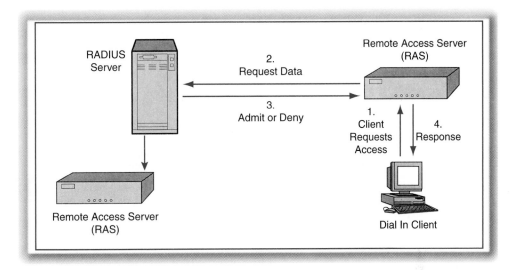

Figure F-7   RADIUS Server

Before PPP

Remote access servers existed long before PPP. These servers give remote users access to all servers on the LAN, so RAS authentication has always been necessary.

Individual RAS Login Authentication

The first step in RAS access control was to put authentication on each remote access server, using proprietary techniques that differed among RAS vendors. This technique worked, but if a company used several RAS vendors, it had to learn and maintain multiple remote access server security processes.

RADIUS Authentication

Another problem with individual RAS login was that a company might have dozens or even hundreds of remote access servers on its LANs. Unless security was implemented uniformly across RASs, an adversary could simply try different RASs until he or she found a RAS with improper security. Individual RAS login security was only as good as the weakest RAS.

To address this "weakest link" problem, vendors collaborated on a way to implement policy-based authentication on remote access servers. Their standard was the **Remote Authentication Dial In User Service (RADIUS)**. Figure F-7 illustrates how RADIUS works.

When a user logs in to the remote access server, the RAS does not do authentication by itself. Instead, it passes the user's login information on to the central RADIUS server. The **RADIUS server** then authenticates the user or refuses the user. It passes this information back to the RAS serving the user. The RAS then accepts or rejects the connection.

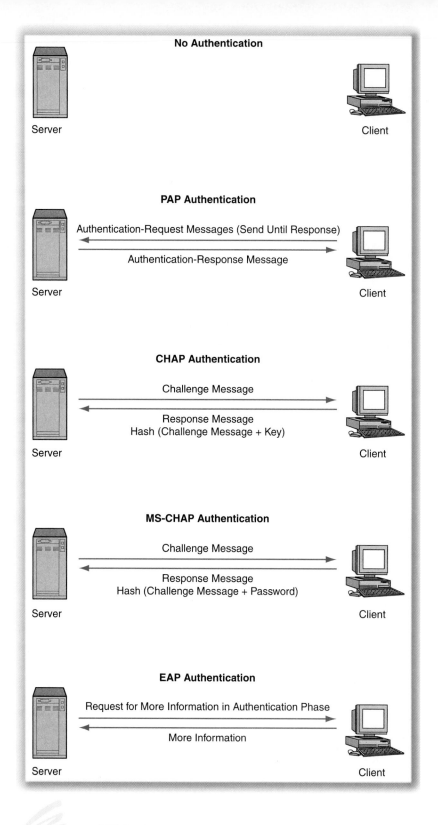

Figure F-8   PPP Authentication

Although RADIUS worked well and is still widely used, we would like to integrate access authentication into our normal Internet protocol suite instead of making it a separate part of network security. We would also like that integration to go beyond authentication to provide confidentiality (privacy) as well.

Point-to-Point Protocol Security: The Negotiation Phase

Developed as a basic Layer 2 (data link layer) transmission standard, PPP has added considerable security since its creation.

PPP communication begins with a negotiation phase, during which the two PPP processes can negotiate the transmission and security processes they will use during transmission. Within PPP, the **Link Control Protocol** is used to govern data link layer negotiation.

PPP Authentication

During negotiation, the two sides can agree upon a process to use for authentication. However, as Figure F-8 notes, *authentication is optional* in PPP. The two sides can decide not to use it at all. If they do decide to use authentication, they have several options.

Password Authentication Protocol (PAP)

The simplest authentication protocol for PPP is the **Password Authentication Protocol (PAP)**. As Figure F-8 indicates, the applicant sends the verifier a stream of PAP authentication-request messages until it receives an authenticate-ACK message (or until the verifier terminates the link).

The PAP authentication-request message contains the user's username and password. Unfortunately, security specialists cringe at the very name PAP because PAP sends user names and passwords **in the clear** (without encryption). Anyone listening to the traffic can steal passwords!

Another limitation of PAP is that it only authenticates the user once, at the beginning of a session. Afterwards, a third party can send messages in the user's name and there will be no authentication testing.

Figure F-9   DES and 3DES Encryption in PPP

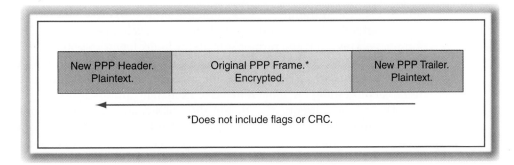

New PPP Header. Plaintext.	Original PPP Frame.* Encrypted.	New PPP Trailer. Plaintext.

*Does not include flags or CRC.

Challenge-Handshake Authentication Protocol (CHAP)

Fortunately, PPP has standardized a much stronger form of authentication, the **Challenge-Handshake Authentication Protocol (CHAP)**. As Figure F-8 illustrates, the verifier sends a challenge message to the applicant. The applicant sends back a response message that should authenticate the applicant to the verifier.

CHAP works on the basis of a shared secret. When the applicant receives the challenge message, it adds the shared secret to the challenge message and then hashes the combined bit stream using MD5 or another agreed-upon hashing algorithm. The applicant sends the resultant hash back to the verifier as its response message.

The verifier also adds the shared secret to the challenge message, hashes the result, and compares the hash with the hash that the applicant sent as its response. If the hashes match, the applicant must know the shared secret and so is authenticated.

Recall that PAP does authentication only once, right after the negotiation phase. CHAP also does authentication then, but it also does so periodically during communication, to thwart an adversary who causes the applicant to crash and then sends a message in the name of the disabled applicant.

Microsoft CHAP (MS-CHAP)

Microsoft has created its own extensions for CHAP. Although not standardized, these are widely used in Windows. Recall that in CHAP, there is a shared secret that must be hashed with the challenge message to create a response message. In **MS-CHAP**, as Figure F-8 shows, this shared secret is the user's password.

Although the Internet Engineering Task Force (IETF) published an informational RFC (2433) to describe MS-CHAP, it warns at the beginning of the RFC that the "protocol described here has significant vulnerabilities." The basic problem is that, as noted in Chapter 9, users often select passwords that are too easy to guess. MS-CHAP security is only as good as the passwords that users select, and security experts consider this to be insufficient. On the other hand, it does address the fact that passwords often do form the basis for authentication in the real world.

Of course, passwords expire and must be renewed. CHAP provides a Change Password message that allows a user to send a new password. There is also a mechanism for the verifier host to tell the applicant that the old password has expired and that a new password is needed. Unfortunately, the first version of the Change Password process had major security vulnerabilities. Fortunately, a second, stronger, version has been released.

Extensible Authentication Protocol (EAP)

One problem with traditional PPP authentication is that the authentication method must be agreed upon with a very simple message exchange during the initial negotiation phase. This limits the verifier's flexibility in dealing with applicants.

The PPP **Extensible Authentication Protocol (EAP)** addresses this weakness. During the initial negotiation phase, the two sides merely select EAP as their authentication method using the limited message exchange options available to them then.

During the subsequent authentication phase, authentication is not done immediately. Rather, the verifier can ask for more information from the applicant in an open-ended manner, so that a more intelligent choice of authentication protocols can be made based on the applicant's identity.

EAP offers a rich set of possible authentication protocols, including MD5-Challenge (which is nearly identical to CHAP), one-time passwords for very high security, and Generic Token Card, which works with certain types of security cards.

PPP Confidentiality

We have been focusing on authentication because remote access servers must guard against impostors gaining access to critical internal resources. However, we would also like to have confidentiality. In other words, we would like to encrypt our messages so that the contents of our PPP frames can be transmitted with privacy.

The IETF has provided an **Encryption Control Protocol** for the PPP negotiation phase to allow the parties to agree upon the encryption process. To date, the IETF has specified two encryption algorithms for confidentiality (but will specify additional algorithms in the future). Not surprisingly, given the popularity of DES and 3DES, these are the two algorithms that the IETF has specified. As noted earlier in this module, DES-CBC and 3DES-CBC were selected.

Figure F-9 shows that the sender encrypts the PPP frame and places it within another PPP frame with a clear text header.

Tunneling

What if a remote access server is far away? Then an expensive long-distance telephone call will be needed for a client to reach the RAS. As Figure F-10 illustrates, another

Figure F-10   Tunneling with the Point-to-Point Tunneling Protocol (PPTP)

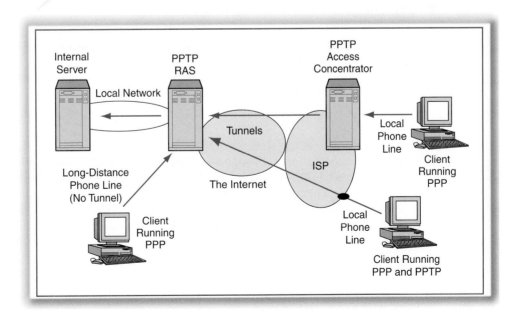

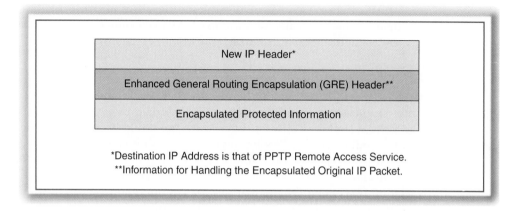

Figure F-11   Point-to-Point Tunneling Protocol (PPTP) Packet

solution is to connect the client with the RAS via the Internet or another network. Packet switched networks are much less expensive than direct long-distance calling.

Point-to-Point Tunneling Protocol (PPTP)

For Windows NT/2000 RASs, the most widely used tunneling protocol is the **Point-to-Point Tunneling Protocol (PPTP)**. As Figure F-10 illustrates, PPTP works in one of two ways. One approach is to implement PPTP on both the client PC and the RAS server. Newer client versions of Microsoft Windows (since Windows 95) have the required PPTP software.

The second approach is to require the ISP (or internal packet switched network) to provide an additional server, the **PPTP access concentrator**, to which the client places the telephone call. When you dial into an ISP, you already give your user name and password to an access server. This access server would also be your PPTP access concentrator. Of course, not all ISP access servers offer PPTP access concentrator support.

PPTP Packet

If the PPTP frame is to pass through an IP network, it must be tunneled inside another IP packet. Figure F-11 shows that the PPP frame[2] is first placed within an enhanced **Generic Routing Encapsulation (GRE)** packet and then within an IP packet.

The enhanced GRE header allows the sender (RAS or PPTP access concentrator) to describe the contents of the GRE data field to the receiver. It is also used for control signaling, including flow control.

---

[2] Before being encapsulated, the PPP frame's start and stop flags and CRC field are removed because they would serve no purpose.

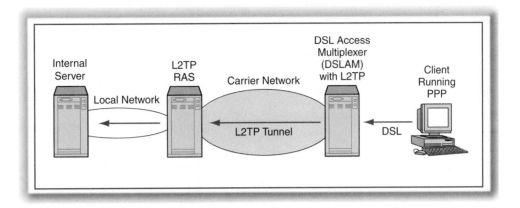

Figure F-12   Layer 2 Tunneling Protocol (L2TP) with DSL

In particular, there can be multiple PPP conversations multiplexed onto a single PPTP connection between a RAS and a PPTP access concentrator. Each conversation is identified in the enhanced GRE header by the value in the *Call ID* field of the enhanced GRE header.

Layer 2 Tunneling Protocol (L2TP)

PPTP is essentially a Microsoft invention. The IETF is also defining the **Layer 2 Tunneling Protocol (L2TP)**, which is viewed by many analysts as a successor to PPTP.

For instance, as Figure F-12 indicates, a user may establish a DSL connection to a DSL access multiplexer (DSLAM), as discussed in Chapter 5. The DSLAM could then establish an L2TP connection to the RAS.

L2TP does not provide security by itself, so Windows requires IPsec to be used with L2TP. In addition, Windows only began supporting L2TP in Windows 2000.

Remote Access Servers (RASs) and Network Access Servers (NASs)

We conclude with a final bit of terminology. This discussion has called the server that connects the user to a particular network the remote access server (RAS). This is traditional terminology. However, IETF documents call these servers **network access servers (NASs)**. This is also a good name, because these servers do provide access to their networks. Fortunately, the two terms can be used interchangeably.

KERBEROS

Windows NT/2000 uses an authentication (plus confidentiality) system called **Kerberos**. As shown in Figure F-13, three parties are involved in Kerberos authentication: an

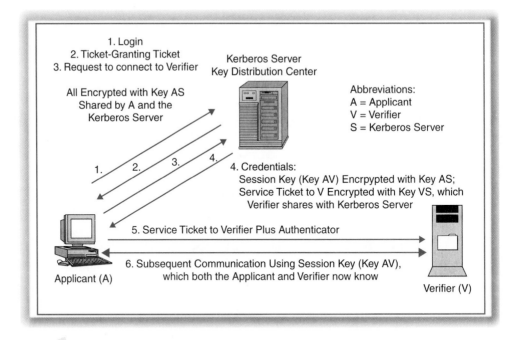

1. Login
2. Ticket-Granting Ticket
3. Request to connect to Verifier

Kerberos Server
Key Distribution Center

All Encrypted with Key AS
Shared by A and the
Kerberos Server

Abbreviations:
A = Applicant
V = Verifier
S = Kerberos Server

1. 2. 3. 4.

4. Credentials:
Session Key (Key AV) Encrpypted with Key AS;
Service Ticket to V Encrypted with Key VS, which
Verifier shares with Kerberos Server

5. Service Ticket to Verifier Plus Authenticator

6. Subsequent Communication Using Session Key (Key AV),
which both the Applicant and Verifier now know

Applicant (A)

Verifier (V)

Figure F-13   Kerberos Authentication

applicant, a verifier, and the Kerberos server.[3] In Chapter 9, we looked at Kerberos simplistically. Here we will give the details.

Initial Login

The first step in Figure F-13 is the applicant's initial login to the Kerberos server. In a login message, the applicant sends its password to the Kerberos server. This login message is encrypted in the permanent symmetric key, Key AS, that the applicant shares with the Kerberos server. Only the applicant and the Kerberos server know Key AS, so they can use it to communicate securely.

Ticket-Granting Ticket

If the applicant's password is correct, the Kerberos server sends the applicant a **Ticket-Granting Ticket (TGT)**. If you go to a movie, your movie ticket grants you the right to admission. Similarly, the TGT grants you the right to make connection requests to the Kerberos server without logging in again. This communication also is protected by symmetric key encryption with Key AS.

---

[3]   In mythology, Kerberos is a three-headed dog monster that guards the gate to the realm of the dead. This is the ultimate in authentication.

Requesting a Connection

As Figure F-13 illustrates, when the applicant wishes to connect to a verifier the applicant first sends a connection request message to the Kerberos server (Step 3). This message also is encrypted Key AS.

Receiving Credentials

Next, the Kerberos server responds to the applicant with a message containing **credentials** for the connection (Step 4). This message also is encrypted with Key AS.

Symmetric Session Key

The credentials come in two parts. First, there is a symmetric session key (Key AV) that the applicant and the verifier will use when they communicate. Recall from Chapter 9 that session keys are one-time keys. If the applicant and verifier communicate again later, they will be given a different session key. In contrast, the key that the applicant shares with the Kerberos server (Key AS) and the key that the verifier shares with the Kerberos server (Key VS) are permanent symmetric keys. The Kerberos server is also called a **Key Distribution Center** because of its function of delivering session keys.

Service Ticket

The credentials also include a **Service Ticket**. The Ticket-Granting Ticket gave you rights to send connection requests to the Kerberos server. In contrast, the Service Ticket should allow you to communicate with a specific verifier.

The Service Ticket contains the symmetric session key (Key AV) that the applicant and the verifier will use in subsequent communication. In other words, the Service Ticket provides a way to exchange the symmetric session key.

The Service Ticket also provides other information. For example, it gives the name of the applicant. If the applicant is a client and the verifier is a server, this will be the client's user name on the server. The Service Ticket also contains a time stamp to prevent its unauthorized replay much later. If the verifier is a server, the Service Ticket may also contain a list of resources to which the applicant should have access, together with the applicant's level of access rights for each resource.

The Service Ticket is encrypted with the permanent shared symmetric key that the verifier shares with the Kerberos server (Key VS). This means that the applicant or an interceptor cannot read the Service Ticket.

Sending the Service Ticket and Authenticator

The applicant sends the Service Ticket to the verifier. However, how can the verifier be certain that the party sending the Service Ticket really is the party that received the Service Ticket from the Kerberos server? To provide this assurance, the message that the applicant sends to the verifier contains more than the Service Ticket itself. It also contains an **authenticator**. This is a string containing several pieces of information, including the applicant's name and a time stamp to thwart replay attacks.

The authenticator is encrypted with the symmetric session key (Key AV) carried within the Service Ticket. If an interceptor has merely stolen the Service Ticket, they would not be able to read it because the Service Ticket is encrypted with Key KV. Therefore, the interceptor would not know the correct symmetric session key.

Therefore, the authenticator, when decrypted with the session key, would not match the comparable data contained within the Service Ticket.

Subsequent Communication

For subsequent communication during this session, the applicant and the verifier will be able to communicate securely, using the symmetric session key given to them by the Kerberos server (Key AV).

Perspective

One problem with Kerberos is that all applications must be "Kerberosized;" that is, must have Kerberos software installed. Microsoft only began to offer Kerberos in Windows 2000.

REVIEW QUESTIONS

REPLAY ATTACKS

1. a) What is a replay attack? b) How is it thwarted?

IPSEC

2. a) Distinguish between transport and tunnel modes in IPsec. b) When is each used?
3. Distinguish between ESP and AH IPsec headers in terms of a) what is protected and b) what protection is given. c) When would you use AH?
4. a) What does an SA specify? b) When two parties wish to communicate in both directions with security, how many SAs must be established?
5. a) What three things are standardized in IKE? b) Distinguish between IKE SAs and IPsec SAs.
6. a) What is the IPsec mandatory default algorithm for getting the two parties a common session key? b) How does it work? c) What useful information, if any, would someone intercepting Diffie-Hellman Key Agreement messages learn?
7. a) Explain why CBC is needed in encryption. b) If one bit is a 1 and the other bit is a 1, what will be the result of an XOR operation? c) What if the other bit is a 0 instead? d) What if both bits are 0? e) Explain how CBC handles blocks beyond the first block.
8. a) In what important way does HMAC authentication differ from digital signature authentication? b) In what way is this difference in HMAC authentication superior to digital signature authentication? c) When is HMAC authentication applied: for one-time authentication, occasional authentication, or message-by-message authentication?
9. In what versions of Windows is IPsec implemented?

PPP SECURITY

10. a) What is the problem with proprietary RAS security approaches? b) What is the benefit of RADIUS?
11. Is authentication mandatory in PPP?
12. a) In PAP, what does the applicant do? b) What does the verifier do? c) How often is PAP authentication done? d) What is the main problem with PAP?
13. a) In CHAP, what does the verifier do? b) What does the applicant do? c) How often is CHAP authentication done?
14. a) In MS-CHAP, what is the shared secret? b) Why is this a potential problem? c) What types of RASs use MS-CHAP?
15. What is the only thing the initial PPP negotiation phase decides when EAP is used?
16. What two encryption algorithms have been defined to date for PPP confidentiality?
17. What is the main benefit of both PPTP and L2TP tunneling?
18. a) For PPTP, what are the two alternatives for the party that communicates with the PPTP RAS? b) Briefly describe the structure of the PPTP packet, including the purposes of the enhanced GRE header.
19. What data link layer tunneling protocol is the IETF developing?
20. Explain the relationship between the terms "remote access server" and "network access server."
21. In what versions of Windows is PPTP implemented?

KERBEROS

22. a) In Kerberos, when does the applicant log into the Kerberos server? b) What is a Ticket-Granting Ticket? c) What are credentials? d) What is a Service Ticket? e) What is an authenticator?
23. In what versions of Windows is Kerberos implemented?

PROJECTS

1. **Getting Current.** Go to the book's website www.prenhall.com/panko, and see the New Information and Errors pages for this module to get new information since this book went to press and to correct any errors in the text.
2. **Internet Exercises.** Go to the book's website www.prenhall.com/panko, and see the Exercises page for this module. Do the Internet exercises.

Index

WELCOME TO THE MTU CAMPUS STORE
OPEN MONDAY THRU FRIDAY 8-4:30
VISIT US ONLINE AT
WWW.BOOKSTORE.MTU.EDU

SALE   001 005   005   065226
CASHIER: JEREMY   08/27/02 10:51

01 PANKO/BUSINESS DATA NETWO
101010 1066527448   1 1   96.00

Subtotal   96.00
6% SALES TAX   5.76

Items   1   Total   101.76

CASH   102.00

Change Due   0.24

TEXTBOOK REFUND POLICY

BOOKS PURCHASED FOR FALL TERM ARE
ELIGIBLE FOR 100% REFUND UNTIL SEPT.9
90% REFUND THIRD WEEK AND 80% REFUND
FOURTH WEEK. YOU MUST HAVE A RECEIPT
QUESTIONS PLEASE CALL 906-487-2410.